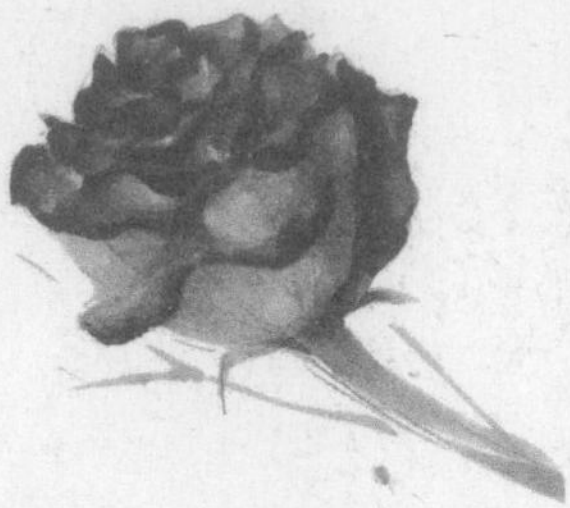

The birthday presents for the characters have been pretty amazing lately... Dom Perignon for Aizen, a hundred roses for Gin, and a blue rose for Rangiku. Honestly, I'm worried about my fans' finances.

-Tite Kubo

Bleach is author Tite Kubo's second title. Kubo made his debut with *ZOMBIEPOWDER.*, a four-volume series for *Weekly Shonen Jump*. To date, *Bleach* has been translated into numerous languages and has also inspired an animated TV series that began airing in the U.S. in 2006. Beginning its serialization in 2001, *Bleach* is still a mainstay in the pages of *Weekly Shonen Jump*. In 2005, *Bleach* was awarded the prestigious Shogakukan Manga Award in the *shonen* (boys) category.

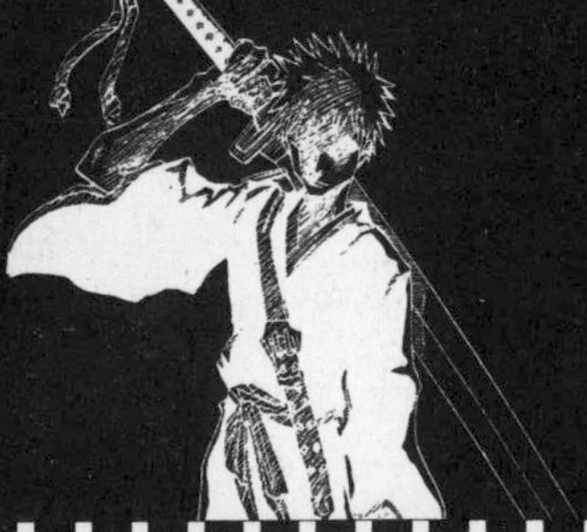

BLEACH
Vol. 36: TURN BACK THE PENDULUM
SHONEN JUMP Manga Edition
This volume contains material that was originally published in English
in SHONEN JUMP #102–105. Artwork in the magazine may have been
altered slightly from what is presented in this volume.

STORY AND ART BY
TITE KUBO

English Adaptation/Lance Caselman
Translation/Joe Yamazaki
Touch-up Art & Lettering/Mark McMurray
Design/Yukiko Whitley
Editor/Alexis Kirsch

Printed in the U.S.A

Published by VIZ Media, LLC
P.O. Box 77010
San Francisco, CA 94107

10 9 8 7 6 5 4 3 2 1
First printing, September 2011

It is still too early to believe.

BLEACH36 TURN BACK THE PENDULUM

STARS AND

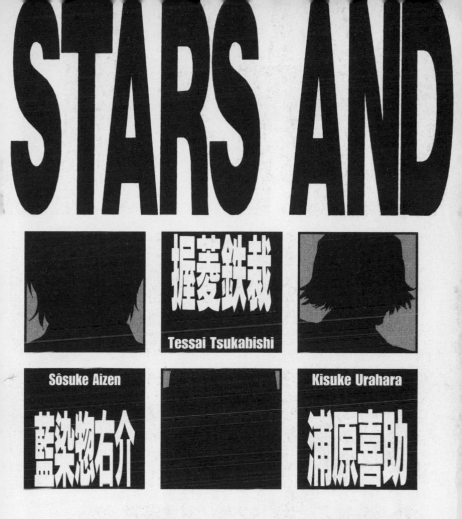

握菱鉄裁

Tessai Tsukabishi

Sôsuke Aizen

Kisuke Urahara

藍染惣右介

浦原喜助

★ plot

When high school student Ichigo Kurosaki meets Soul Reaper Rukia Kuchiki his life is changed forever. Soon Ichigo is a soul-cleansing Soul Reaper too, and he finds himself having adventures, as well as problems, that he never would have imagined. Now Ichigo and his friends must stop renegade Soul Reaper Aizen and his army of Arrancars from destroying the Soul Society and wiping out KarakuraTown as well.

Having penetrated the enemy's stronghold in order to rescue Orihime, Ichigo and his friends manage to defeat the fearsome Espadas with the help of reinforcements from the Soul Society. But the thrill of victory is short-lived as Orihime is soon recaptured and placed in a tower while Aizen and his forces go to attack the Soul Society! As the fight continues, the scene shifts to the past where it all began!

BLEACH ALL

猿柿ひよ里
Hiyori Sarugaki

市丸ギン
Gin Ichimaru

Shinji Hirako
平子真子

STORIES

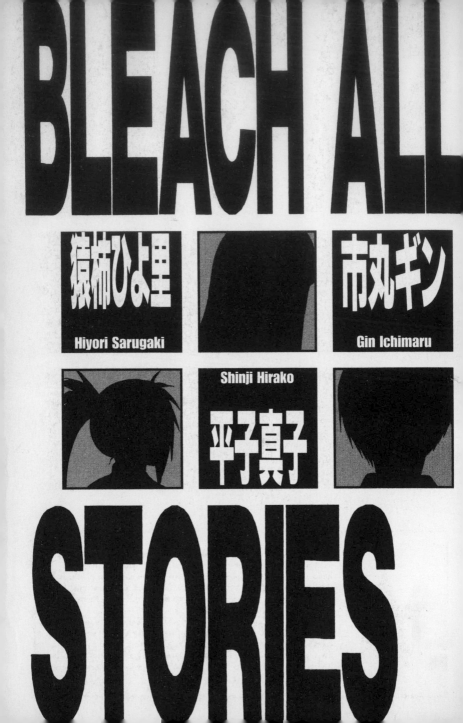

BLEACH36

TURN BACK THE PENDULUM

Contents

-108. Turn Back the Pendulum		7
-107. Turn Back the Pendulum 2		27
-106. Turn Back the Pendulum 3		51
-105. Turn Back the Pendulum 4		71
-104. Turn Back the Pendulum 5		91
-103. Turn Back the Pendulum 6		111
-102. Turn Back the Pendulum 7		135
-101. Turn Back the Pendulum 8		155
-100. Turn Back the Pendulum 9		175

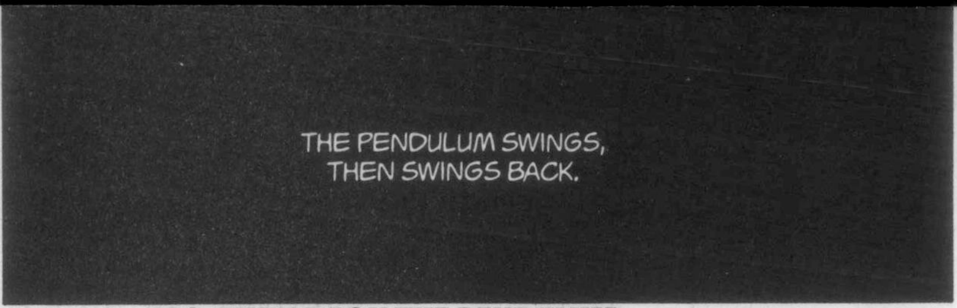
THE PENDULUM SWINGS,
THEN SWINGS BACK.

-108. TURN BACK THE PENDULUM

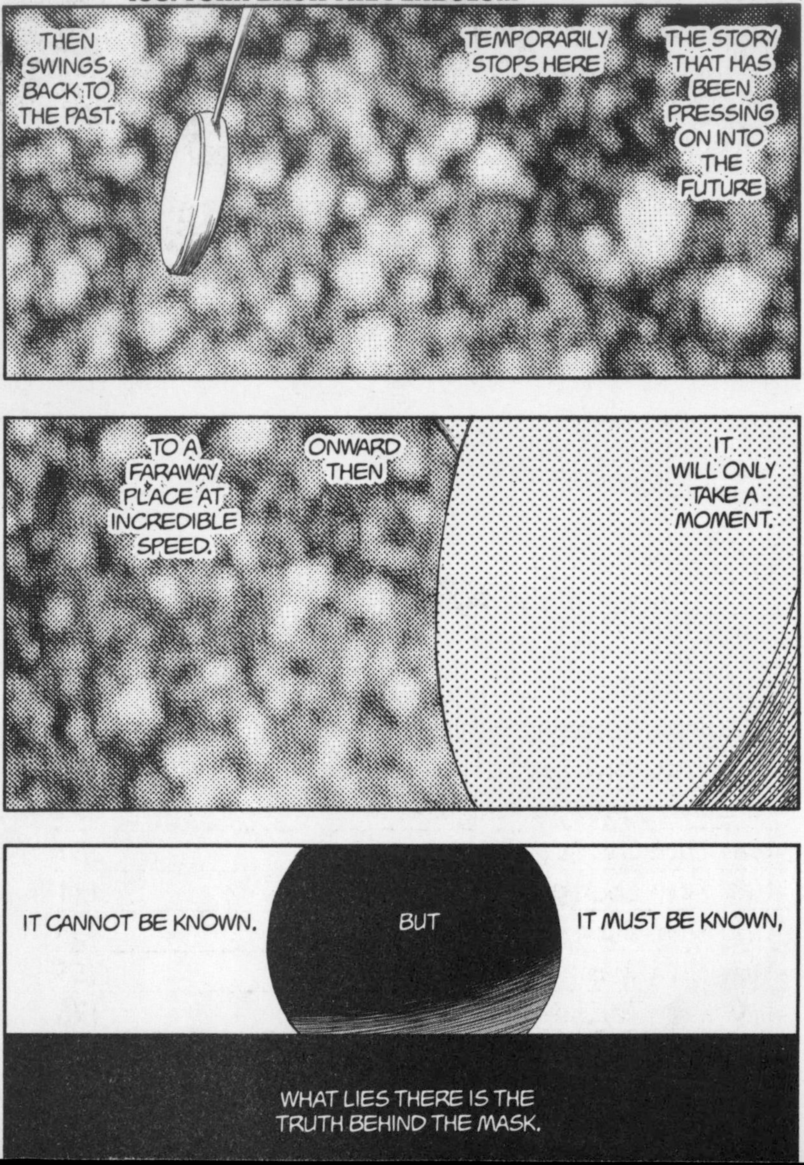
THE STORY THAT HAS BEEN PRESSING ON INTO THE FUTURE
TEMPORARILY STOPS HERE
THEN SWINGS BACK TO THE PAST.
IT WILL ONLY TAKE A MOMENT.
ONWARD THEN
TO A FARAWAY PLACE AT INCREDIBLE SPEED.
IT MUST BE KNOWN,
BUT
IT CANNOT BE KNOWN.
WHAT LIES THERE IS THE
TRUTH BEHIND THE MASK.

H-108.

HE PENDULUM

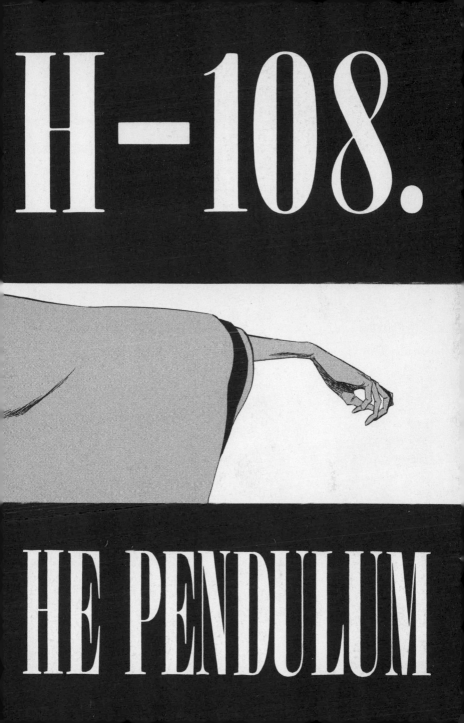

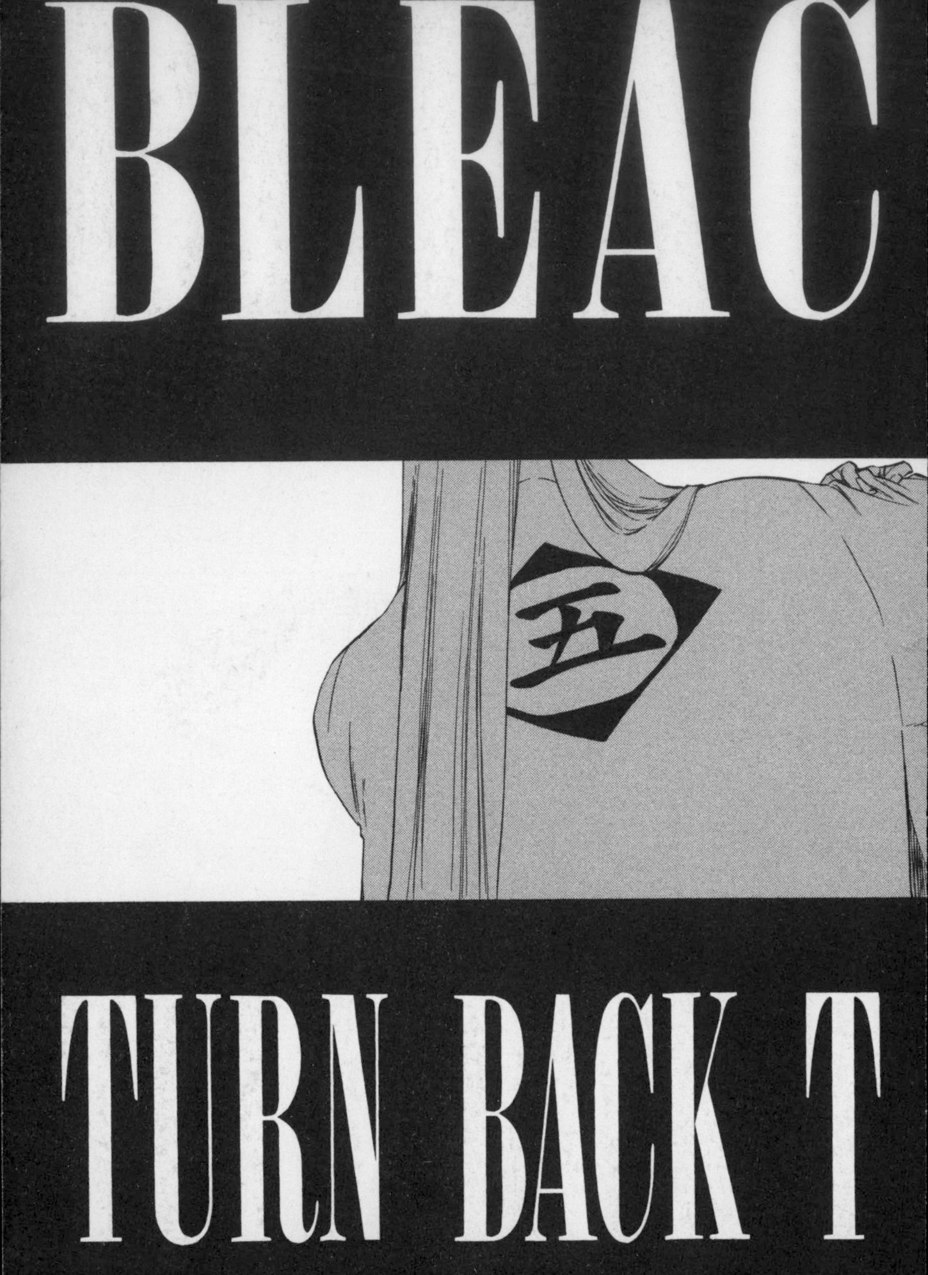
BLEAC
五
TURN BACK T

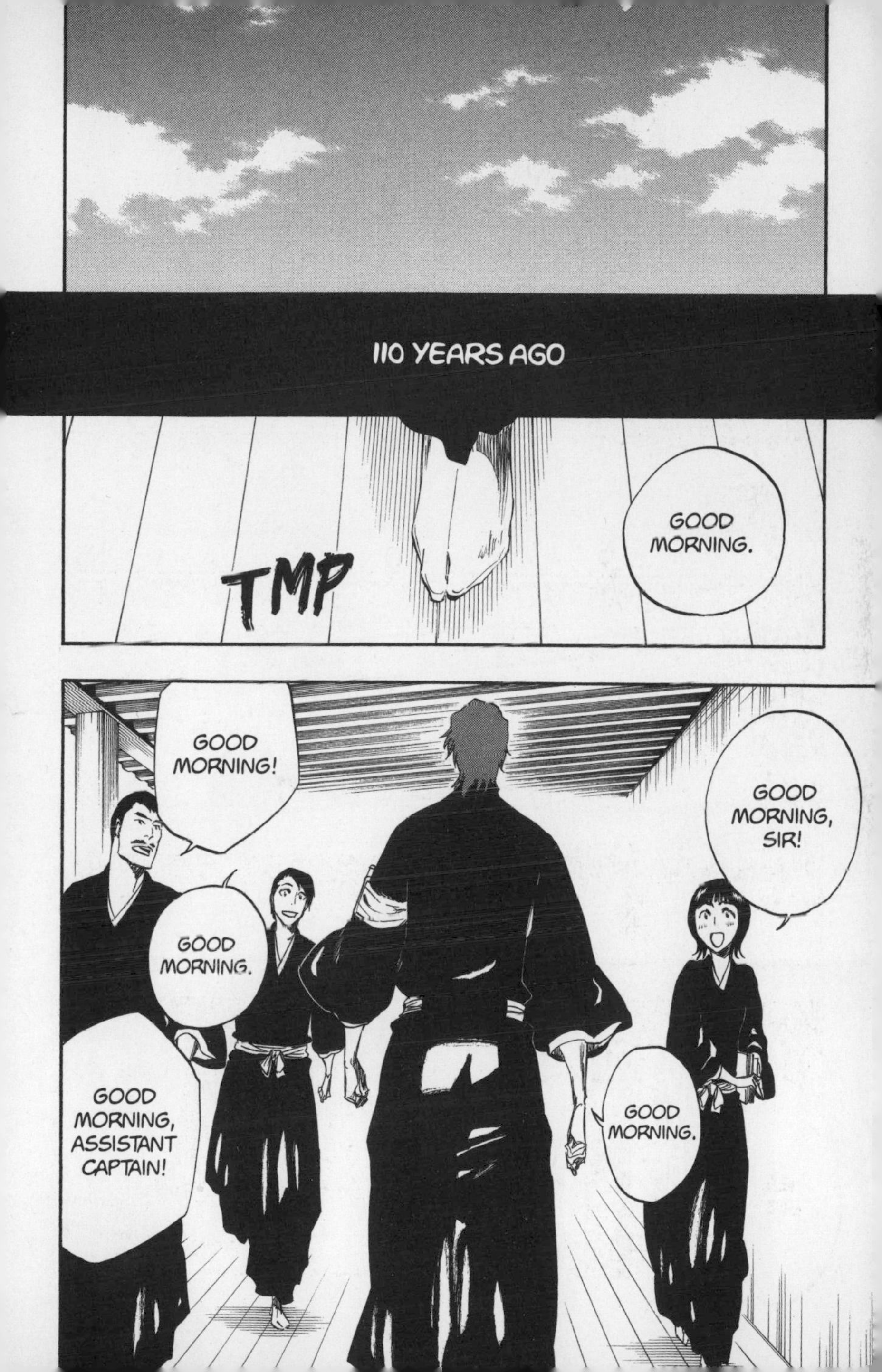
110 YEARS AGO
TMP
GOOD MORNING.
GOOD MORNING, SIR!
GOOD MORNING!
GOOD MORNING.
GOOD MORNING.
GOOD MORNING, ASSISTANT CAPTAIN!

GOOD MORNING.

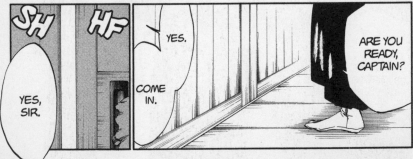

YES, SIR.

YES.

COME IN.

ARE YOU READY, CAPTAIN?

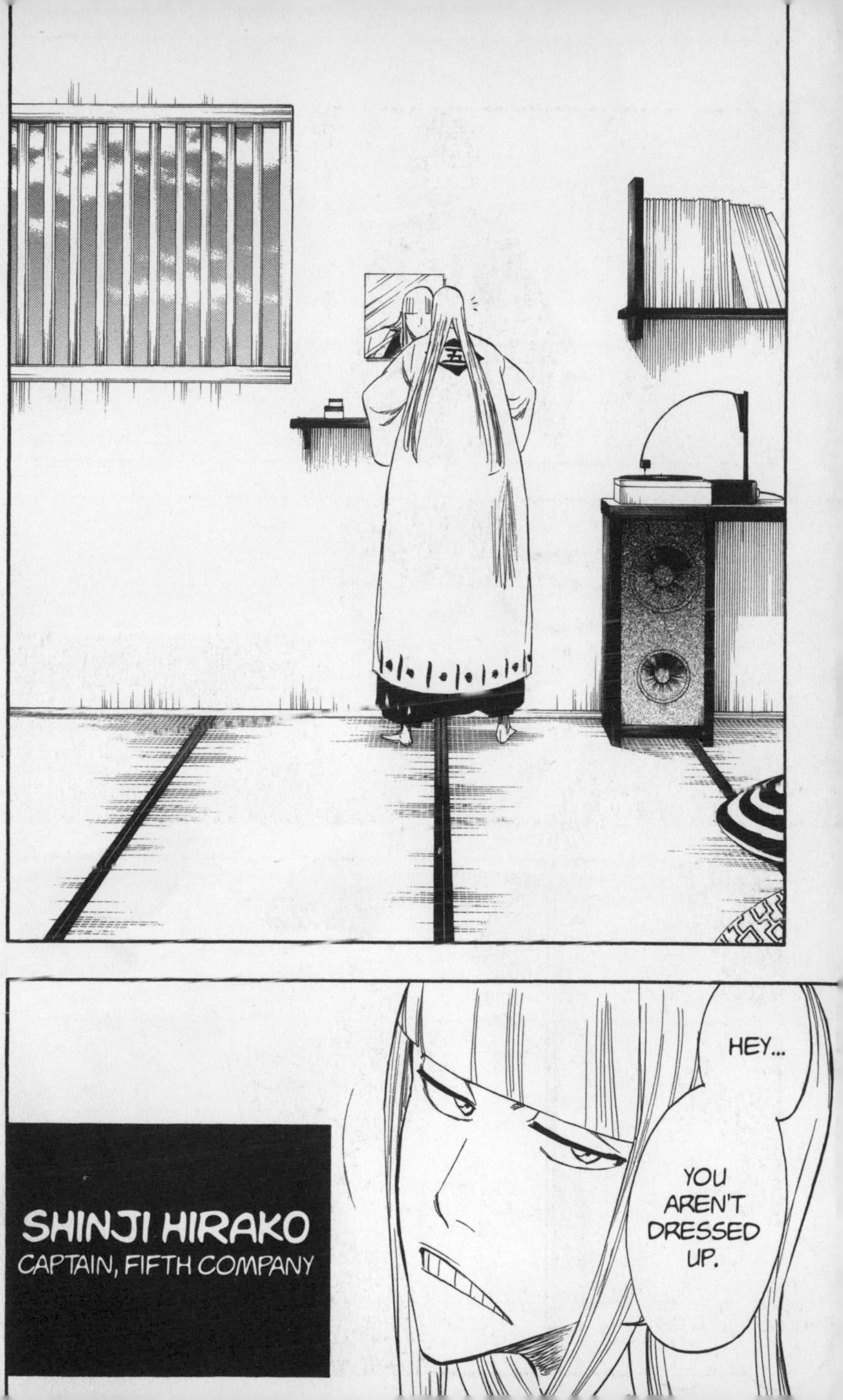
HEY...
YOU AREN'T DRESSED UP.
SHINJI HIRAKO
CAPTAIN, FIFTH COMPANY

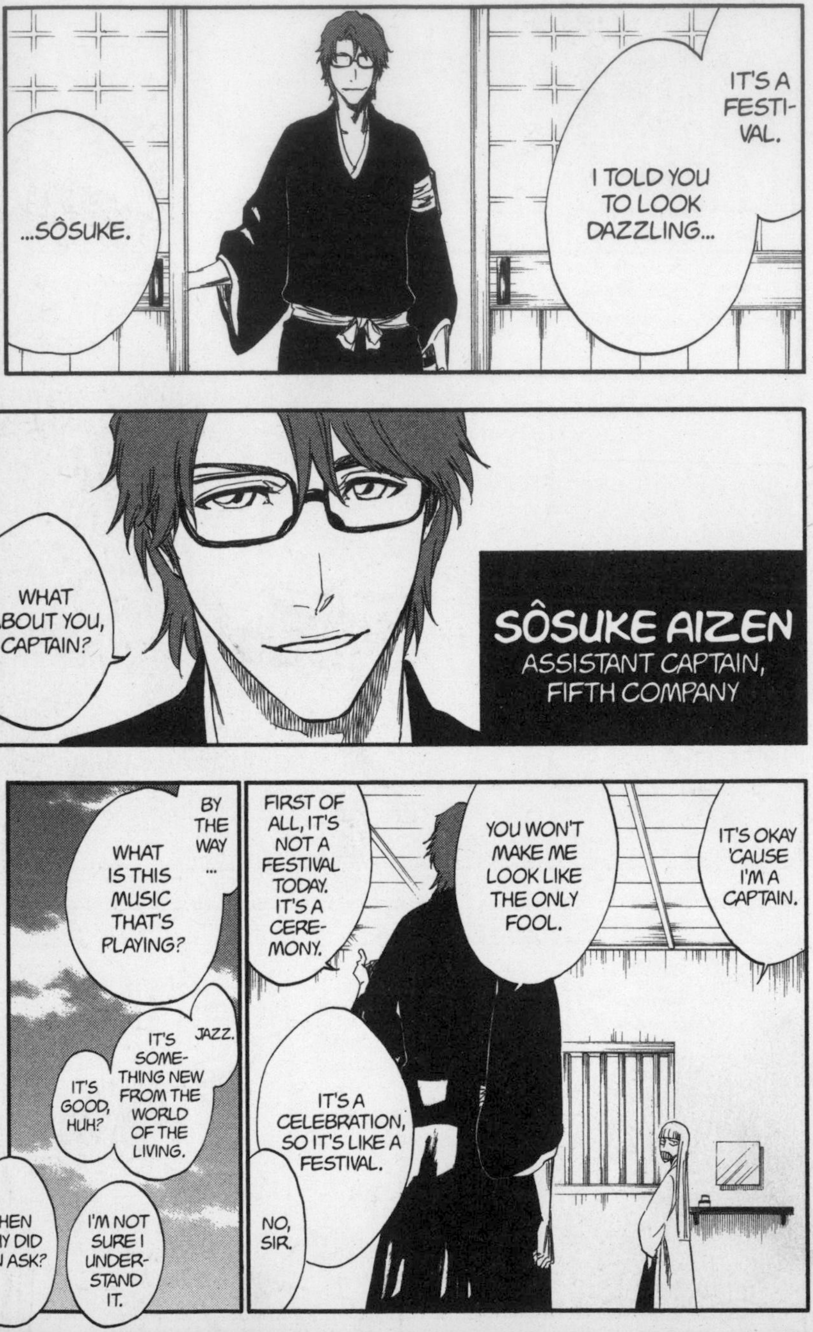
IT'S A FESTIVAL.
I TOLD YOU TO LOOK DAZZLING...
...SÔSUKE.
SÔSUKE AIZEN
ASSISTANT CAPTAIN, FIFTH COMPANY
WHAT ABOUT YOU, CAPTAIN?
IT'S OKAY 'CAUSE I'M A CAPTAIN.
YOU WON'T MAKE ME LOOK LIKE THE ONLY FOOL.
FIRST OF ALL, IT'S NOT A FESTIVAL TODAY. IT'S A CEREMONY.
IT'S A CELEBRATION, SO IT'S LIKE A FESTIVAL.
NO, SIR.
BY THE WAY...
WHAT IS THIS MUSIC THAT'S PLAYING?
JAZZ.
IT'S SOMETHING NEW FROM THE WORLD OF THE LIVING.
IT'S GOOD, HUH?
I'M NOT SURE I UNDERSTAND IT.
THEN WHY DID YOU ASK?

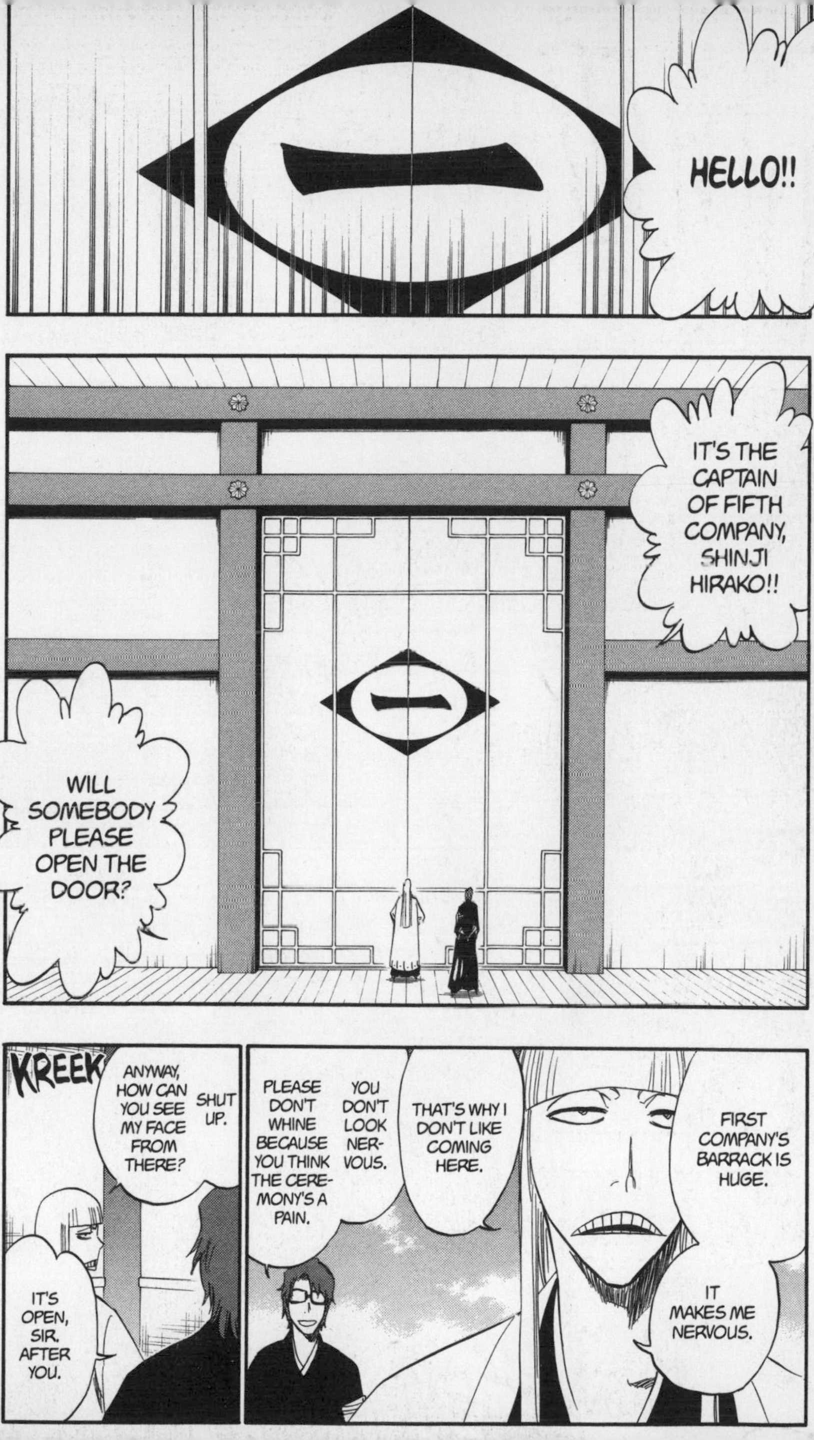
HELLO!!
IT'S THE CAPTAIN OF FIFTH COMPANY, SHINJI HIRAKO!!
WILL SOMEBODY PLEASE OPEN THE DOOR?
FIRST COMPANY'S BARRACK IS HUGE.
IT MAKES ME NERVOUS.
THAT'S WHY I DON'T LIKE COMING HERE.
YOU DON'T LOOK NER-VOUS.
PLEASE DON'T WHINE BECAUSE YOU THINK THE CERE-MONY'S A PAIN.
SHUT UP.
ANYWAY, HOW CAN YOU SEE MY FACE FROM THERE?
KREEK
IT'S OPEN, SIR. AFTER YOU.

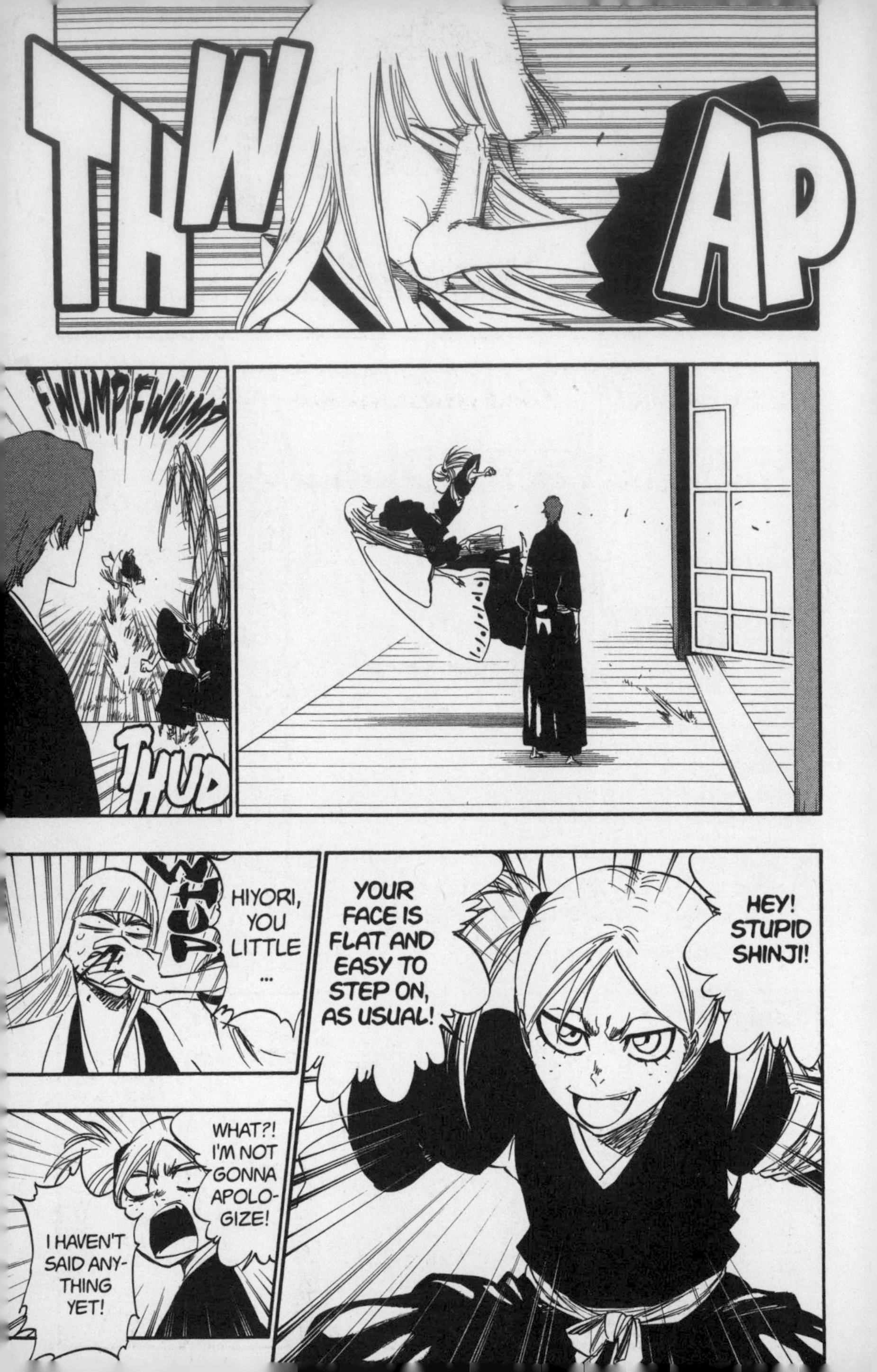
THWAP
FWUMP FWUMP
THUD
HEY! STUPID SHINJI!
YOUR FACE IS FLAT AND EASY TO STEP ON, AS USUAL!
HIYORI, YOU LITTLE ...
WHAT?! I'M NOT GONNA APOLOGIZE!
I HAVEN'T SAID ANYTHING YET!

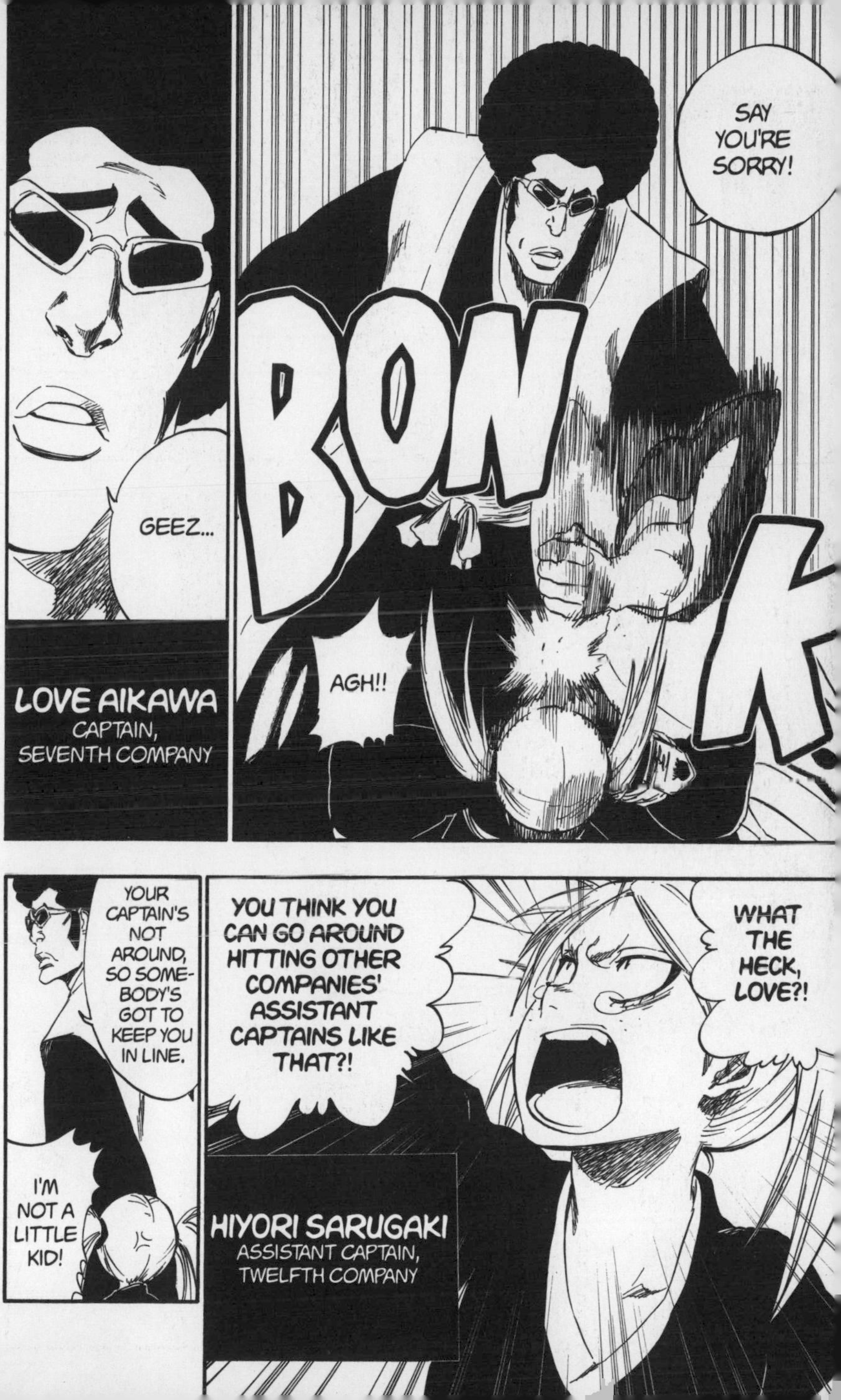
SAY YOU'RE SORRY!
BONK
AGH!!
GEEZ...
LOVE AIKAWA
CAPTAIN, SEVENTH COMPANY
WHAT THE HECK, LOVE?!
YOU THINK YOU CAN GO AROUND HITTING OTHER COMPANIES' ASSISTANT CAPTAINS LIKE THAT?!
HIYORI SARUGAKI
ASSISTANT CAPTAIN, TWELFTH COMPANY
YOUR CAPTAIN'S NOT AROUND, SO SOMEBODY'S GOT TO KEEP YOU IN LINE.
I'M NOT A LITTLE KID!

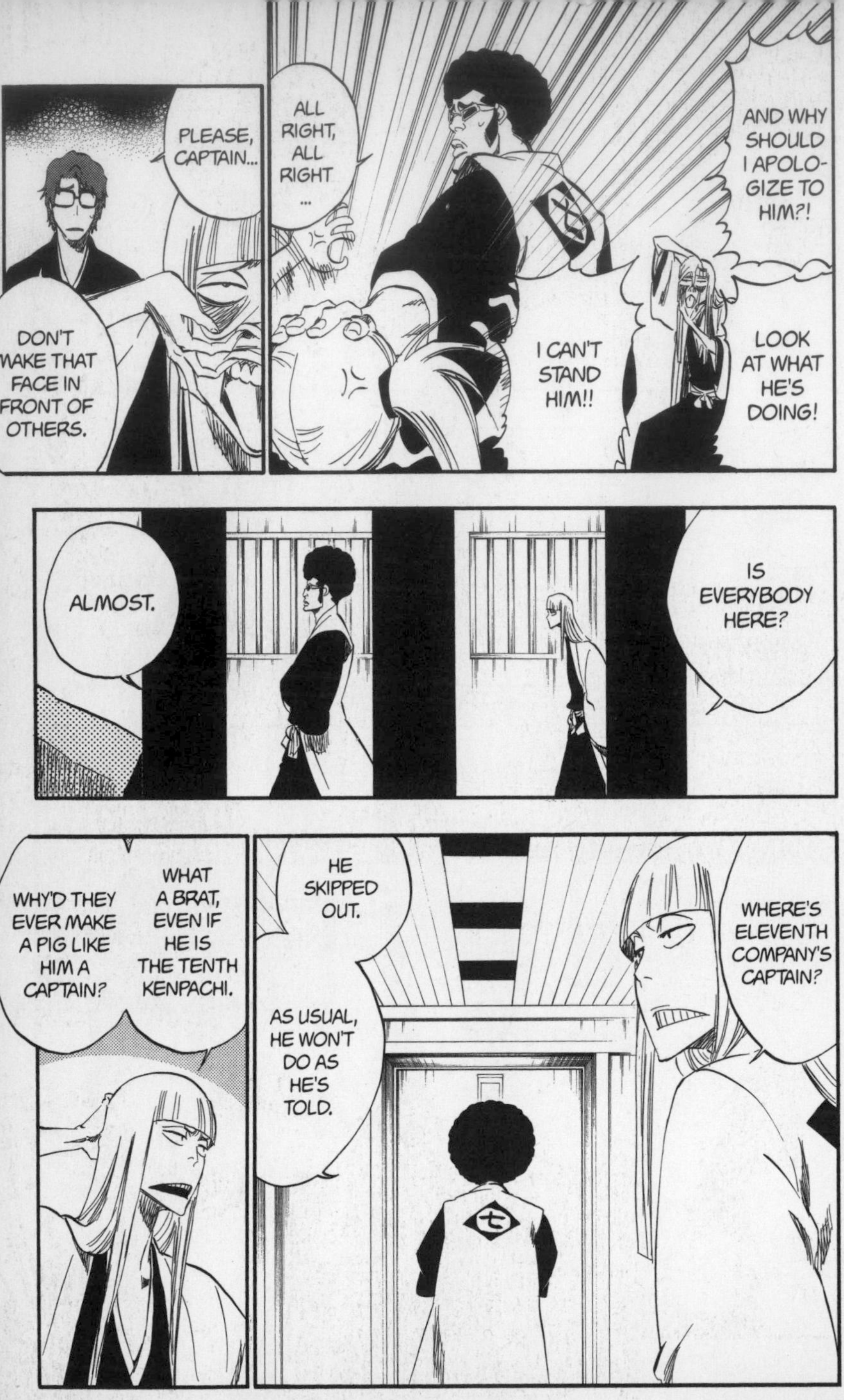
AND WHY SHOULD I APOLOGIZE TO HIM?!
ALL RIGHT, ALL RIGHT ...
LOOK AT WHAT HE'S DOING!
I CAN'T STAND HIM!!
PLEASE, CAPTAIN...
DON'T MAKE THAT FACE IN FRONT OF OTHERS.
IS EVERYBODY HERE?
ALMOST.
WHERE'S ELEVENTH COMPANY'S CAPTAIN?
HE SKIPPED OUT.
AS USUAL, HE WON'T DO AS HE'S TOLD.
WHAT A BRAT, EVEN IF HE IS THE TENTH KENPACHI.
WHY'D THEY EVER MAKE A PIG LIKE HIM A CAPTAIN?

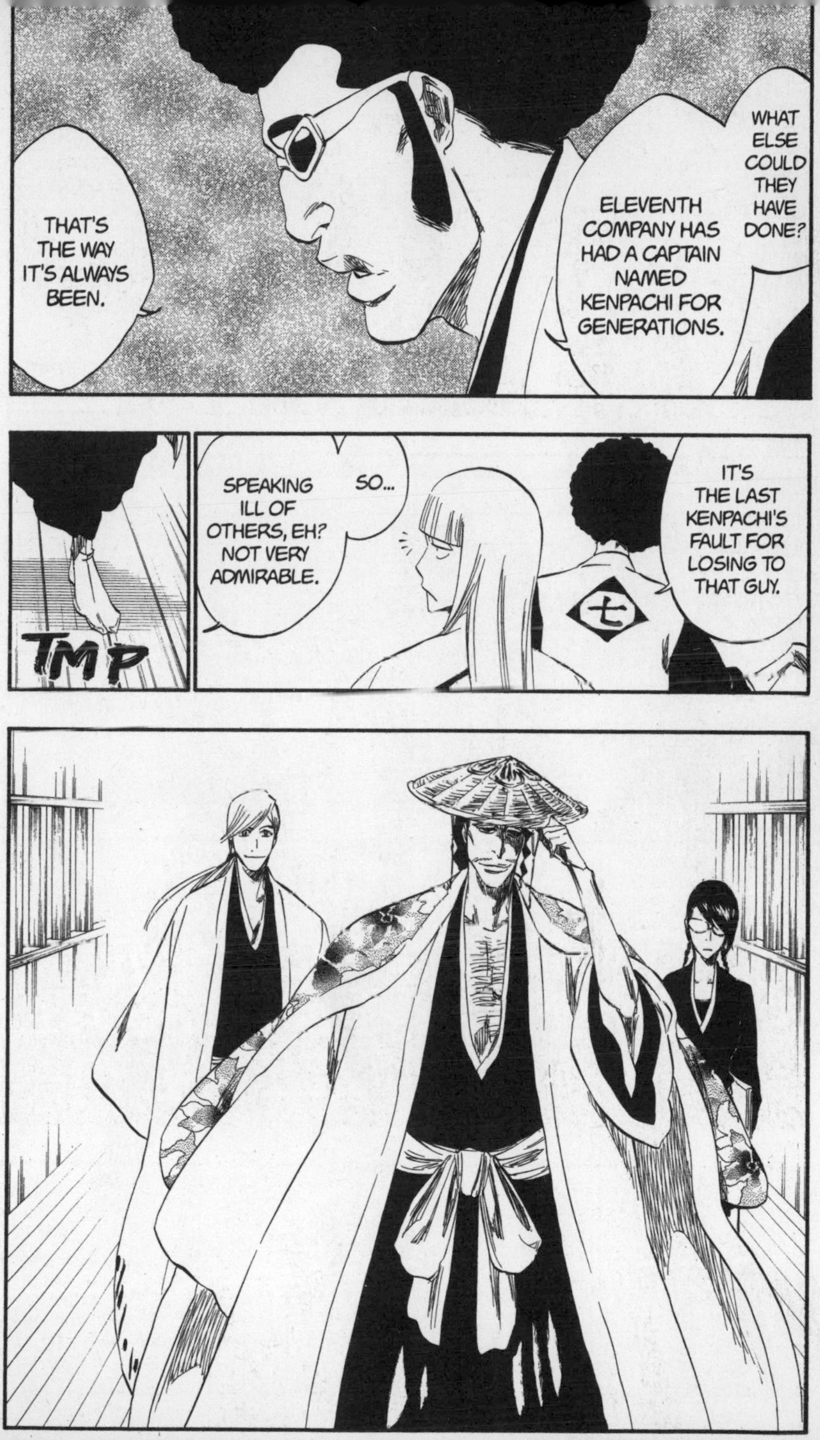
WHAT ELSE COULD THEY HAVE DONE?
ELEVENTH COMPANY HAS HAD A CAPTAIN NAMED KENPACHI FOR GENERATIONS.
THAT'S THE WAY IT'S ALWAYS BEEN.
IT'S THE LAST KENPACHI'S FAULT FOR LOSING TO THAT GUY.
SO...
SPEAKING ILL OF OTHERS, EH? NOT VERY ADMIRABLE.
TMP

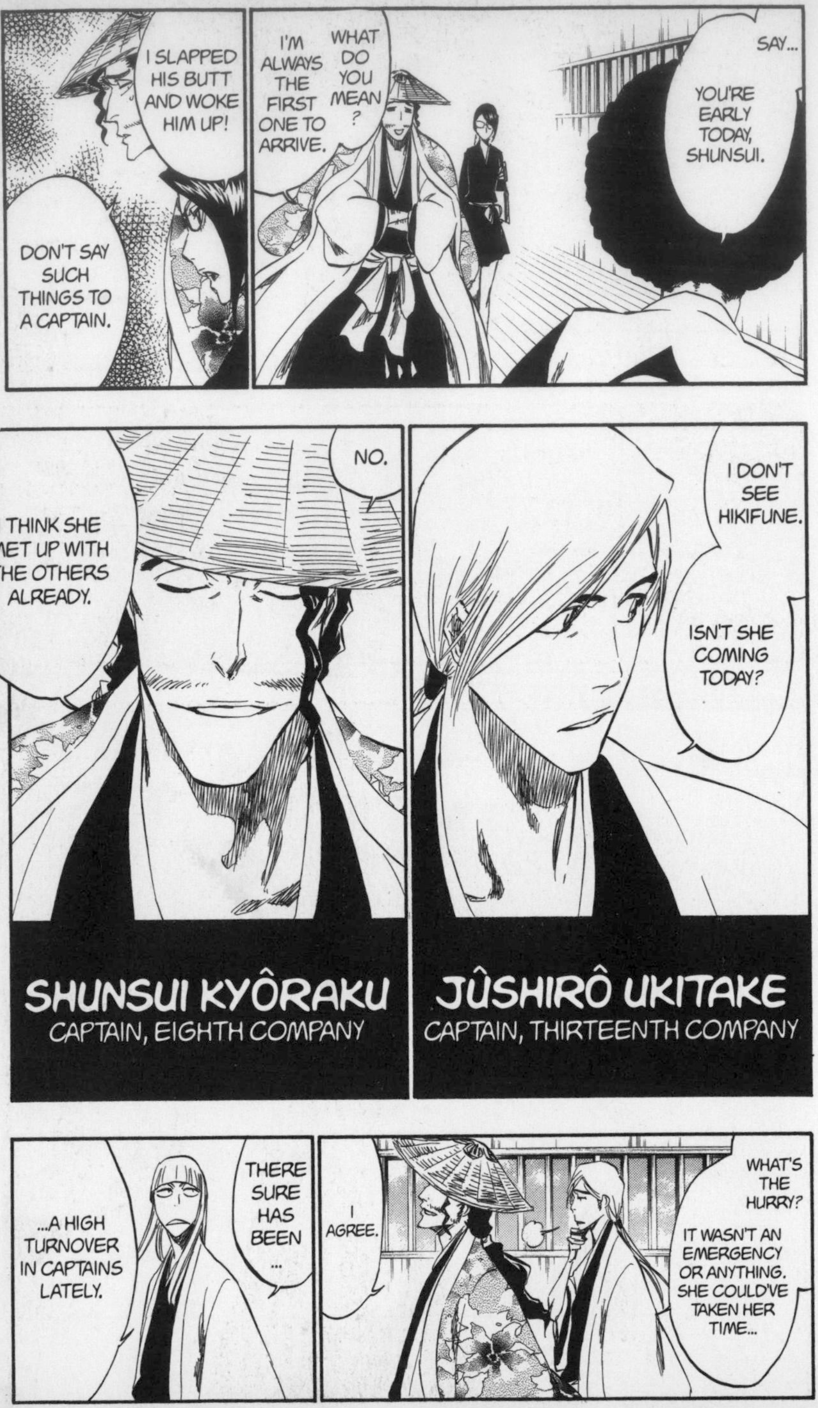
SAY...
YOU'RE EARLY TODAY, SHUNSUI.
WHAT DO YOU MEAN?
I'M ALWAYS THE FIRST ONE TO ARRIVE.
I SLAPPED HIS BUTT AND WOKE HIM UP!
DON'T SAY SUCH THINGS TO A CAPTAIN.
I DON'T SEE HIKIFUNE.
ISN'T SHE COMING TODAY?
JÛSHIRÔ UKITAKE
CAPTAIN, THIRTEENTH COMPANY
NO.
I THINK SHE MET UP WITH THE OTHERS ALREADY.
SHUNSUI KYÔRAKU
CAPTAIN, EIGHTH COMPANY
WHAT'S THE HURRY?
IT WASN'T AN EMERGENCY OR ANYTHING. SHE COULD'VE TAKEN HER TIME...
I AGREE.
THERE SURE HAS BEEN...
...A HIGH TURNOVER IN CAPTAINS LATELY.

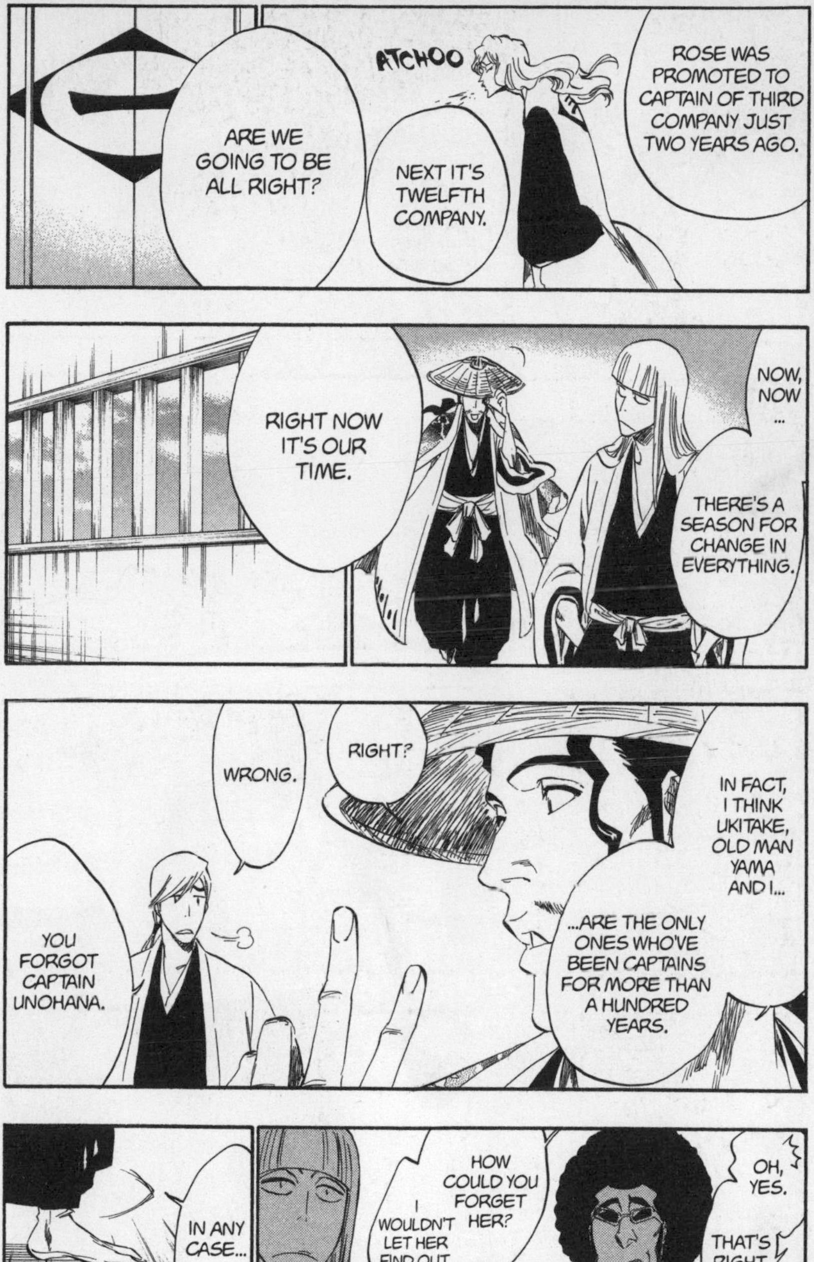
ROSE WAS PROMOTED TO CAPTAIN OF THIRD COMPANY JUST TWO YEARS AGO.
ATCHOO
NEXT IT'S TWELFTH COMPANY.
ARE WE GOING TO BE ALL RIGHT?
NOW, NOW ...
THERE'S A SEASON FOR CHANGE IN EVERYTHING.
RIGHT NOW IT'S OUR TIME.
IN FACT, I THINK UKITAKE, OLD MAN YAMA AND I...
...ARE THE ONLY ONES WHO'VE BEEN CAPTAINS FOR MORE THAN A HUNDRED YEARS.
RIGHT?
WRONG.
YOU FORGOT CAPTAIN UNOHANA.
OH, YES.
THAT'S RIGHT.
HOW COULD YOU FORGET HER?
I WOULDN'T LET HER FIND OUT YOU DID.
IN ANY CASE...

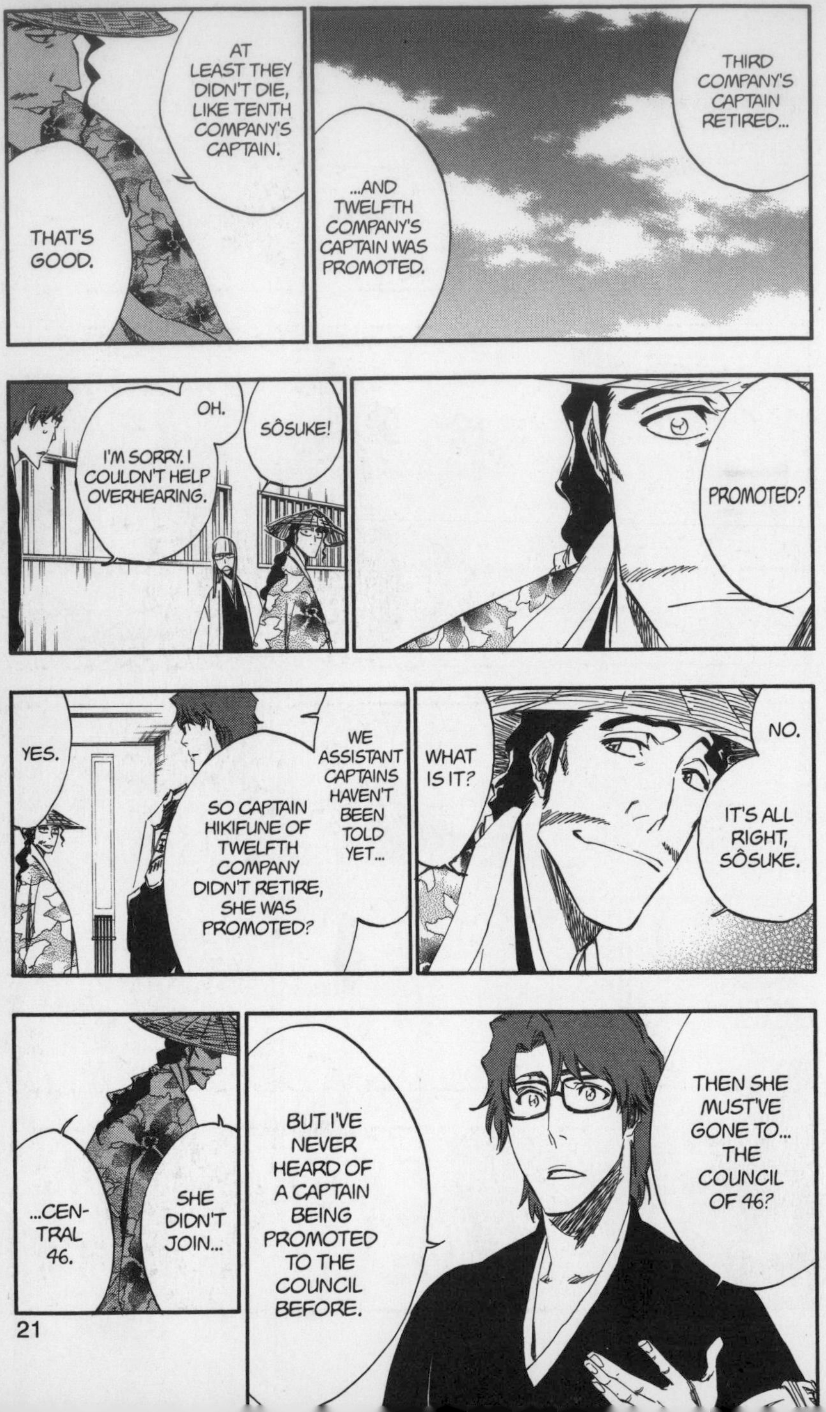
THIRD COMPANY'S CAPTAIN RETIRED...
...AND TWELFTH COMPANY'S CAPTAIN WAS PROMOTED.
AT LEAST THEY DIDN'T DIE, LIKE TENTH COMPANY'S CAPTAIN.
THAT'S GOOD.
PROMOTED?
SÔSUKE!
OH.
I'M SORRY. I COULDN'T HELP OVERHEARING.
NO.
IT'S ALL RIGHT, SÔSUKE.
WHAT IS IT?
WE ASSISTANT CAPTAINS HAVEN'T BEEN TOLD YET...
SO CAPTAIN HIKIFUNE OF TWELFTH COMPANY DIDN'T RETIRE, SHE WAS PROMOTED?
YES.
THEN SHE MUST'VE GONE TO... THE COUNCIL OF 46?
BUT I'VE NEVER HEARD OF A CAPTAIN BEING PROMOTED TO THE COUNCIL BEFORE.
SHE DIDN'T JOIN...
...CEN-TRAL 46.

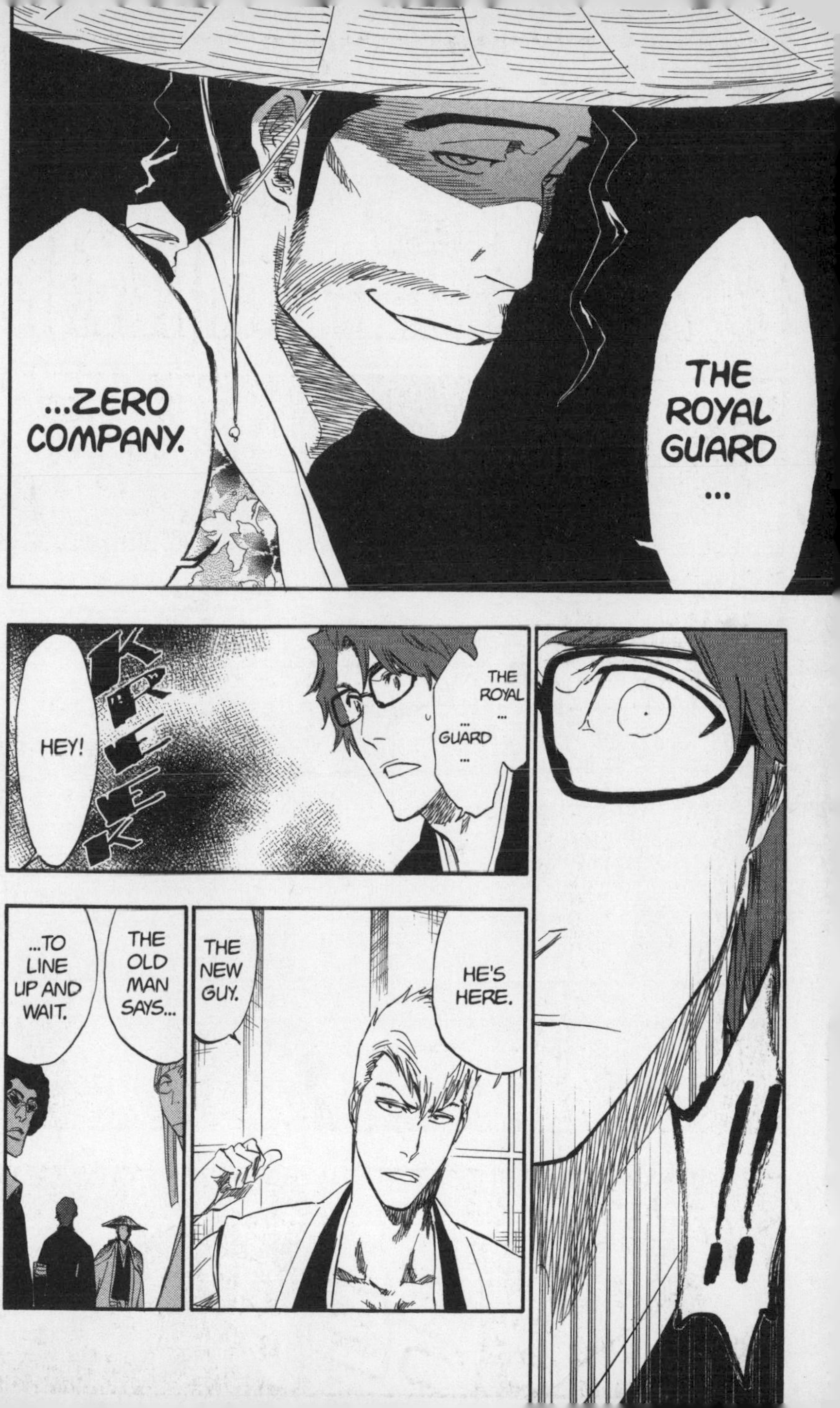
THE ROYAL GUARD ...
...ZERO COMPANY.
!!
THE ROYAL ... GUARD ...
HEY!
KREEK
HE'S HERE.
THE NEW GUY.
THE OLD MAN SAYS...
...TO LINE UP AND WAIT.

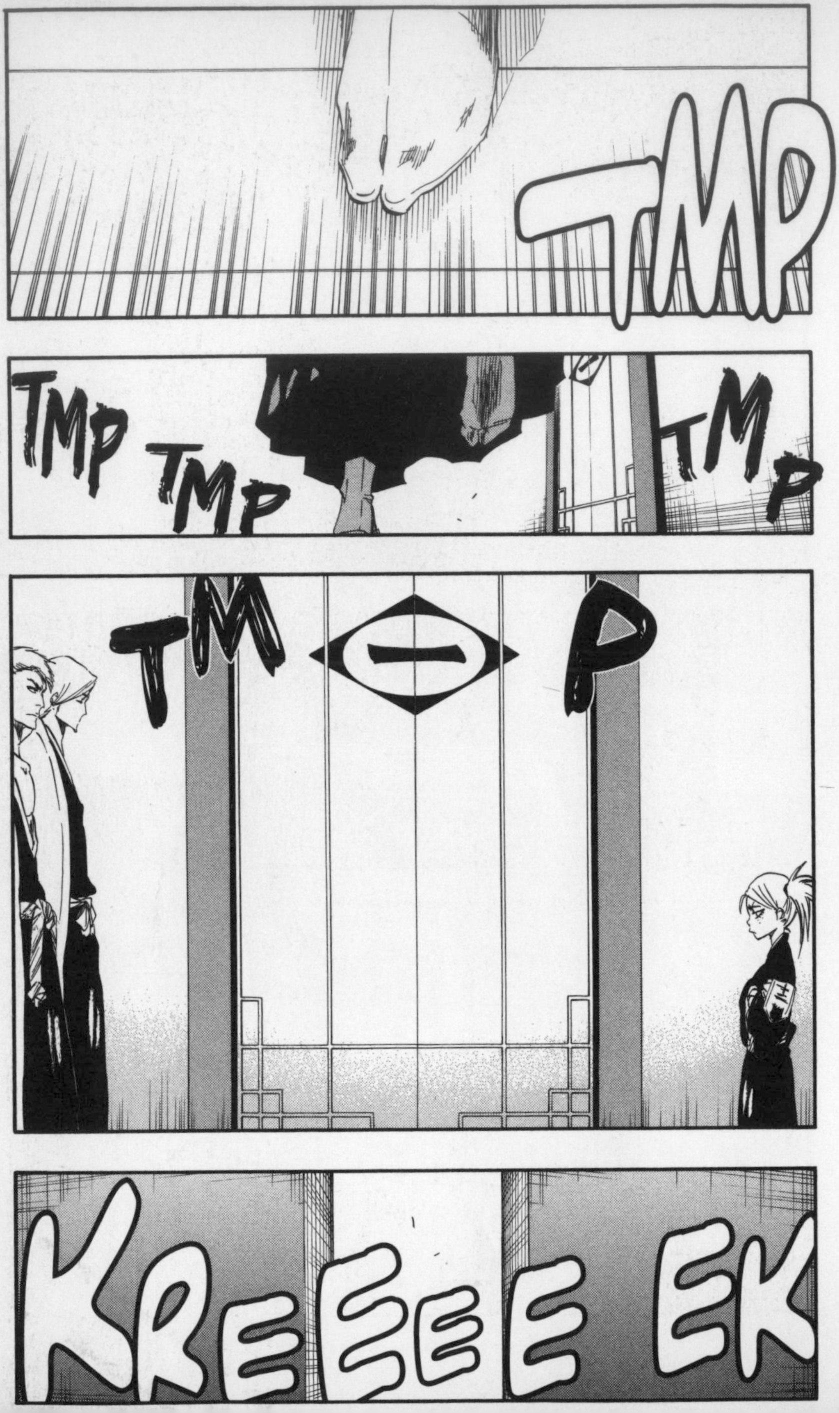
TMP
TMP
TMP
TMP
TMP
KREEEEEK

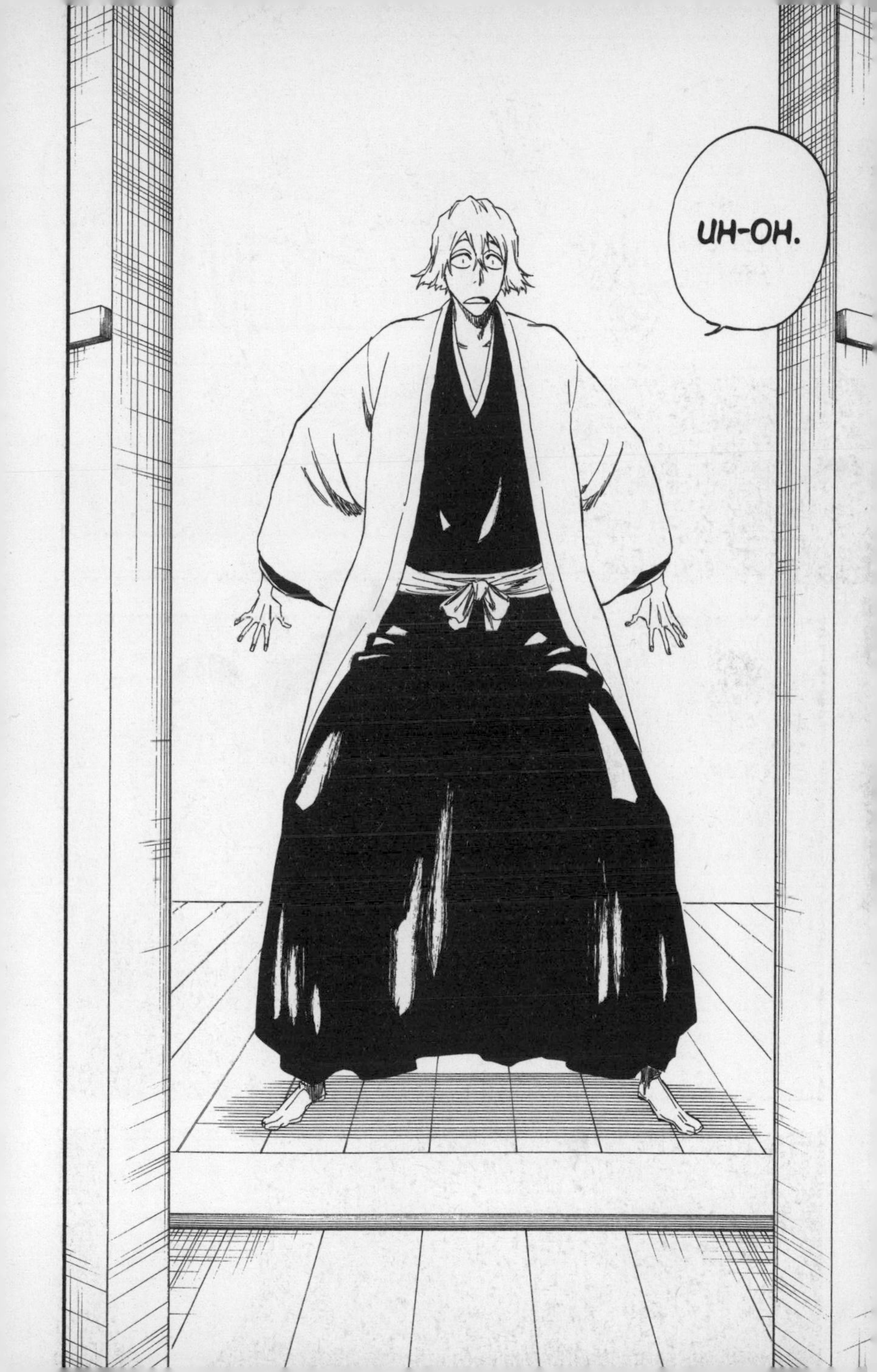
UH-OH.

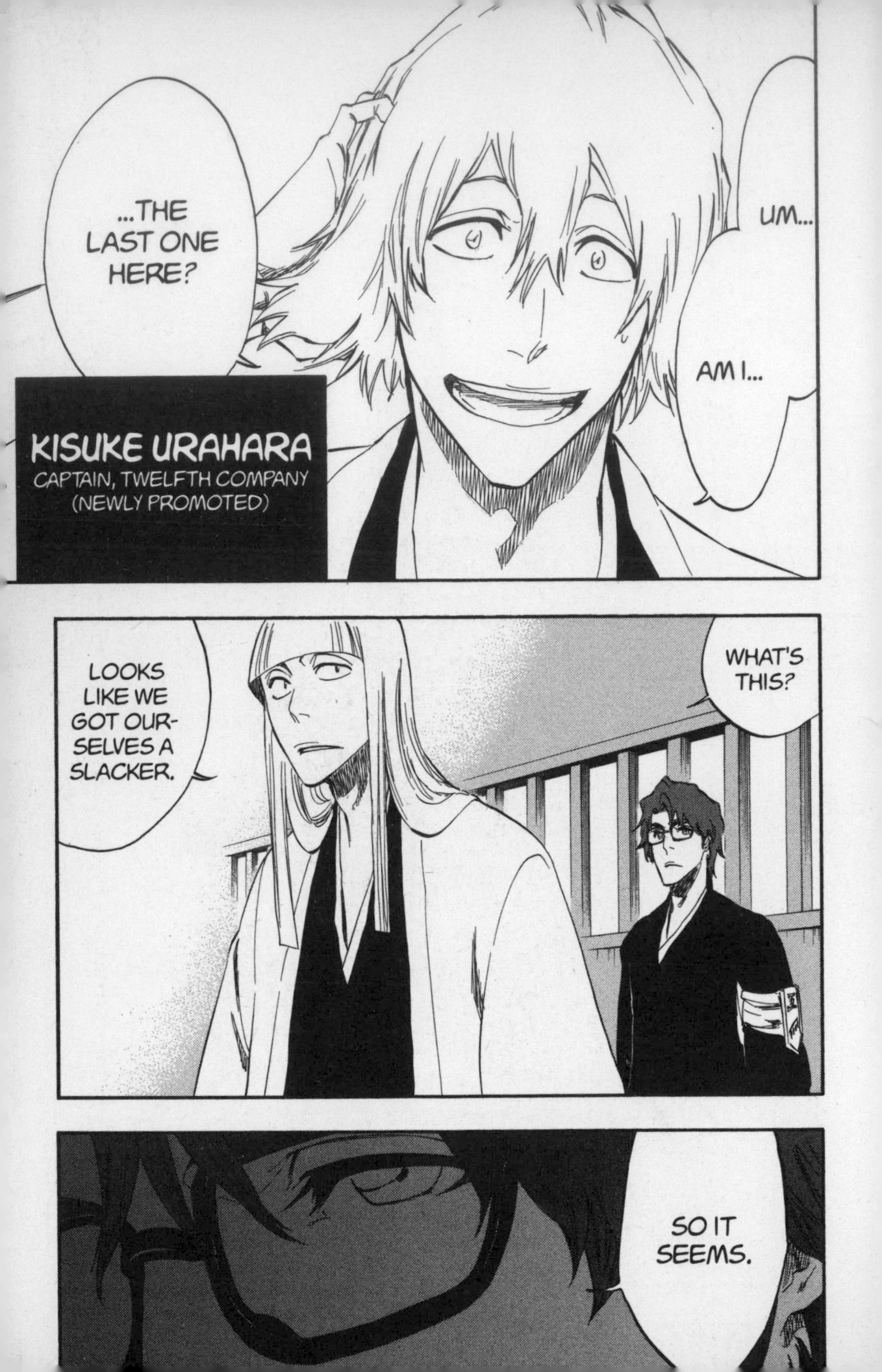
UM...
AM I...
...THE LAST ONE HERE?
KISUKE URAHARA
CAPTAIN, TWELFTH COMPANY
(NEWLY PROMOTED)
WHAT'S THIS?
LOOKS LIKE WE GOT OUR-SELVES A SLACKER.
SO IT SEEMS.

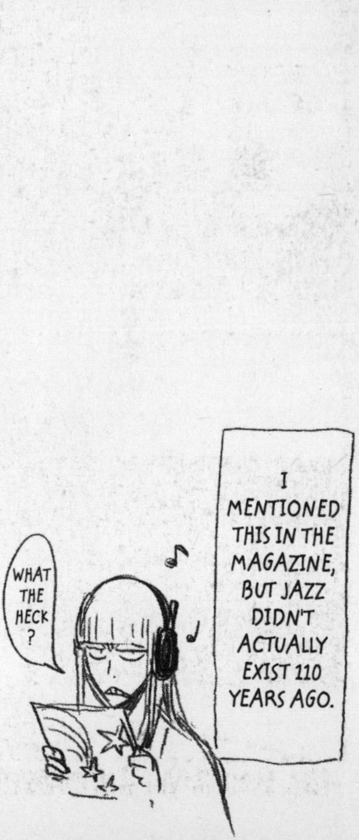
I MENTIONED THIS IN THE MAGAZINE, BUT JAZZ DIDN'T ACTUALLY EXIST 110 YEARS AGO.
WHAT THE HECK ?

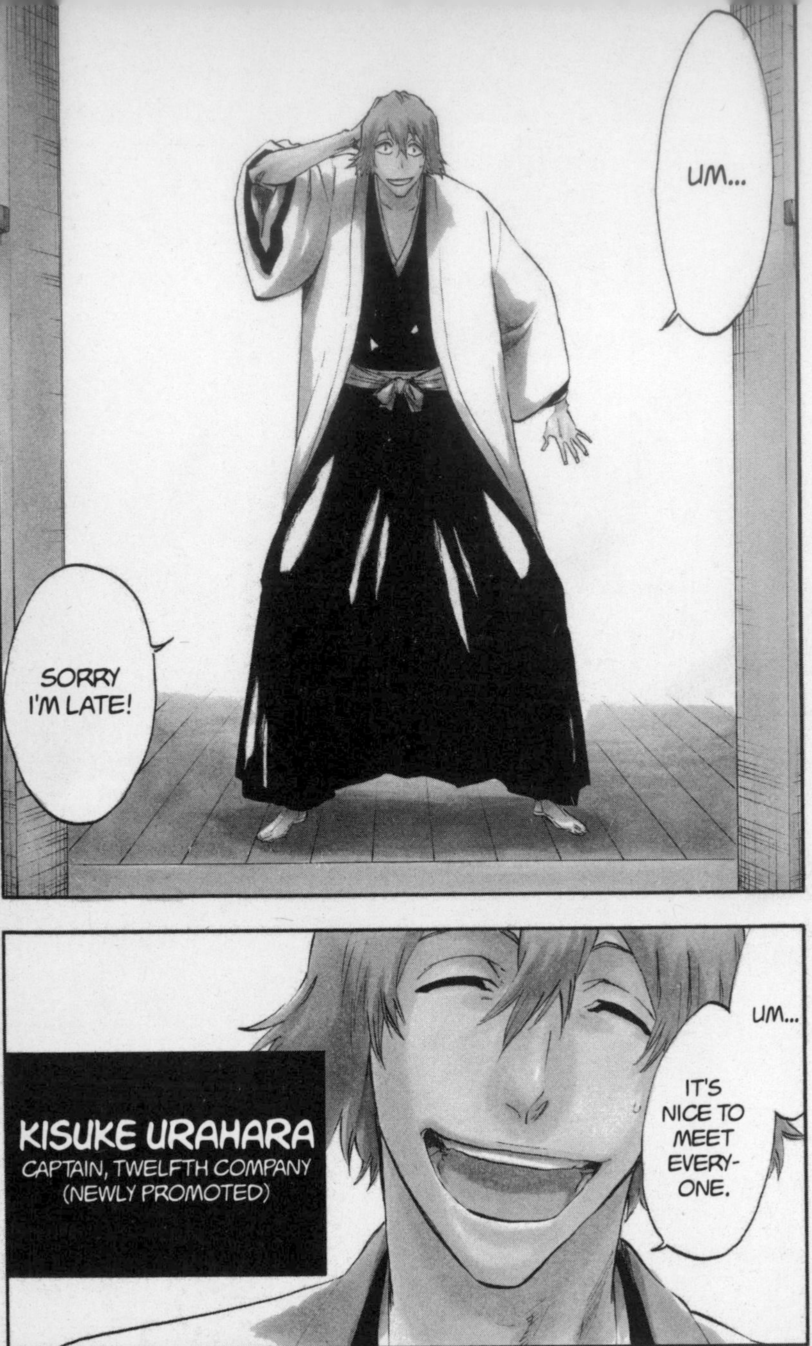
UM...
SORRY I'M LATE!
UM...
IT'S NICE TO MEET EVERY-ONE.
KISUKE URAHARA
CAPTAIN, TWELFTH COMPANY (NEWLY PROMOTED)

-107. Turn Back the Pendulum 2

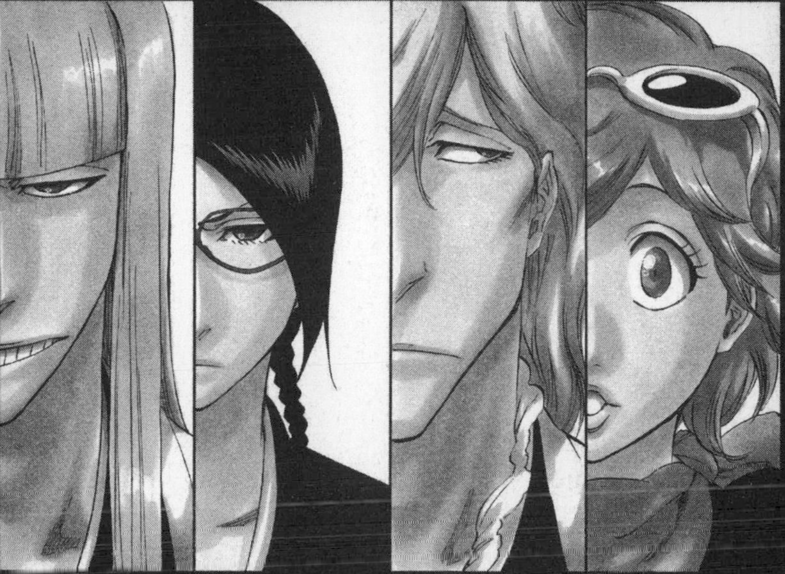

Turn Back the Pendulum 2

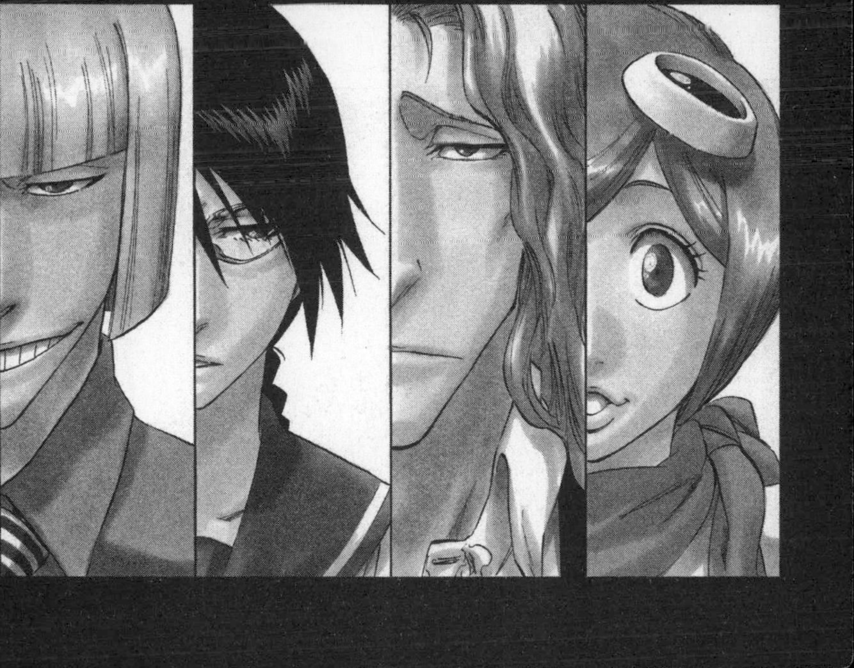

BLEACH -107.

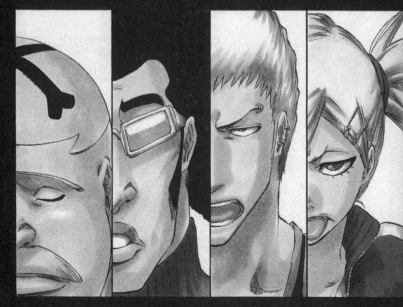

BLEACH
ブリーチ

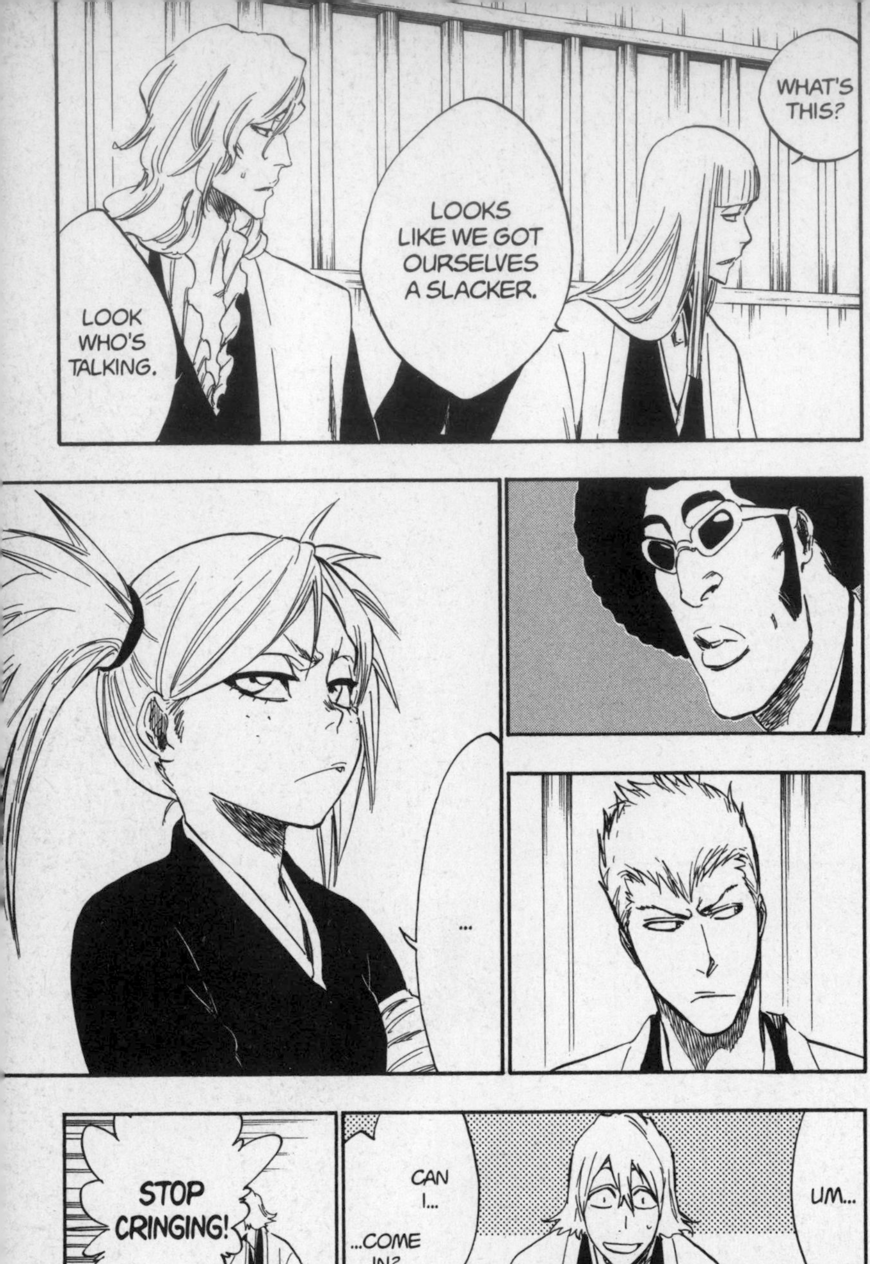
WHAT'S THIS?
LOOKS LIKE WE GOT OURSELVES A SLACKER.
LOOK WHO'S TALKING.
...
UM...
CAN I...
...COME IN?
STOP CRINGING!

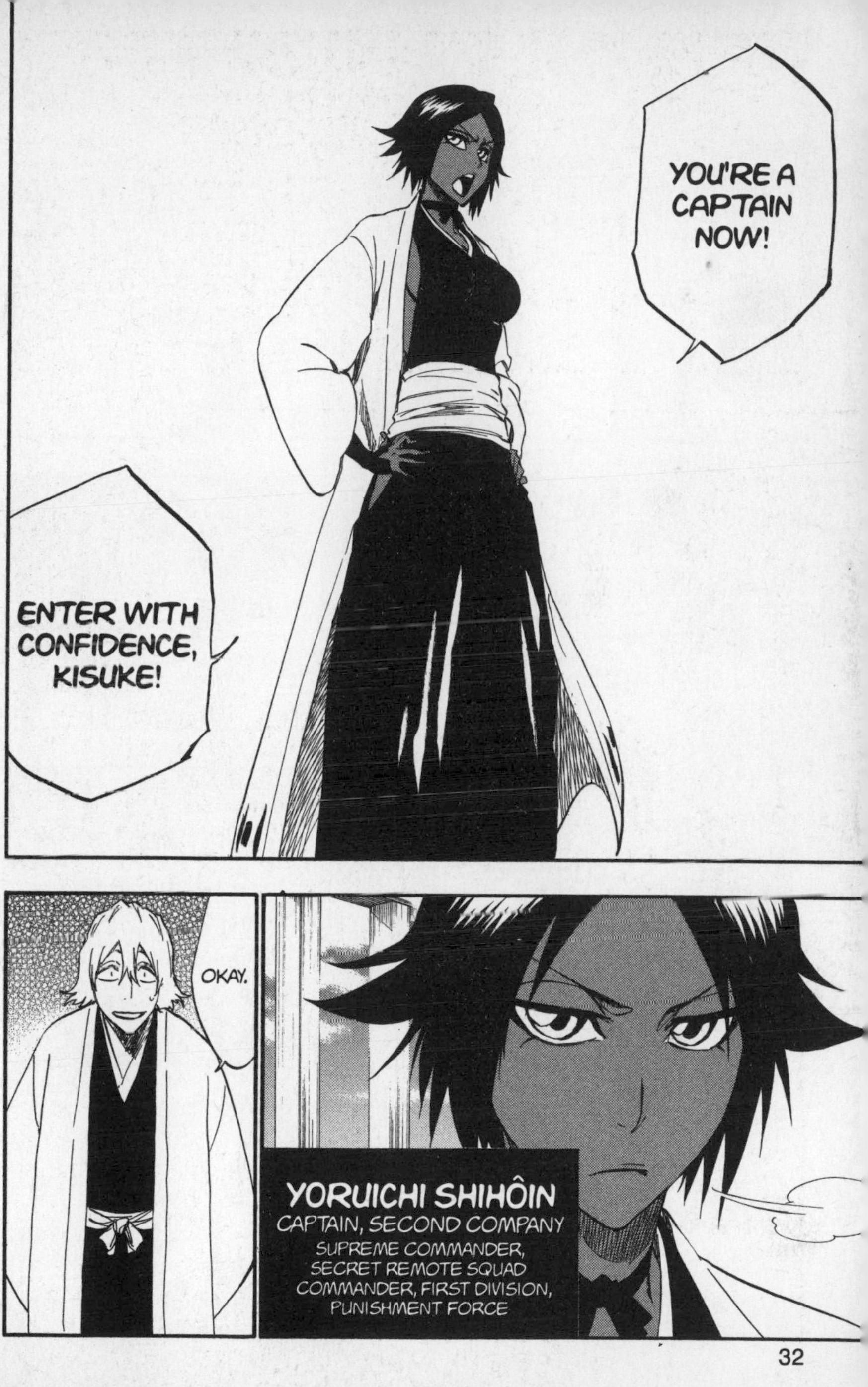
YOU'RE A CAPTAIN NOW!
ENTER WITH CONFIDENCE, KISUKE!
YORUICHI SHIHÔIN
CAPTAIN, SECOND COMPANY
SUPREME COMMANDER, SECRET REMOTE SQUAD
COMMANDER, FIRST DIVISION, PUNISHMENT FORCE
OKAY.

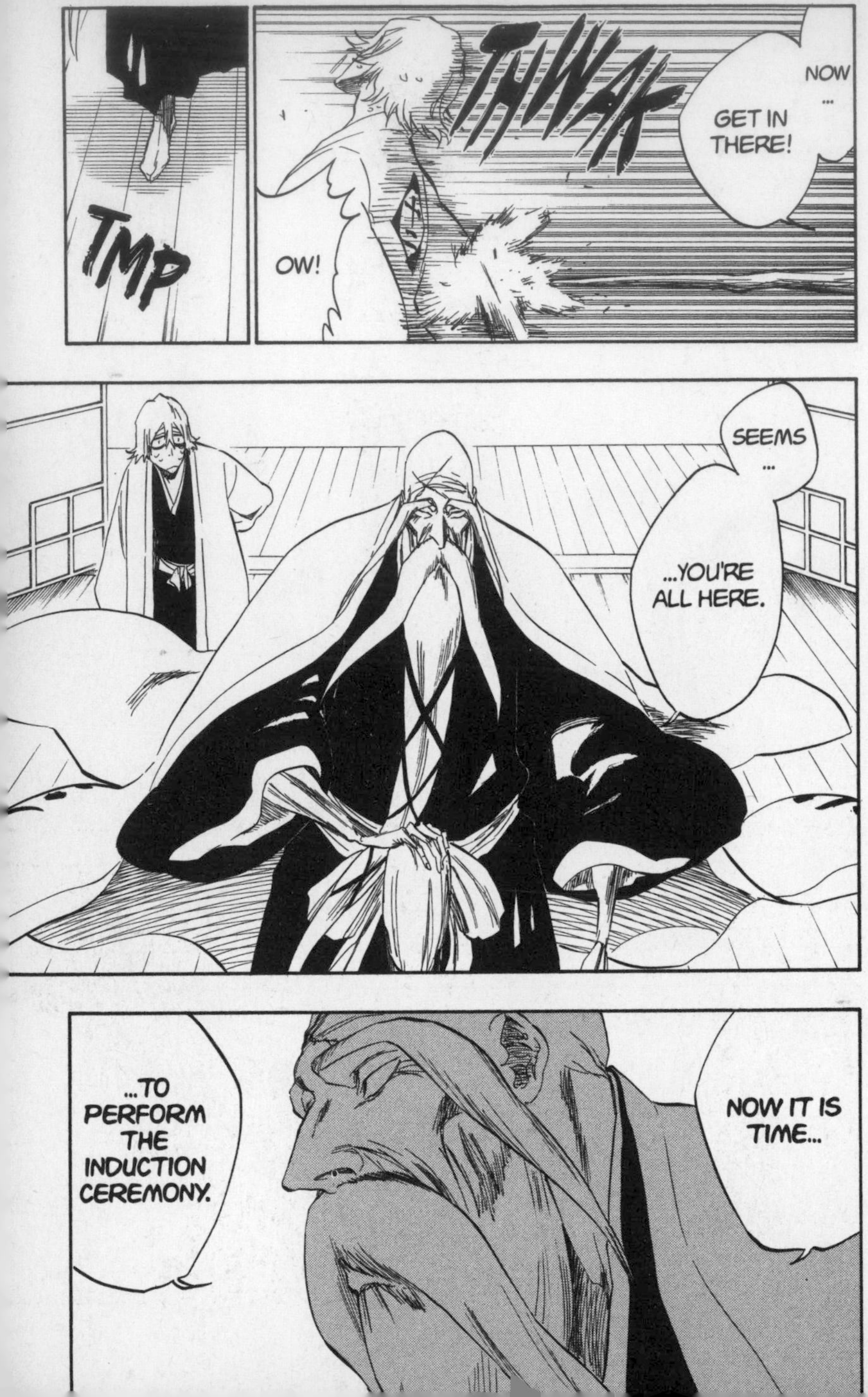
NOW ... GET IN THERE!
THWAK
OW!
TMP
SEEMS ...
...YOU'RE ALL HERE.
NOW IT IS TIME...
...TO PERFORM THE INDUCTION CEREMONY.

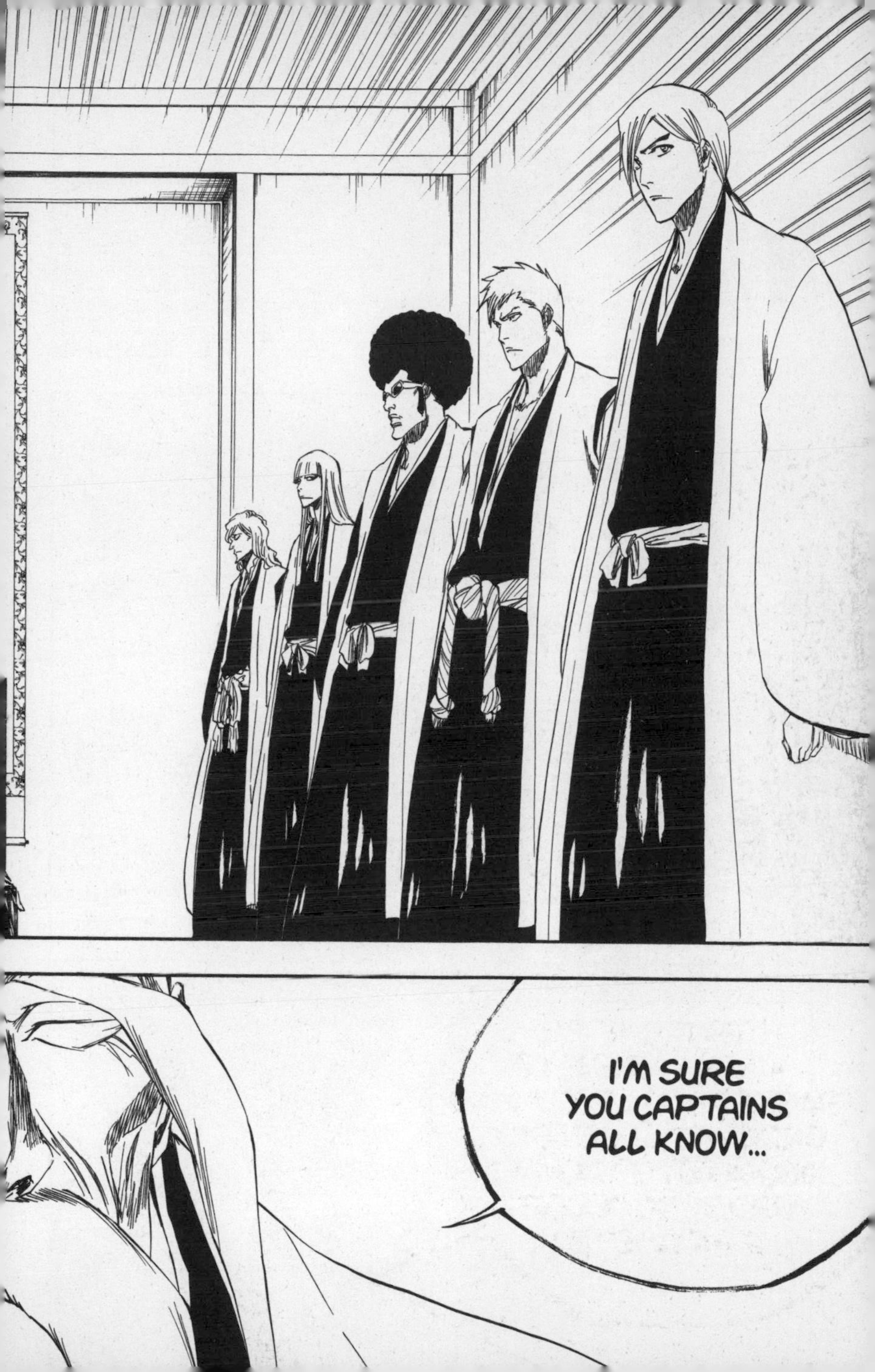
I'M SURE YOU CAPTAINS ALL KNOW...

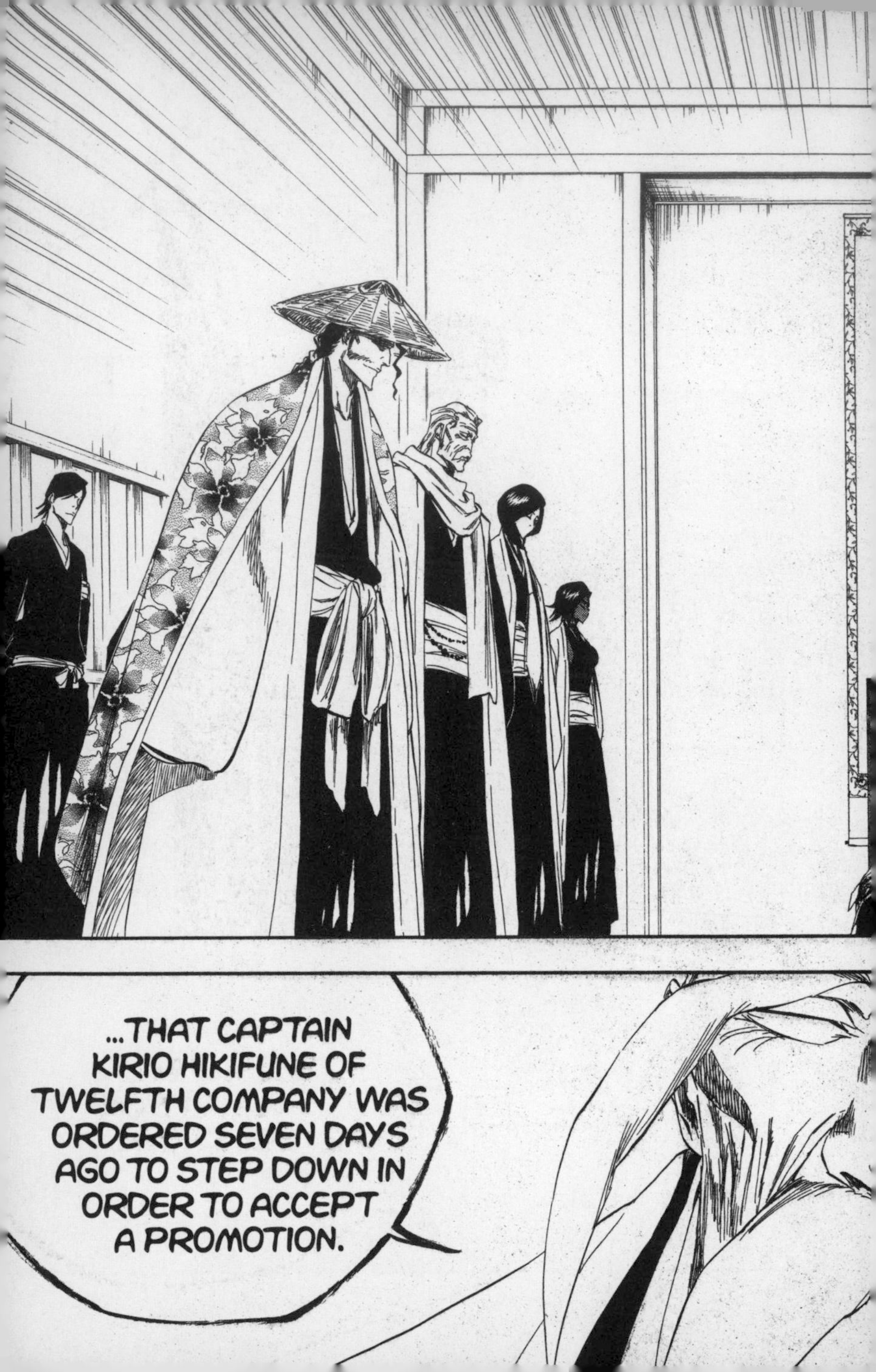
...THAT CAPTAIN KIRIO HIKIFUNE OF TWELFTH COMPANY WAS ORDERED SEVEN DAYS AGO TO STEP DOWN IN ORDER TO ACCEPT A PROMOTION.

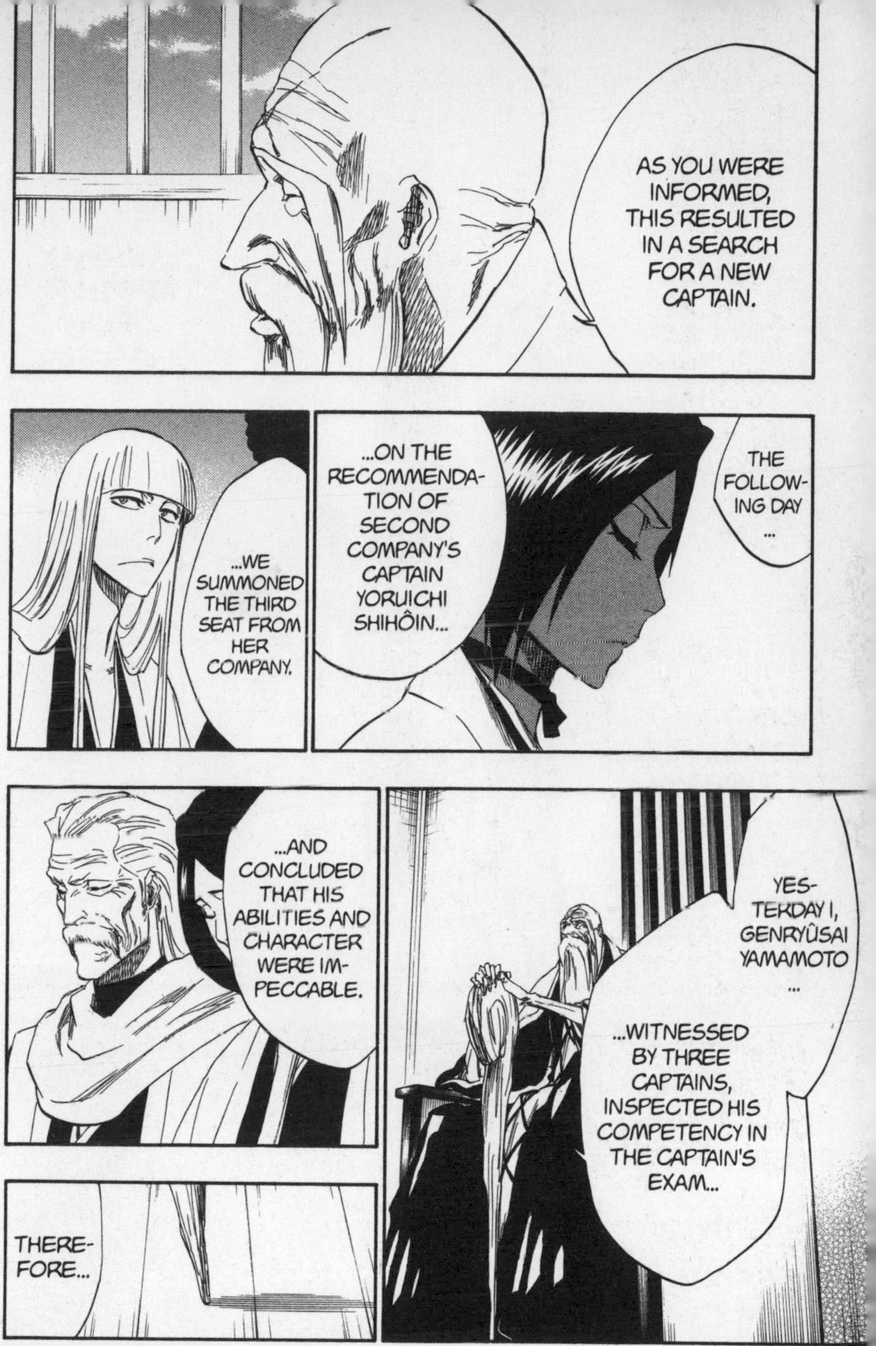
AS YOU WERE INFORMED, THIS RESULTED IN A SEARCH FOR A NEW CAPTAIN.
THE FOLLOW-ING DAY ...
...ON THE RECOMMENDA-TION OF SECOND COMPANY'S CAPTAIN YORUICHI SHIHÔIN...
...WE SUMMONED THE THIRD SEAT FROM HER COMPANY.
YES-TERDAY I, GENRYÛSAI YAMAMOTO ...
...WITNESSED BY THREE CAPTAINS, INSPECTED HIS COMPETENCY IN THE CAPTAIN'S EXAM...
...AND CONCLUDED THAT HIS ABILITIES AND CHARACTER WERE IM-PECCABLE.
THERE-FORE...

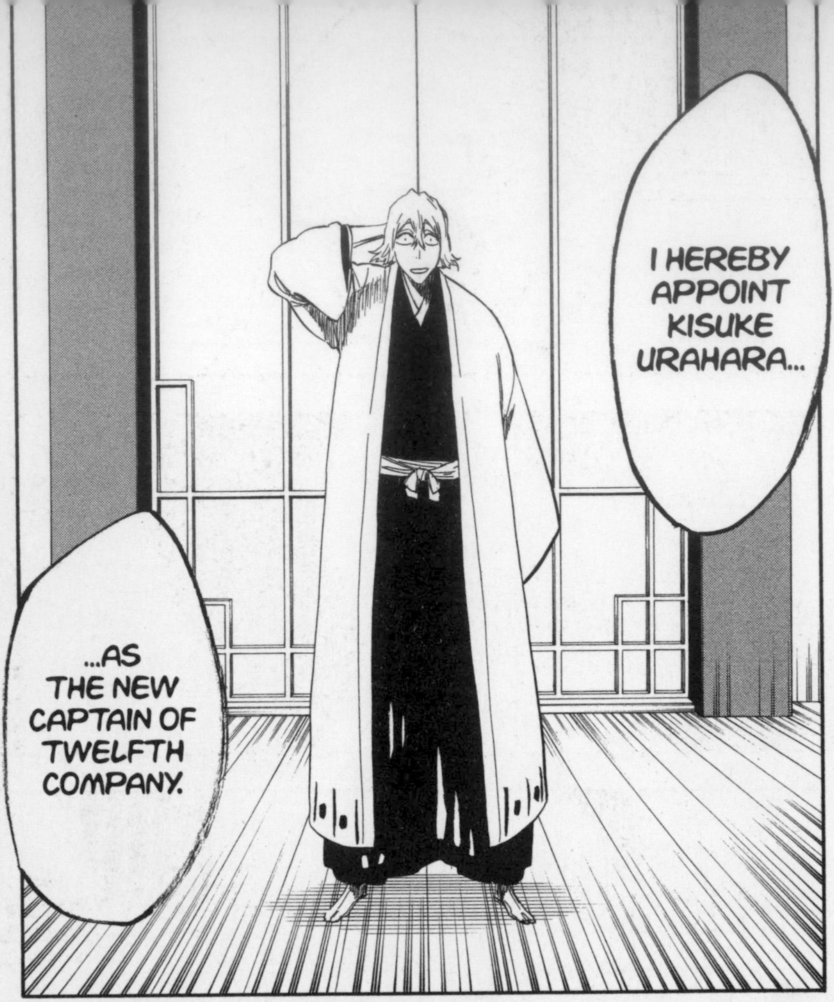
I HEREBY APPOINT KISUKE URAHARA...
...AS THE NEW CAPTAIN OF TWELFTH COMPANY.
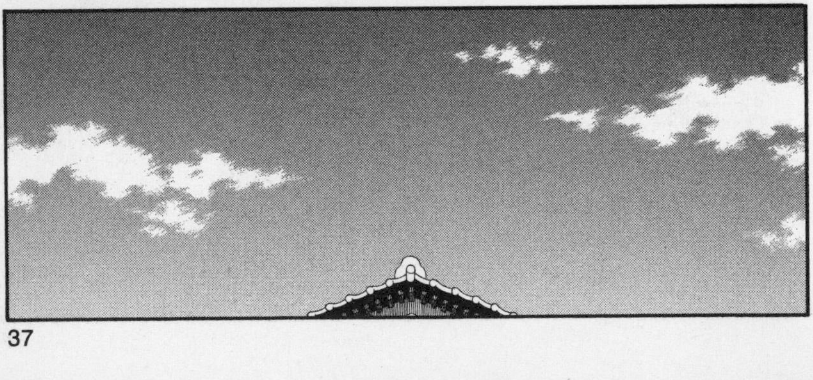

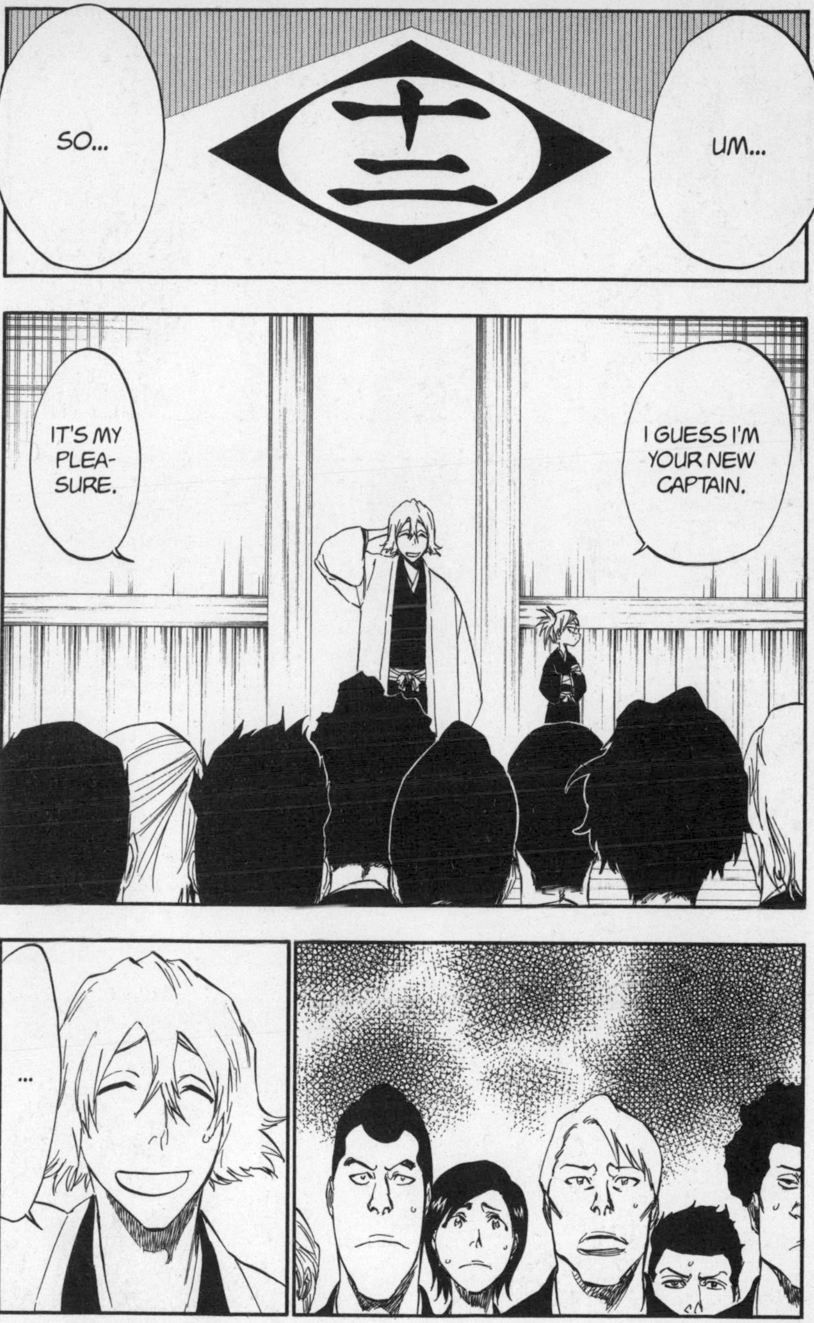
UM...
SO...
I GUESS I'M YOUR NEW CAPTAIN.
IT'S MY PLEA-SURE.
...

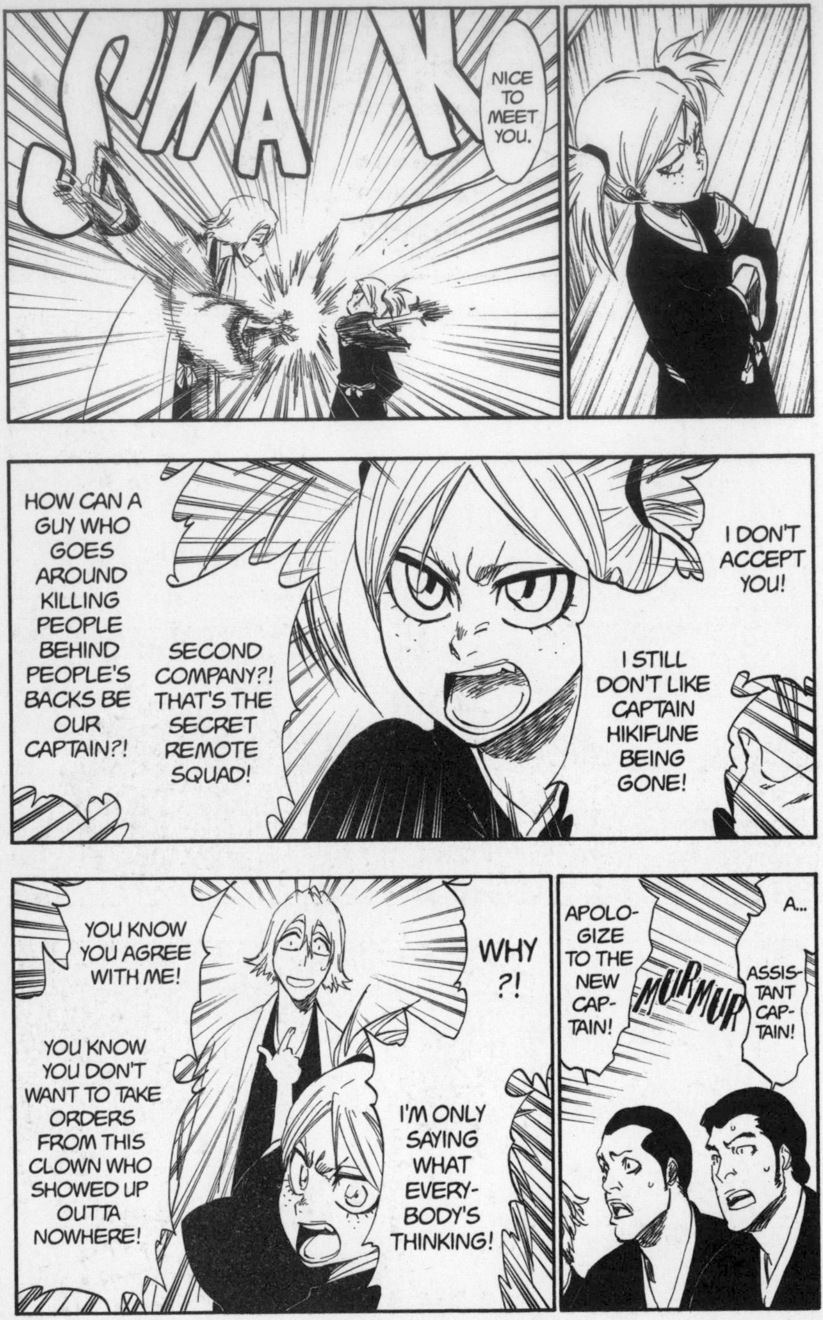
NICE TO MEET YOU.
SWAK
I DON'T ACCEPT YOU!
I STILL DON'T LIKE CAPTAIN HIKIFUNE BEING GONE!
SECOND COMPANY?! THAT'S THE SECRET REMOTE SQUAD!
HOW CAN A GUY WHO GOES AROUND KILLING PEOPLE BEHIND PEOPLE'S BACKS BE OUR CAPTAIN?!
A...
ASSISTANT CAPTAIN!
MURMUR
APOLOGIZE TO THE NEW CAPTAIN!
WHY?!
I'M ONLY SAYING WHAT EVERYBODY'S THINKING!
YOU KNOW YOU AGREE WITH ME!
YOU KNOW YOU DON'T WANT TO TAKE ORDERS FROM THIS CLOWN WHO SHOWED UP OUTTA NOWHERE!

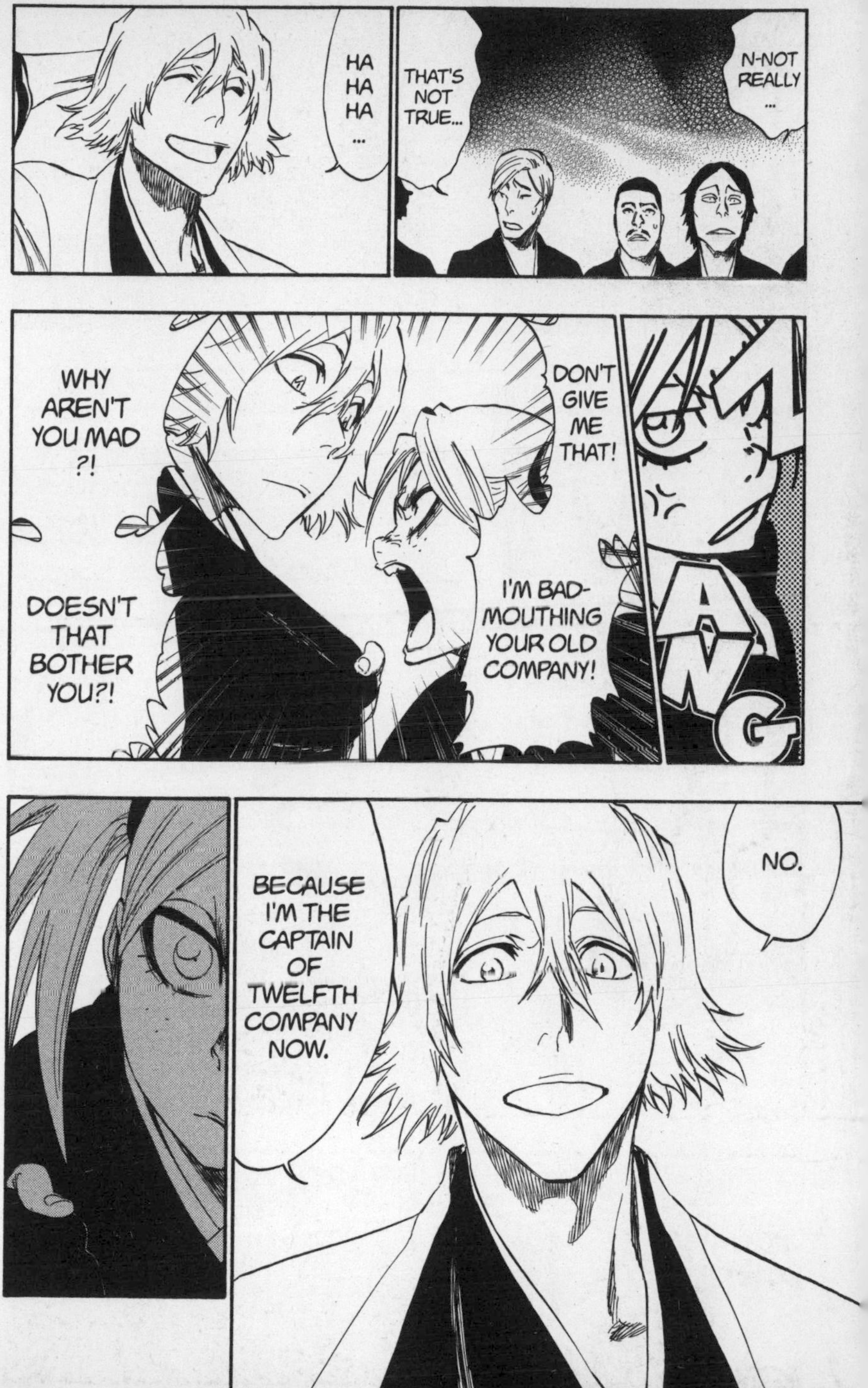
N-NOT REALLY ...
THAT'S NOT TRUE...
HA HA HA ...
ANG
DON'T GIVE ME THAT!
I'M BAD-MOUTHING YOUR OLD COMPANY!
WHY AREN'T YOU MAD ?!
DOESN'T THAT BOTHER YOU?!
NO.
BECAUSE I'M THE CAPTAIN OF TWELFTH COMPANY NOW.

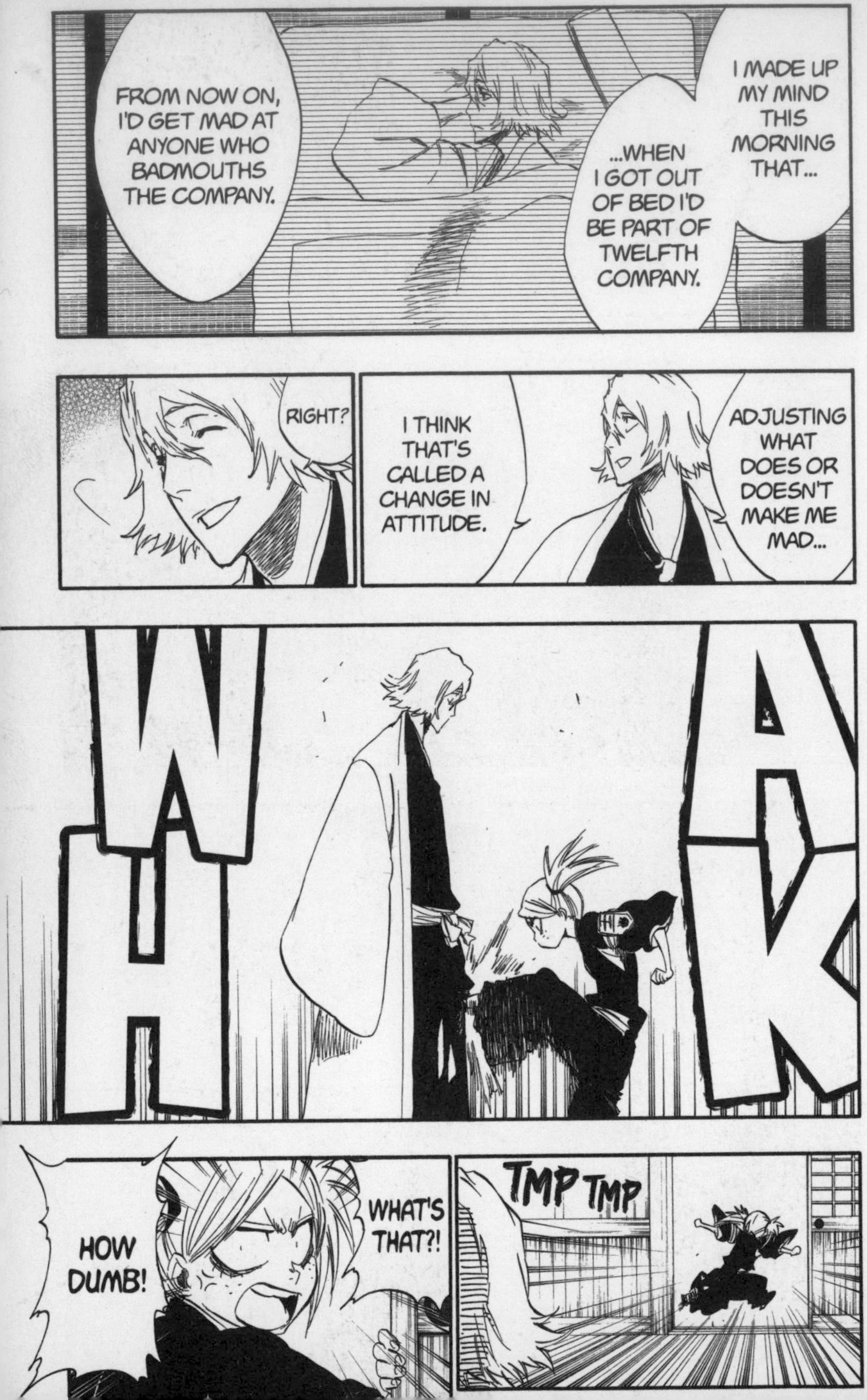
I MADE UP MY MIND THIS MORNING THAT...
...WHEN I GOT OUT OF BED I'D BE PART OF TWELFTH COMPANY.
FROM NOW ON, I'D GET MAD AT ANYONE WHO BADMOUTHS THE COMPANY.
ADJUSTING WHAT DOES OR DOESN'T MAKE ME MAD...
I THINK THAT'S CALLED A CHANGE IN ATTITUDE.
RIGHT?
WHAK
TMP TMP
WHAT'S THAT?!
HOW DUMB!

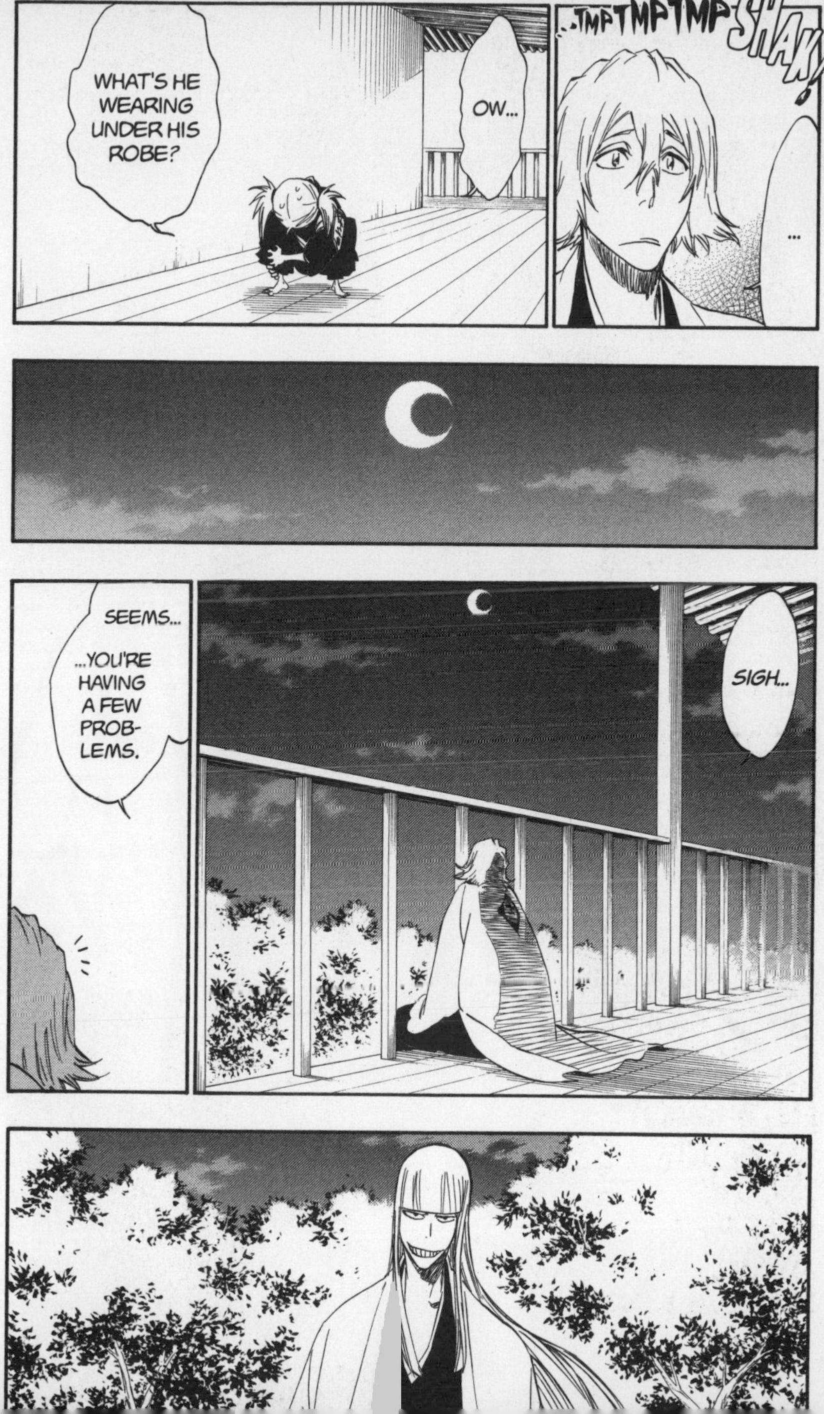
...TMP TMP TMP
SHAK!
...
OW...
WHAT'S HE WEARING UNDER HIS ROBE?
SIGH...
SEEMS...
...YOU'RE HAVING A FEW PROB-LEMS.

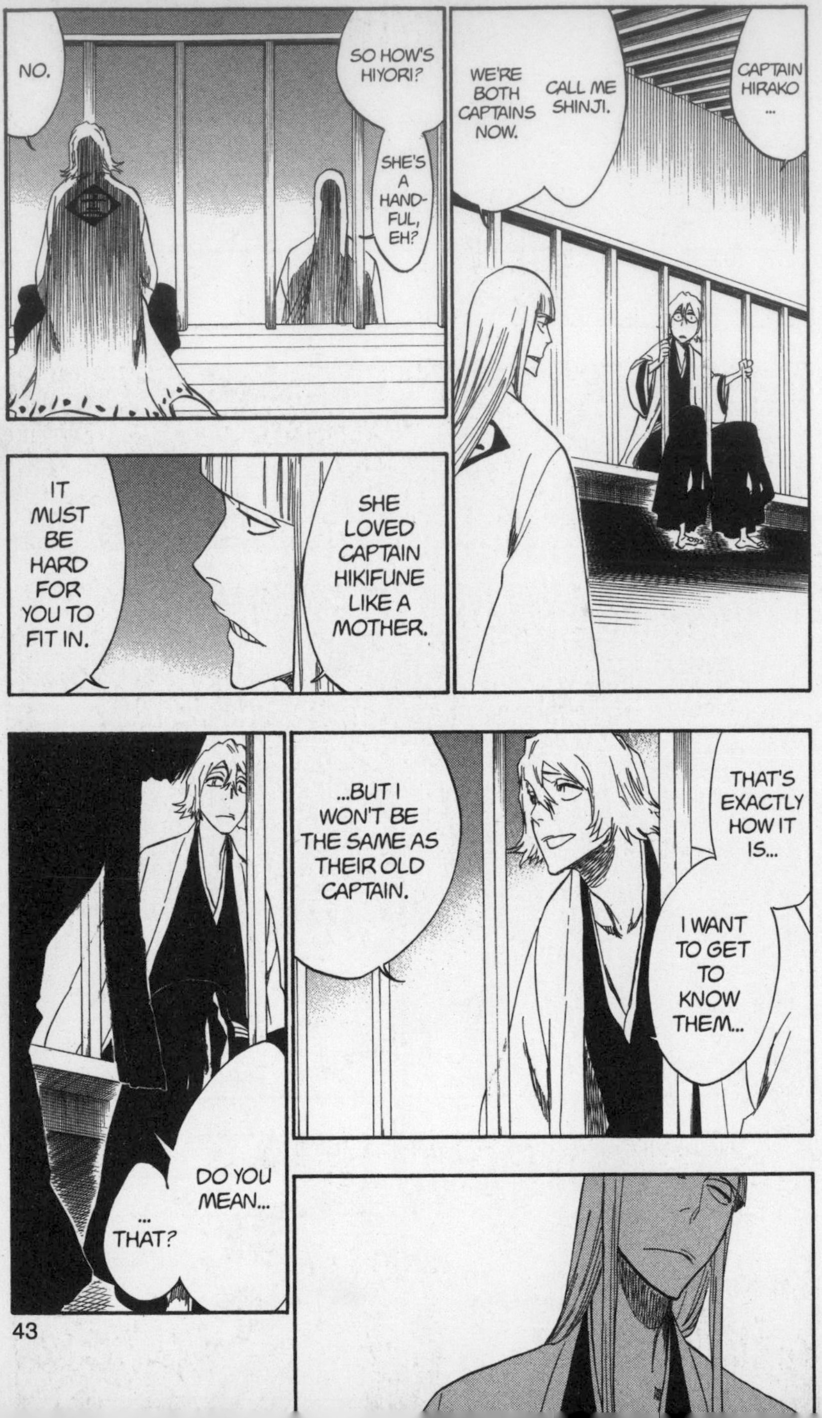
CAPTAIN HIRAKO ...
CALL ME SHINJI.
WE'RE BOTH CAPTAINS NOW.
SO HOW'S HIYORI?
SHE'S A HAND-FUL, EH?
NO.
SHE LOVED CAPTAIN HIKIFUNE LIKE A MOTHER.
IT MUST BE HARD FOR YOU TO FIT IN.
THAT'S EXACTLY HOW IT IS...
I WANT TO GET TO KNOW THEM...
...BUT I WON'T BE THE SAME AS THEIR OLD CAPTAIN.
DO YOU MEAN...
... THAT?

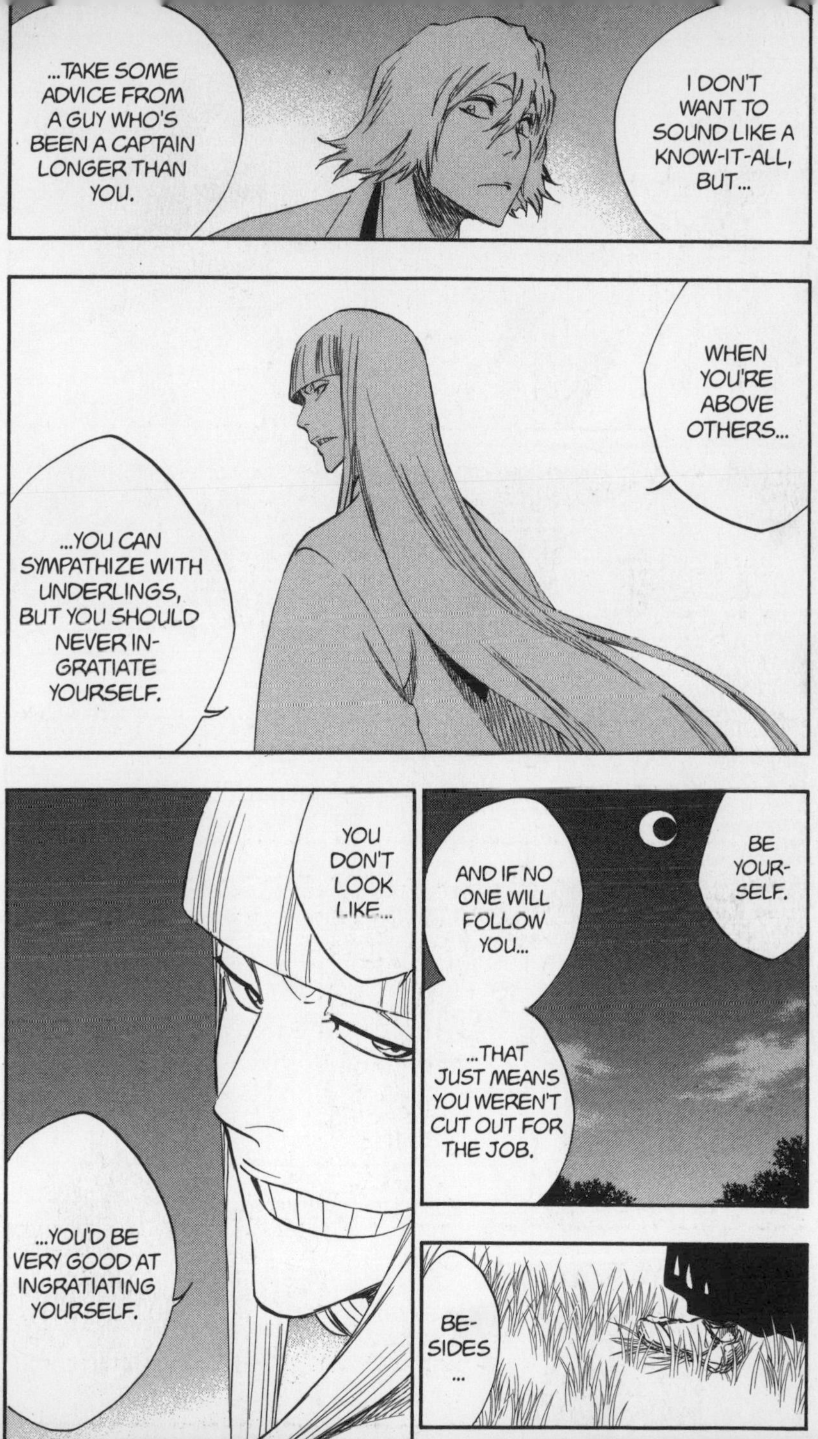
I DON'T WANT TO SOUND LIKE A KNOW-IT-ALL, BUT...
...TAKE SOME ADVICE FROM A GUY WHO'S BEEN A CAPTAIN LONGER THAN YOU.
WHEN YOU'RE ABOVE OTHERS...
...YOU CAN SYMPATHIZE WITH UNDERLINGS, BUT YOU SHOULD NEVER INGRATIATE YOURSELF.
BE YOURSELF.
AND IF NO ONE WILL FOLLOW YOU...
...THAT JUST MEANS YOU WEREN'T CUT OUT FOR THE JOB.
BESIDES...
YOU DON'T LOOK LIKE...
...YOU'D BE VERY GOOD AT INGRATIATING YOURSELF.

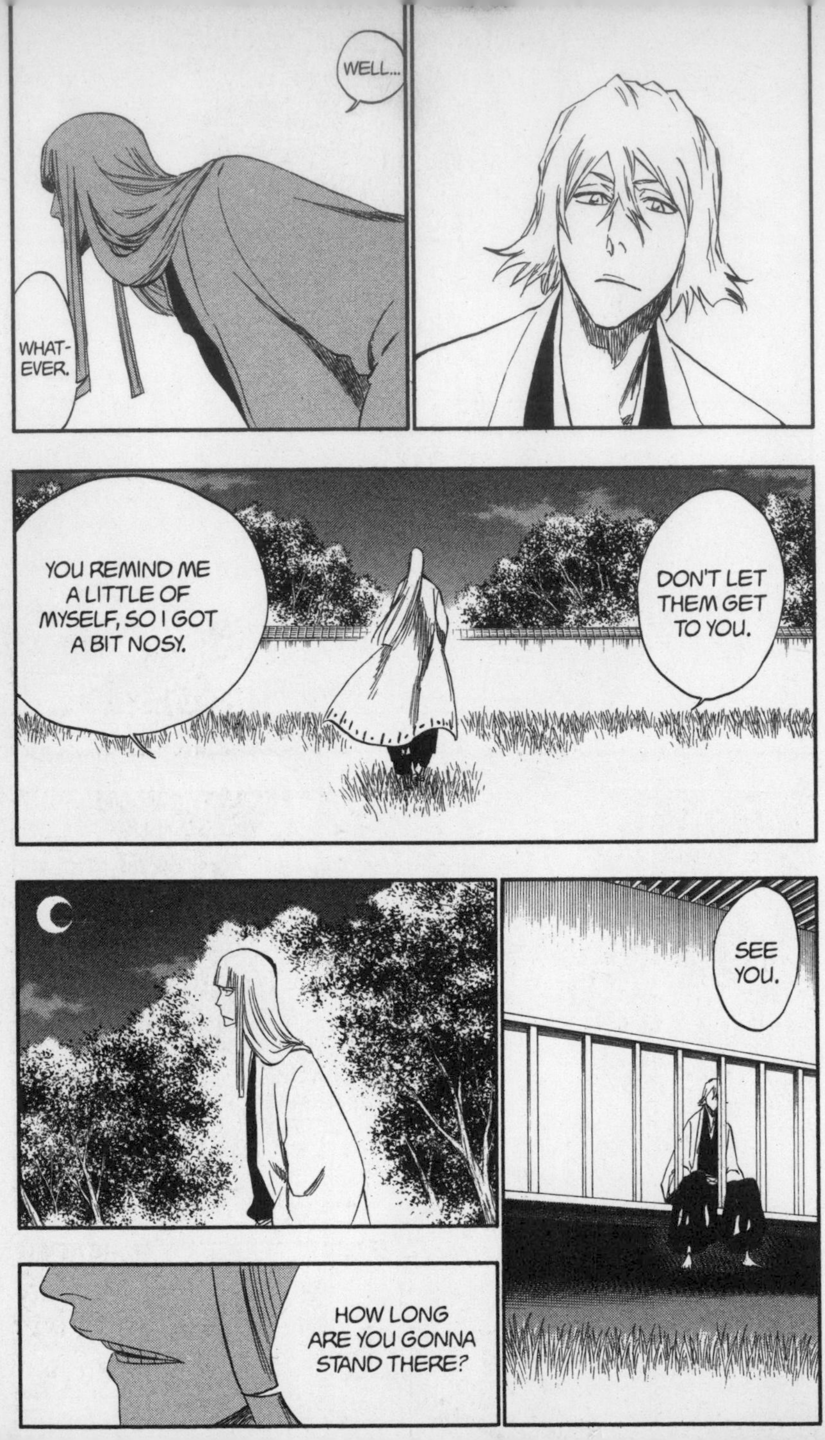
WELL...
WHAT-EVER.
DON'T LET THEM GET TO YOU.
YOU REMIND ME A LITTLE OF MYSELF, SO I GOT A BIT NOSY.
SEE YOU.
HOW LONG ARE YOU GONNA STAND THERE?

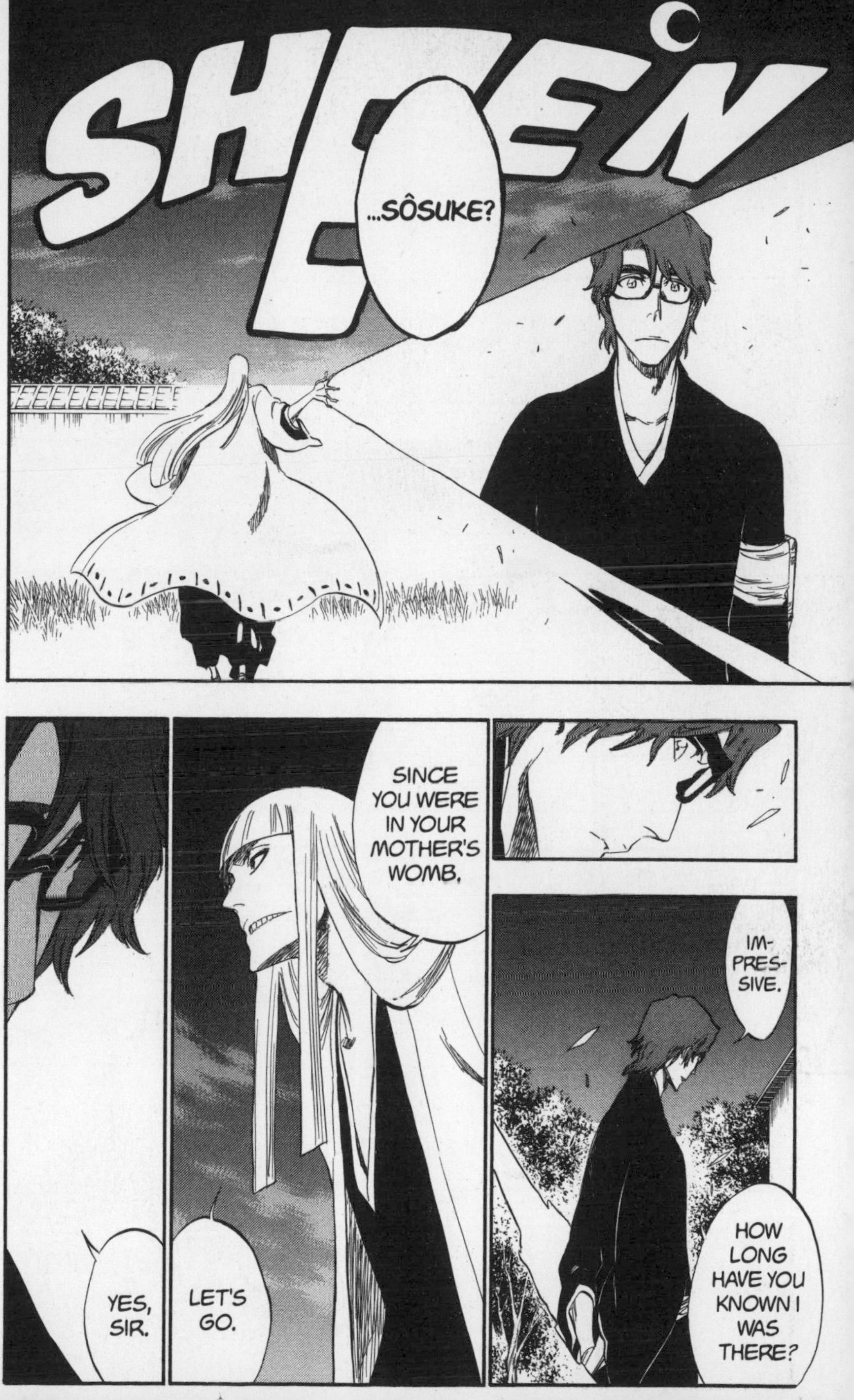
SHEEN
...SÔSUKE?
IMPRESSIVE.
HOW LONG HAVE YOU KNOWN I WAS THERE?
SINCE YOU WERE IN YOUR MOTHER'S WOMB.
LET'S GO.
YES, SIR.

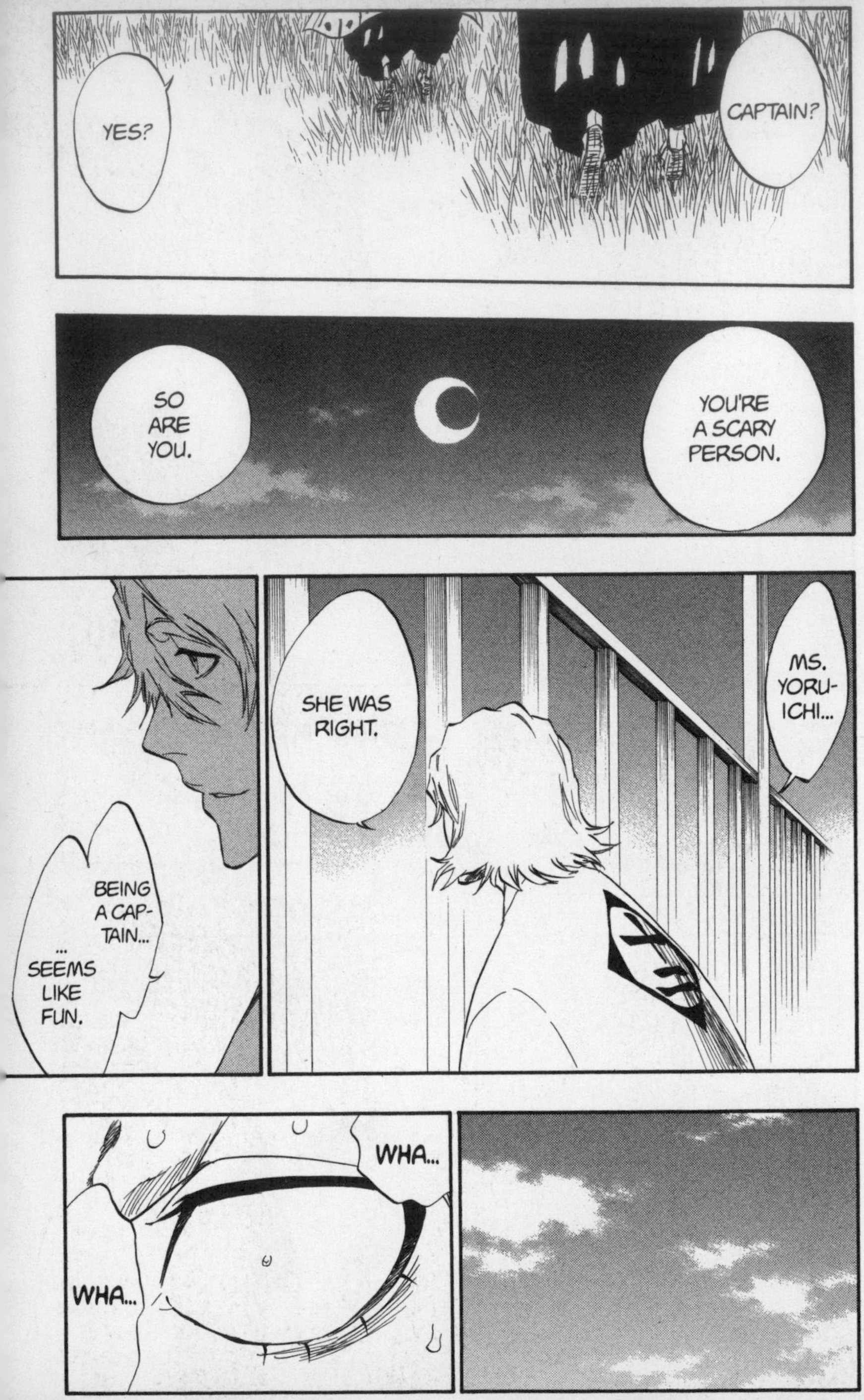
CAPTAIN?
YES?
YOU'RE A SCARY PERSON.
SO ARE YOU.
MS. YORU-ICHI...
SHE WAS RIGHT.
BEING A CAP-TAIN...
... SEEMS LIKE FUN.
WHA...
WHA...

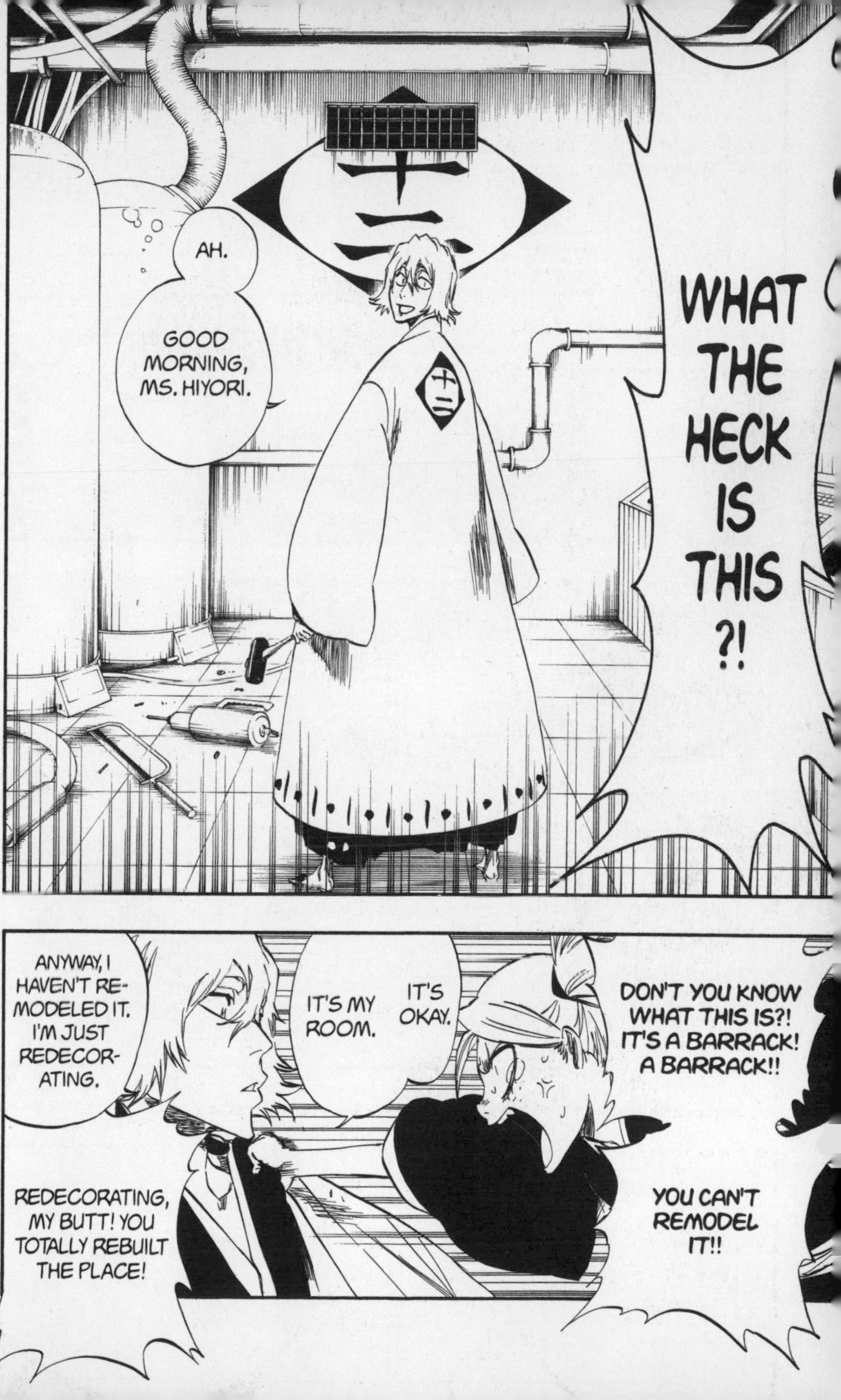
WHAT THE HECK IS THIS ?!
AH.
GOOD MORNING, MS. HIYORI.
DON'T YOU KNOW WHAT THIS IS?! IT'S A BARRACK! A BARRACK!!
YOU CAN'T REMODEL IT!!
IT'S OKAY.
IT'S MY ROOM.
ANYWAY, I HAVEN'T RE-MODELED IT. I'M JUST REDECOR-ATING.
REDECORATING, MY BUTT! YOU TOTALLY REBUILT THE PLACE!

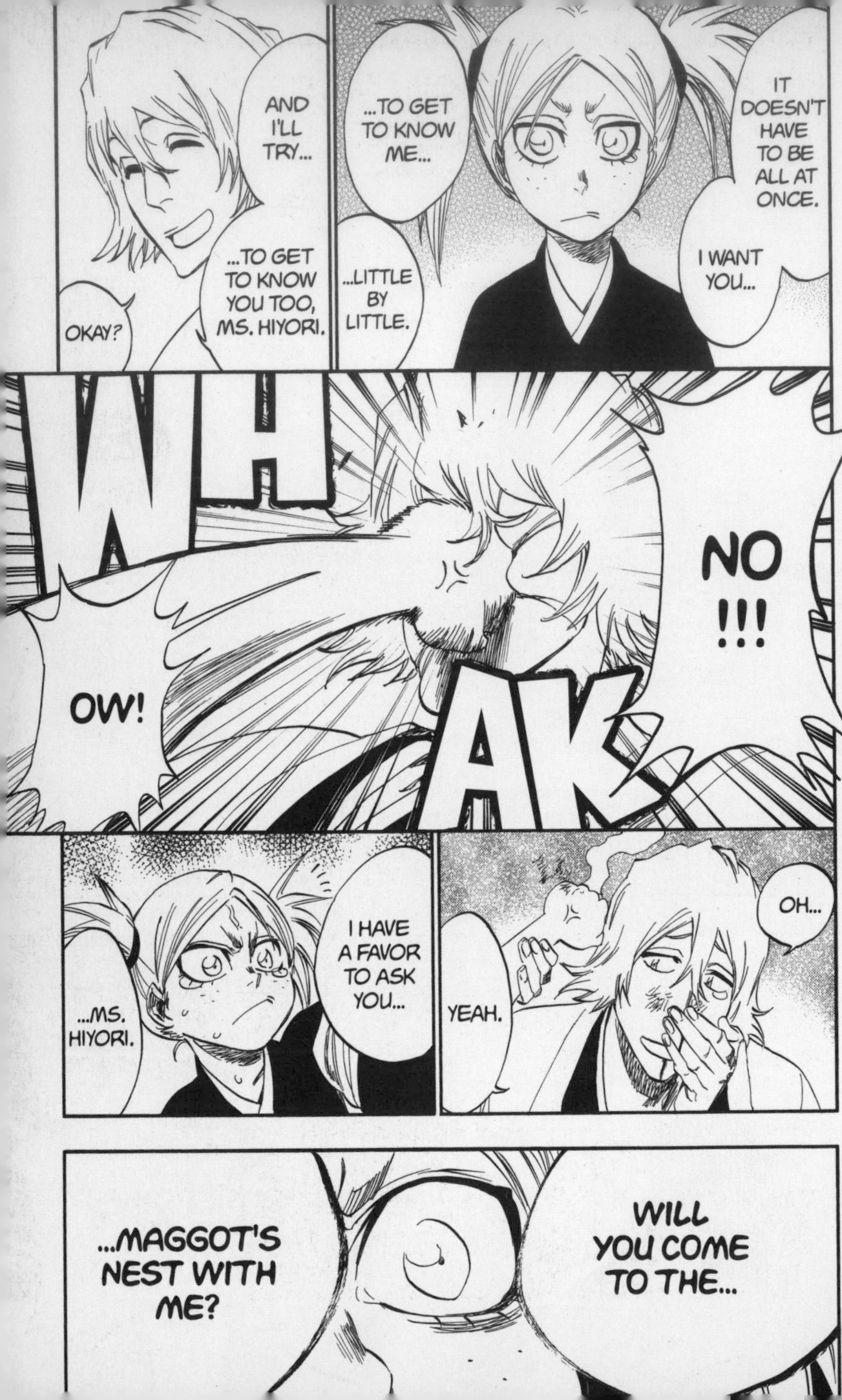
IT DOESN'T HAVE TO BE ALL AT ONCE.
I WANT YOU...
...TO GET TO KNOW ME...
...LITTLE BY LITTLE.
AND I'LL TRY...
...TO GET TO KNOW YOU TOO, MS. HIYORI.
OKAY?
NO !!!
WHAK
OW!
OH...
YEAH.
I HAVE A FAVOR TO ASK YOU...
...MS. HIYORI.
WILL YOU COME TO THE...
...MAGGOT'S NEST WITH ME?

SEINOSUKE YAMADA
ASSISTANT CAPTAIN,
FOURTH COMPANY

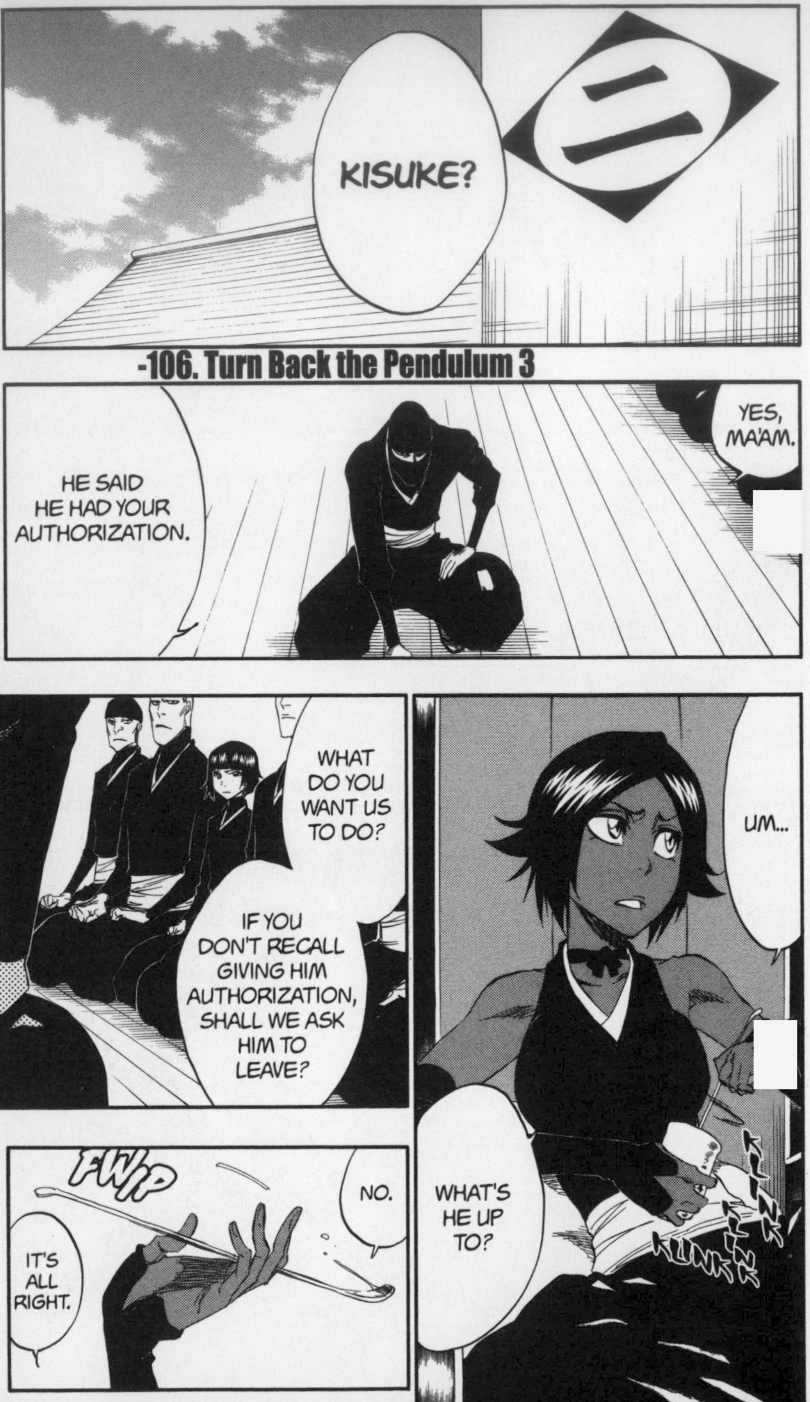
KISUKE?
-106. Turn Back the Pendulum 3
YES, MA'AM.
HE SAID HE HAD YOUR AUTHORIZATION.
UM...
WHAT'S HE UP TO?
WHAT DO YOU WANT US TO DO?
IF YOU DON'T RECALL GIVING HIM AUTHORIZATION, SHALL WE ASK HIM TO LEAVE?
NO.
FWIP
IT'S ALL RIGHT.

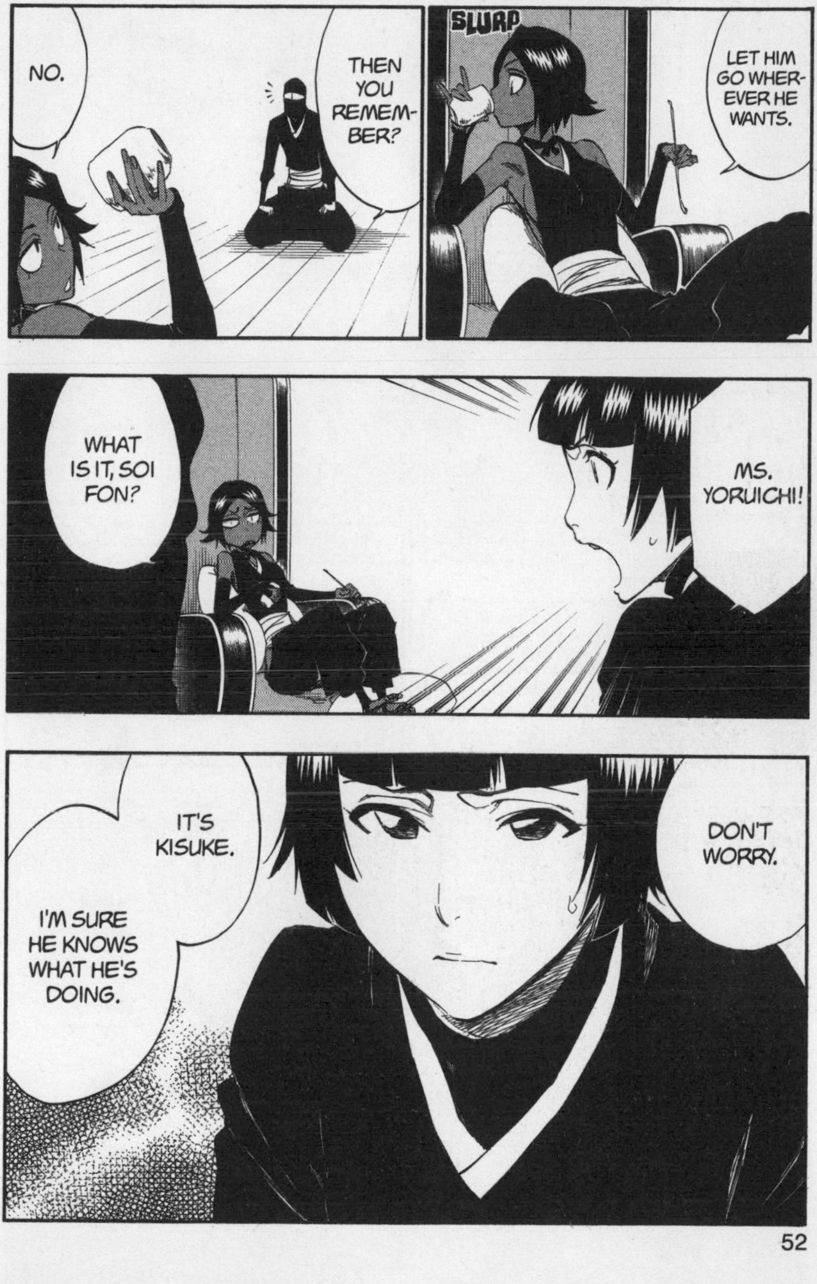
SLURP
LET HIM GO WHEREVER HE WANTS.
THEN YOU REMEMBER?
NO.
MS. YORUICHI!
WHAT IS IT, SOI FON?
DON'T WORRY.
IT'S KISUKE.
I'M SURE HE KNOWS WHAT HE'S DOING.

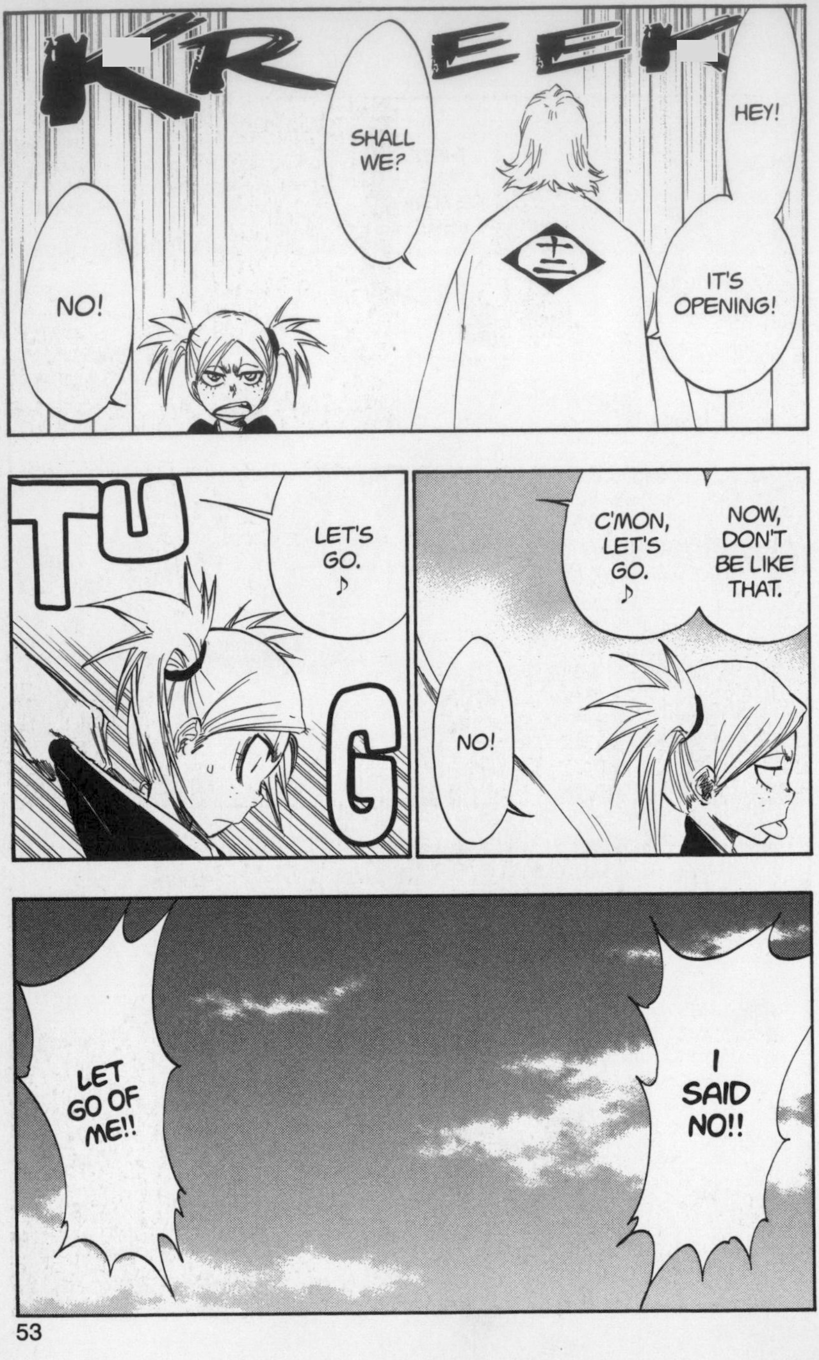
KREEK
HEY!
IT'S OPENING!
SHALL WE?
NO!
NOW, DON'T BE LIKE THAT.
C'MON, LET'S GO. ♪
NO!
TUG
LET'S GO. ♪
I SAID NO!!
LET GO OF ME!!

THE SECRET REMOTE SQUAD

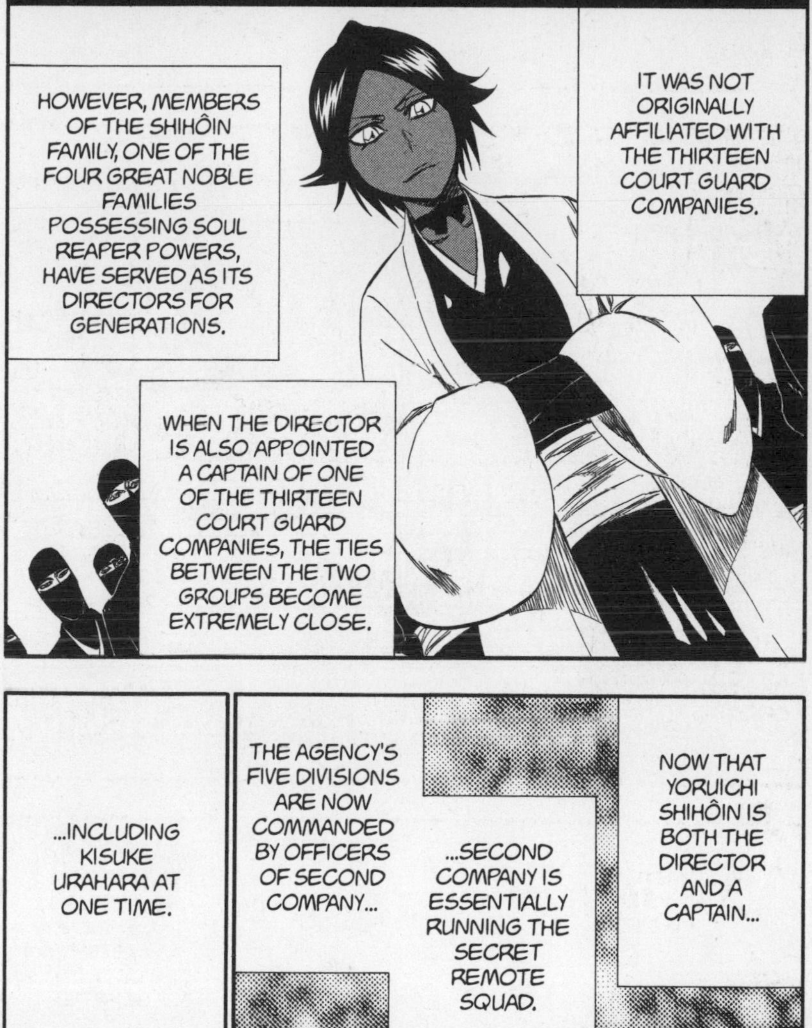
IT WAS NOT ORIGINALLY AFFILIATED WITH THE THIRTEEN COURT GUARD COMPANIES.
HOWEVER, MEMBERS OF THE SHIHÔIN FAMILY, ONE OF THE FOUR GREAT NOBLE FAMILIES POSSESSING SOUL REAPER POWERS, HAVE SERVED AS ITS DIRECTORS FOR GENERATIONS.
WHEN THE DIRECTOR IS ALSO APPOINTED A CAPTAIN OF ONE OF THE THIRTEEN COURT GUARD COMPANIES, THE TIES BETWEEN THE TWO GROUPS BECOME EXTREMELY CLOSE.
NOW THAT YORUICHI SHIHÔIN IS BOTH THE DIRECTOR AND A CAPTAIN...
...SECOND COMPANY IS ESSENTIALLY RUNNING THE SECRET REMOTE SQUAD.
THE AGENCY'S FIVE DIVISIONS ARE NOW COMMANDED BY OFFICERS OF SECOND COMPANY...
...INCLUDING KISUKE URAHARA AT ONE TIME.

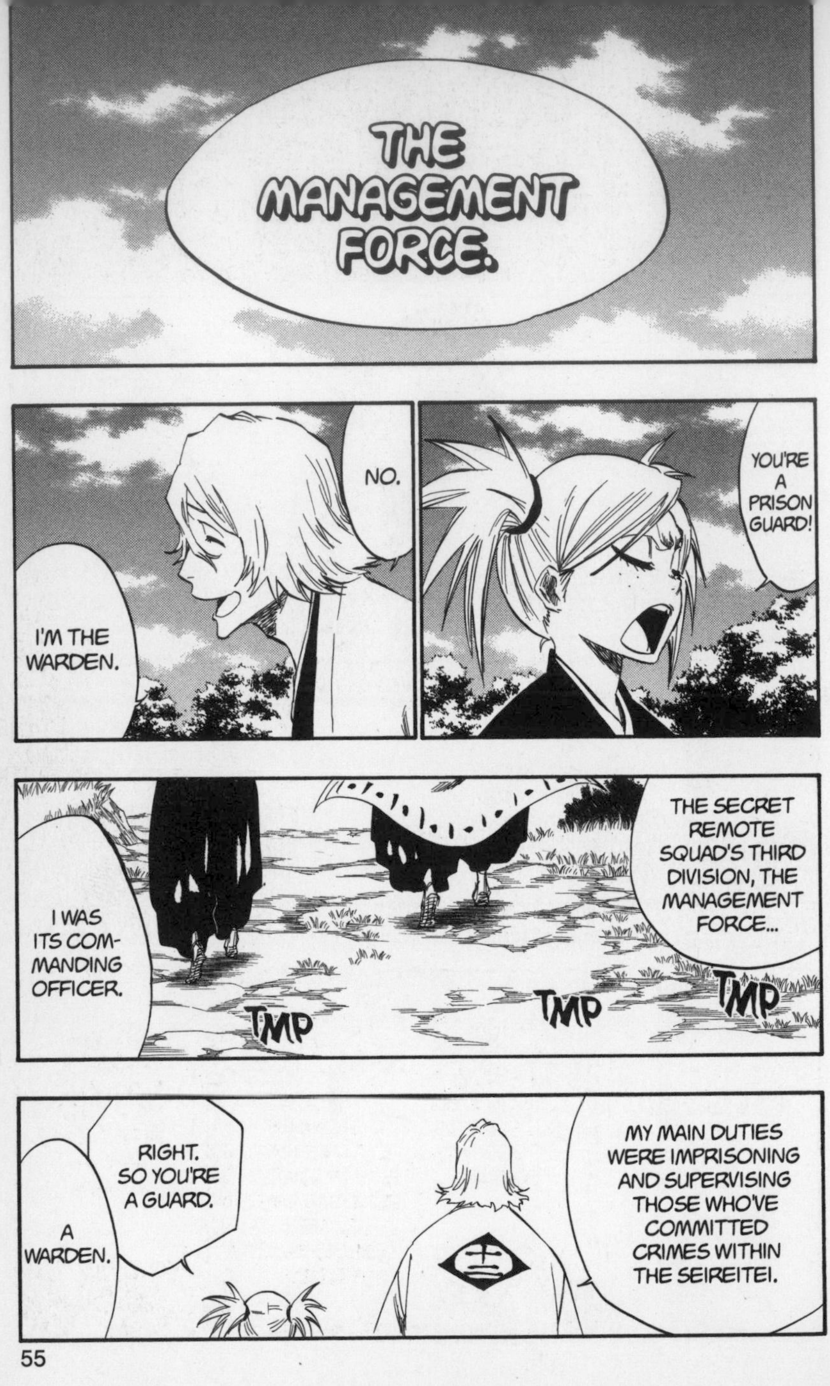
THE MANAGEMENT FORCE.
YOU'RE A PRISON GUARD!
NO.
I'M THE WARDEN.
THE SECRET REMOTE SQUAD'S THIRD DIVISION, THE MANAGEMENT FORCE...
TMP
TMP
TMP
I WAS ITS COM-MANDING OFFICER.
MY MAIN DUTIES WERE IMPRISONING AND SUPERVISING THOSE WHO'VE COMMITTED CRIMES WITHIN THE SEIREITEI.
RIGHT. SO YOU'RE A GUARD.
A WARDEN.

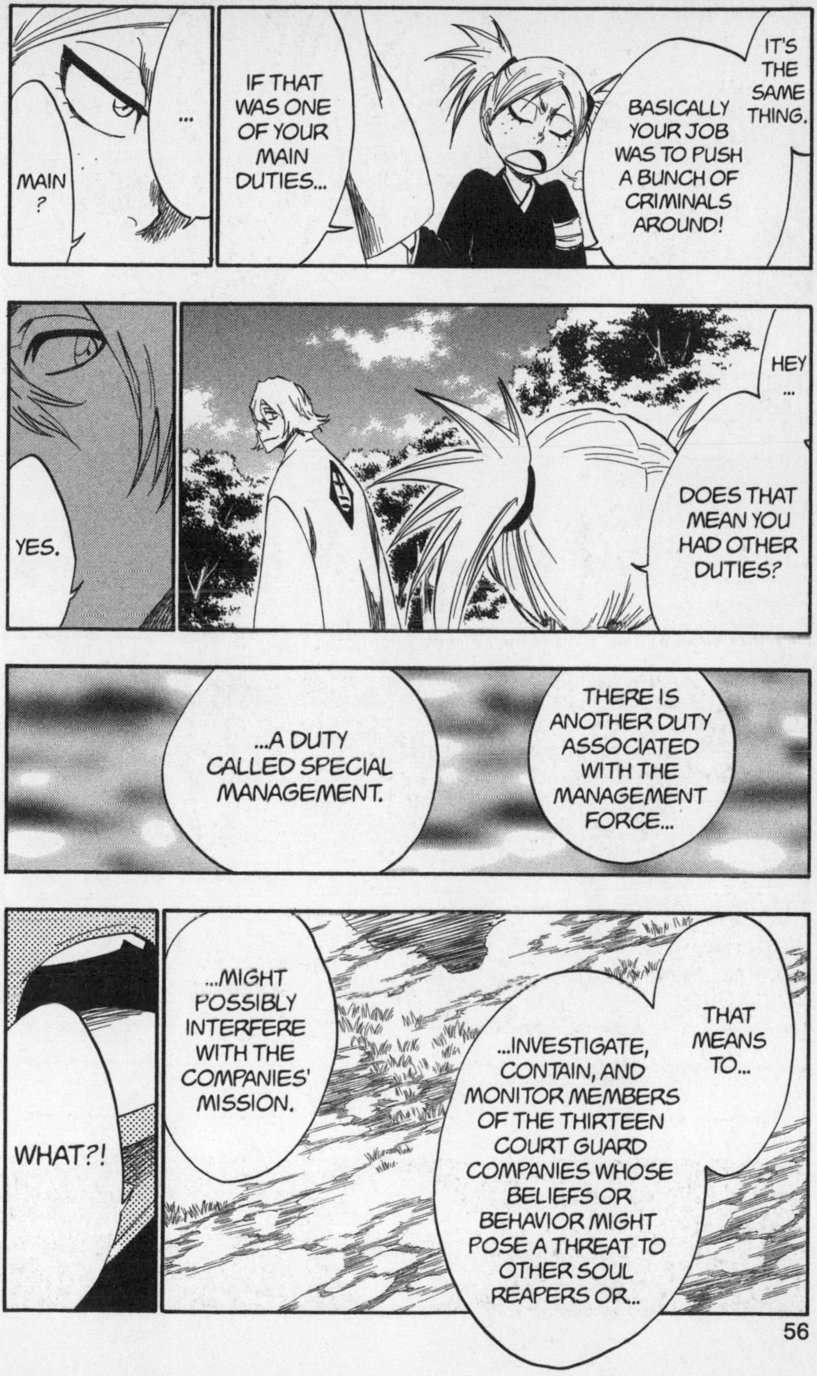
IT'S THE SAME THING.
BASICALLY YOUR JOB WAS TO PUSH A BUNCH OF CRIMINALS AROUND!
IF THAT WAS ONE OF YOUR MAIN DUTIES...
...
MAIN ?
HEY ...
DOES THAT MEAN YOU HAD OTHER DUTIES?
YES.
THERE IS ANOTHER DUTY ASSOCIATED WITH THE MANAGEMENT FORCE...
...A DUTY CALLED SPECIAL MANAGEMENT.
THAT MEANS TO...
...INVESTIGATE, CONTAIN, AND MONITOR MEMBERS OF THE THIRTEEN COURT GUARD COMPANIES WHOSE BELIEFS OR BEHAVIOR MIGHT POSE A THREAT TO OTHER SOUL REAPERS OR...
...MIGHT POSSIBLY INTERFERE WITH THE COMPANIES' MISSION.
WHAT?!

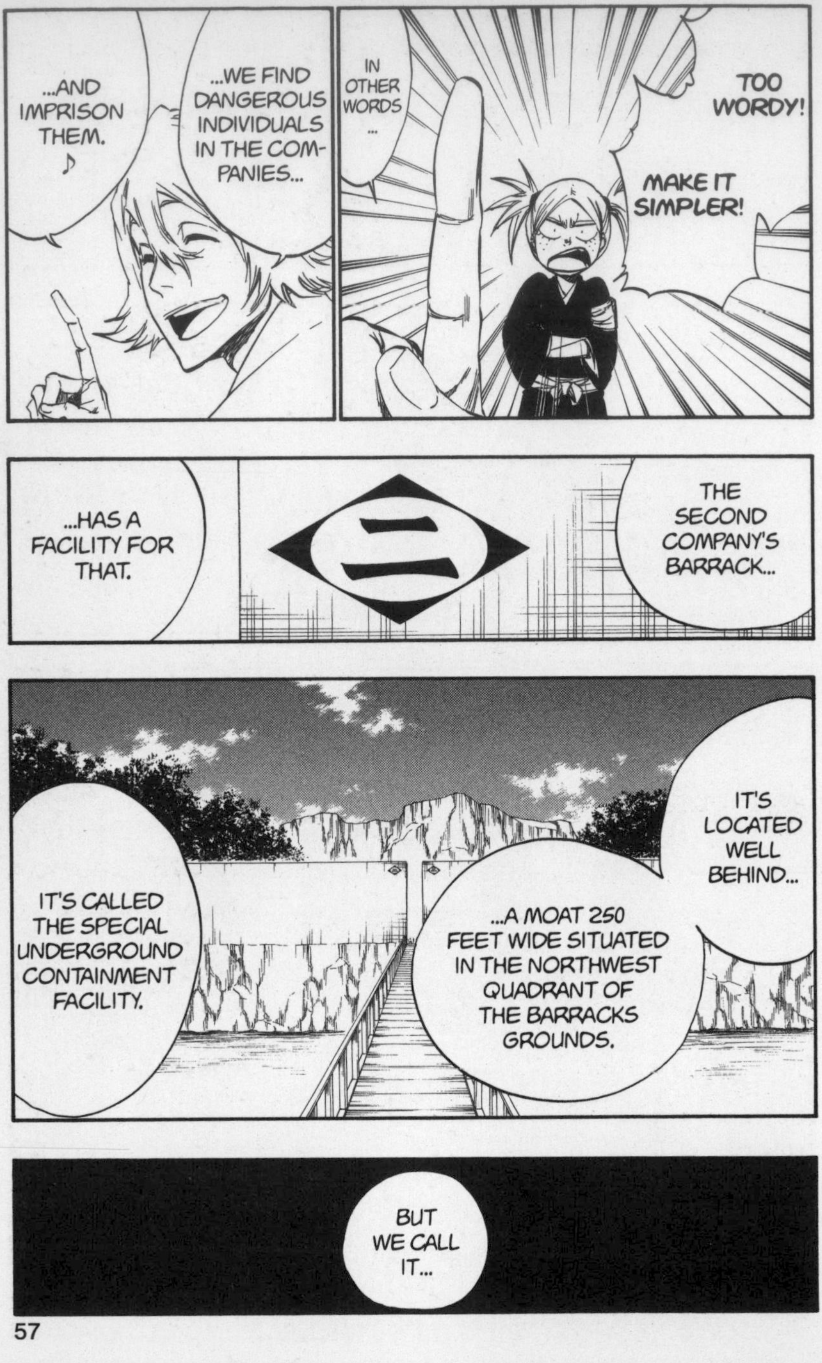
TOO WORDY!
MAKE IT SIMPLER!
IN OTHER WORDS ...
...WE FIND DANGEROUS INDIVIDUALS IN THE COMPANIES...
...AND IMPRISON THEM. ♪
THE SECOND COMPANY'S BARRACK...
...HAS A FACILITY FOR THAT.
IT'S LOCATED WELL BEHIND...
...A MOAT 250 FEET WIDE SITUATED IN THE NORTHWEST QUADRANT OF THE BARRACKS GROUNDS.
IT'S CALLED THE SPECIAL UNDERGROUND CONTAINMENT FACILITY.
BUT WE CALL IT...

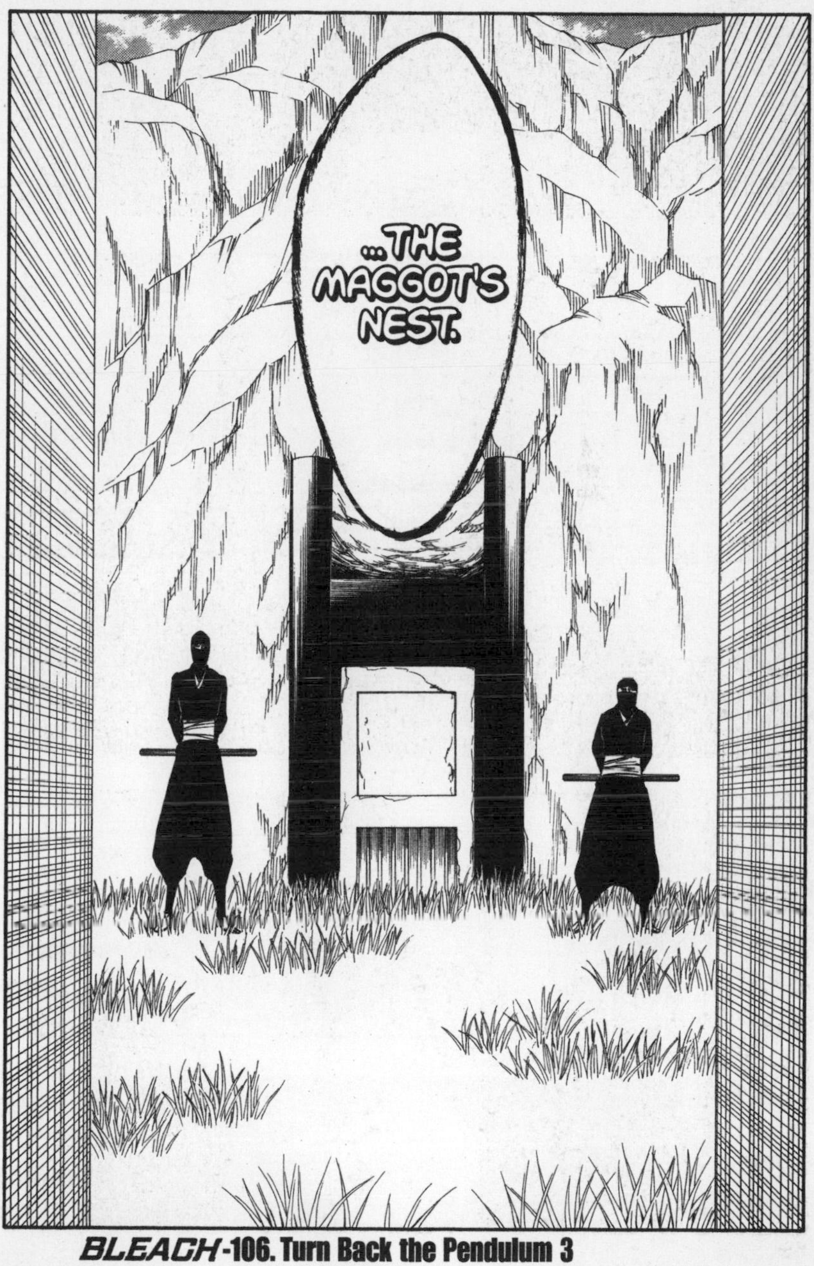
...THE MAGGOT'S NEST.

BLEACH -106. Turn Back the Pendulum 3

READ THIS WAY

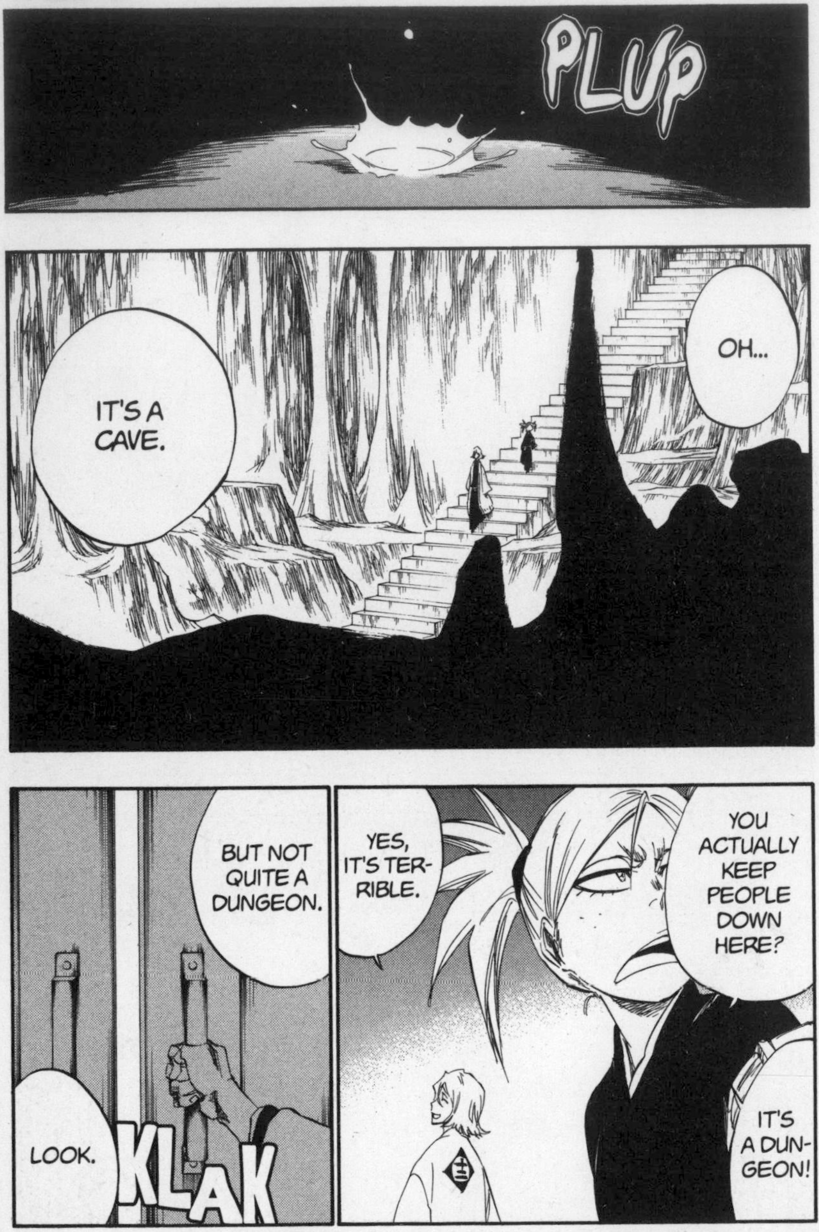
PLUP
OH...
IT'S A CAVE.
YOU ACTUALLY KEEP PEOPLE DOWN HERE?
YES, IT'S TERRIBLE.
IT'S A DUNGEON!
BUT NOT QUITE A DUNGEON.
LOOK.
KLAK

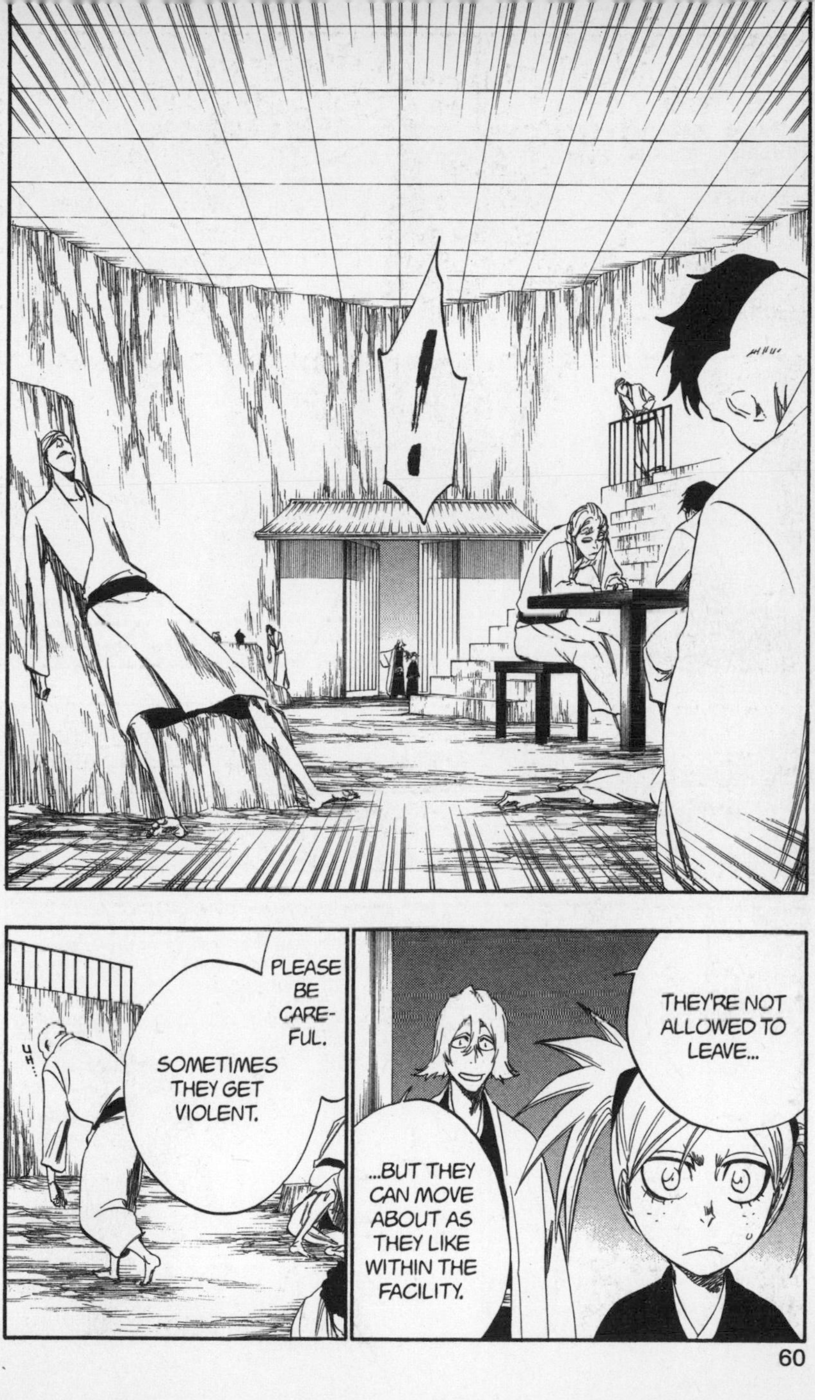
!
THEY'RE NOT ALLOWED TO LEAVE...
...BUT THEY CAN MOVE ABOUT AS THEY LIKE WITHIN THE FACILITY.
PLEASE BE CARE-FUL.
SOMETIMES THEY GET VIOLENT.
UH...

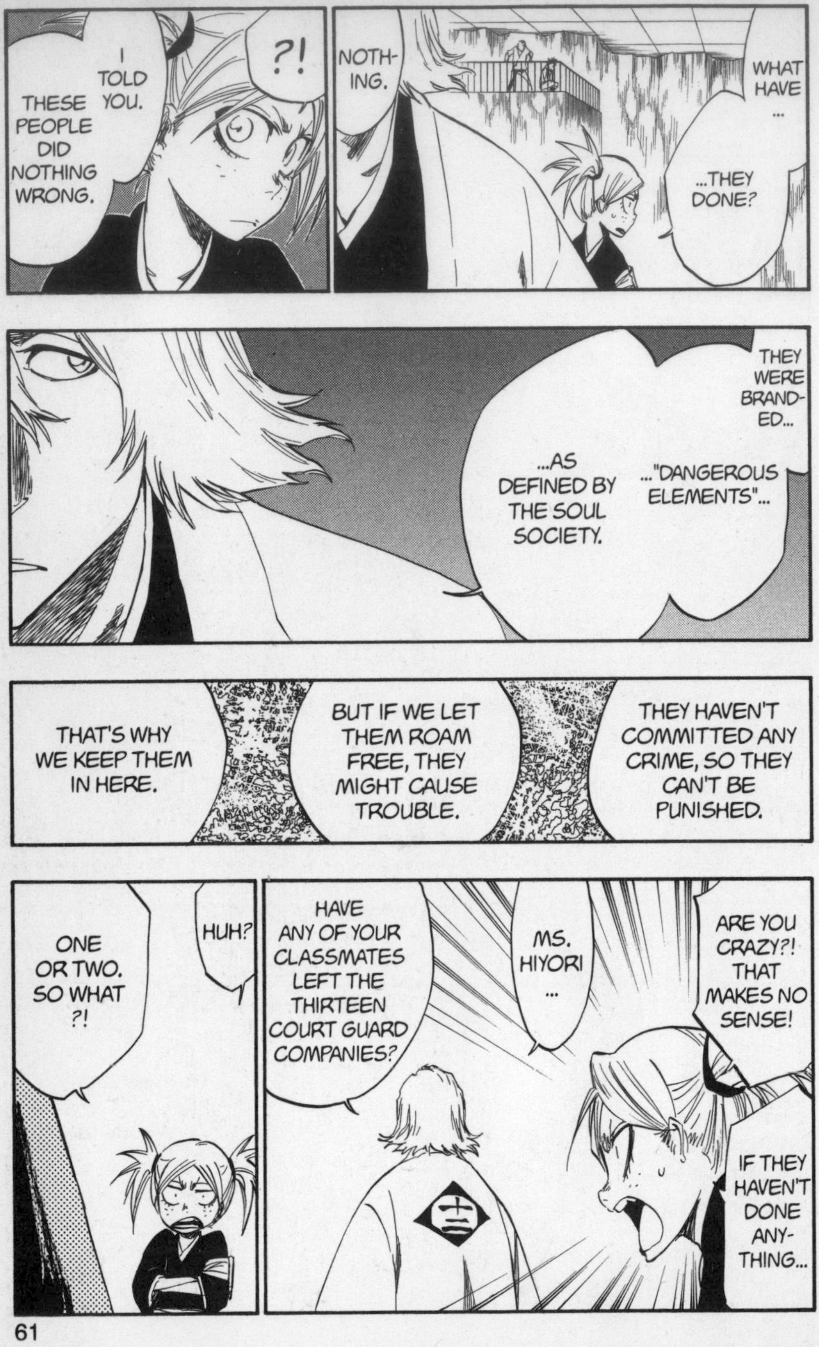
WHAT HAVE ...
...THEY DONE?
NOTHING.
?!
I TOLD YOU.
THESE PEOPLE DID NOTHING WRONG.
THEY WERE BRANDED...
..."DANGEROUS ELEMENTS"...
...AS DEFINED BY THE SOUL SOCIETY.
THEY HAVEN'T COMMITTED ANY CRIME, SO THEY CAN'T BE PUNISHED.
BUT IF WE LET THEM ROAM FREE, THEY MIGHT CAUSE TROUBLE.
THAT'S WHY WE KEEP THEM IN HERE.
ARE YOU CRAZY?! THAT MAKES NO SENSE!
IF THEY HAVEN'T DONE ANYTHING...
MS. HIYORI ...
HAVE ANY OF YOUR CLASSMATES LEFT THE THIRTEEN COURT GUARD COMPANIES?
HUH?
ONE OR TWO. SO WHAT ?!

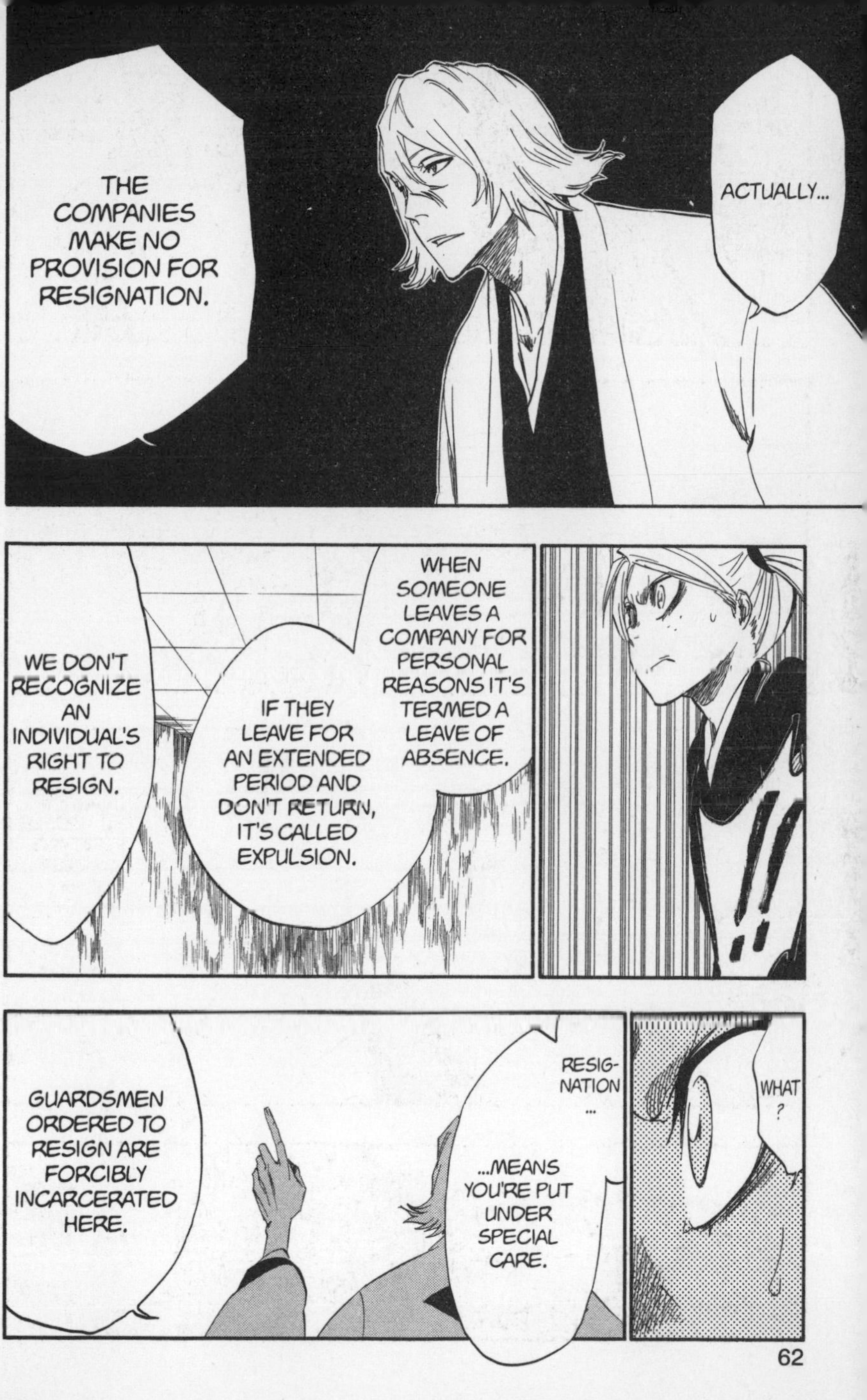
ACTUALLY...
THE COMPANIES MAKE NO PROVISION FOR RESIGNATION.
WHEN SOMEONE LEAVES A COMPANY FOR PERSONAL REASONS IT'S TERMED A LEAVE OF ABSENCE.
IF THEY LEAVE FOR AN EXTENDED PERIOD AND DON'T RETURN, IT'S CALLED EXPULSION.
WE DON'T RECOGNIZE AN INDIVIDUAL'S RIGHT TO RESIGN.
WHAT?
RESIG-NATION...
...MEANS YOU'RE PUT UNDER SPECIAL CARE.
GUARDSMEN ORDERED TO RESIGN ARE FORCIBLY INCARCERATED HERE.

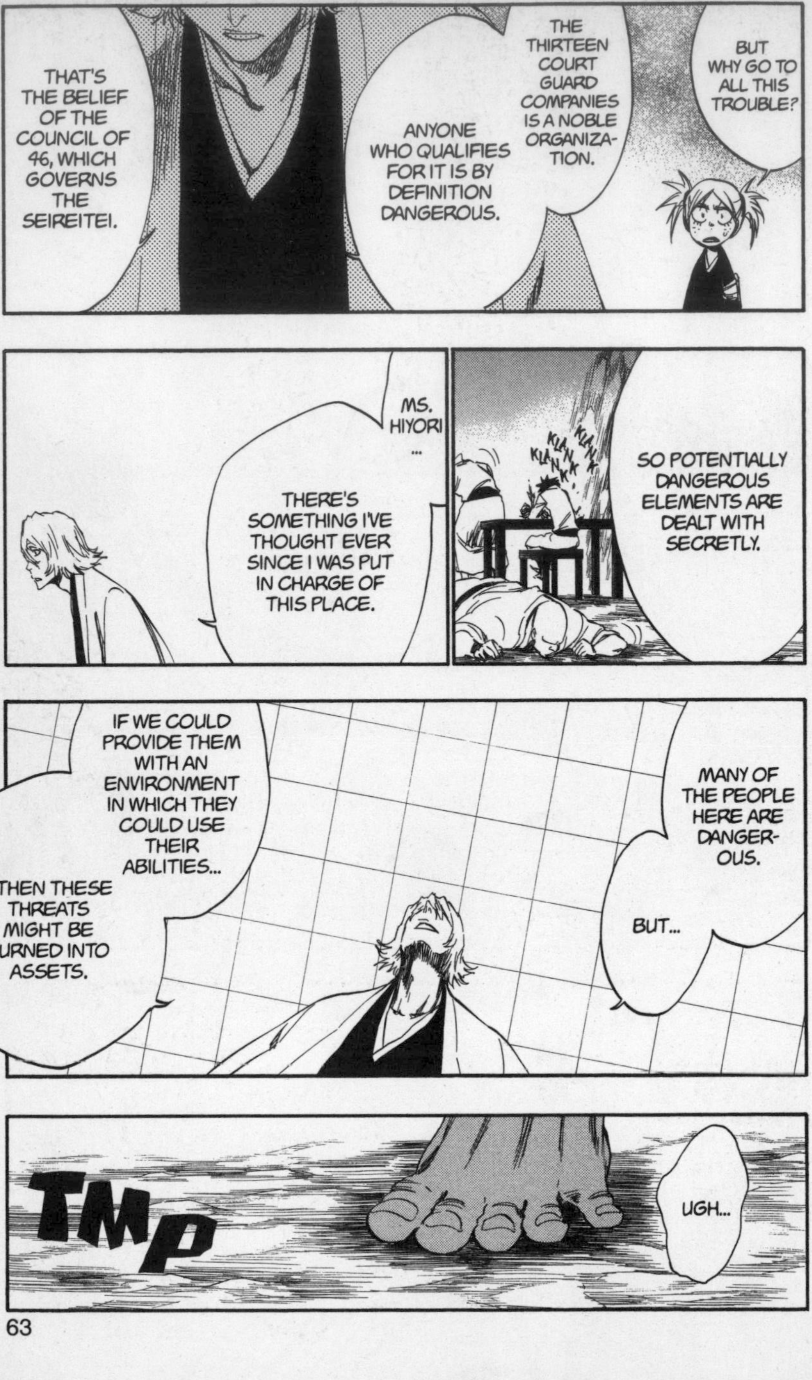
BUT WHY GO TO ALL THIS TROUBLE?
THE THIRTEEN COURT GUARD COMPANIES IS A NOBLE ORGANIZATION.
ANYONE WHO QUALIFIES FOR IT IS BY DEFINITION DANGEROUS.
THAT'S THE BELIEF OF THE COUNCIL OF 46, WHICH GOVERNS THE SEIREITEI.
KLANK KLANK KLANK
SO POTENTIALLY DANGEROUS ELEMENTS ARE DEALT WITH SECRETLY.
MS. HIYORI...
THERE'S SOMETHING I'VE THOUGHT EVER SINCE I WAS PUT IN CHARGE OF THIS PLACE.
MANY OF THE PEOPLE HERE ARE DANGEROUS.
BUT...
IF WE COULD PROVIDE THEM WITH AN ENVIRONMENT IN WHICH THEY COULD USE THEIR ABILITIES...
...THEN THESE THREATS MIGHT BE TURNED INTO ASSETS.
UGH...
TMP

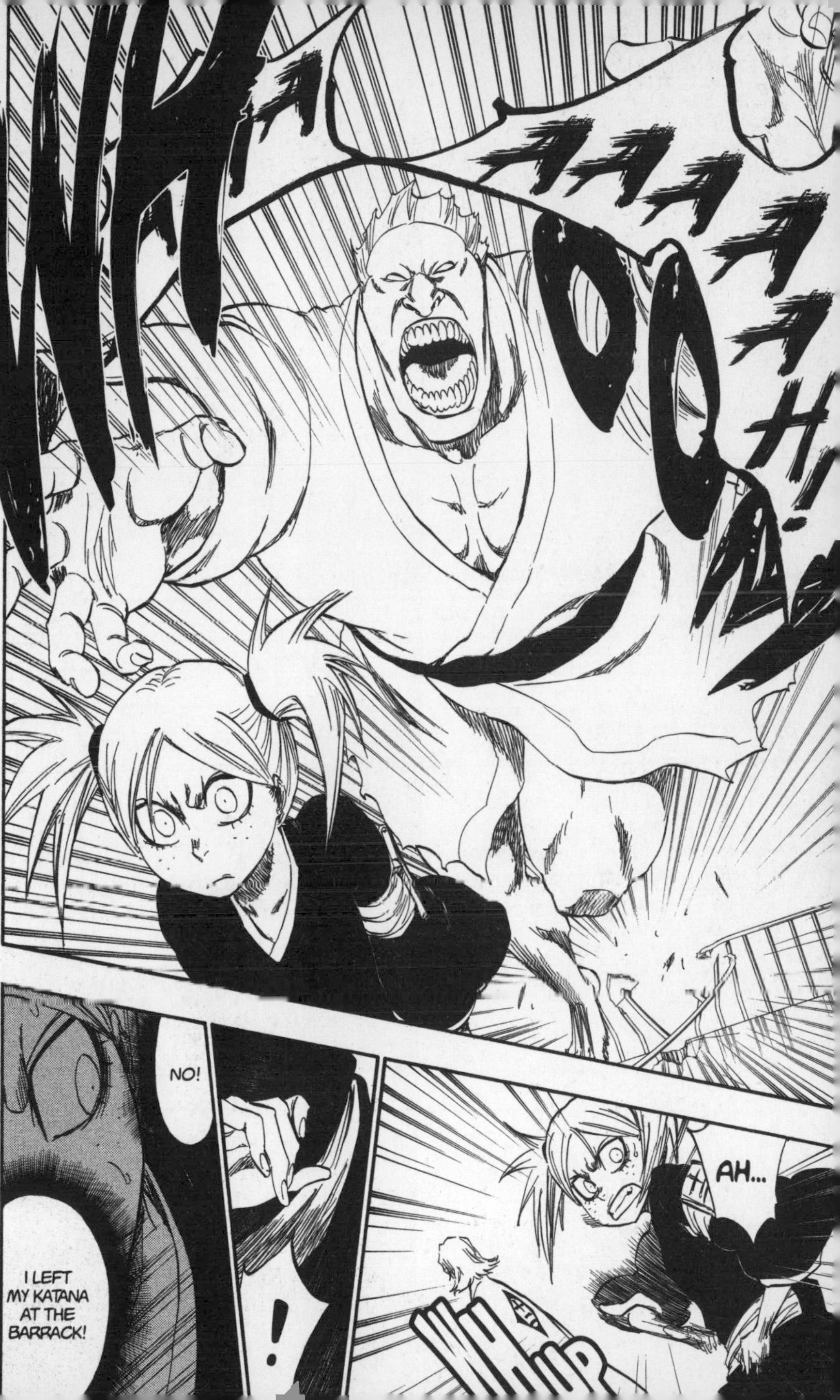
AH...
NO!
!
I LEFT MY KATANA AT THE BARRACK!

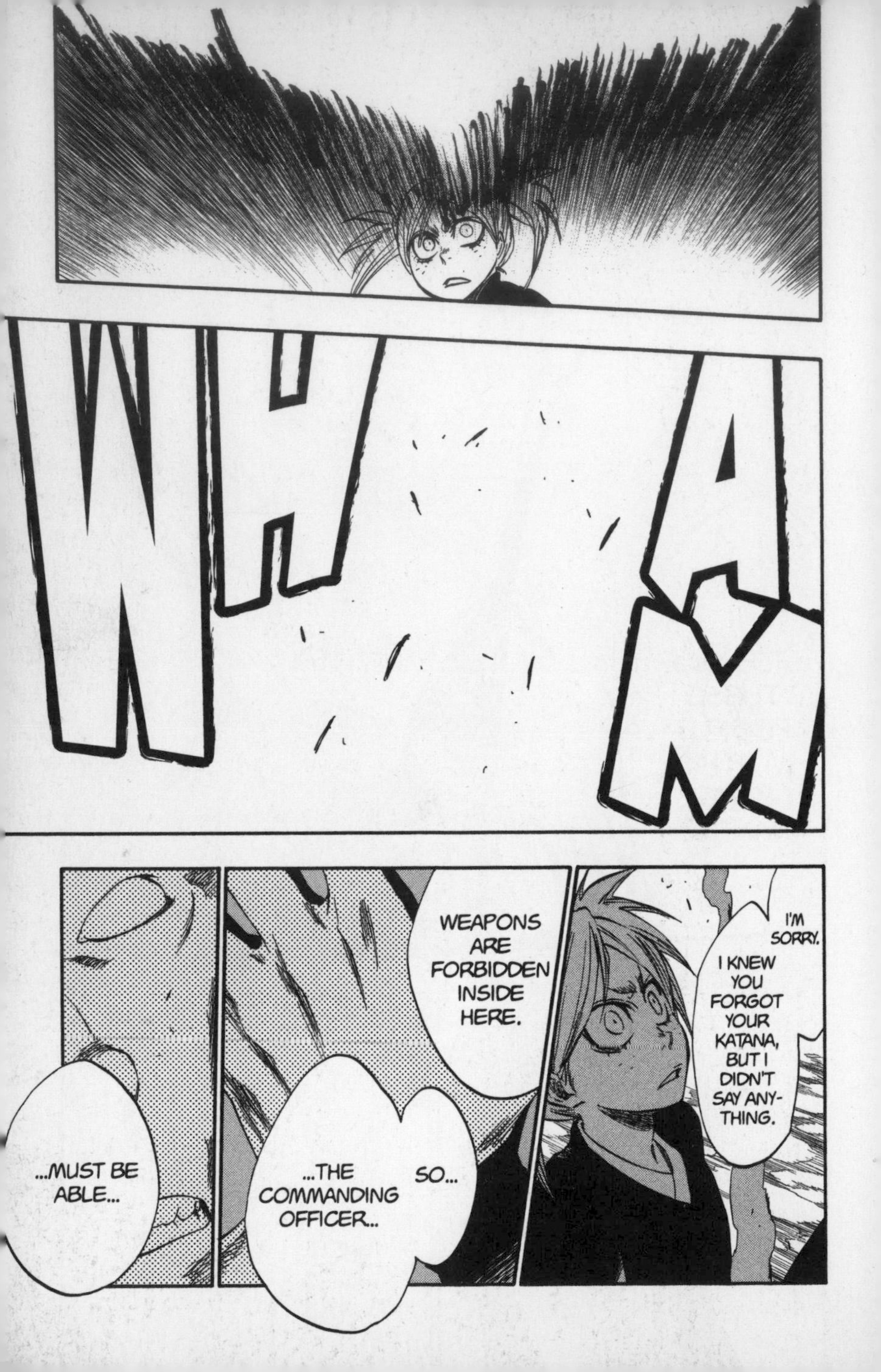
WHAM
I'M SORRY.
I KNEW YOU FORGOT YOUR KATANA, BUT I DIDN'T SAY ANYTHING.
WEAPONS ARE FORBIDDEN INSIDE HERE.
SO...
...THE COMMANDING OFFICER...
...MUST BE ABLE...

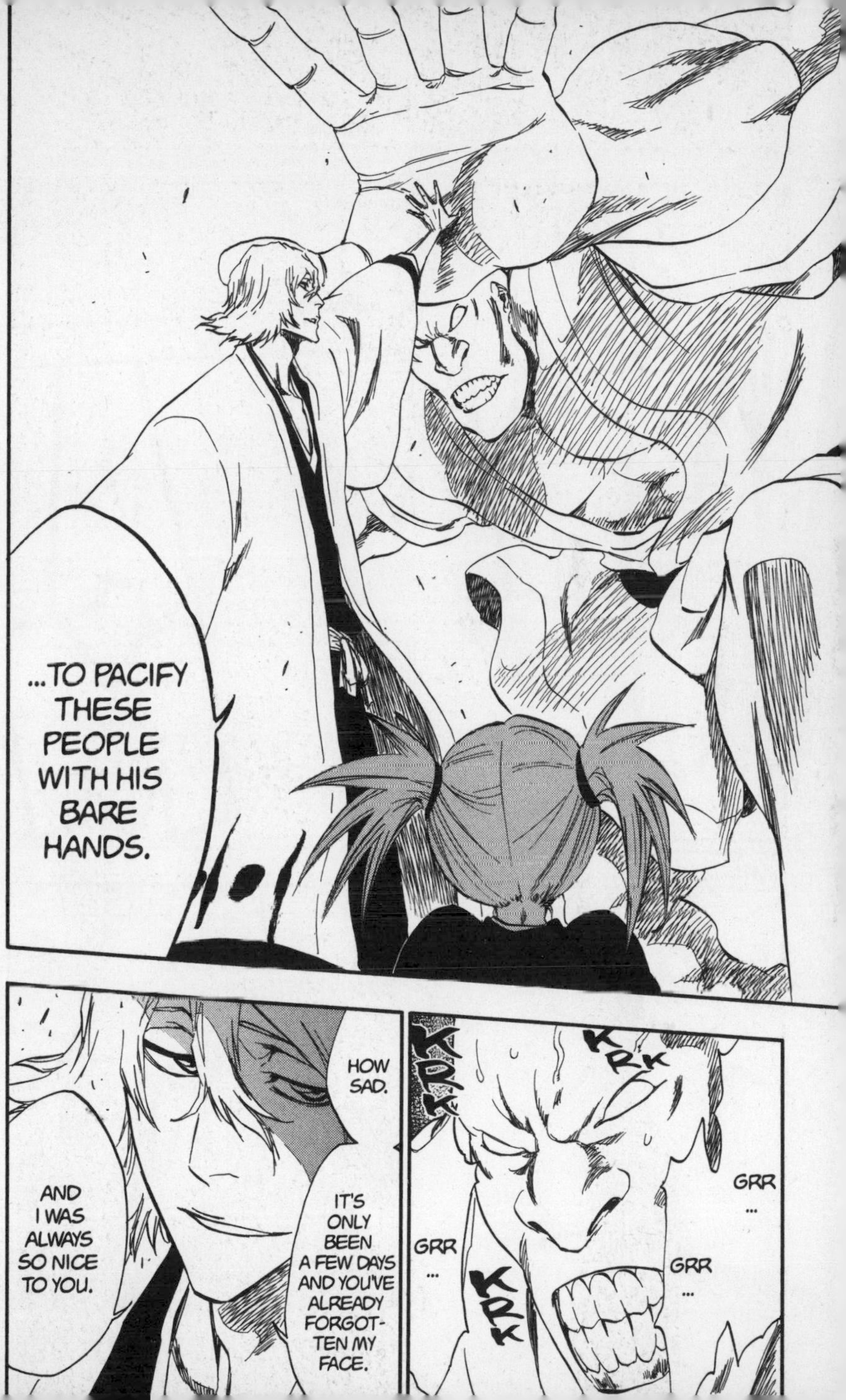
...TO PACIFY THESE PEOPLE WITH HIS BARE HANDS.
KRK
KRK
GRR...
GRR...
GRR...
KRK
HOW SAD.
IT'S ONLY BEEN A FEW DAYS AND YOU'VE ALREADY FORGOT-TEN MY FACE.
AND I WAS ALWAYS SO NICE TO YOU.

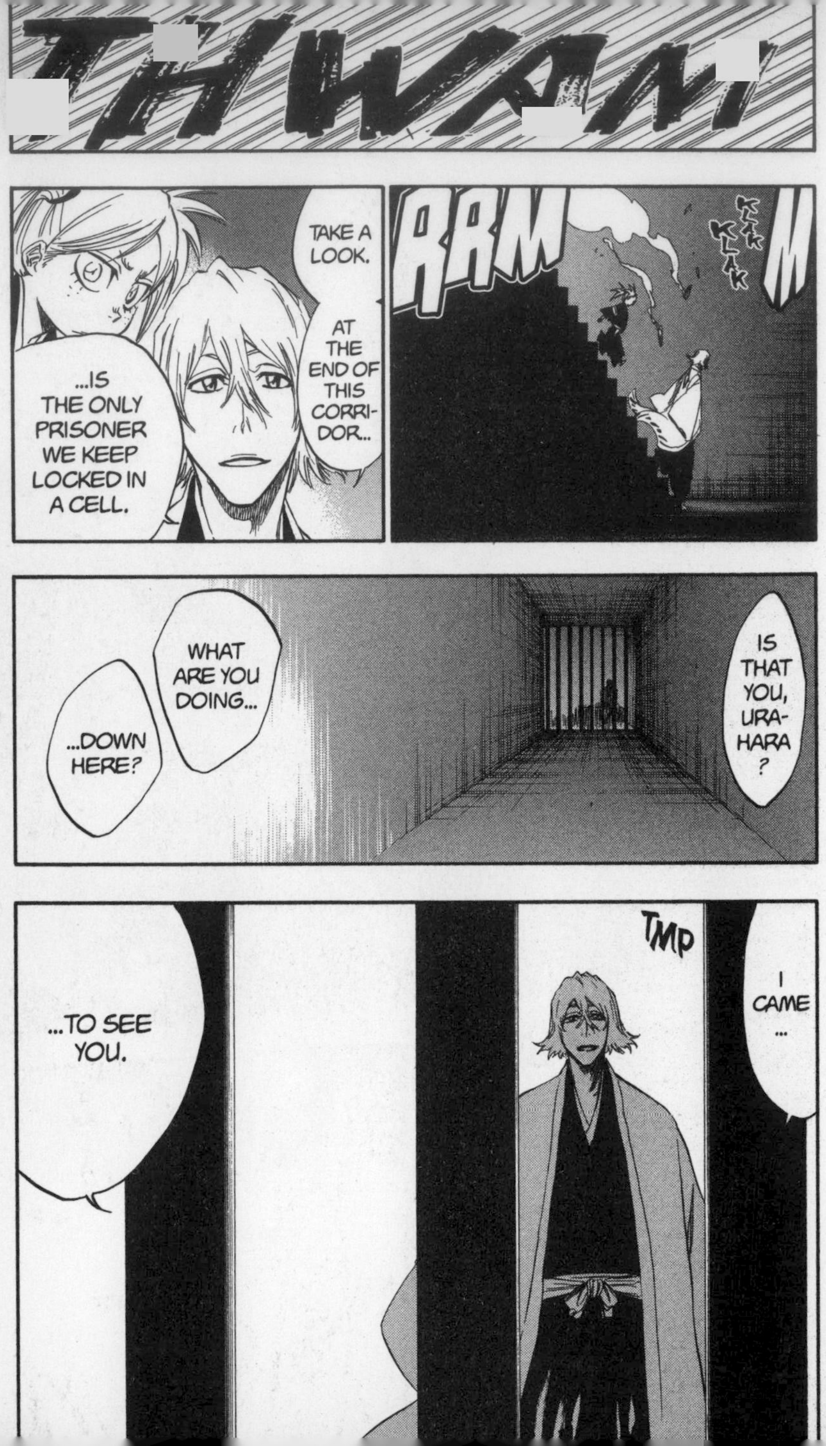
THWAM
RRM
M
KLAK KLAK
TAKE A LOOK.
AT THE END OF THIS CORRIDOR...
...IS THE ONLY PRISONER WE KEEP LOCKED IN A CELL.
IS THAT YOU, URAHARA?
WHAT ARE YOU DOING...
...DOWN HERE?
TMP
I CAME...
...TO SEE YOU.

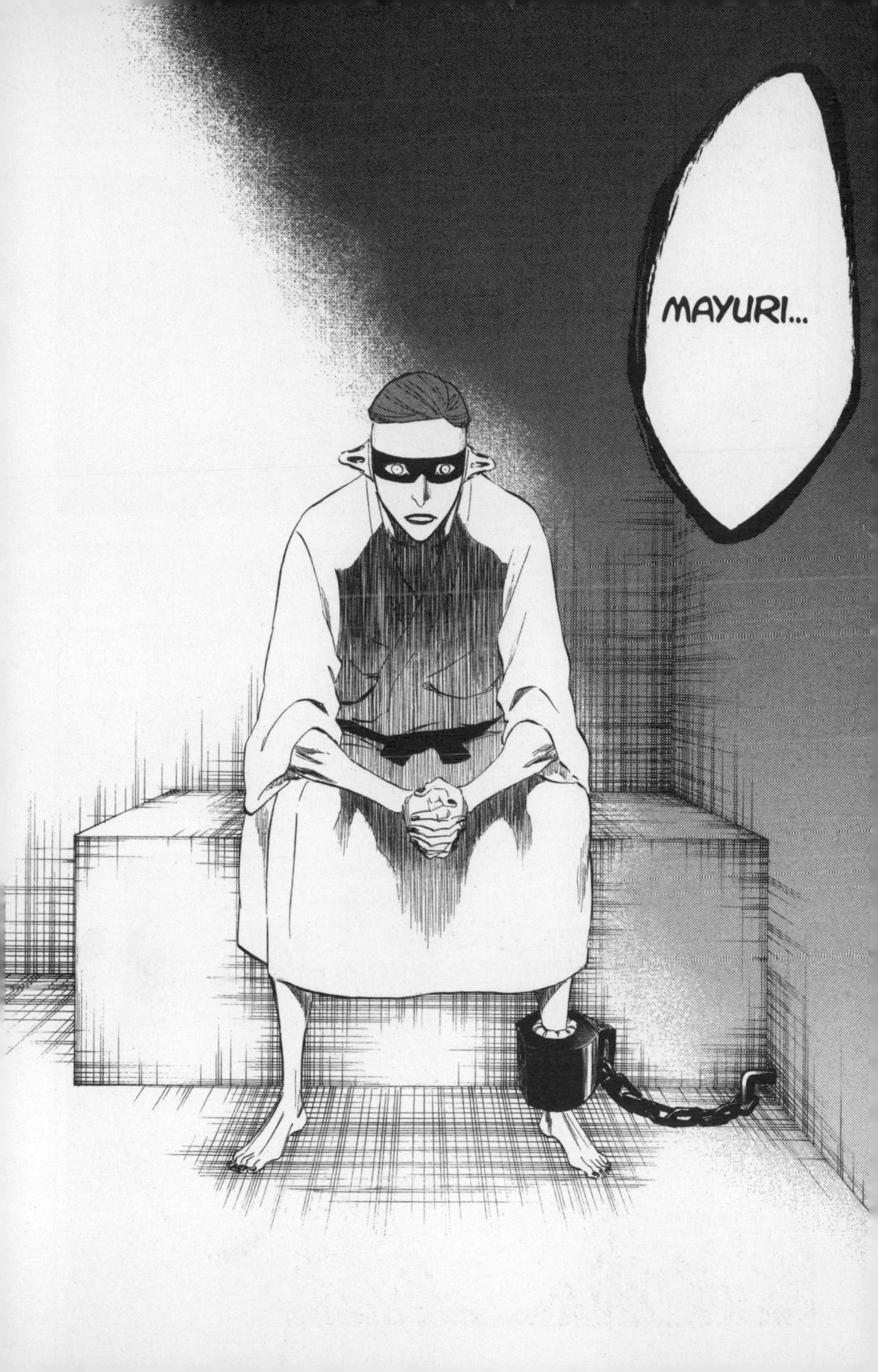
MAYURI...

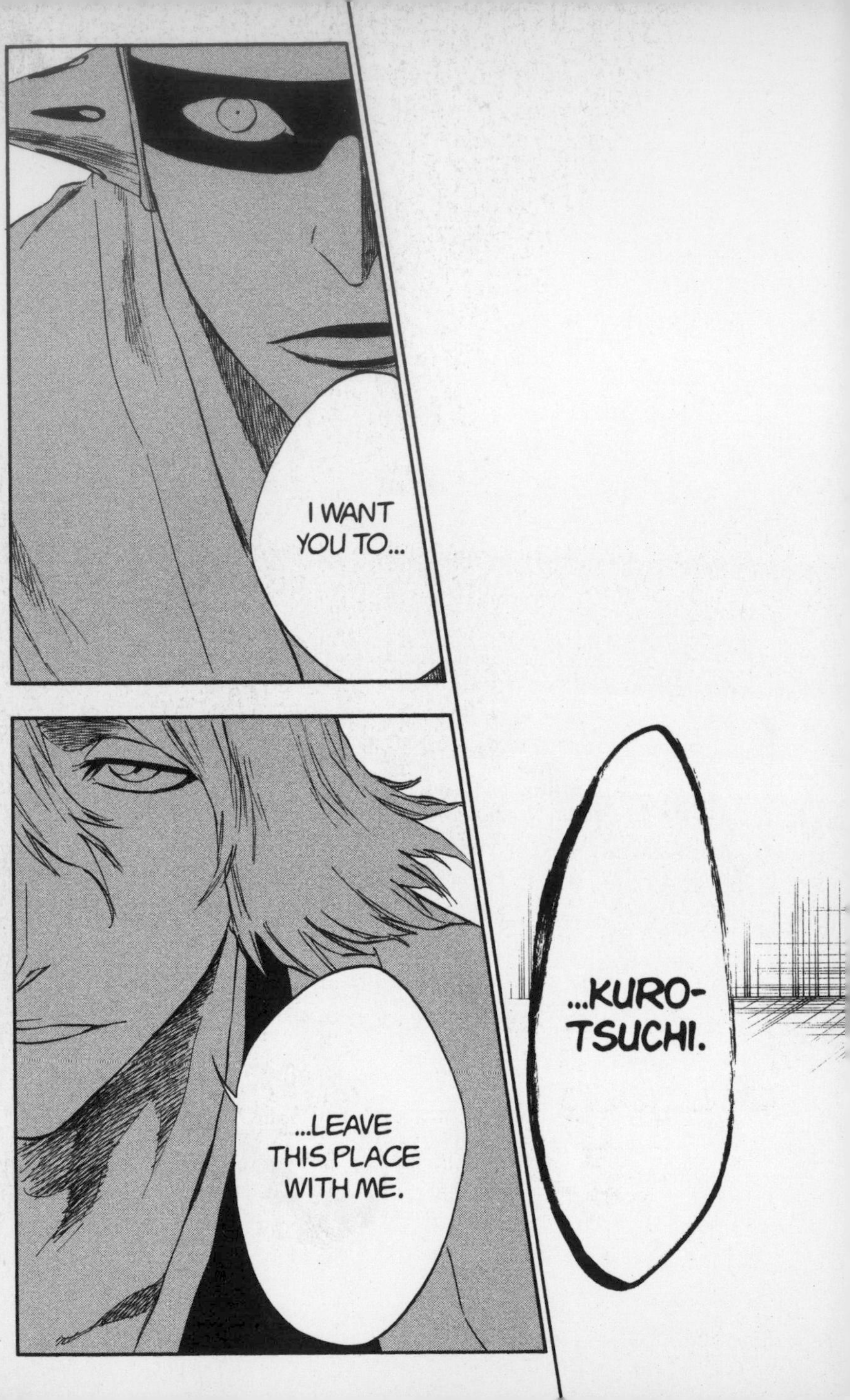
...KURO-TSUCHI.
I WANT YOU TO...
...LEAVE THIS PLACE WITH ME.

THE MAGGOT'S NEST... YOU ONLY SEE HIM FROM BEHIND, BUT AKON WAS THERE TOO.

KLANK KLANK

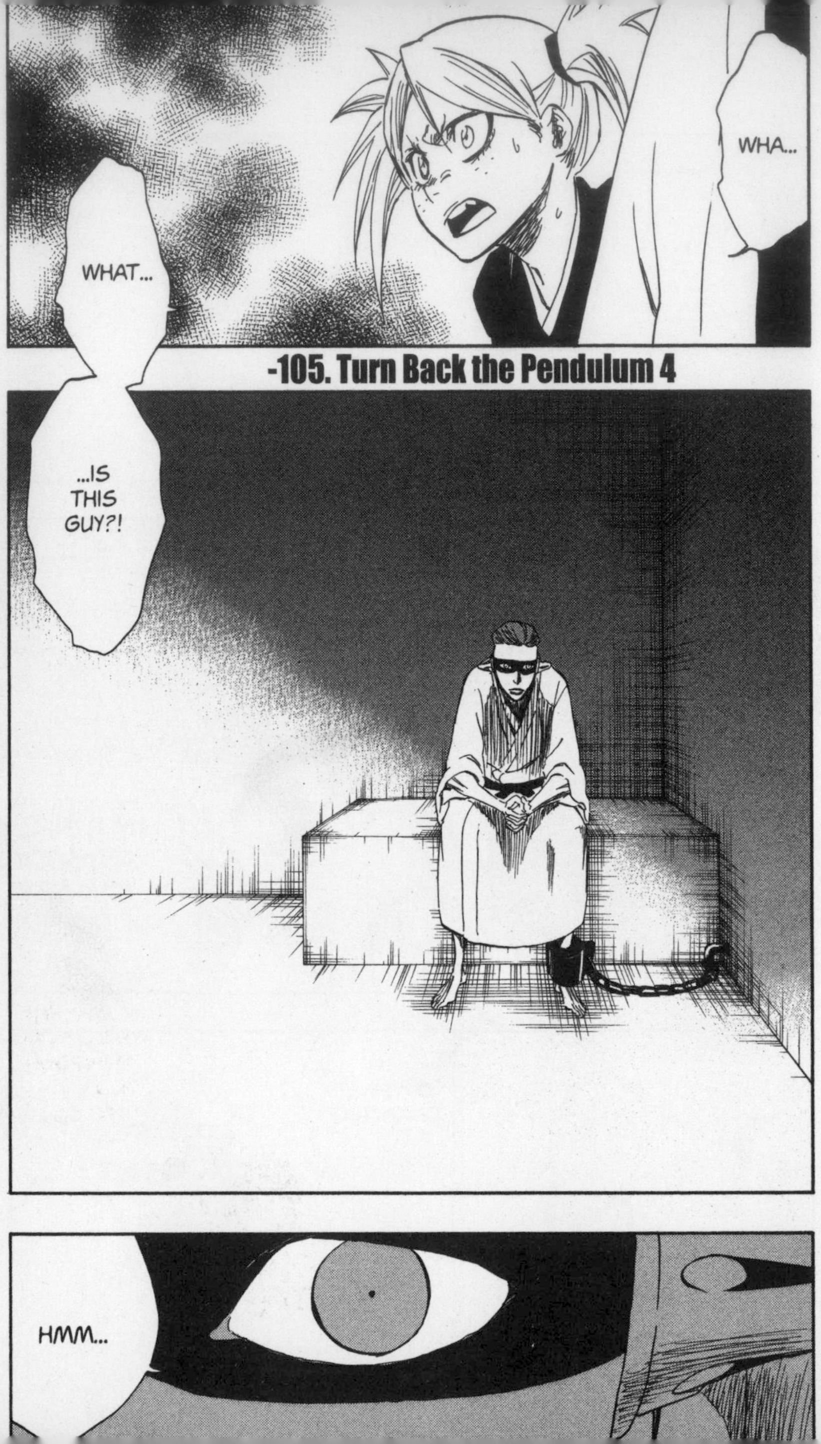
WHA...
WHAT...
...IS THIS GUY?!
-105. Turn Back the Pendulum 4
HMM...

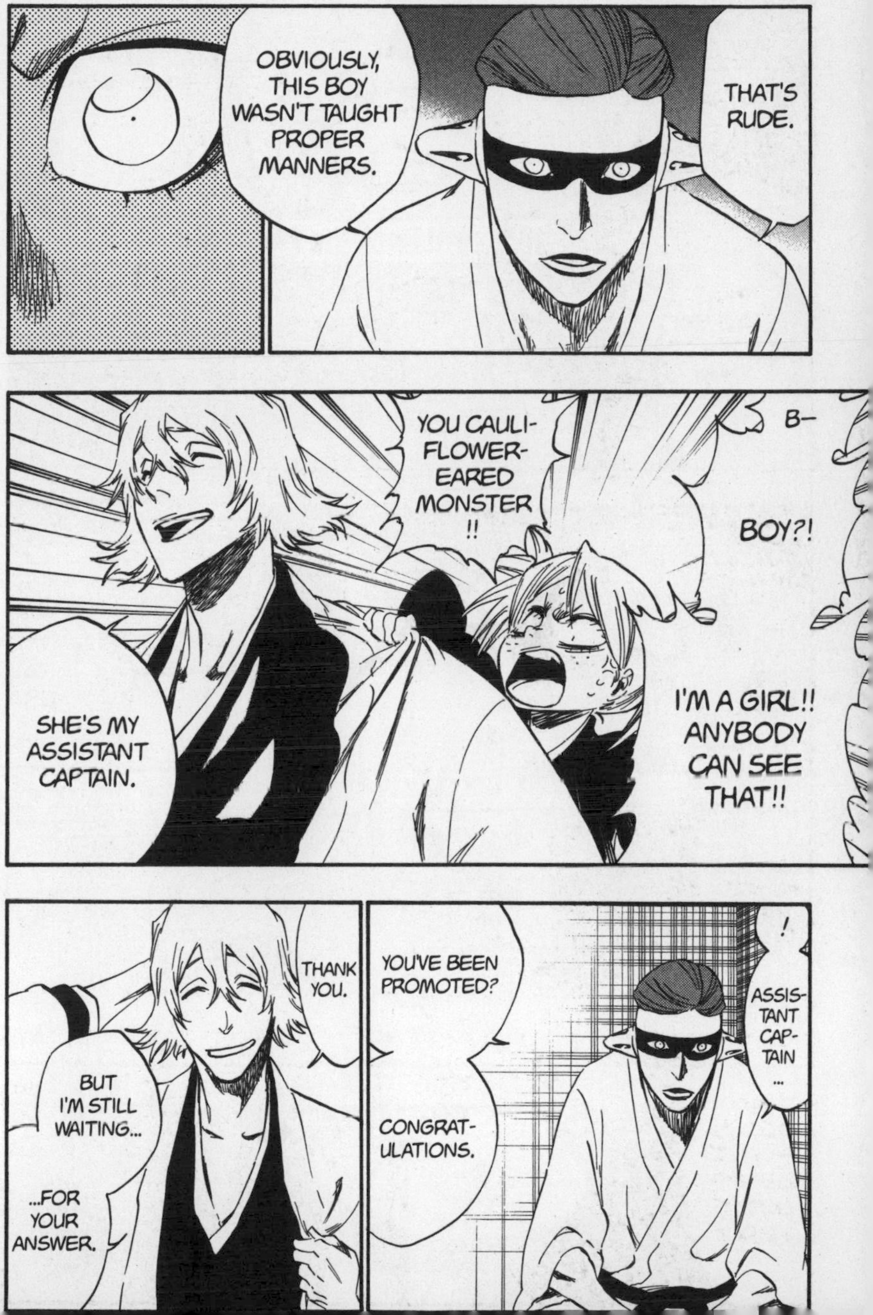
THAT'S RUDE.
OBVIOUSLY, THIS BOY WASN'T TAUGHT PROPER MANNERS.
B—
BOY?!
I'M A GIRL!! ANYBODY CAN SEE THAT!!
YOU CAULI-FLOWER-EARED MONSTER!!
SHE'S MY ASSISTANT CAPTAIN.
!
ASSIS-TANT CAP-TAIN...
YOU'VE BEEN PROMOTED?
CONGRAT-ULATIONS.
THANK YOU.
BUT I'M STILL WAITING...
...FOR YOUR ANSWER.

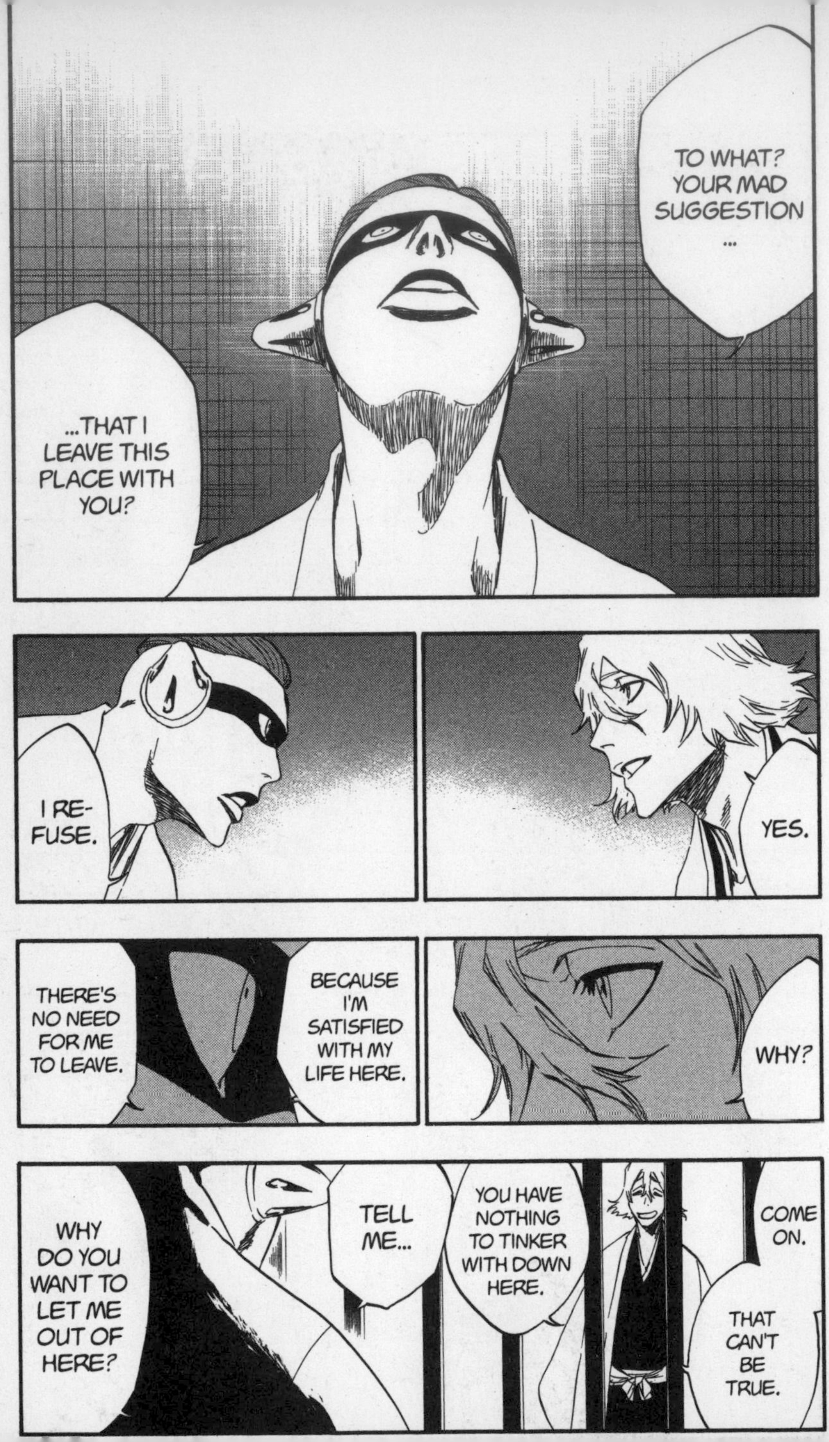
TO WHAT? YOUR MAD SUGGESTION ...
...THAT I LEAVE THIS PLACE WITH YOU?
YES.
I RE-FUSE.
WHY?
BECAUSE I'M SATISFIED WITH MY LIFE HERE.
THERE'S NO NEED FOR ME TO LEAVE.
COME ON.
THAT CAN'T BE TRUE.
YOU HAVE NOTHING TO TINKER WITH DOWN HERE.
TELL ME...
WHY DO YOU WANT TO LET ME OUT OF HERE?

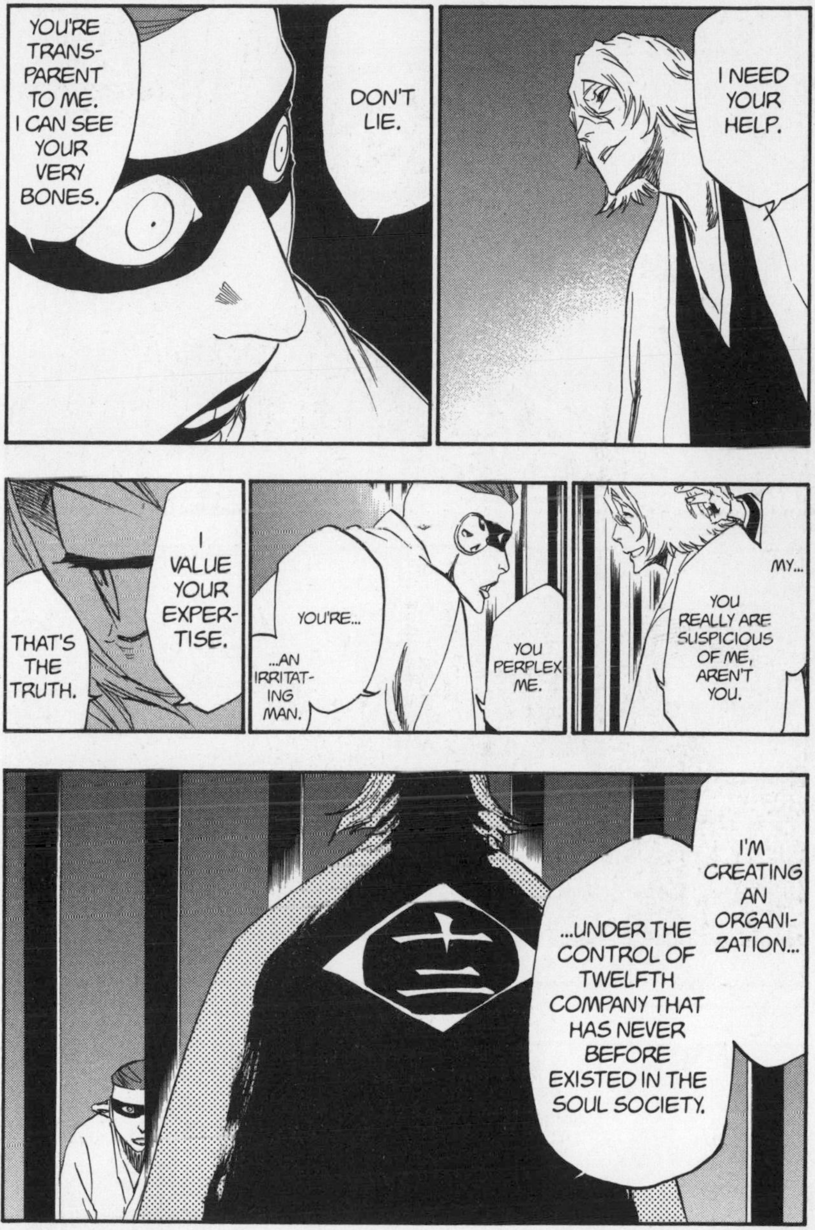
I NEED YOUR HELP.
DON'T LIE.
YOU'RE TRANS-PARENT TO ME. I CAN SEE YOUR VERY BONES.
MY...
YOU REALLY ARE SUSPICIOUS OF ME, AREN'T YOU.
YOU PERPLEX ME.
YOU'RE...
...AN IRRITAT-ING MAN.
I VALUE YOUR EXPER-TISE.
THAT'S THE TRUTH.
I'M CREATING AN ORGANI-ZATION...
...UNDER THE CONTROL OF TWELFTH COMPANY THAT HAS NEVER BEFORE EXISTED IN THE SOUL SOCIETY.

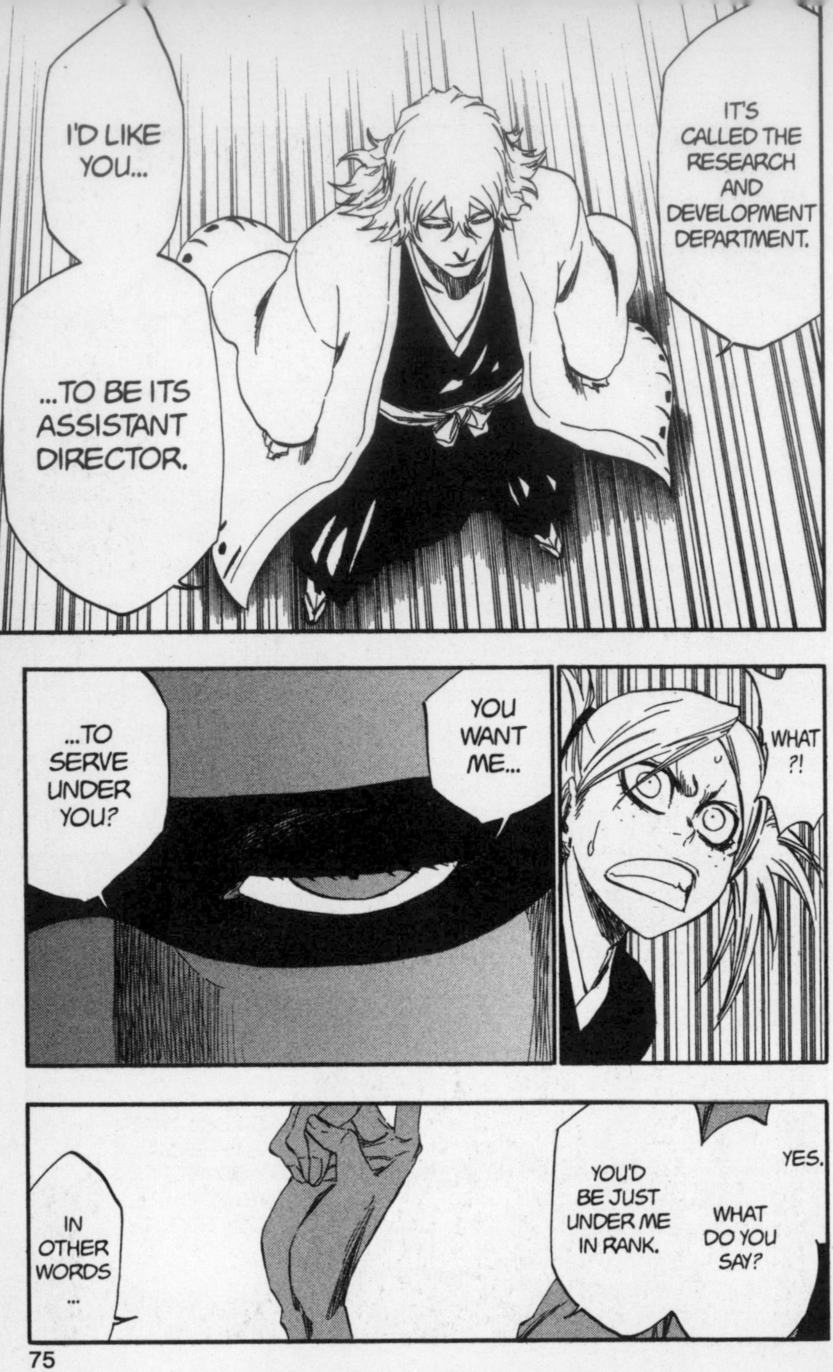
IT'S CALLED THE RESEARCH AND DEVELOPMENT DEPARTMENT.
I'D LIKE YOU...
...TO BE ITS ASSISTANT DIRECTOR.
WHAT ?!
YOU WANT ME...
...TO SERVE UNDER YOU?
YES.
YOU'D BE JUST UNDER ME IN RANK.
WHAT DO YOU SAY?
IN OTHER WORDS ...

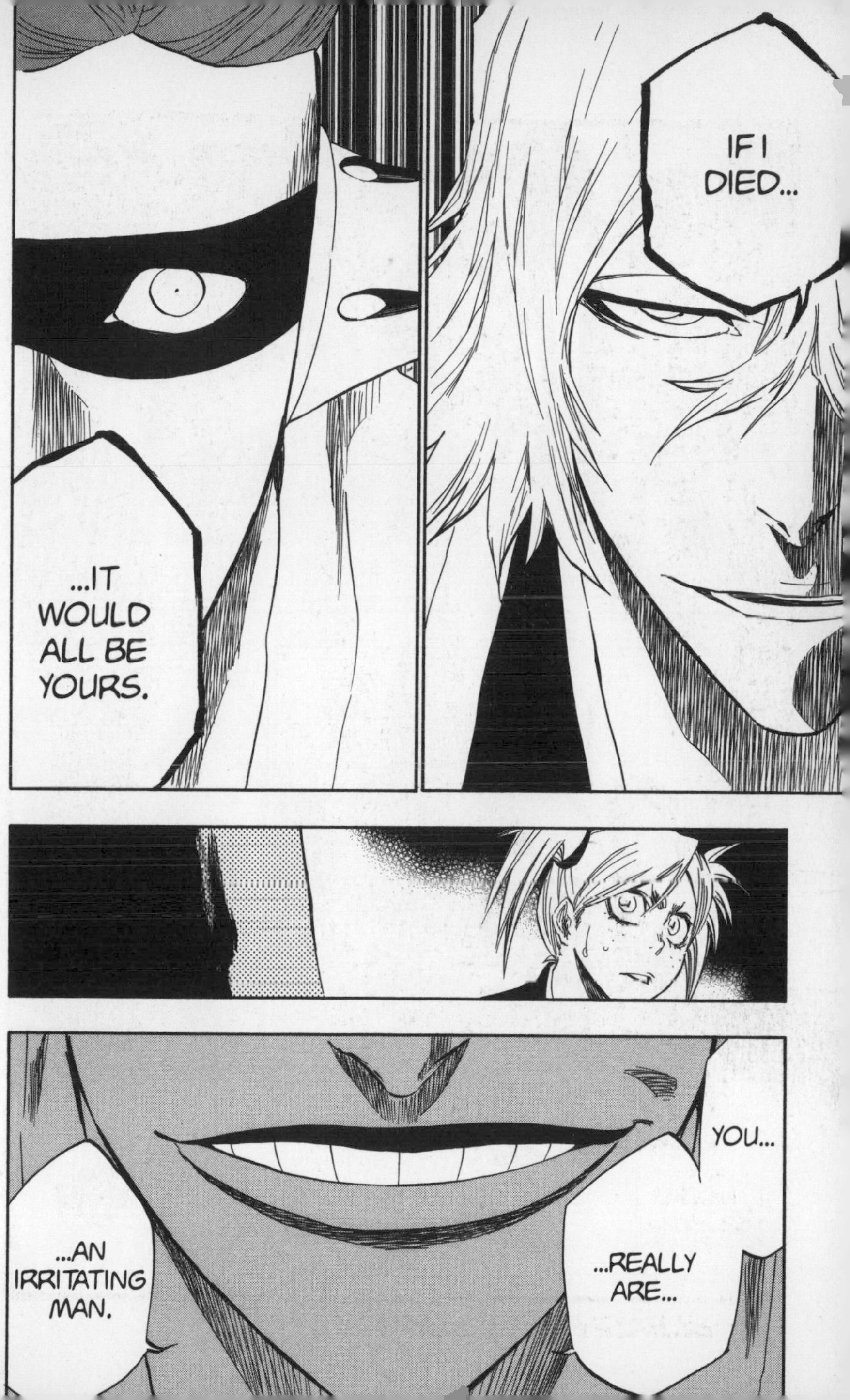
IF I DIED...
...IT WOULD ALL BE YOURS.
YOU...
...REALLY ARE...
...AN IRRITATING MAN.

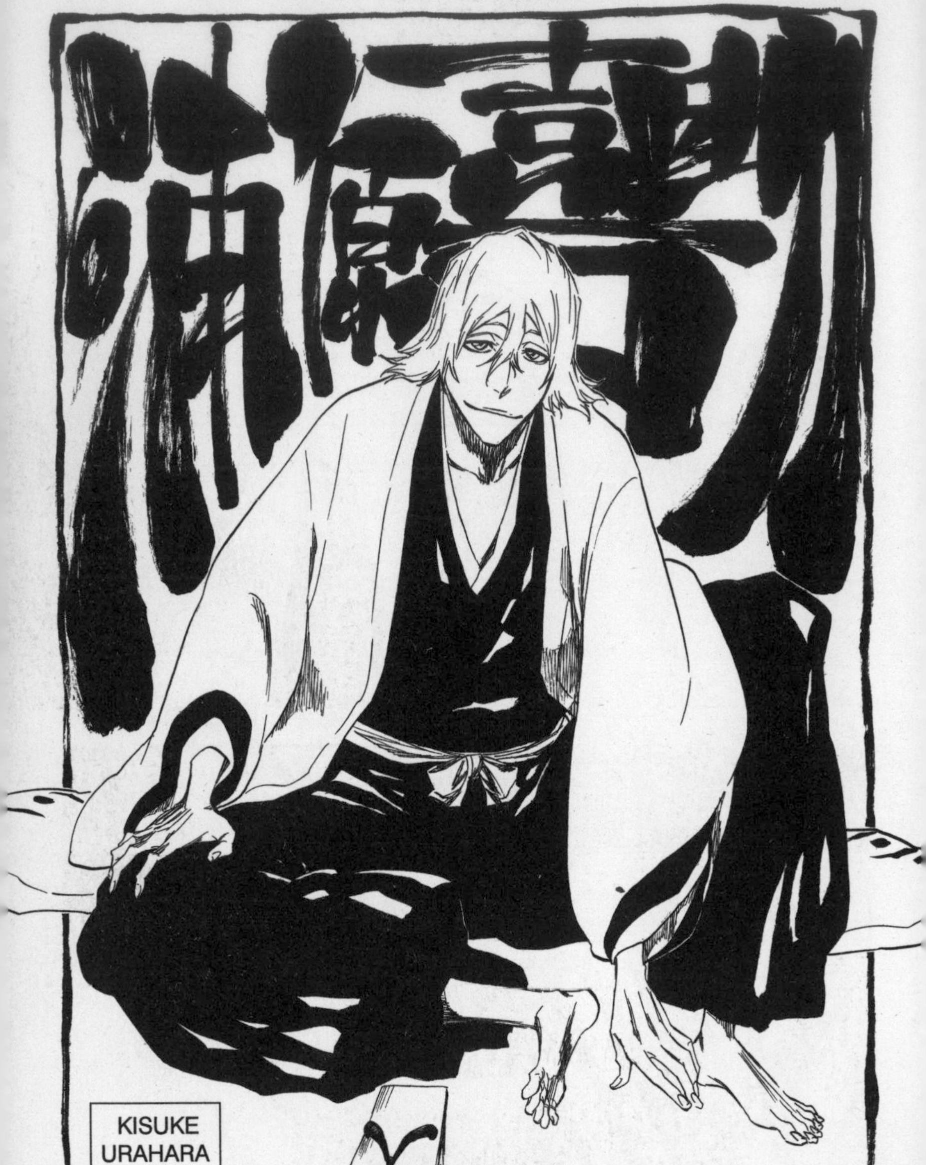
KISUKE
URAHARA

***BLEACH*-105. Turn Back the Pendulum 4**

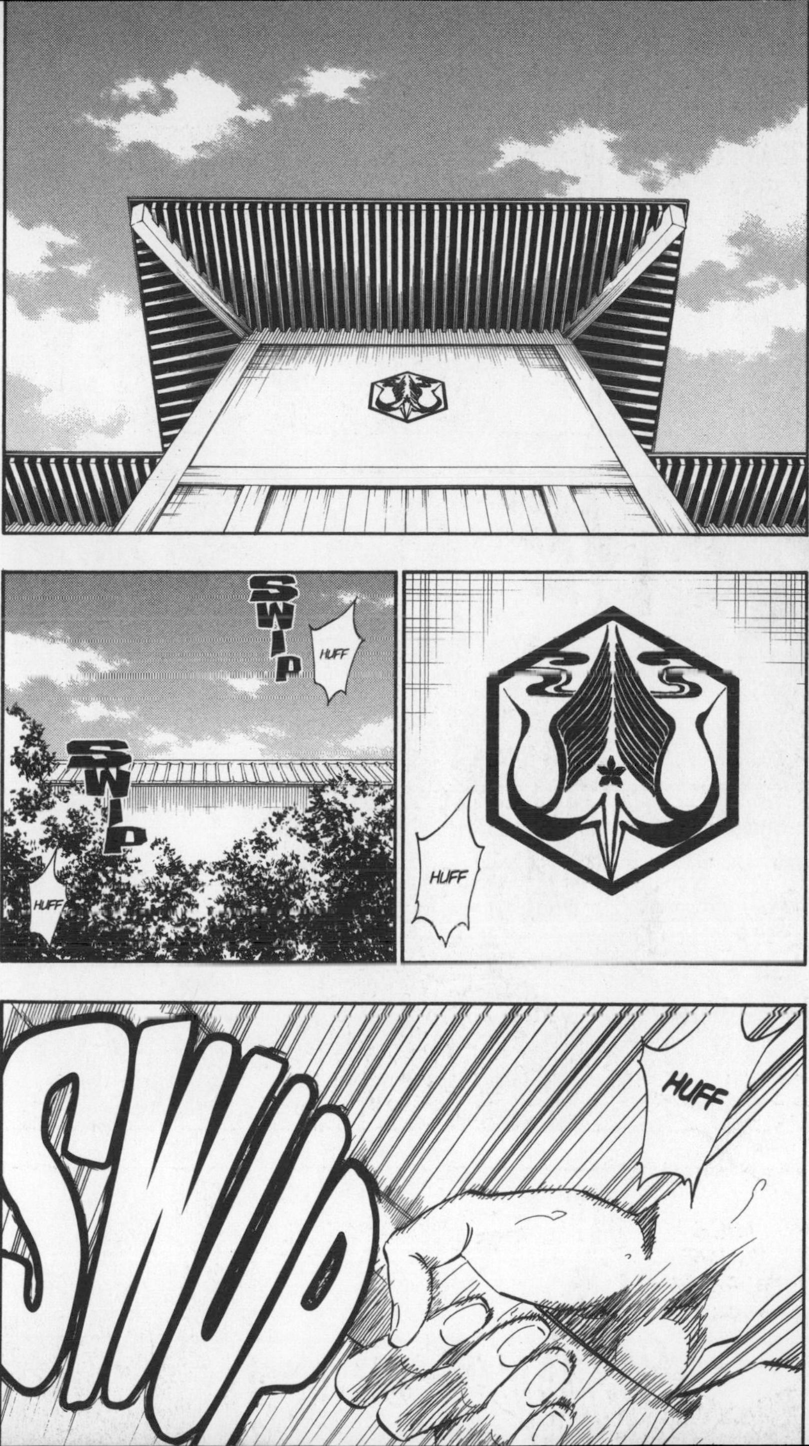
HUFF
HUFF
SWIP
SWIP
HUFF
HUFF
SWUP

READ THIS WAY

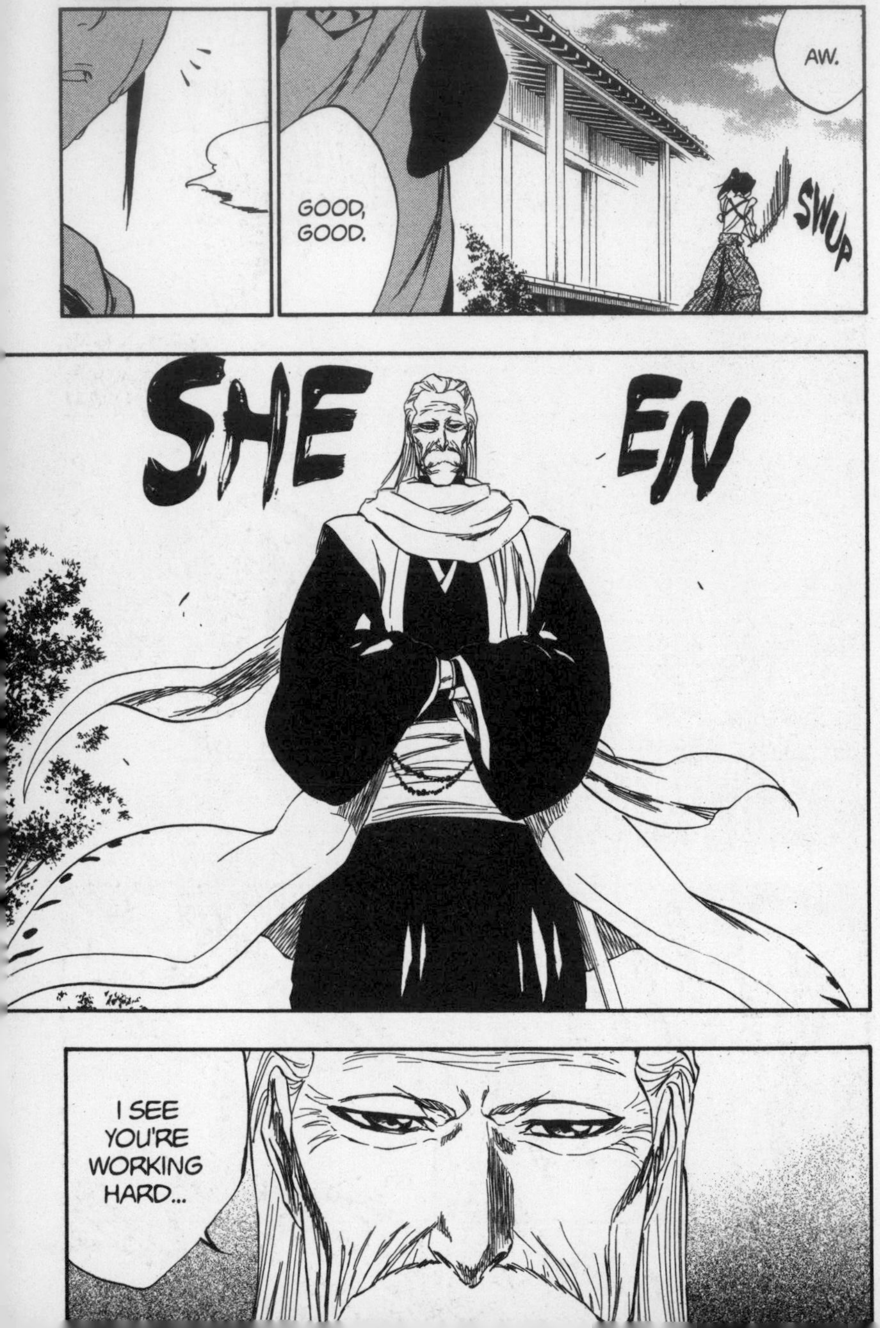
AW.
SWUP
GOOD, GOOD.
SHE EN
I SEE YOU'RE WORKING HARD...

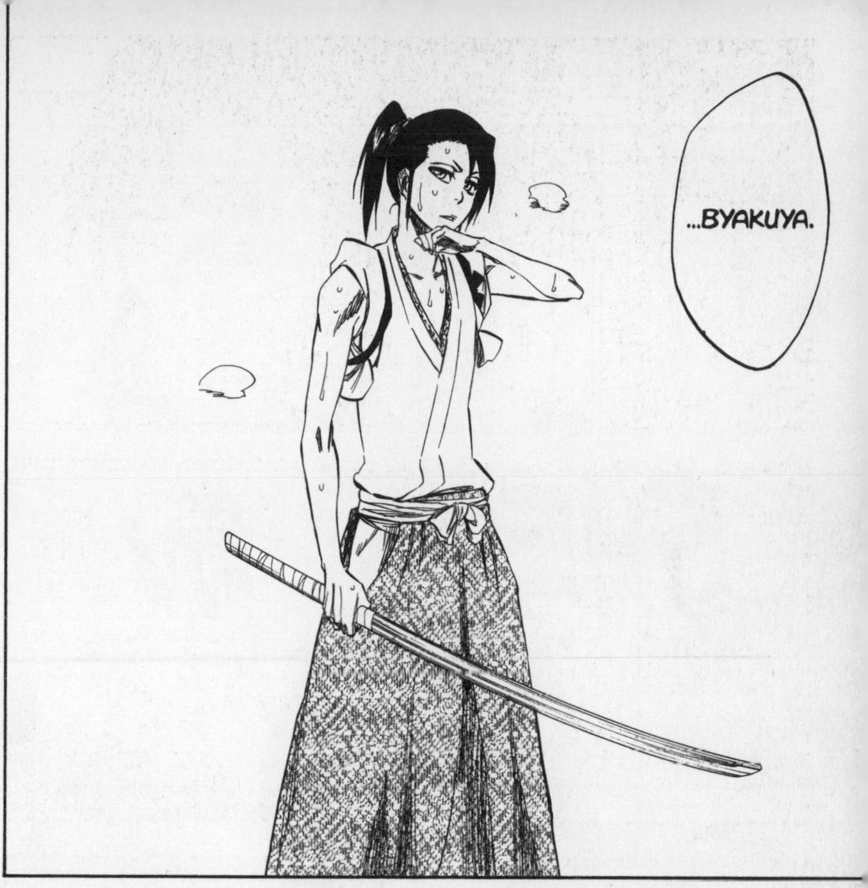
...BYAKUYA.

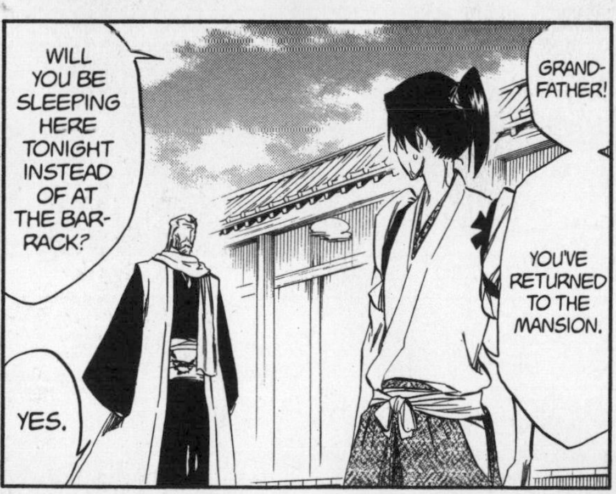
GRAND-FATHER!
YOU'VE RETURNED TO THE MANSION.
WILL YOU BE SLEEPING HERE TONIGHT INSTEAD OF AT THE BAR-RACK?
YES.

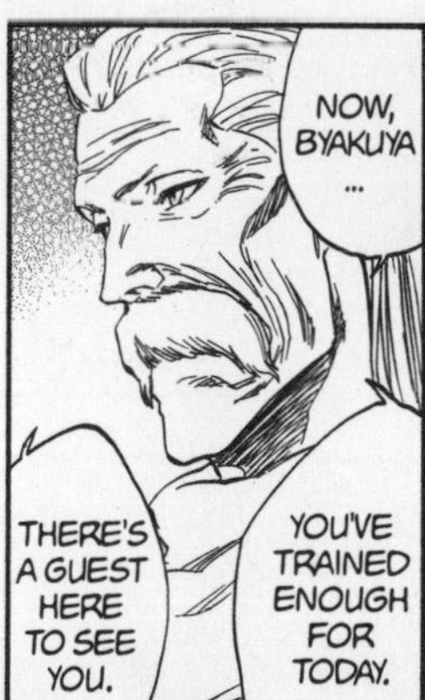
NOW, BYAKUYA ...
YOU'VE TRAINED ENOUGH FOR TODAY.
THERE'S A GUEST HERE TO SEE YOU.

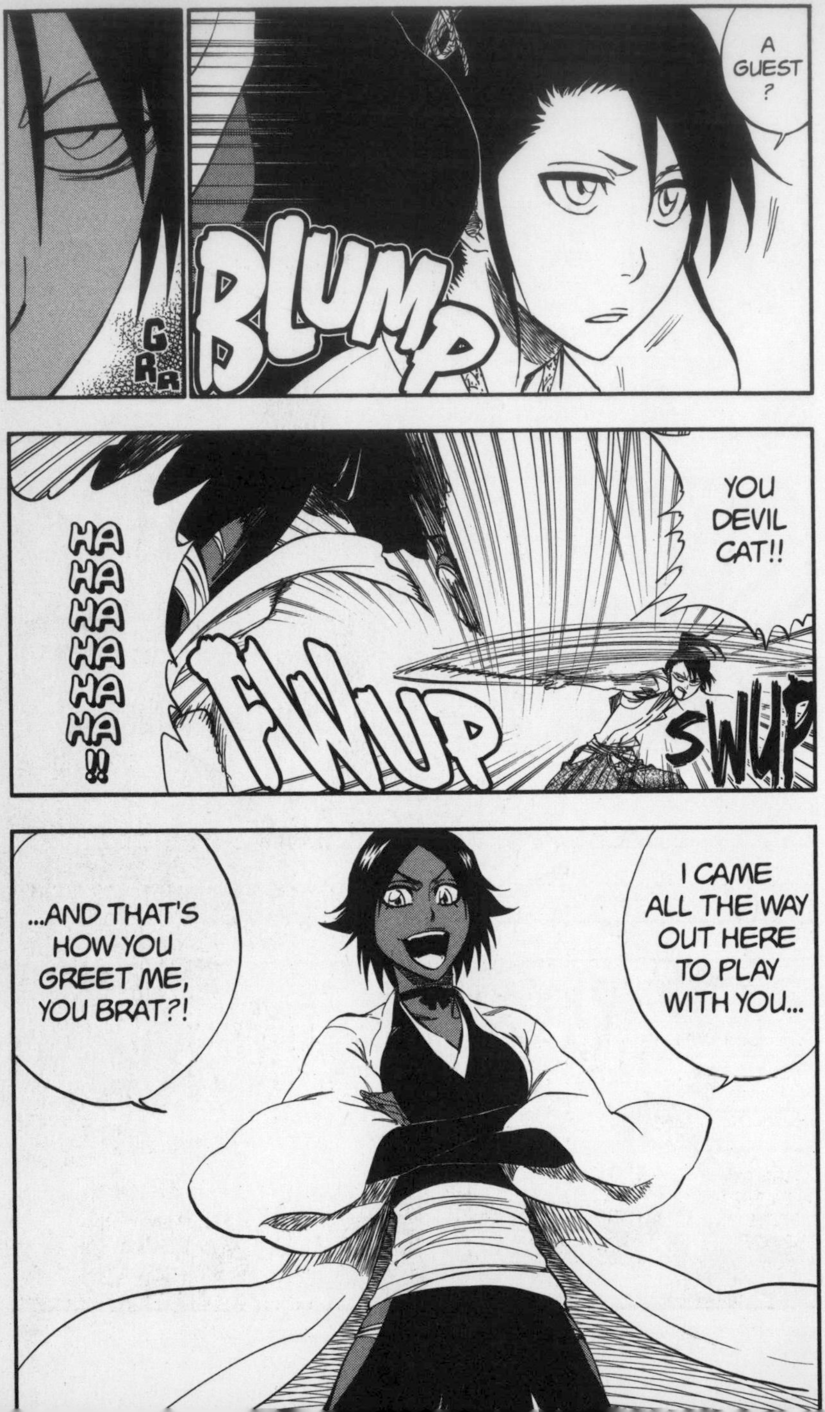
A GUEST?
BLUMP
GRR
YOU DEVIL CAT!!
SWUP
FWUP
HA HA HA HA HA HA!!
I CAME ALL THE WAY OUT HERE TO PLAY WITH YOU...
...AND THAT'S HOW YOU GREET ME, YOU BRAT?!

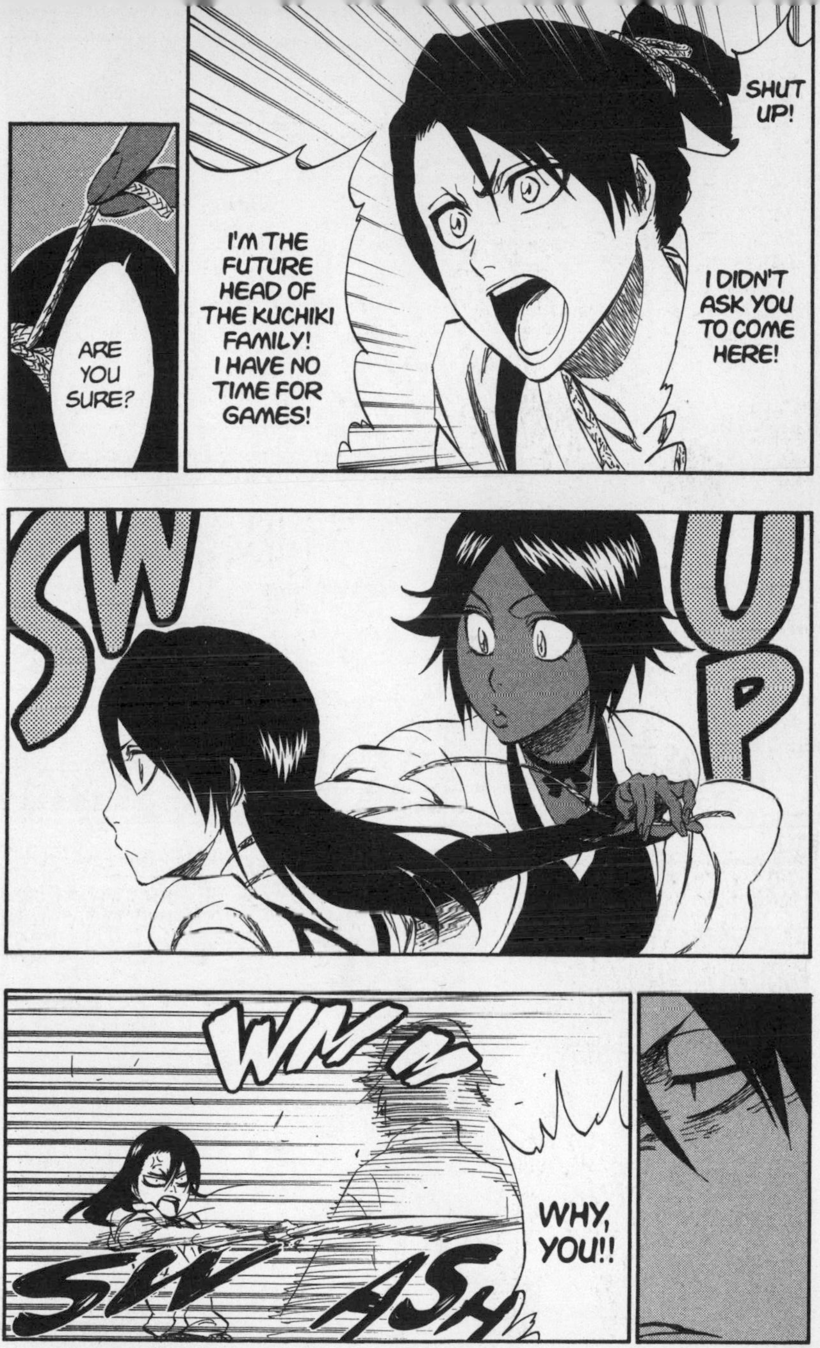
SHUT UP!
I DIDN'T ASK YOU TO COME HERE!
I'M THE FUTURE HEAD OF THE KUCHIKI FAMILY! I HAVE NO TIME FOR GAMES!
ARE YOU SURE?
SWUP
WHY, YOU!!
WHN
SWASH

READ THIS WAY

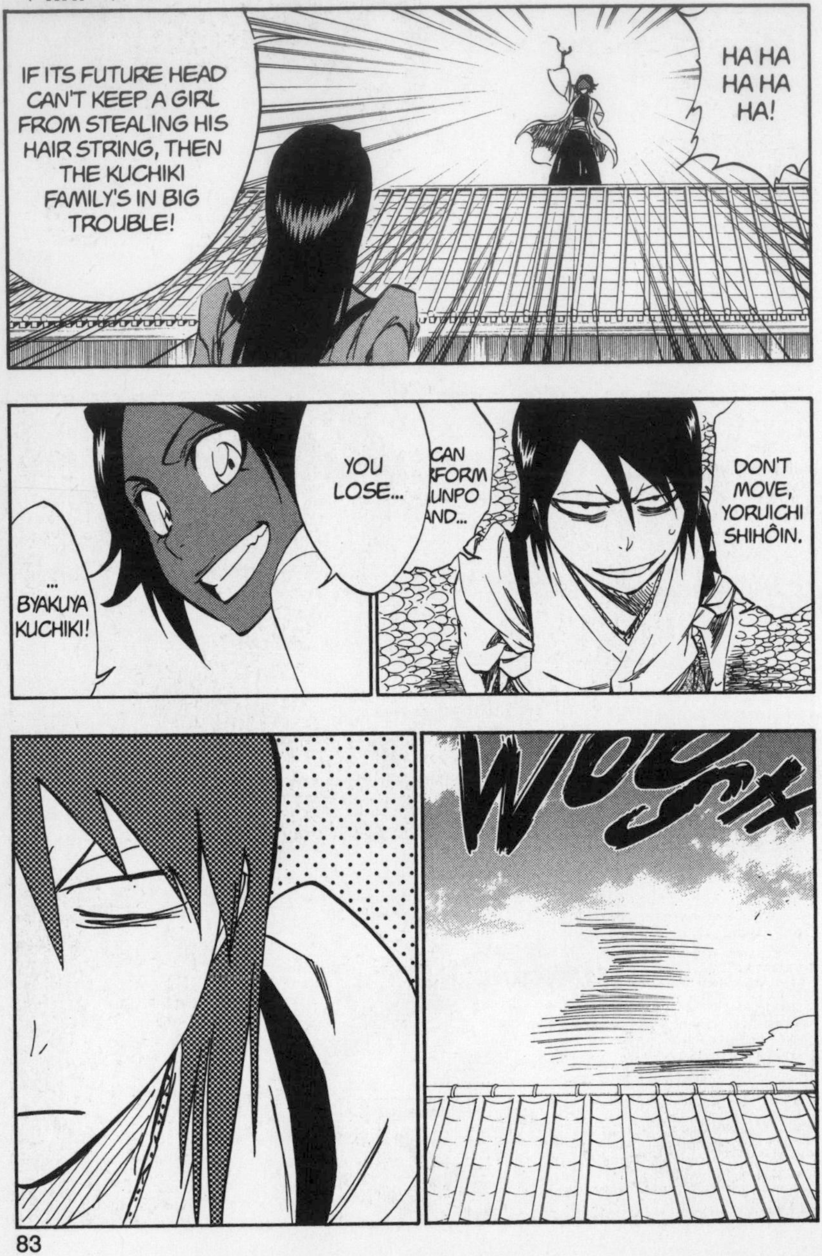

HA HA HA HA HA!
IF ITS FUTURE HEAD CAN'T KEEP A GIRL FROM STEALING HIS HAIR STRING, THEN THE KUCHIKI FAMILY'S IN BIG TROUBLE!
DON'T MOVE, YORUICHI SHIHÔIN.
CAN RFORM UNPO AND...
YOU LOSE...
... BYAKUYA KUCHIKI!
WOOSH

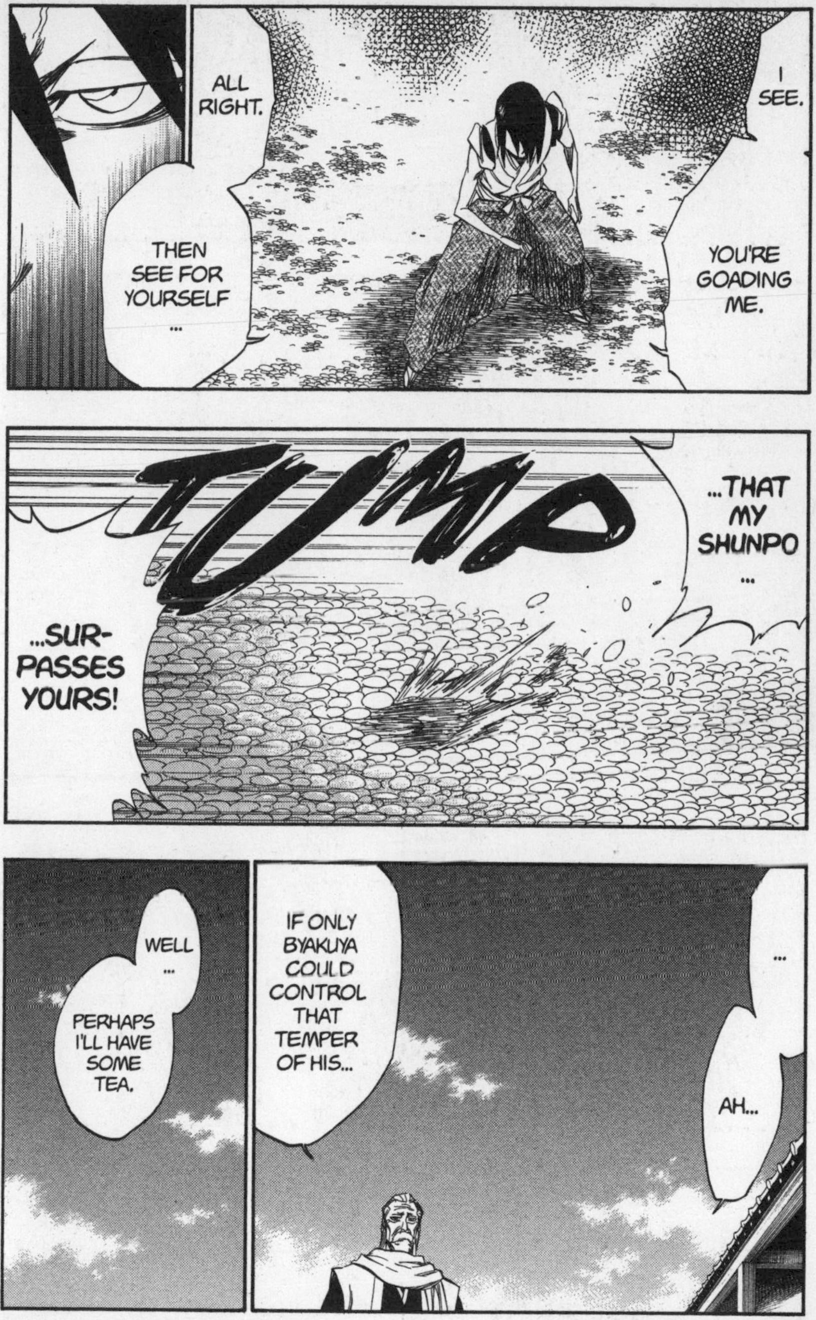
I SEE.
YOU'RE GOADING ME.
ALL RIGHT.
THEN SEE FOR YOURSELF ...
...THAT MY SHUNPO ...
TUMP
...SUR-PASSES YOURS!
...
AH...
IF ONLY BYAKUYA COULD CONTROL THAT TEMPER OF HIS...
WELL ...
PERHAPS I'LL HAVE SOME TEA.

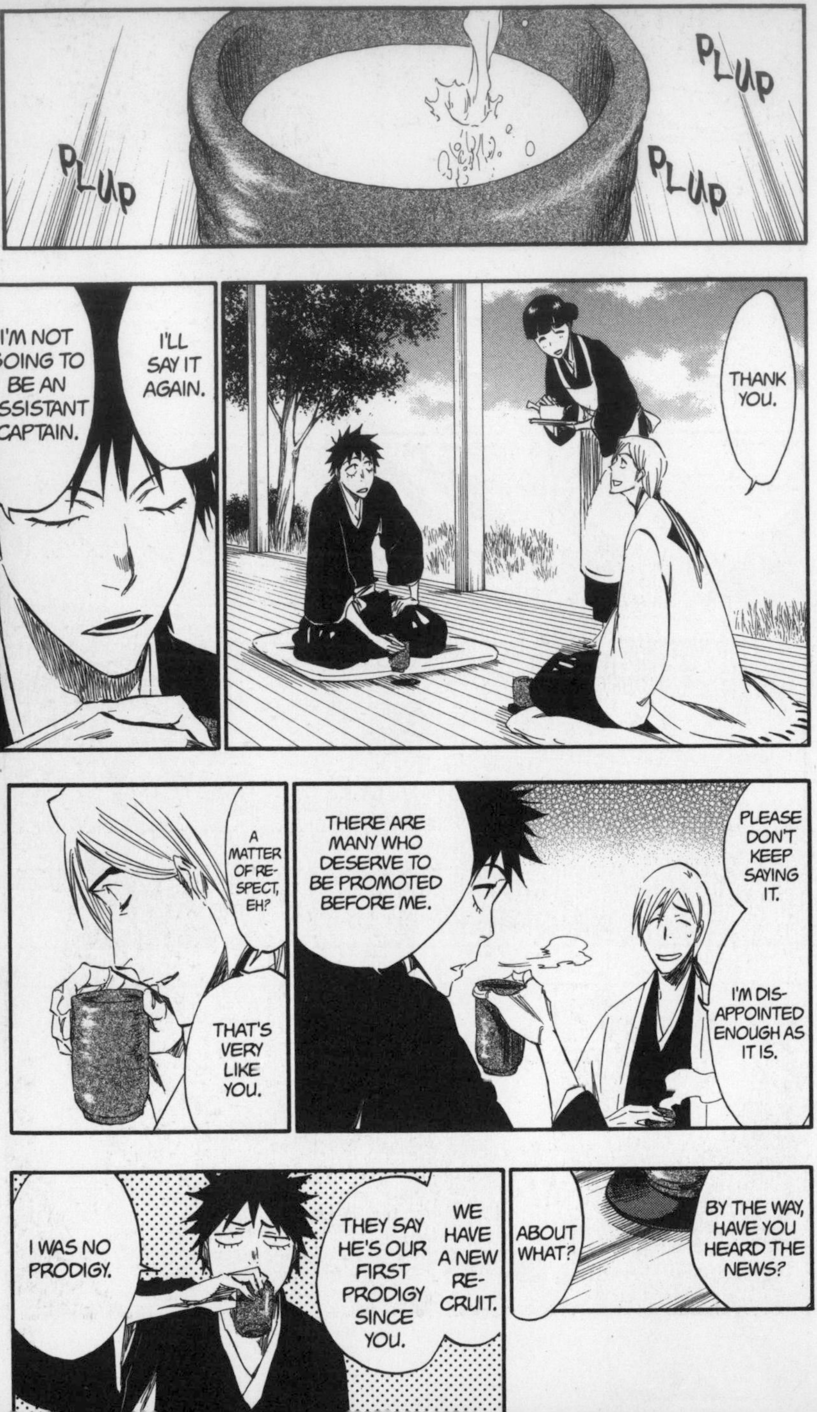
PLUP
PLUP
PLUP
THANK YOU.
I'LL SAY IT AGAIN.
I'M NOT GOING TO BE AN ASSISTANT CAPTAIN.
PLEASE DON'T KEEP SAYING IT.
I'M DISAPPOINTED ENOUGH AS IT IS.
THERE ARE MANY WHO DESERVE TO BE PROMOTED BEFORE ME.
A MATTER OF RESPECT, EH?
THAT'S VERY LIKE YOU.
BY THE WAY, HAVE YOU HEARD THE NEWS?
ABOUT WHAT?
WE HAVE A NEW RECRUIT.
THEY SAY HE'S OUR FIRST PRODIGY SINCE YOU.
I WAS NO PRODIGY.

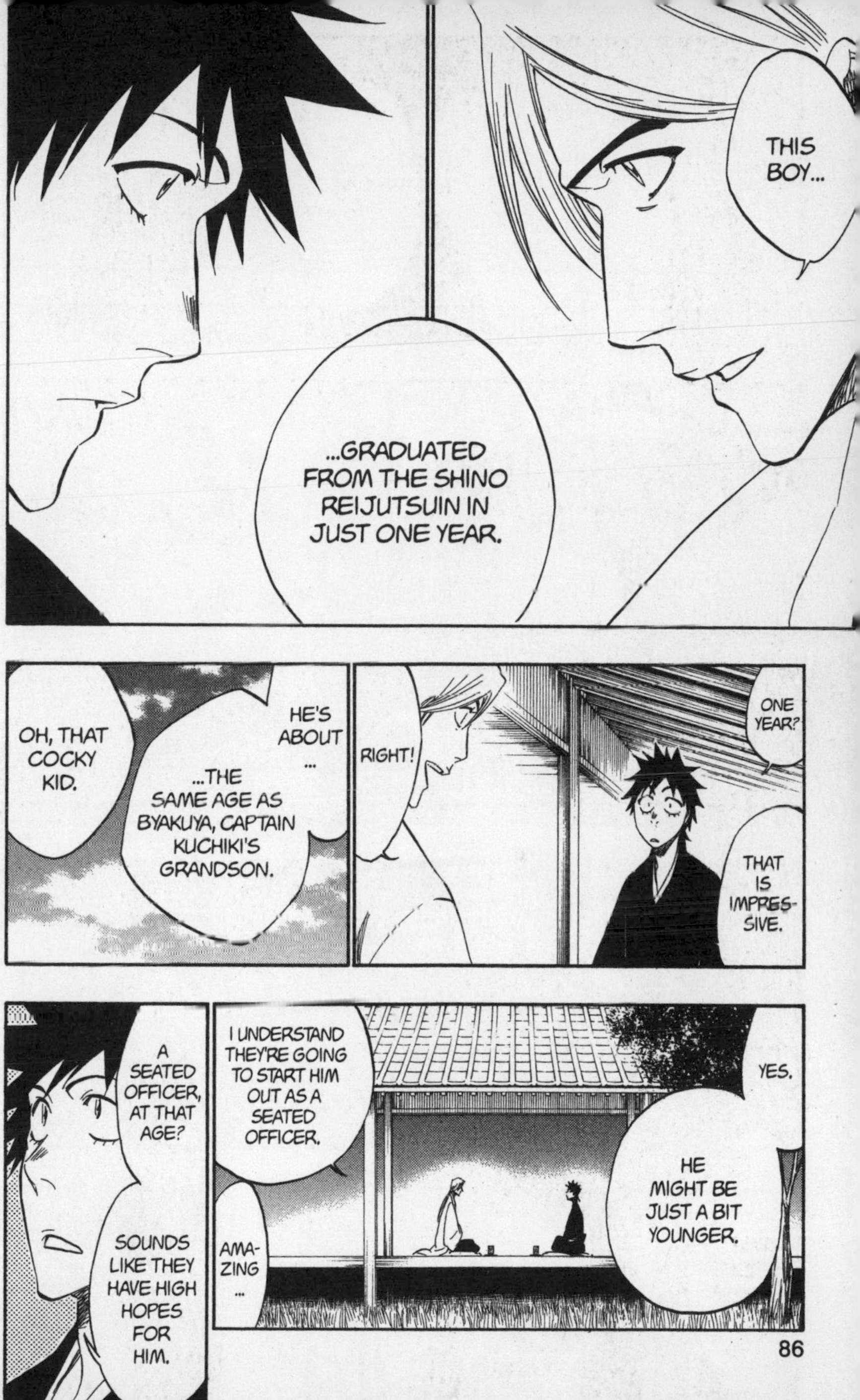
THIS BOY...
...GRADUATED FROM THE SHINO REIJUTSUIN IN JUST ONE YEAR.
ONE YEAR?
THAT IS IMPRES-SIVE.
RIGHT!
HE'S ABOUT...
...THE SAME AGE AS BYAKUYA, CAPTAIN KUCHIKI'S GRANDSON.
OH, THAT COCKY KID.
YES.
HE MIGHT BE JUST A BIT YOUNGER.
I UNDERSTAND THEY'RE GOING TO START HIM OUT AS A SEATED OFFICER.
AMA-ZING...
A SEATED OFFICER, AT THAT AGE?
SOUNDS LIKE THEY HAVE HIGH HOPES FOR HIM.

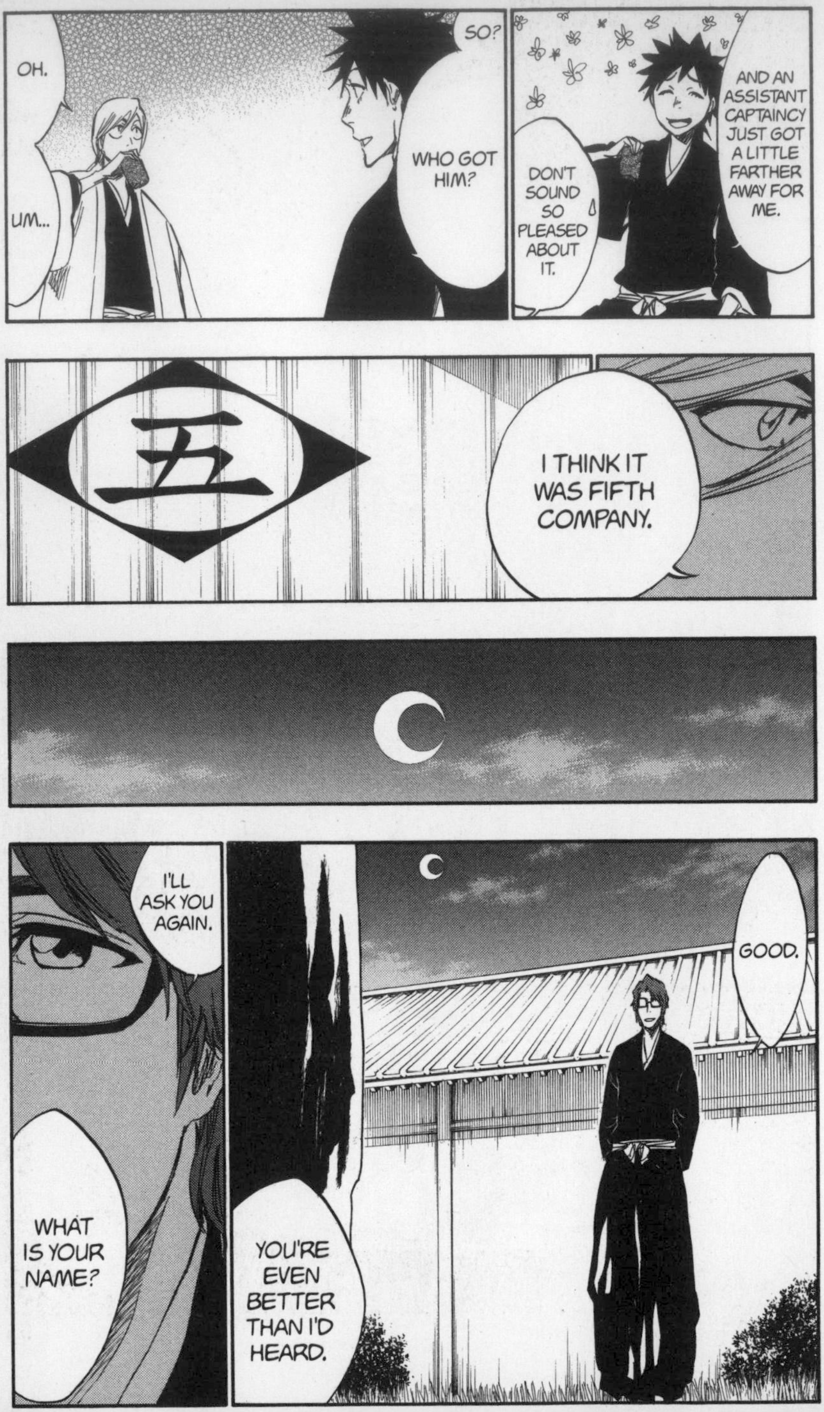
AND AN ASSISTANT CAPTAINCY JUST GOT A LITTLE FARTHER AWAY FOR ME.
DON'T SOUND SO PLEASED ABOUT IT.
SO?
WHO GOT HIM?
OH.
UM...
I THINK IT WAS FIFTH COMPANY.
五
GOOD.
YOU'RE EVEN BETTER THAN I'D HEARD.
I'LL ASK YOU AGAIN.
WHAT IS YOUR NAME?

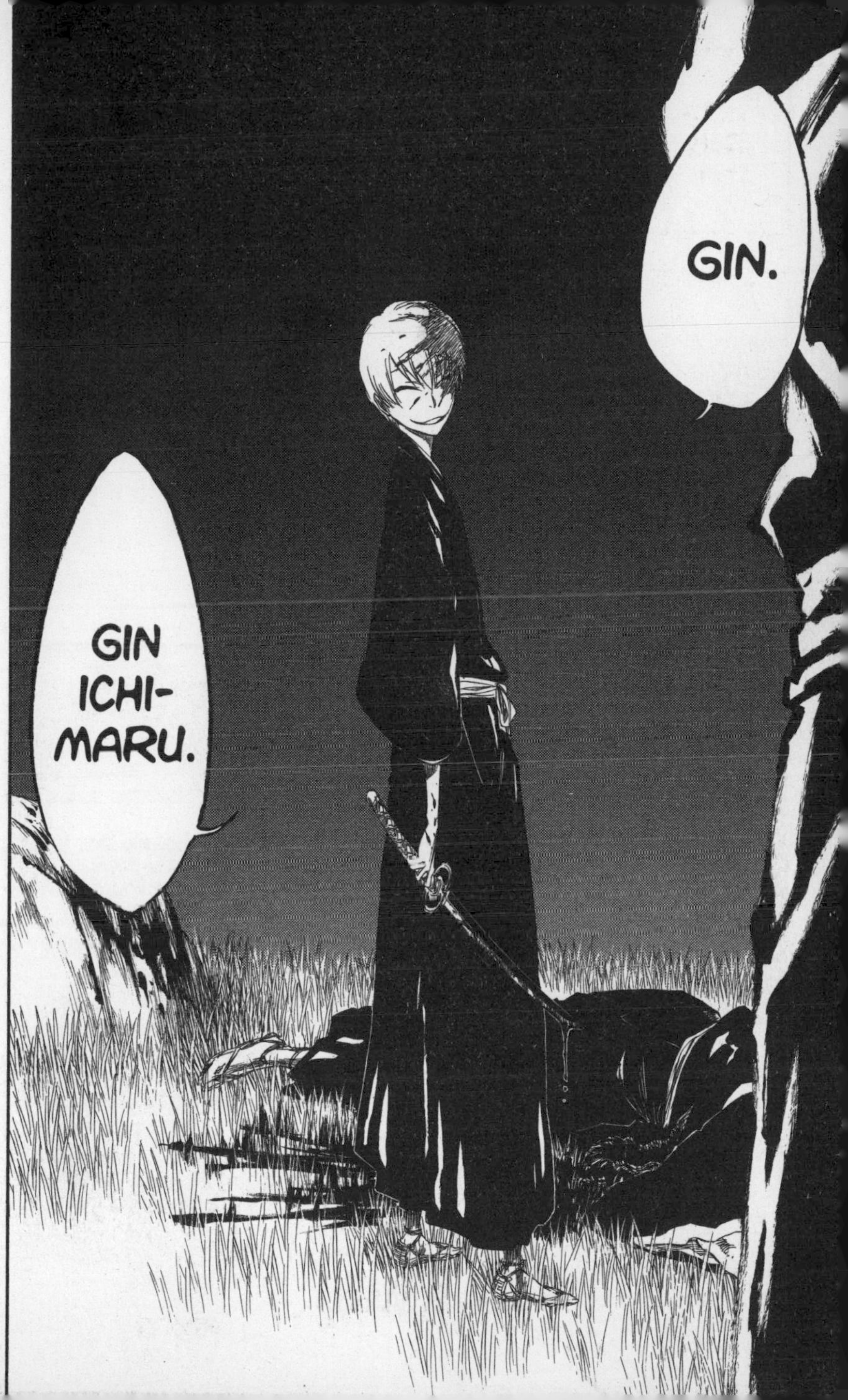
GIN.
GIN ICHI-MARU.

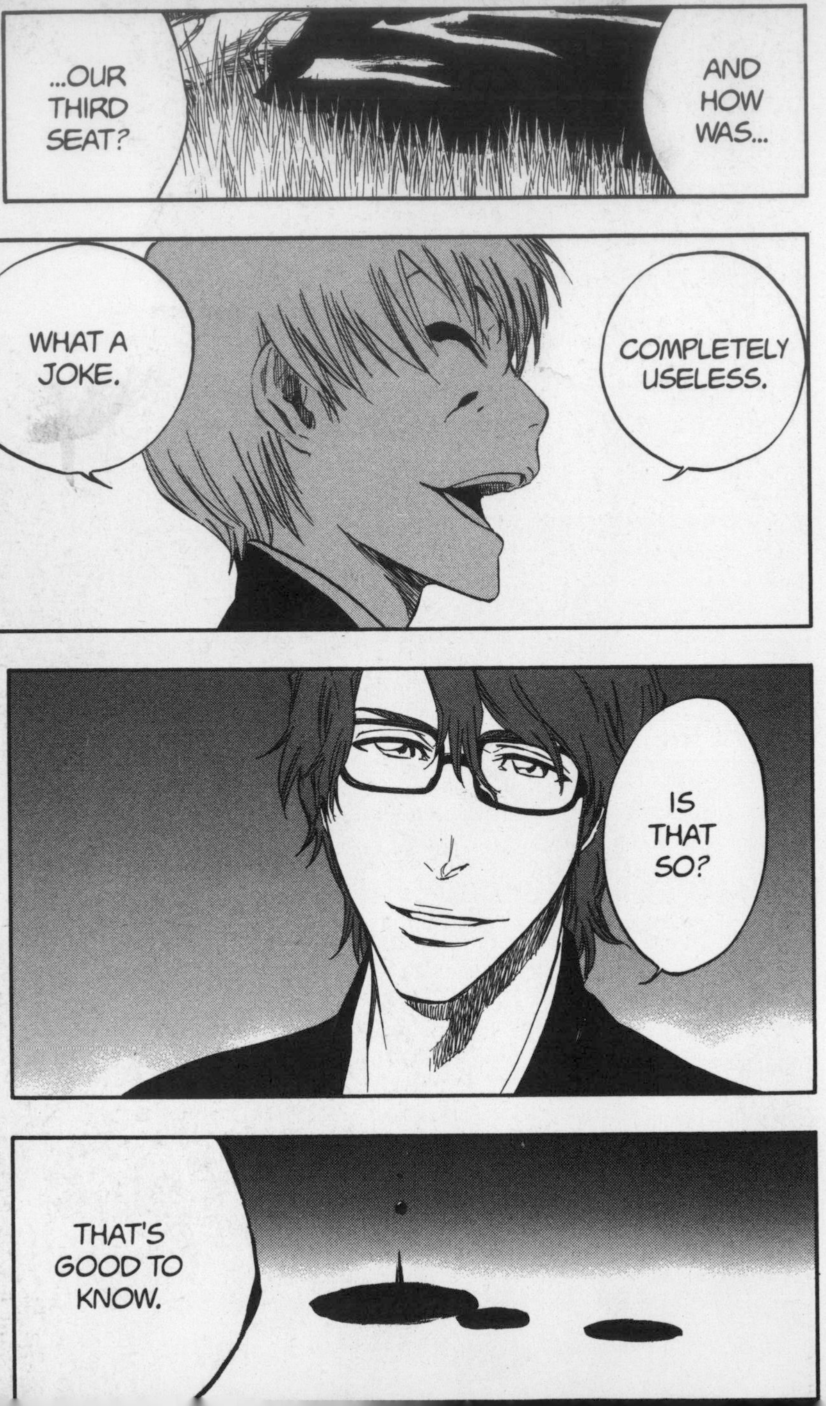
AND HOW WAS...
...OUR THIRD SEAT?
COMPLETELY USELESS.
WHAT A JOKE.
IS THAT SO?
THAT'S GOOD TO KNOW.

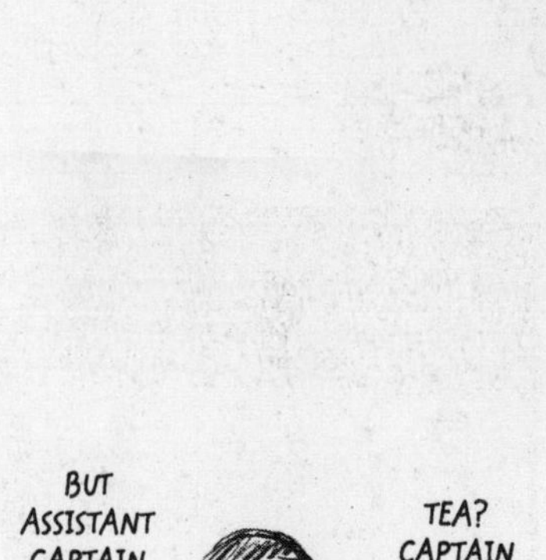
TEA? CAPTAIN UKITAKE LIKES THE SWEETER TEAS, SO WE SERVE HIM *HAGOROMO*, OUR FINEST *GYOKURO* GREEN TEA.
BUT ASSISTANT CAPTAIN SHIBA THINKS IT'S TOO SWEET, SO WE SERVE HIM OUR CHEAPEST.

-104. Turn Back the Pendulum 5

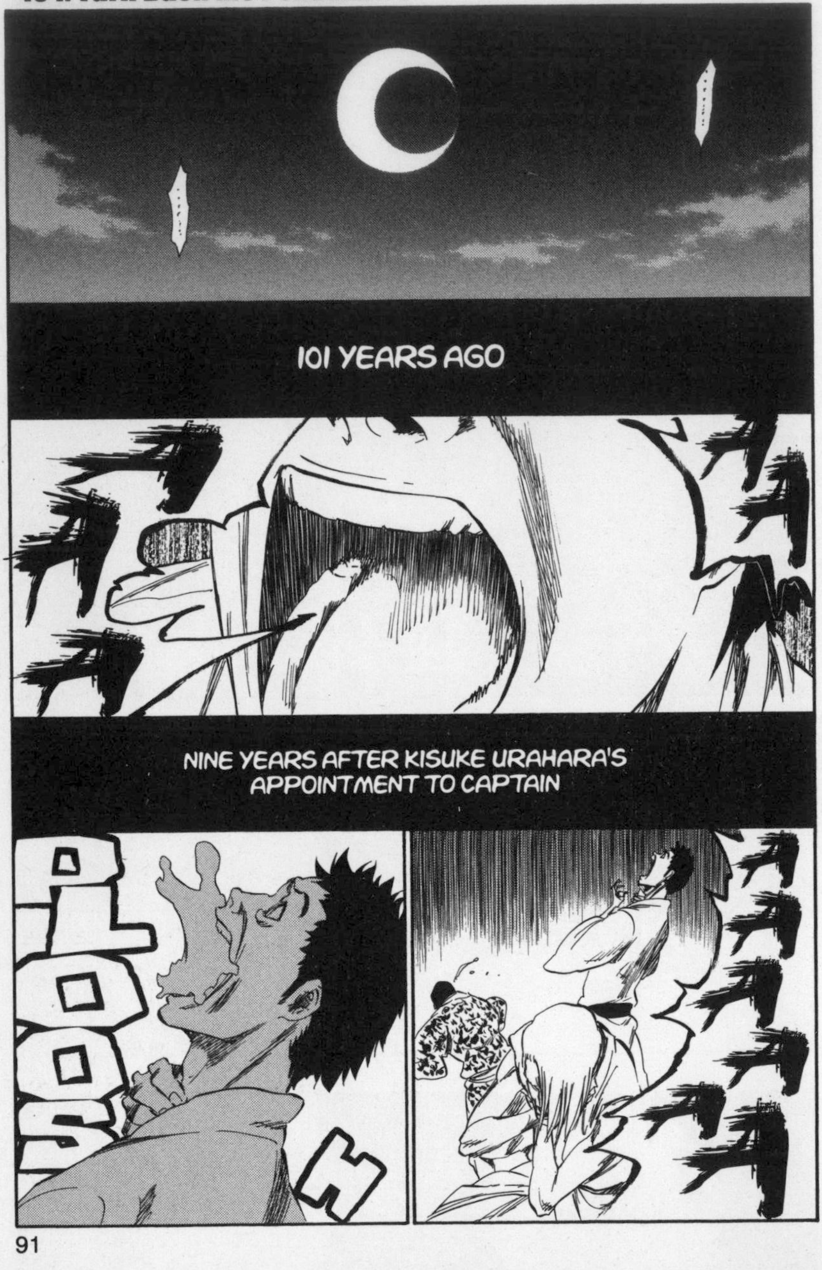
101 YEARS AGO
NINE YEARS AFTER KISUKE URAHARA'S APPOINTMENT TO CAPTAIN
PLOOSH

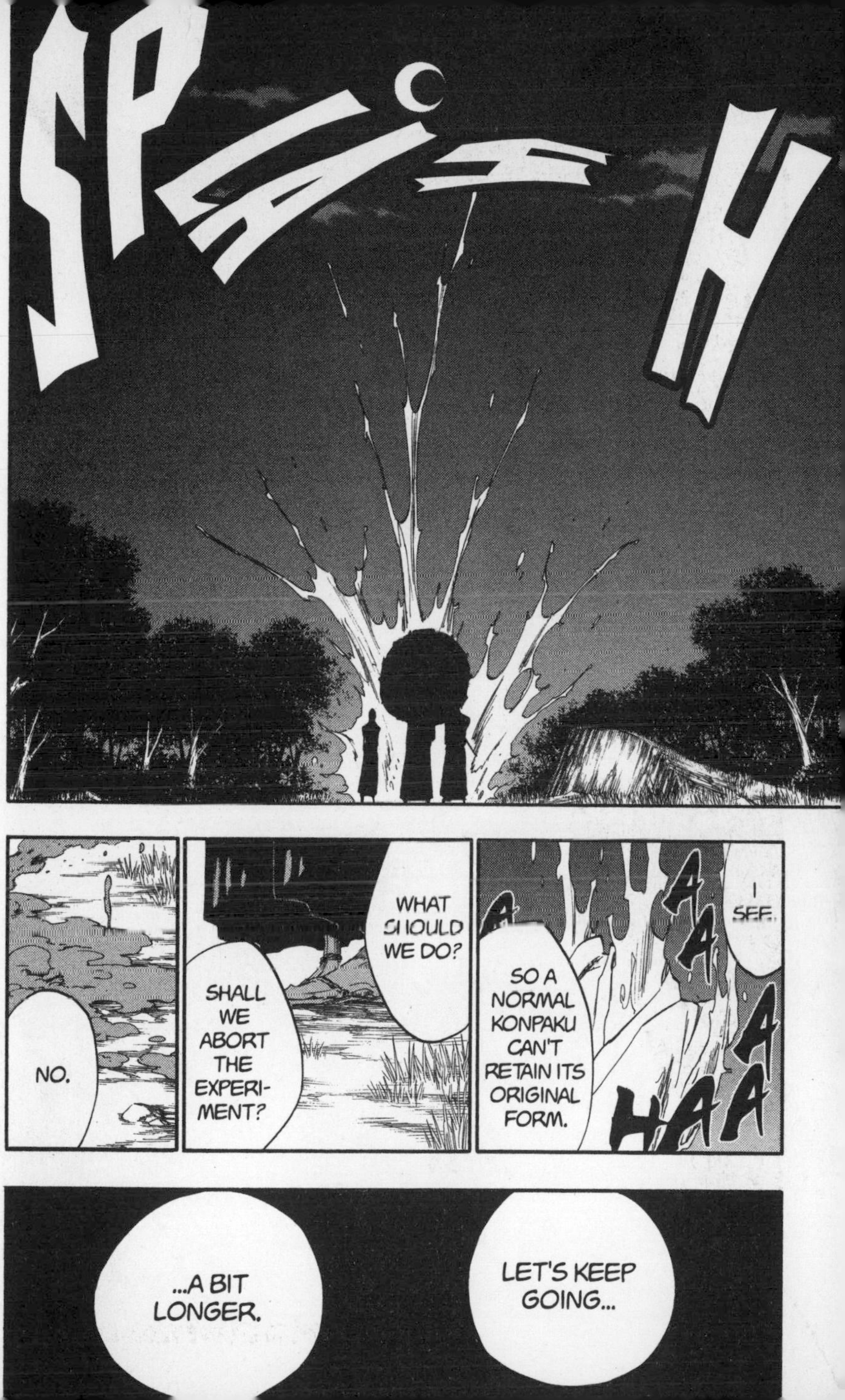
SPLASH
I SEE.
SO A NORMAL KONPAKU CAN'T RETAIN ITS ORIGINAL FORM.
HAA
WHAT SHOULD WE DO?
SHALL WE ABORT THE EXPERIMENT?
NO.
LET'S KEEP GOING...
...A BIT LONGER.

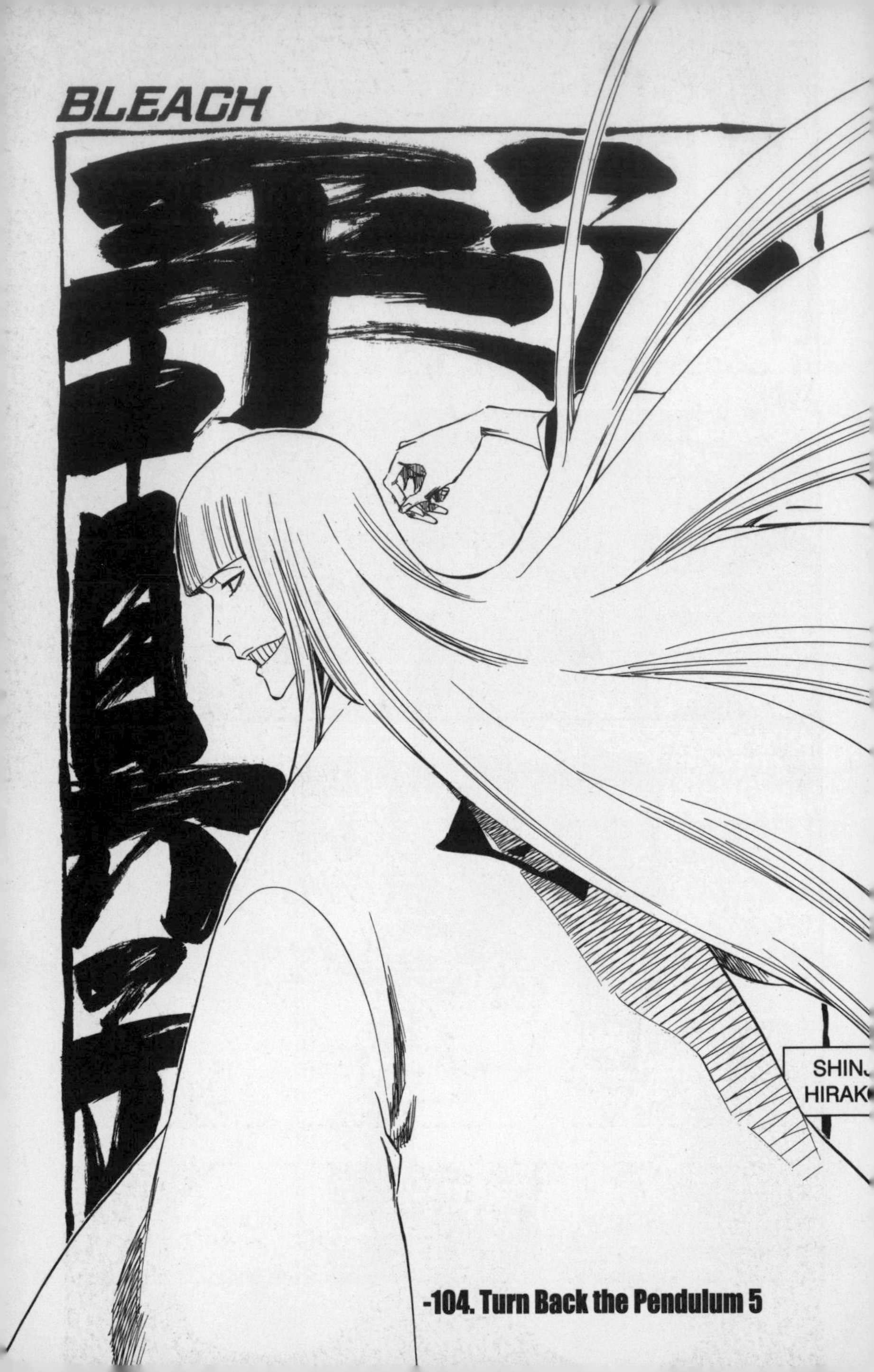
BLEACH
SHINJ
HIRAK
-104. Turn Back the Pendulum 5

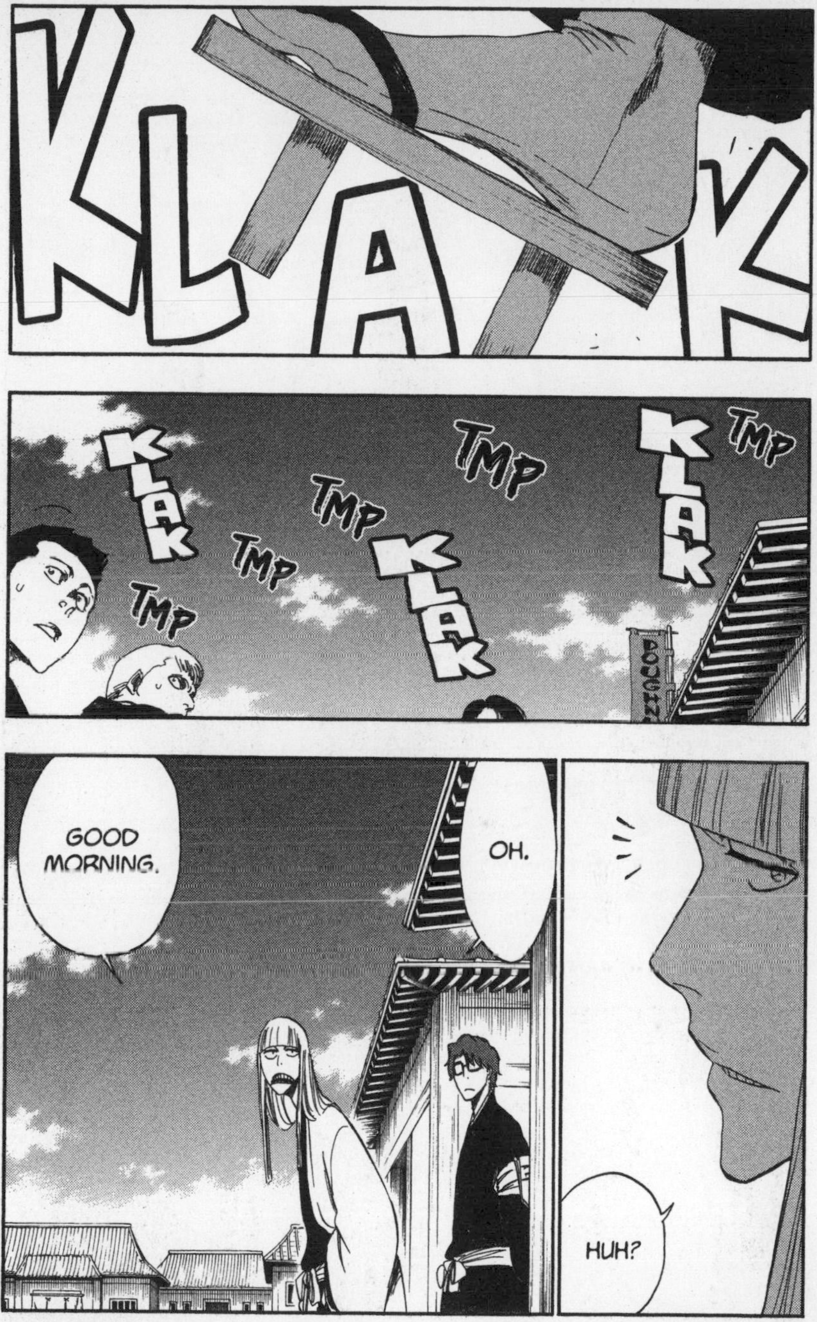
KLAK
TMP
KLAK
TMP
KLAK
TMP
TMP
KLAK
TMP
DOUGHN
HUH?
OH.
GOOD MORNING.

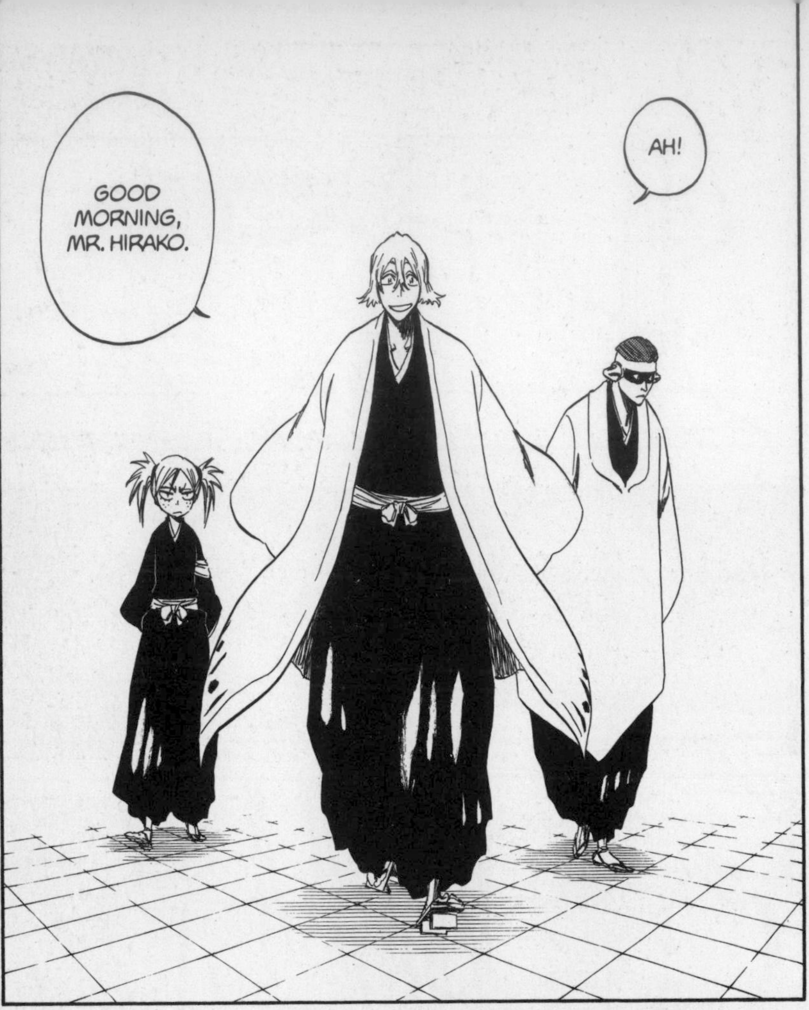
AH!
GOOD MORNING, MR. HIRAKO.

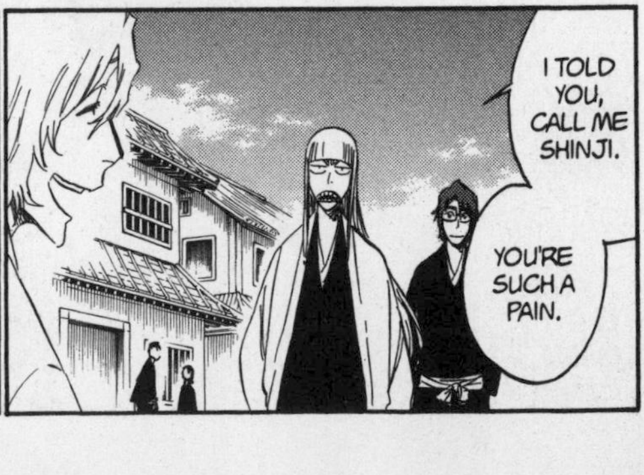
I TOLD YOU, CALL ME SHINJI.
YOU'RE SUCH A PAIN.

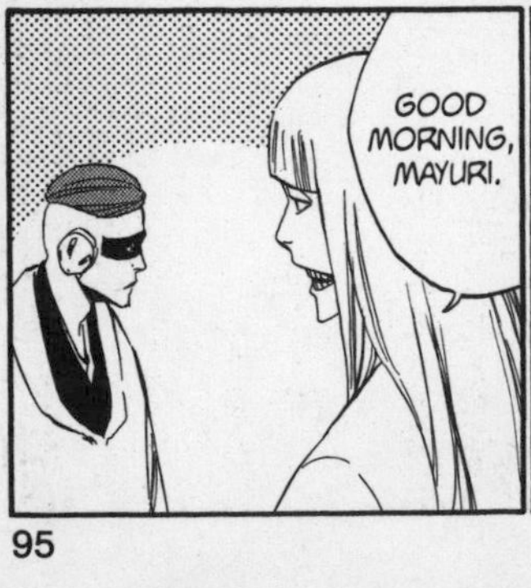
GOOD MORNING, MAYURI.

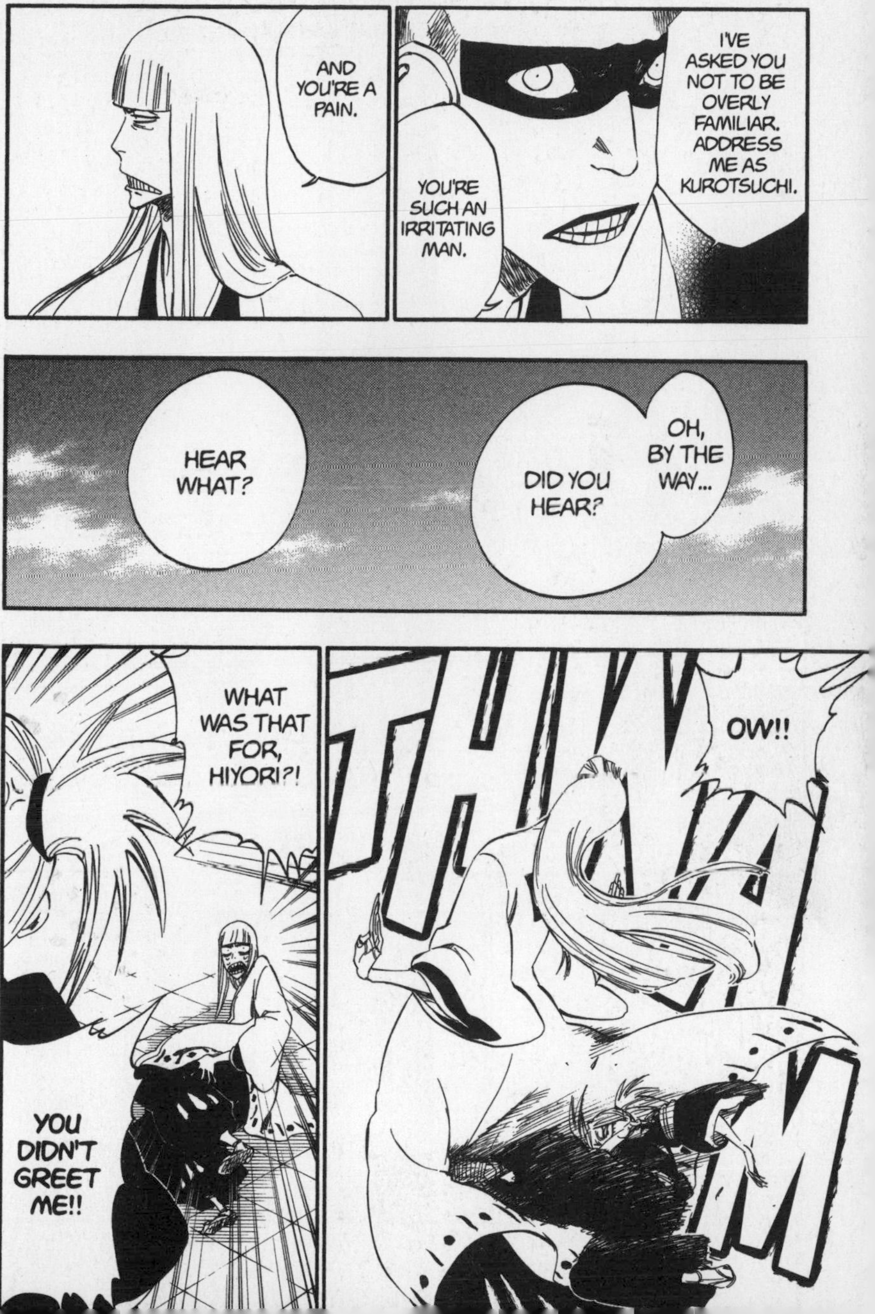
I'VE ASKED YOU NOT TO BE OVERLY FAMILIAR. ADDRESS ME AS KUROTSUCHI.
YOU'RE SUCH AN IRRITATING MAN.
AND YOU'RE A PAIN.
OH, BY THE WAY...
DID YOU HEAR?
HEAR WHAT?
OW!!
THWAM
WHAT WAS THAT FOR, HIYORI?!
YOU DIDN'T GREET ME!!

READ THIS WAY

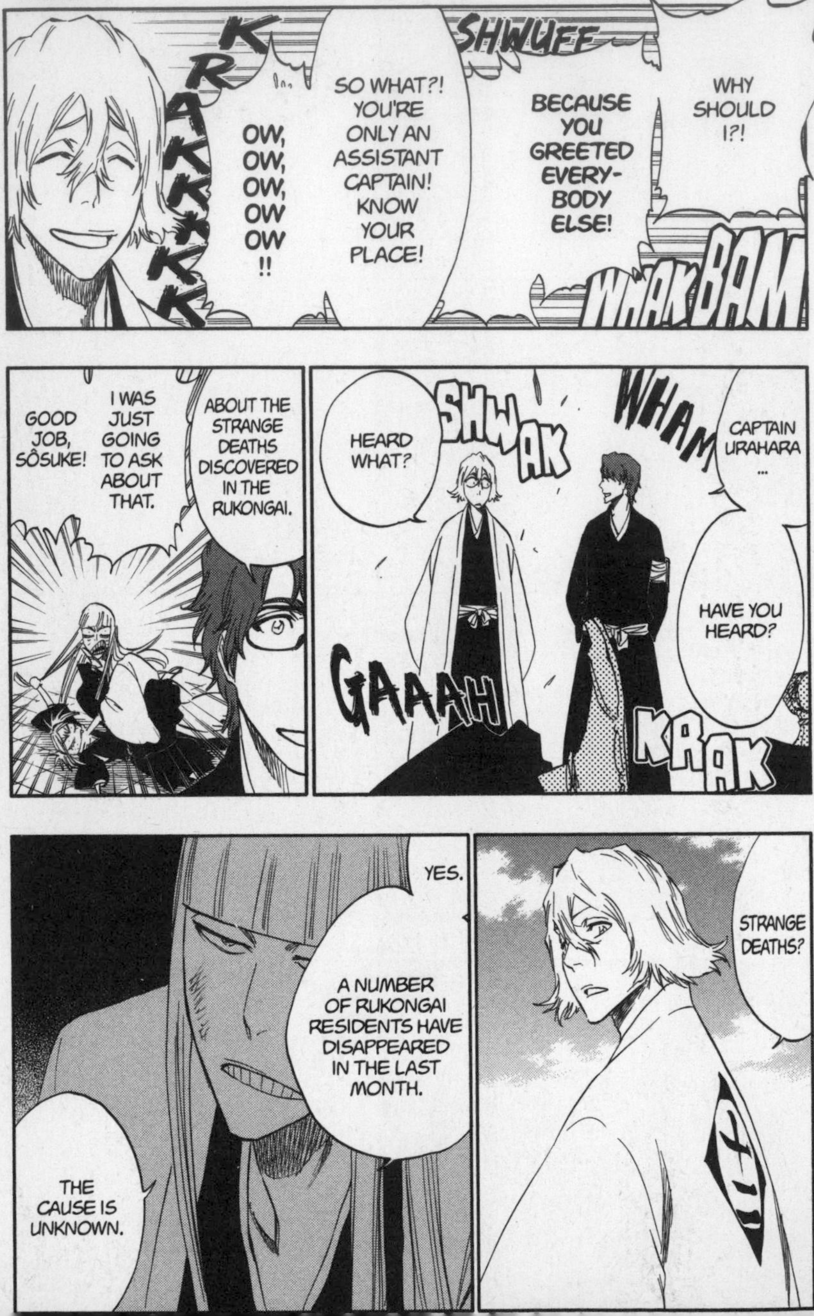
WHY SHOULD I?!
SHWUFF
BECAUSE YOU GREETED EVERY-BODY ELSE!
WHAK BAM
SO WHAT?! YOU'RE ONLY AN ASSISTANT CAPTAIN! KNOW YOUR PLACE!
OW, OW, OW, OW OW !!
KRAKKKKK
CAPTAIN URAHARA ...
HAVE YOU HEARD?
WHAM
SHWAK
HEARD WHAT?
KRAK
GAAAH
ABOUT THE STRANGE DEATHS DISCOVERED IN THE RUKONGAI.
I WAS JUST GOING TO ASK ABOUT THAT.
GOOD JOB, SÔSUKE!
STRANGE DEATHS?
YES.
A NUMBER OF RUKONGAI RESIDENTS HAVE DISAPPEARED IN THE LAST MONTH.
THE CAUSE IS UNKNOWN.

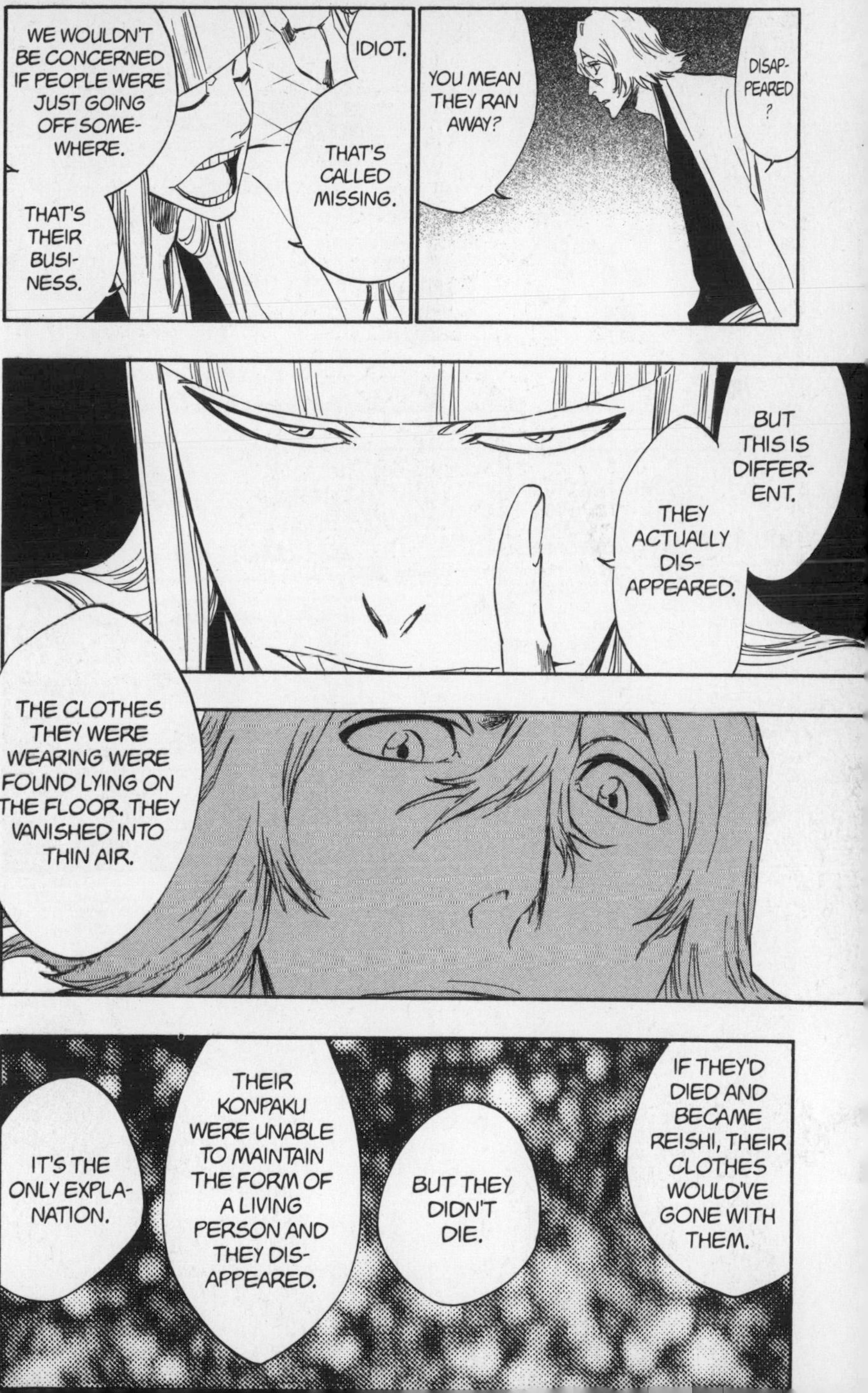
DISAPPEARED?
YOU MEAN THEY RAN AWAY?
IDIOT.
THAT'S CALLED MISSING.
WE WOULDN'T BE CONCERNED IF PEOPLE WERE JUST GOING OFF SOMEWHERE.
THAT'S THEIR BUSINESS.
BUT THIS IS DIFFERENT.
THEY ACTUALLY DISAPPEARED.
THE CLOTHES THEY WERE WEARING WERE FOUND LYING ON THE FLOOR. THEY VANISHED INTO THIN AIR.
IF THEY'D DIED AND BECAME REISHI, THEIR CLOTHES WOULD'VE GONE WITH THEM.
BUT THEY DIDN'T DIE.
THEIR KONPAKU WERE UNABLE TO MAINTAIN THE FORM OF A LIVING PERSON AND THEY DISAPPEARED.
IT'S THE ONLY EXPLANATION.

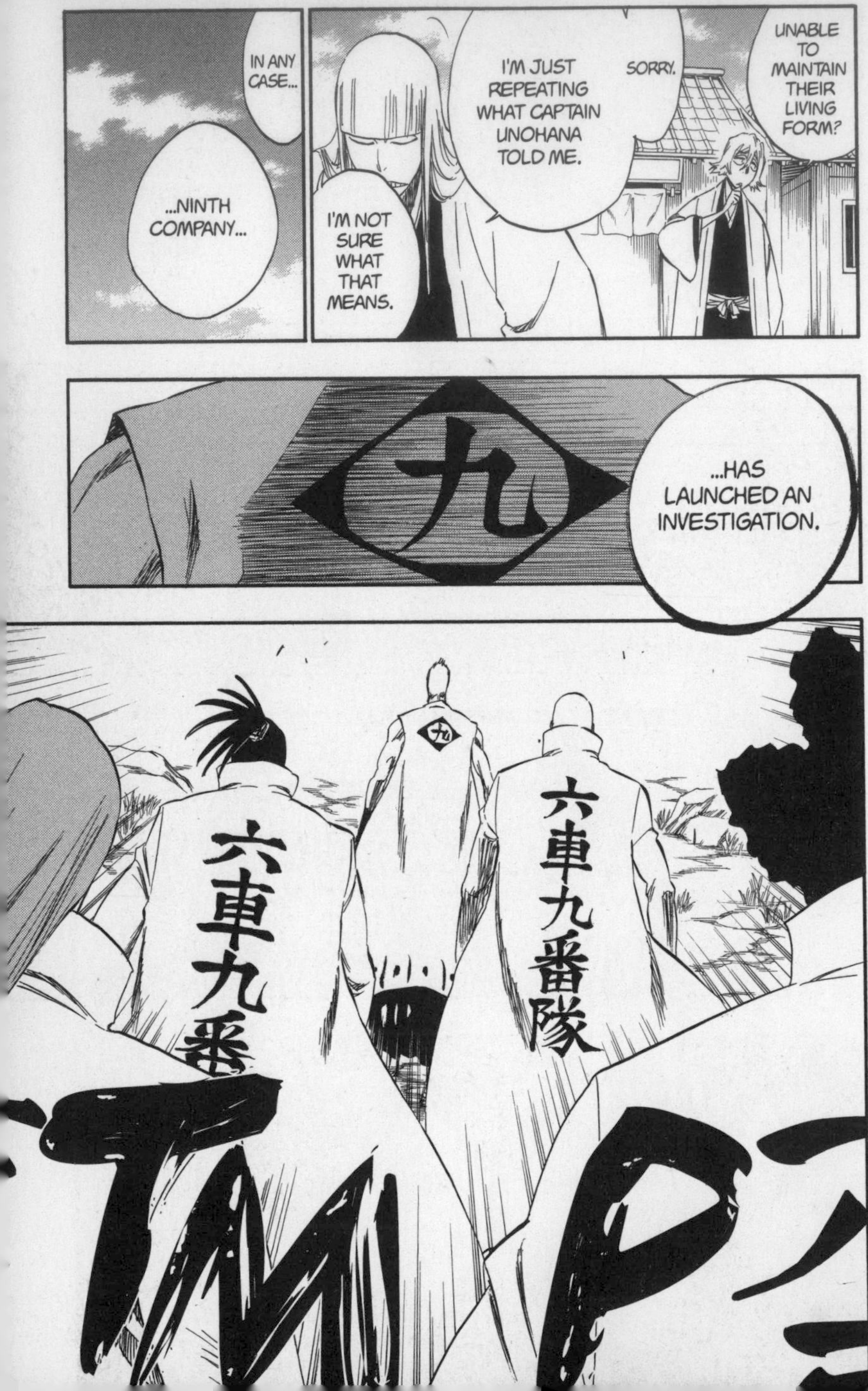
UNABLE TO MAINTAIN THEIR LIVING FORM?
SORRY.
I'M JUST REPEATING WHAT CAPTAIN UNOHANA TOLD ME.
I'M NOT SURE WHAT THAT MEANS.
IN ANY CASE...
...NINTH COMPANY...
九
...HAS LAUNCHED AN INVESTIGATION.
六車九番隊
六車九番
TMP

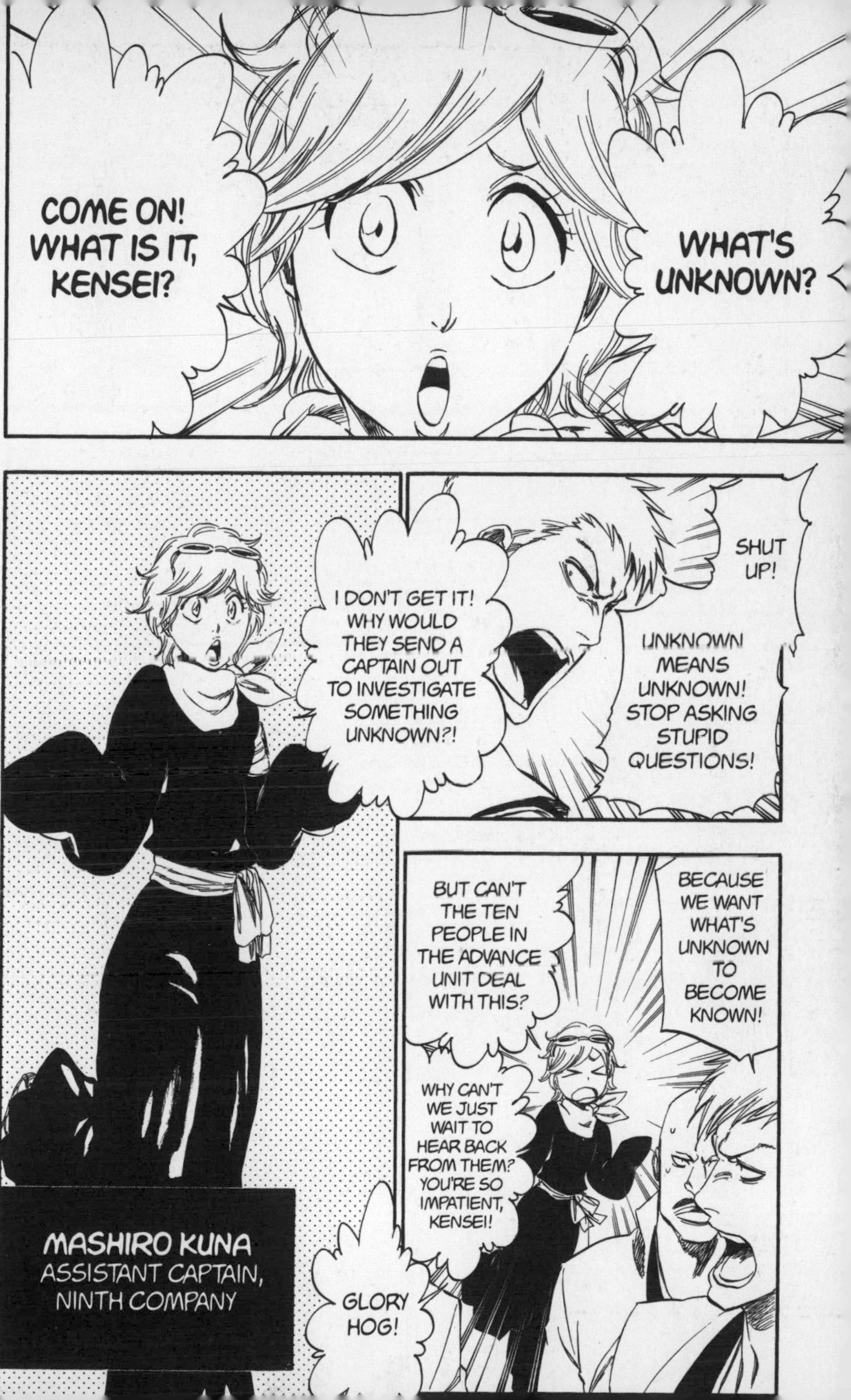
WHAT'S UNKNOWN?
COME ON! WHAT IS IT, KENSEI?
SHUT UP!
UNKNOWN MEANS UNKNOWN! STOP ASKING STUPID QUESTIONS!
I DON'T GET IT! WHY WOULD THEY SEND A CAPTAIN OUT TO INVESTIGATE SOMETHING UNKNOWN?!
BECAUSE WE WANT WHAT'S UNKNOWN TO BECOME KNOWN!
BUT CAN'T THE TEN PEOPLE IN THE ADVANCE UNIT DEAL WITH THIS?
WHY CAN'T WE JUST WAIT TO HEAR BACK FROM THEM? YOU'RE SO IMPATIENT, KENSEI!
GLORY HOG!
MASHIRO KUNA
ASSISTANT CAPTAIN, NINTH COMPANY

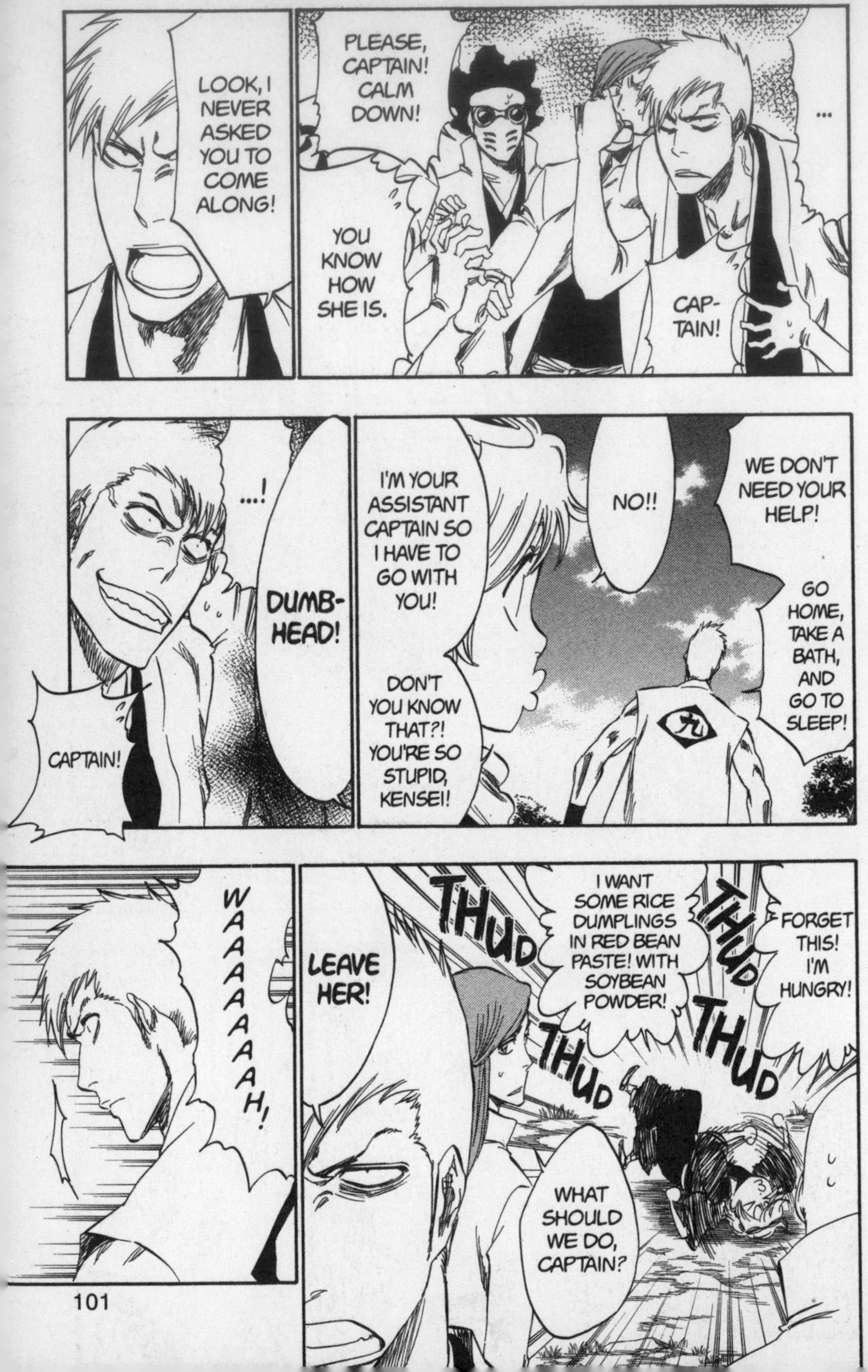
...
CAP-TAIN!
PLEASE, CAPTAIN! CALM DOWN!
YOU KNOW HOW SHE IS.
LOOK, I NEVER ASKED YOU TO COME ALONG!
WE DON'T NEED YOUR HELP!
GO HOME, TAKE A BATH, AND GO TO SLEEP!
NO!!
I'M YOUR ASSISTANT CAPTAIN SO I HAVE TO GO WITH YOU!
DON'T YOU KNOW THAT?! YOU'RE SO STUPID, KENSEI!
DUMB-HEAD!
...!
CAPTAIN!
FORGET THIS! I'M HUNGRY!
THUD
THUD
I WANT SOME RICE DUMPLINGS IN RED BEAN PASTE! WITH SOYBEAN POWDER!
THUD
THUD
LEAVE HER!
WHAT SHOULD WE DO, CAPTAIN?
WAAAAAAAAAH!

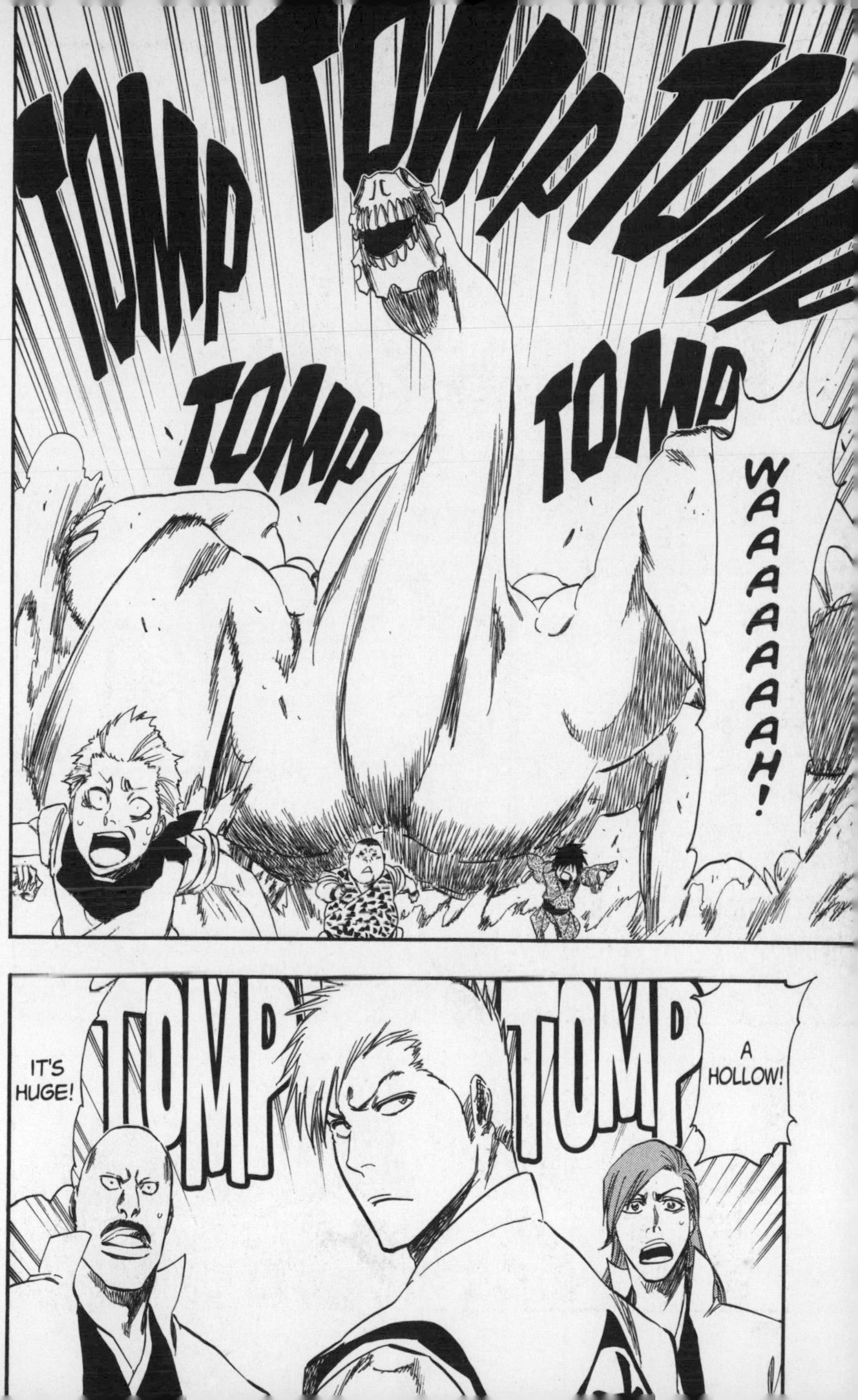
TOMP TOMP TOMP
TOMP TOMP
WAAAAAAAH!
TOMP TOMP
A HOLLOW!
IT'S HUGE!

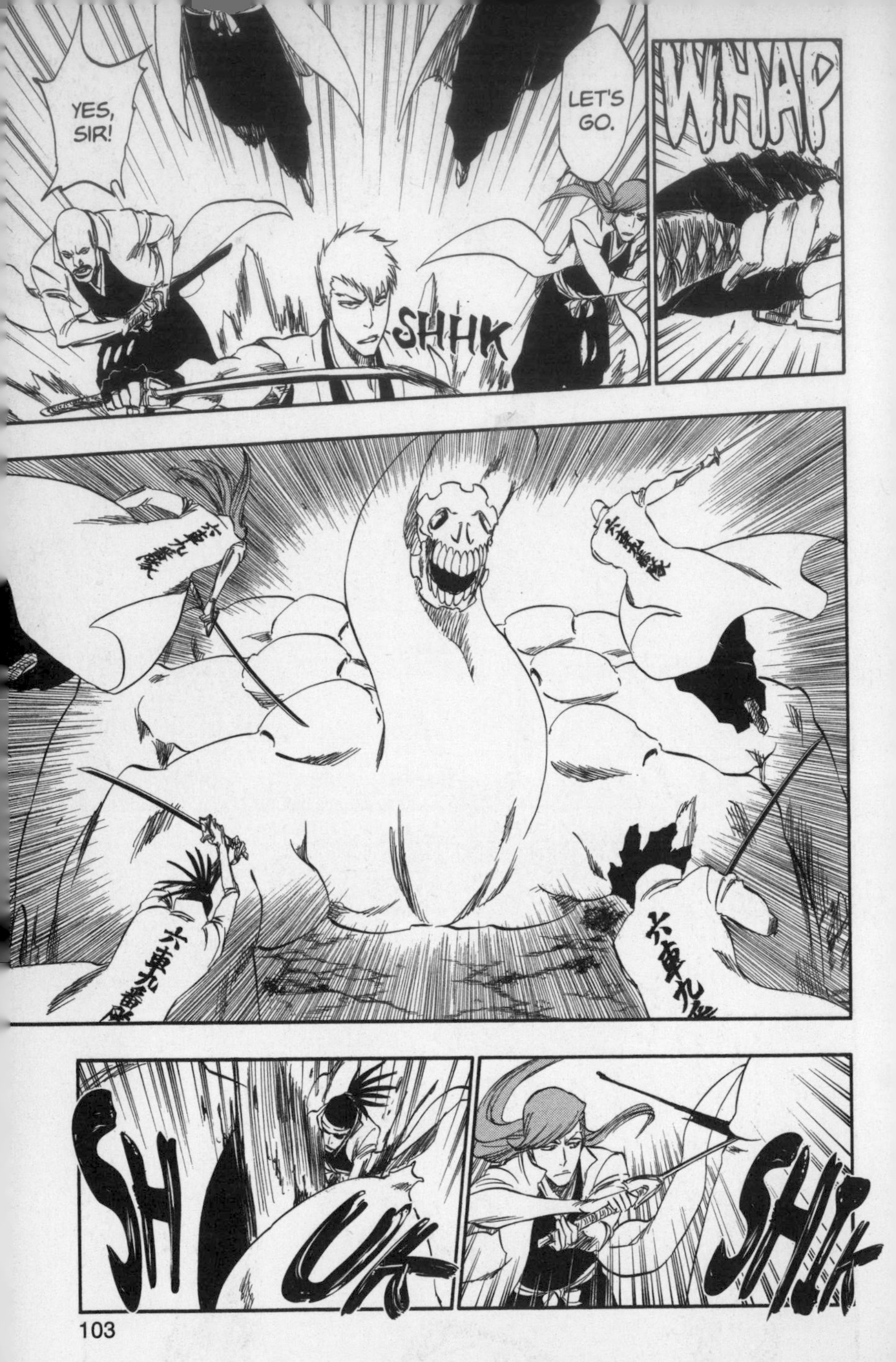
WHAP
LET'S GO.
YES, SIR!
SHHK
六車九番隊
SHIK
SHUK

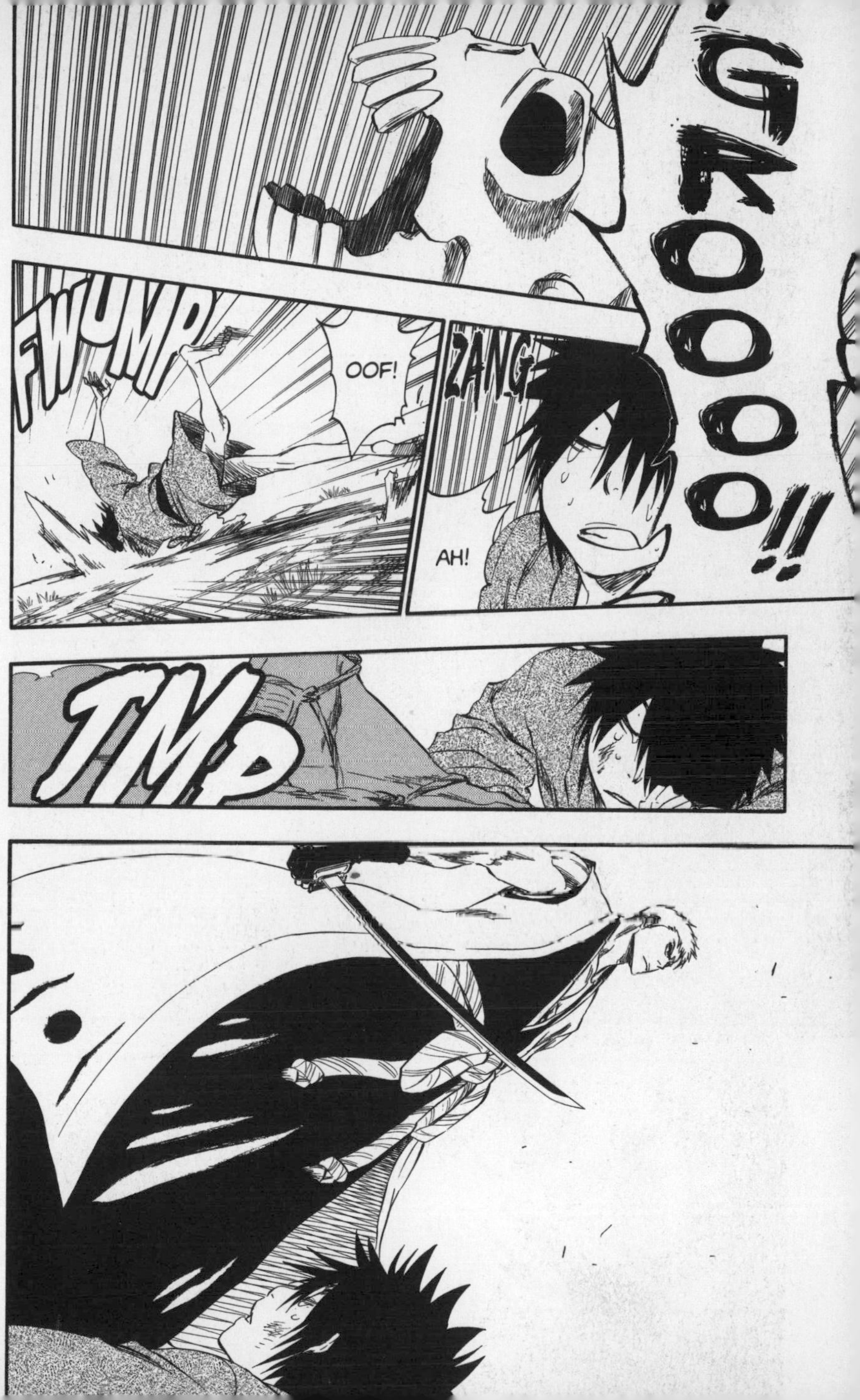
¡GROOOOO!!
ZANG
AH!
FWUMP
OOF!
TMP

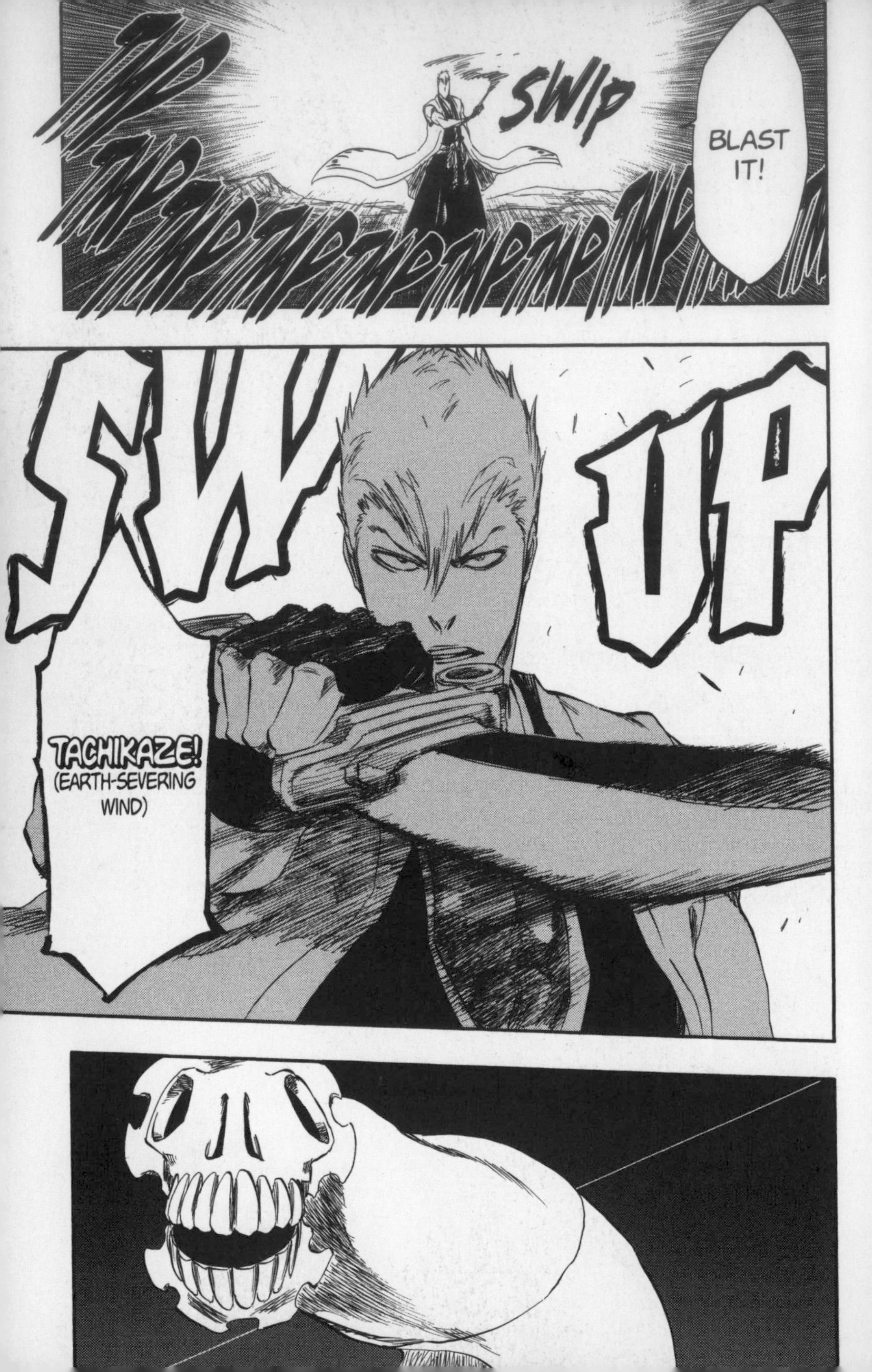
BLAST IT!
SWIP
SWUP
TACHIKAZE!
(EARTH-SEVERING WIND)

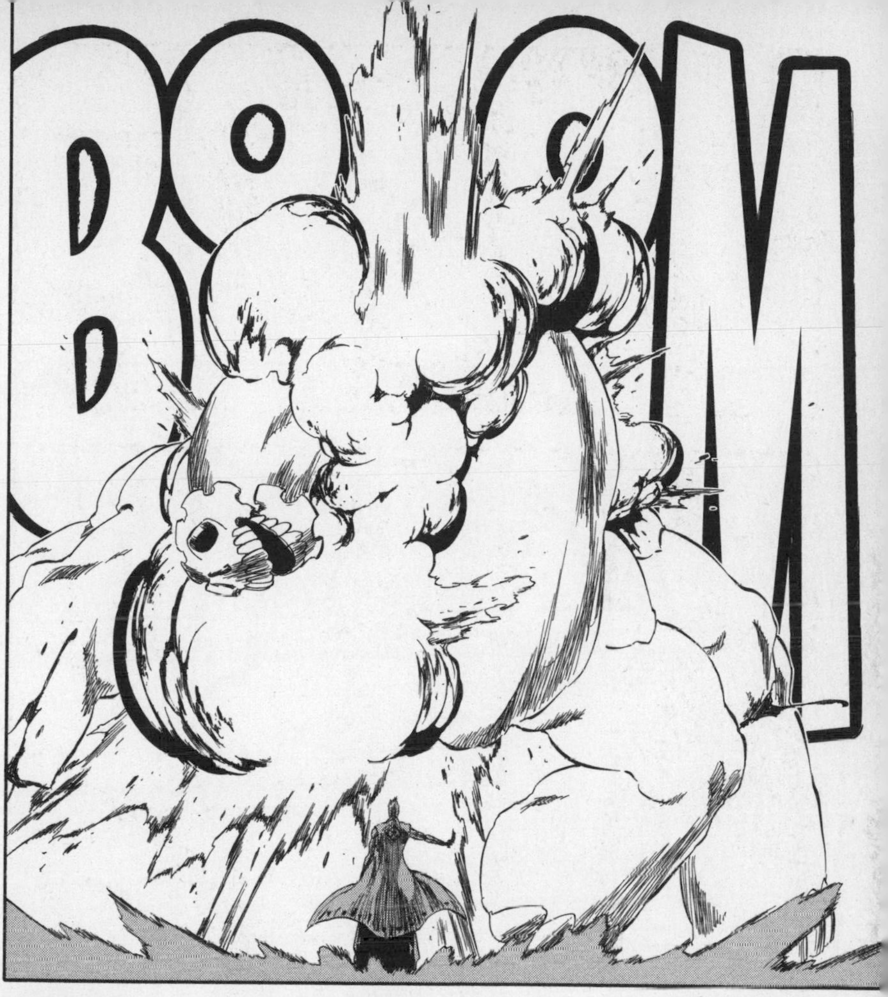
BOOM
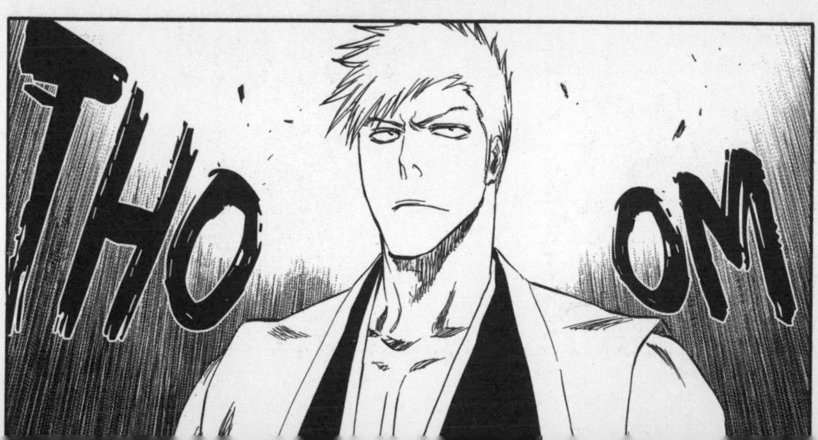
THO OM

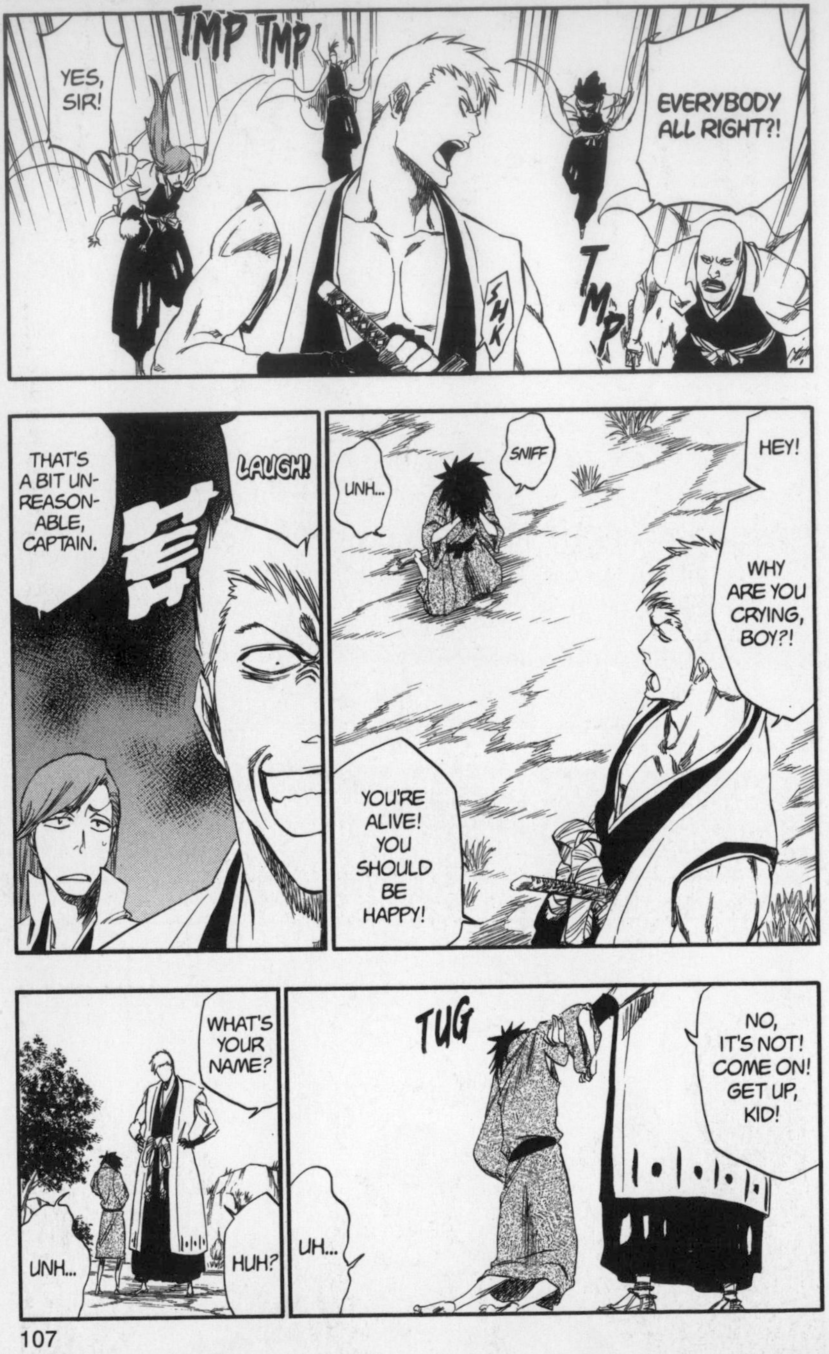
EVERYBODY ALL RIGHT?!
TMP TMP
YES, SIR!
SHK
TMP
HEY!
SNIFF
UNH...
WHY ARE YOU CRYING, BOY?!
YOU'RE ALIVE! YOU SHOULD BE HAPPY!
LAUGH!
THAT'S A BIT UN-REASON-ABLE, CAPTAIN.
NO, IT'S NOT! COME ON! GET UP, KID!
TUG
UH...
WHAT'S YOUR NAME?
HUH?
UNH...

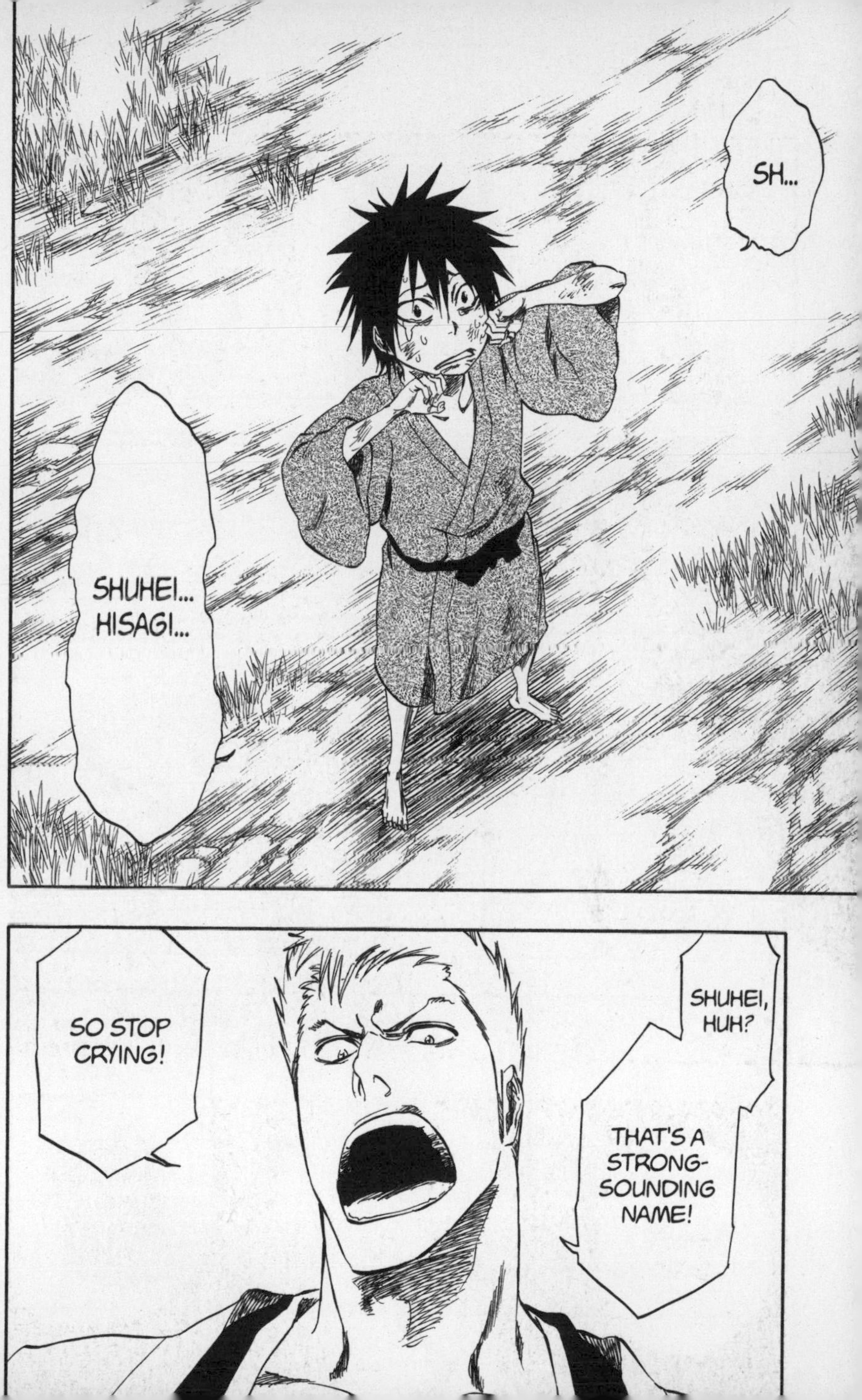
SH...
SHUHEI... HISAGI...
SHUHEI, HUH?
THAT'S A STRONG-SOUNDING NAME!
SO STOP CRYING!

READ THIS WAY

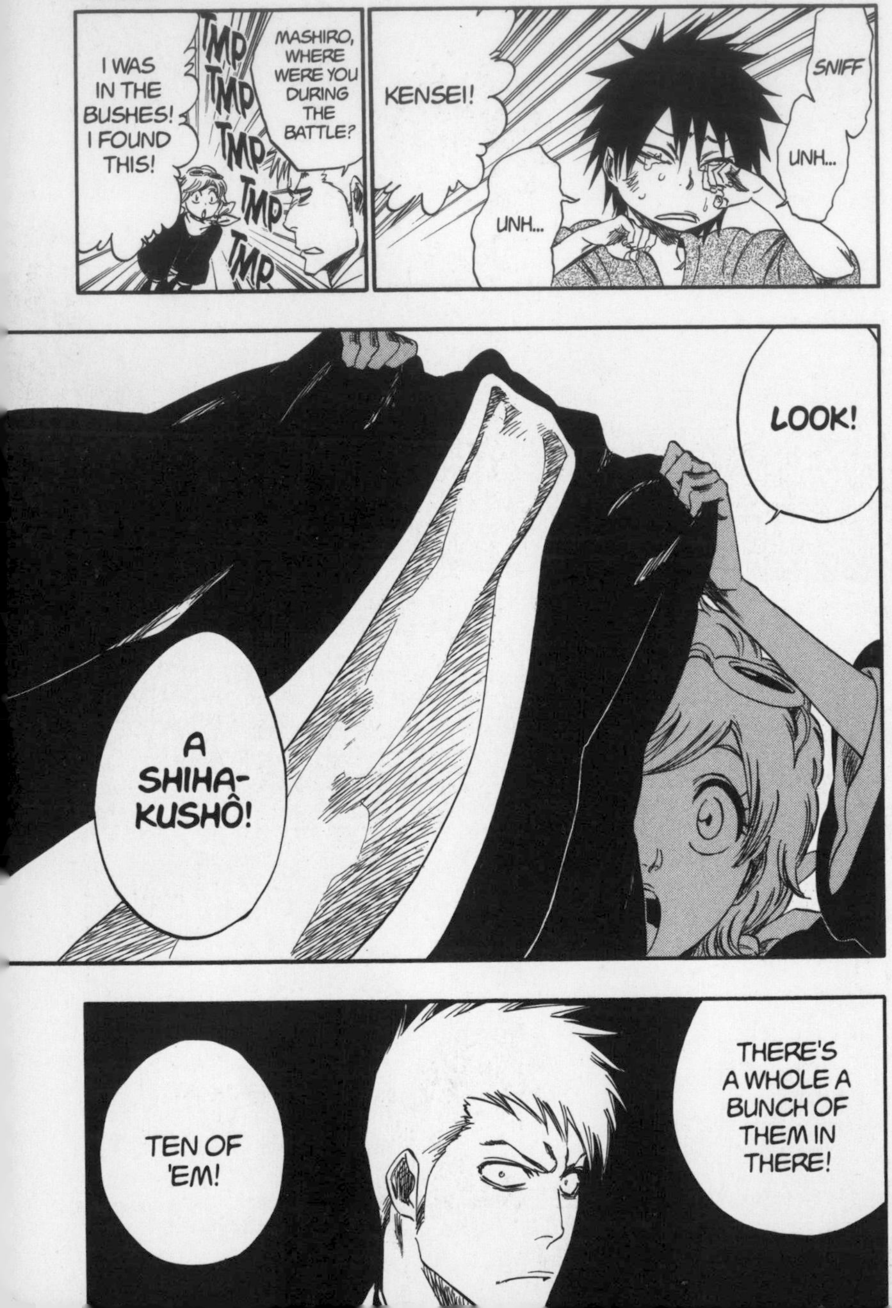
SNIFF
UNH...
KENSEI!
UNH...
MASHIRO, WHERE WERE YOU DURING THE BATTLE?
TMP TMP TMP TMP TMP TMP
I WAS IN THE BUSHES! I FOUND THIS!
LOOK!
A SHIHAKUSHÔ!
THERE'S A WHOLE A BUNCH OF THEM IN THERE!
TEN OF 'EM!

SHUHEI'S FRIENDS

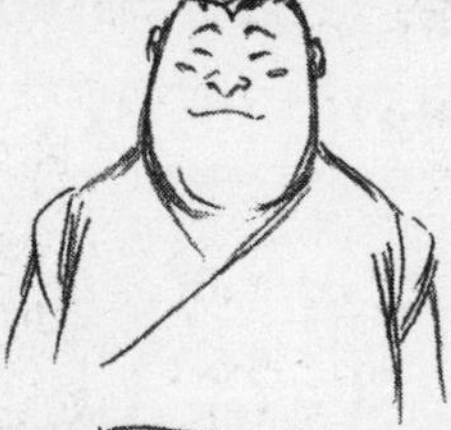

GYUJI

THOUGH NOT AS BOLD AS SHUHEI, HE CONSIDERS HIMSELF SUPERIOR.

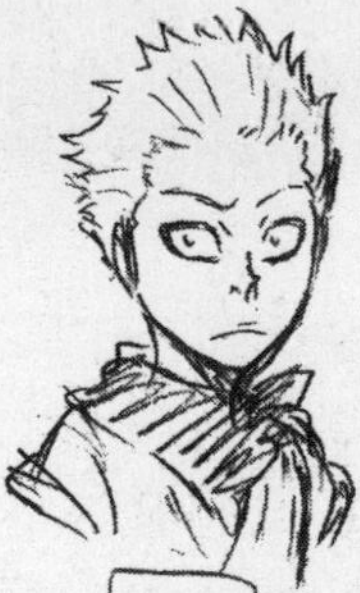

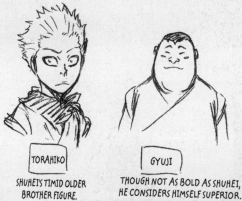

TORAHIKO

SHUHEI'S TIMID OLDER BROTHER FIGURE.

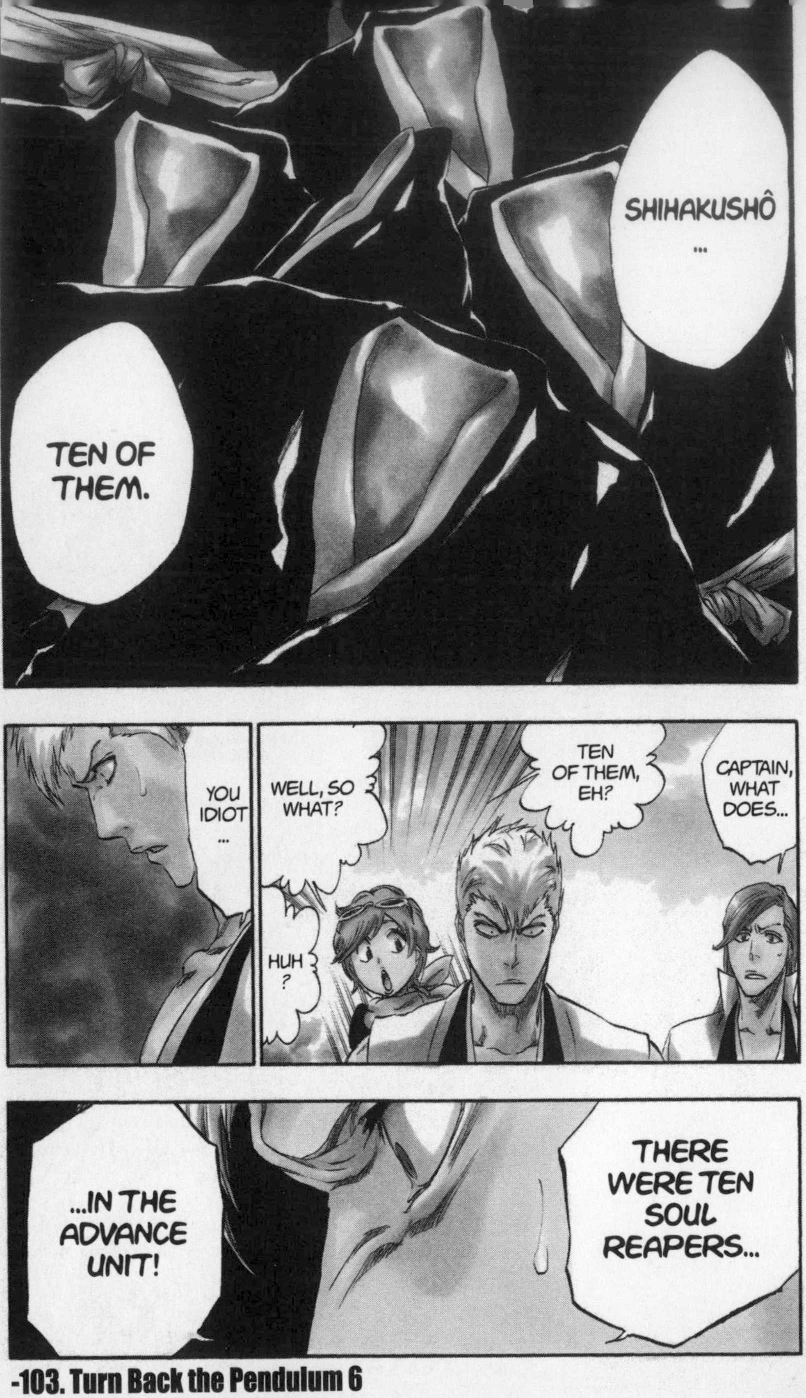
SHIHAKUSHÔ ...
TEN OF THEM.
CAPTAIN, WHAT DOES...
TEN OF THEM, EH?
WELL, SO WHAT?
HUH ?
YOU IDIOT ...
THERE WERE TEN SOUL REAPERS...
...IN THE ADVANCE UNIT!

-103. Turn Back the Pendulum 6

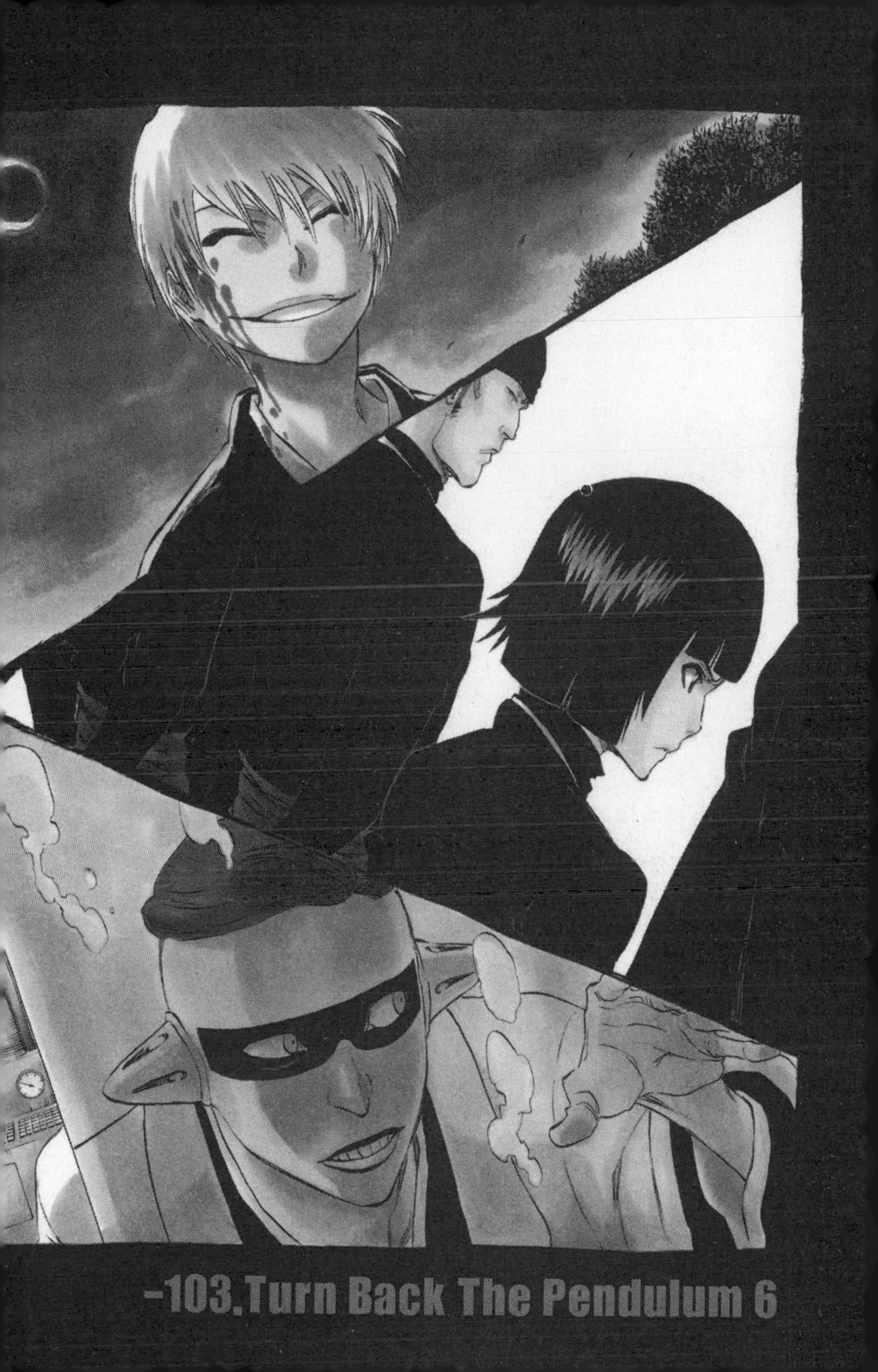

-103.Turn Back The Pendulum 6

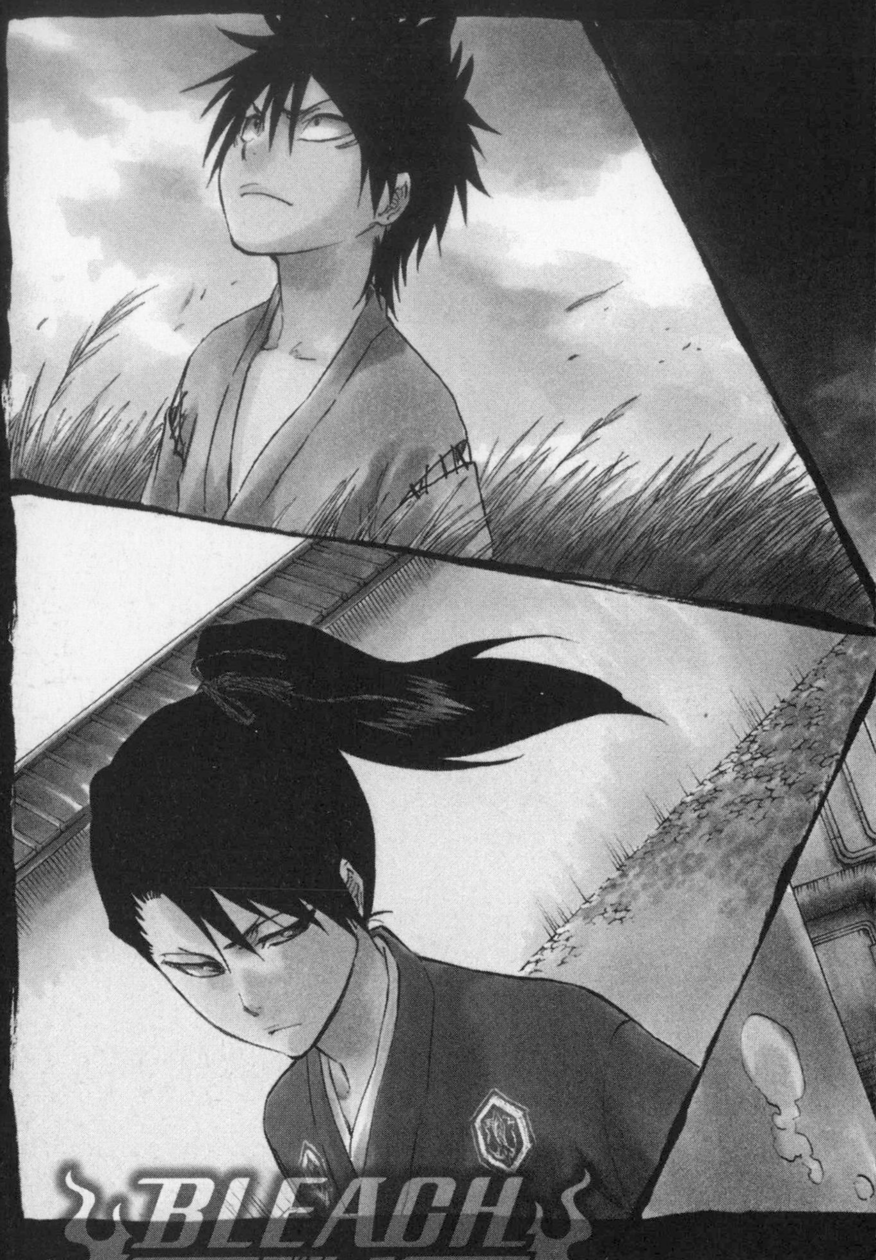
BLEACH
ブリーチ

BLEACH
ブリーチ

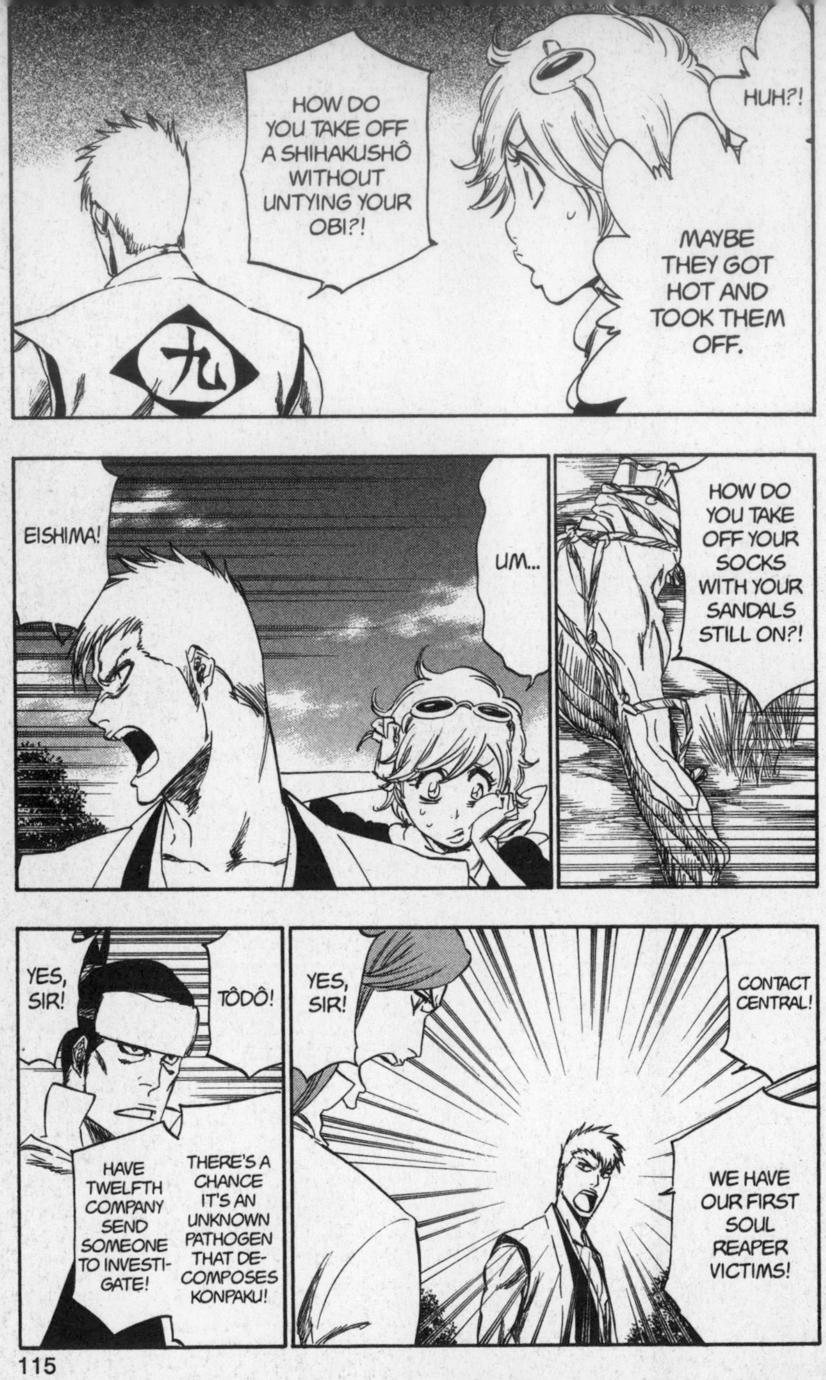
HUH?!
MAYBE THEY GOT HOT AND TOOK THEM OFF.
HOW DO YOU TAKE OFF A SHIHAKUSHÔ WITHOUT UNTYING YOUR OBI?!
HOW DO YOU TAKE OFF YOUR SOCKS WITH YOUR SANDALS STILL ON?!
UM...
EISHIMA!
YES, SIR!
CONTACT CENTRAL!
WE HAVE OUR FIRST SOUL REAPER VICTIMS!
TÔDÔ!
YES, SIR!
THERE'S A CHANCE IT'S AN UNKNOWN PATHOGEN THAT DE-COMPOSES KONPAKU!
HAVE TWELFTH COMPANY SEND SOMEONE TO INVESTI-GATE!

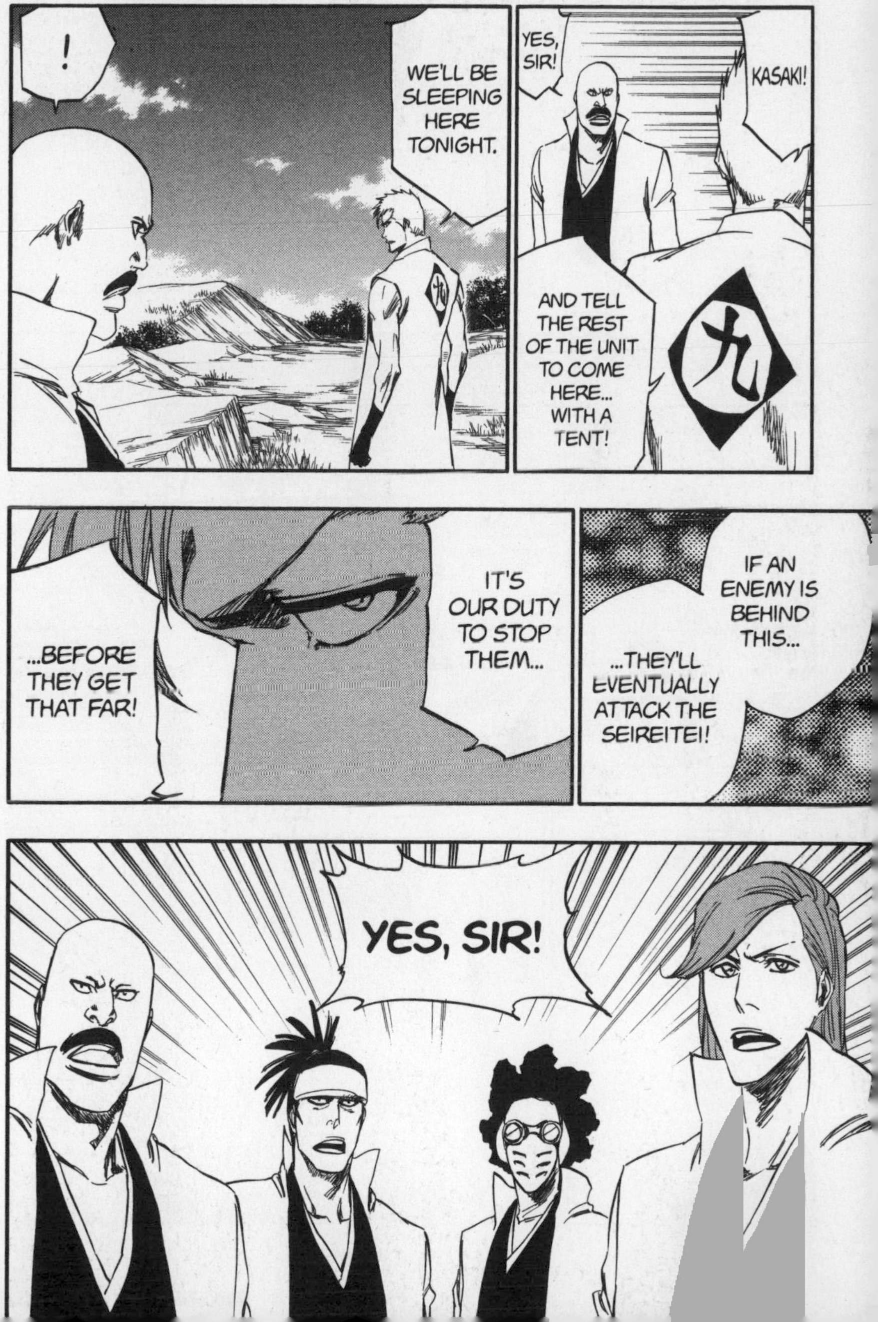
KASAKI!
YES, SIR!
AND TELL THE REST OF THE UNIT TO COME HERE... WITH A TENT!
WE'LL BE SLEEPING HERE TONIGHT.
!
IF AN ENEMY IS BEHIND THIS...
...THEY'LL EVENTUALLY ATTACK THE SEIREITEI!
IT'S OUR DUTY TO STOP THEM...
...BEFORE THEY GET THAT FAR!
YES, SIR!

READ THIS WAY

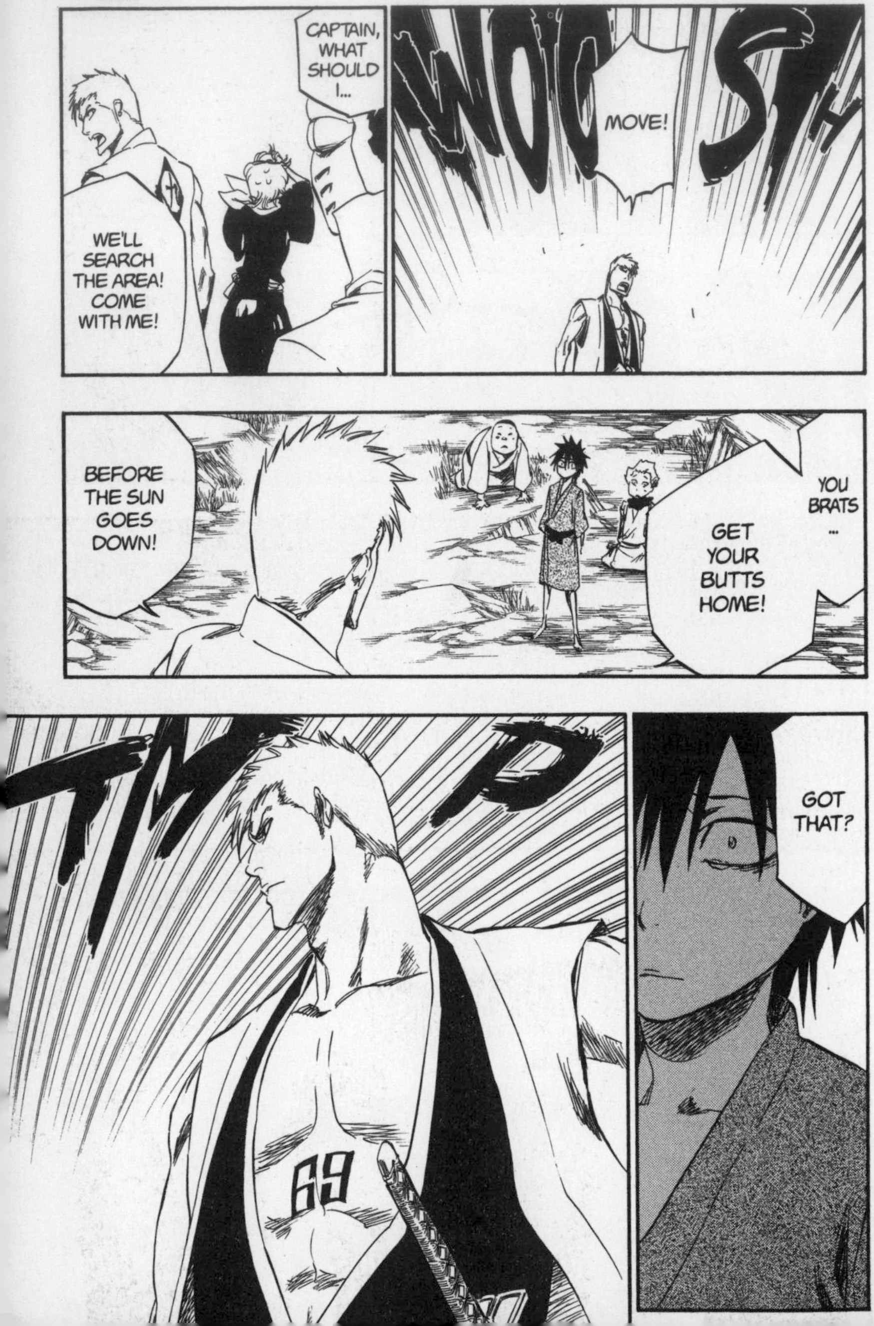
WOOSH
MOVE!
CAPTAIN, WHAT SHOULD I...
WE'LL SEARCH THE AREA! COME WITH ME!
YOU BRATS ...
GET YOUR BUTTS HOME!
BEFORE THE SUN GOES DOWN!
GOT THAT?

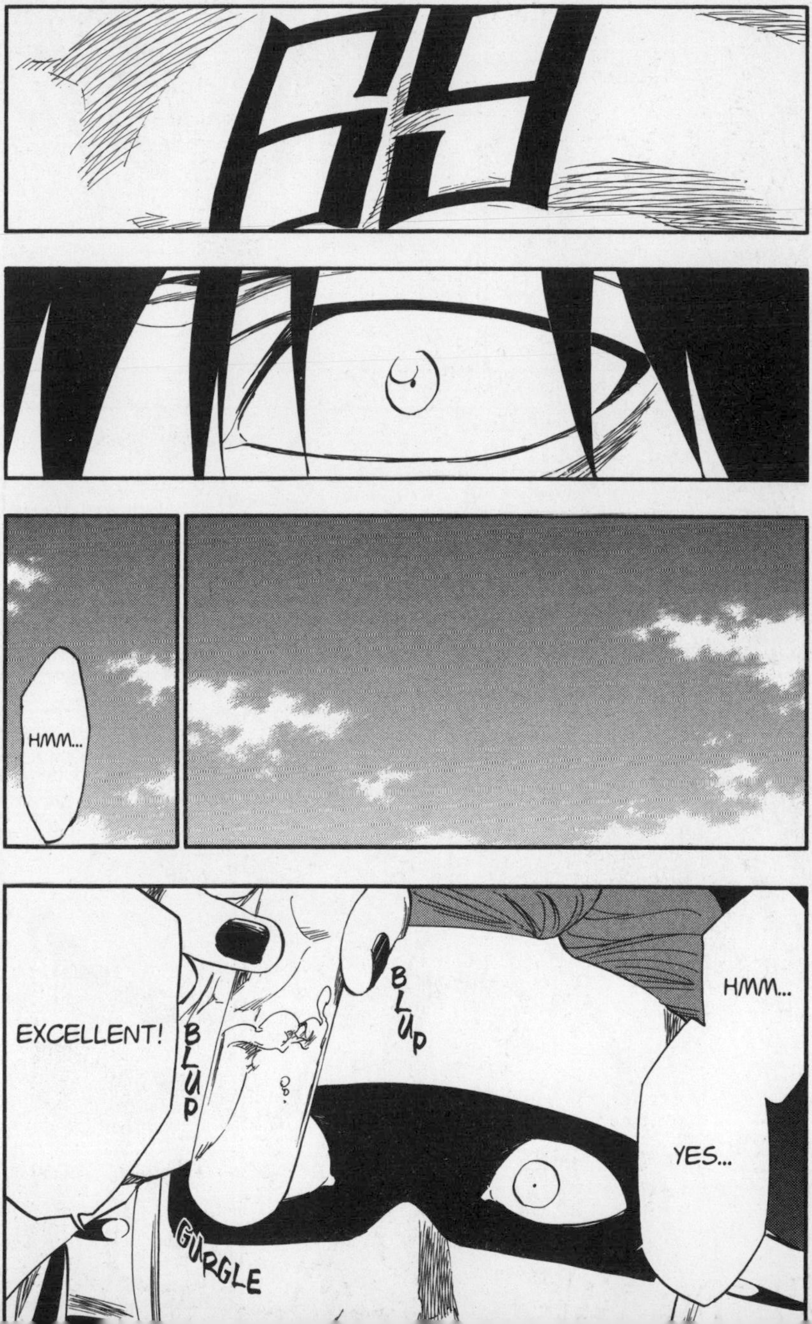
HMM...
HMM...
BLUP
YES...
EXCELLENT!
BLUP
GURGLE

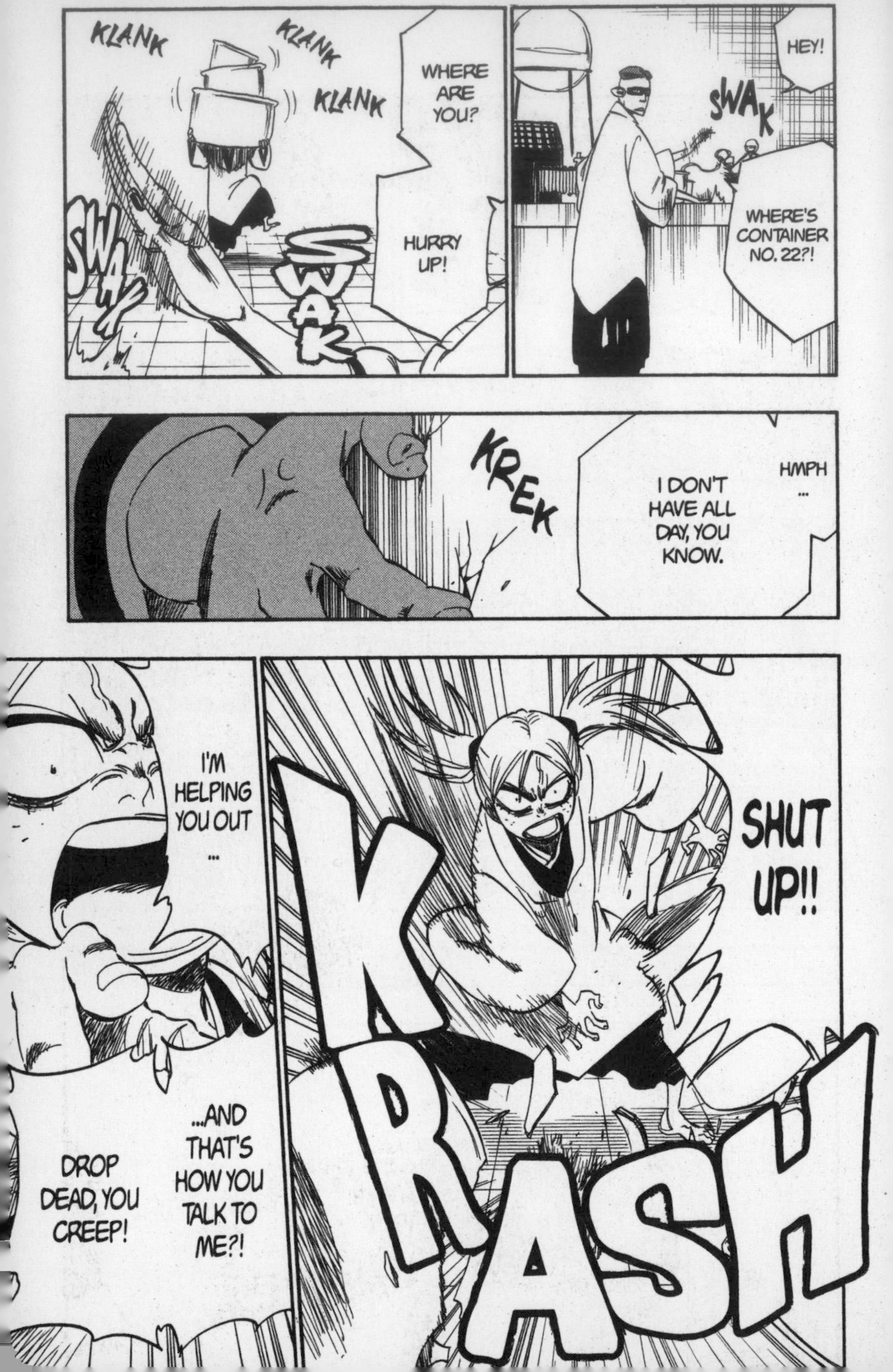
HEY!
SWAK
WHERE'S CONTAINER NO. 22?!
WHERE ARE YOU?
KLANK
KLANK
KLANK
HURRY UP!
SWAK
SWAK
HMPH ...
I DON'T HAVE ALL DAY, YOU KNOW.
KREK
SHUT UP!!
KRASH
I'M HELPING YOU OUT ...
...AND THAT'S HOW YOU TALK TO ME?!
DROP DEAD, YOU CREEP!

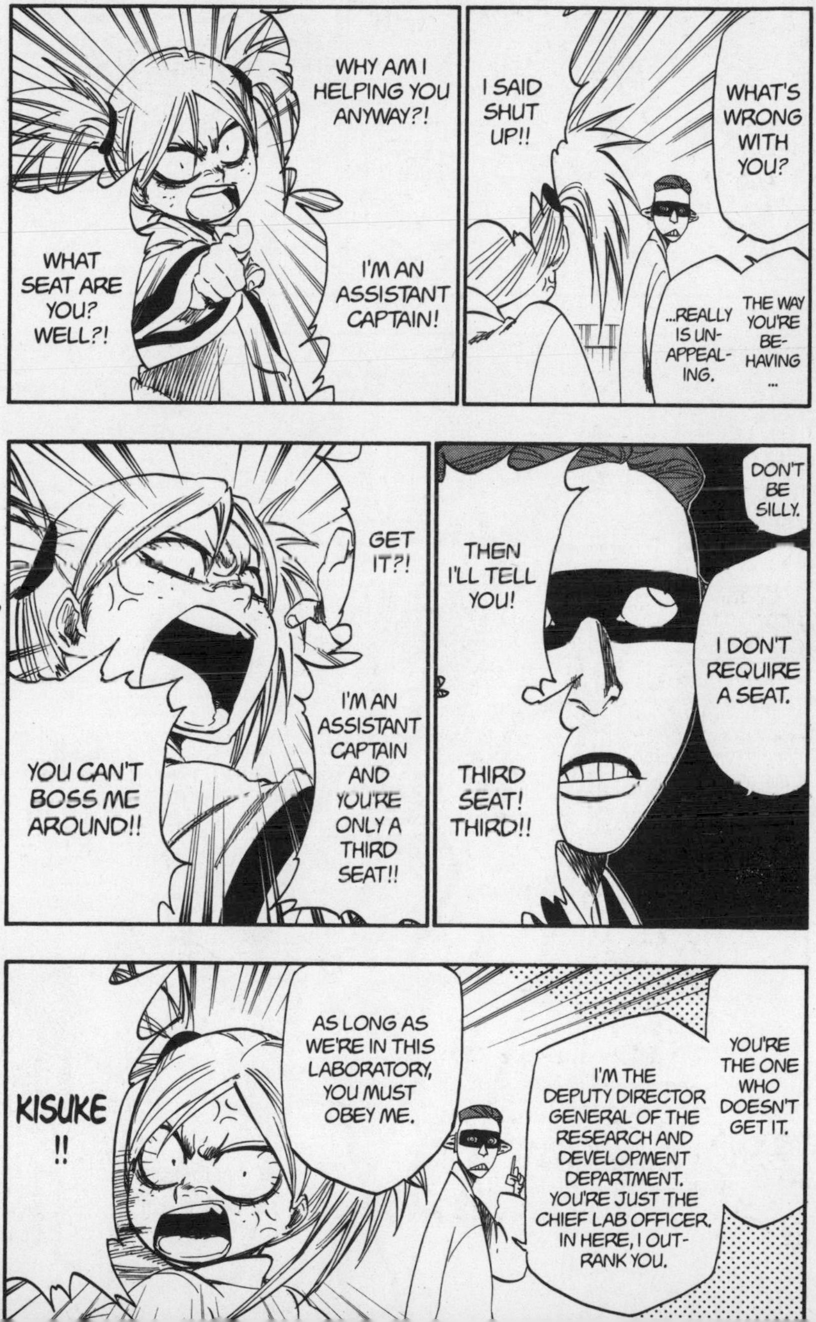
WHAT'S WRONG WITH YOU?
THE WAY YOU'RE BE-HAVING ...
...REALLY IS UN-APPEAL-ING.
I SAID SHUT UP!!
WHY AM I HELPING YOU ANYWAY?!
I'M AN ASSISTANT CAPTAIN!
WHAT SEAT ARE YOU? WELL?!
DON'T BE SILLY.
I DON'T REQUIRE A SEAT.
THEN I'LL TELL YOU!
THIRD SEAT! THIRD!!
GET IT?!
I'M AN ASSISTANT CAPTAIN AND YOU'RE ONLY A THIRD SEAT!!
YOU CAN'T BOSS ME AROUND!!
YOU'RE THE ONE WHO DOESN'T GET IT.
I'M THE DEPUTY DIRECTOR GENERAL OF THE RESEARCH AND DEVELOPMENT DEPARTMENT. YOU'RE JUST THE CHIEF LAB OFFICER. IN HERE, I OUT-RANK YOU.
AS LONG AS WE'RE IN THIS LABORATORY, YOU MUST OBEY ME.
KISUKE !!

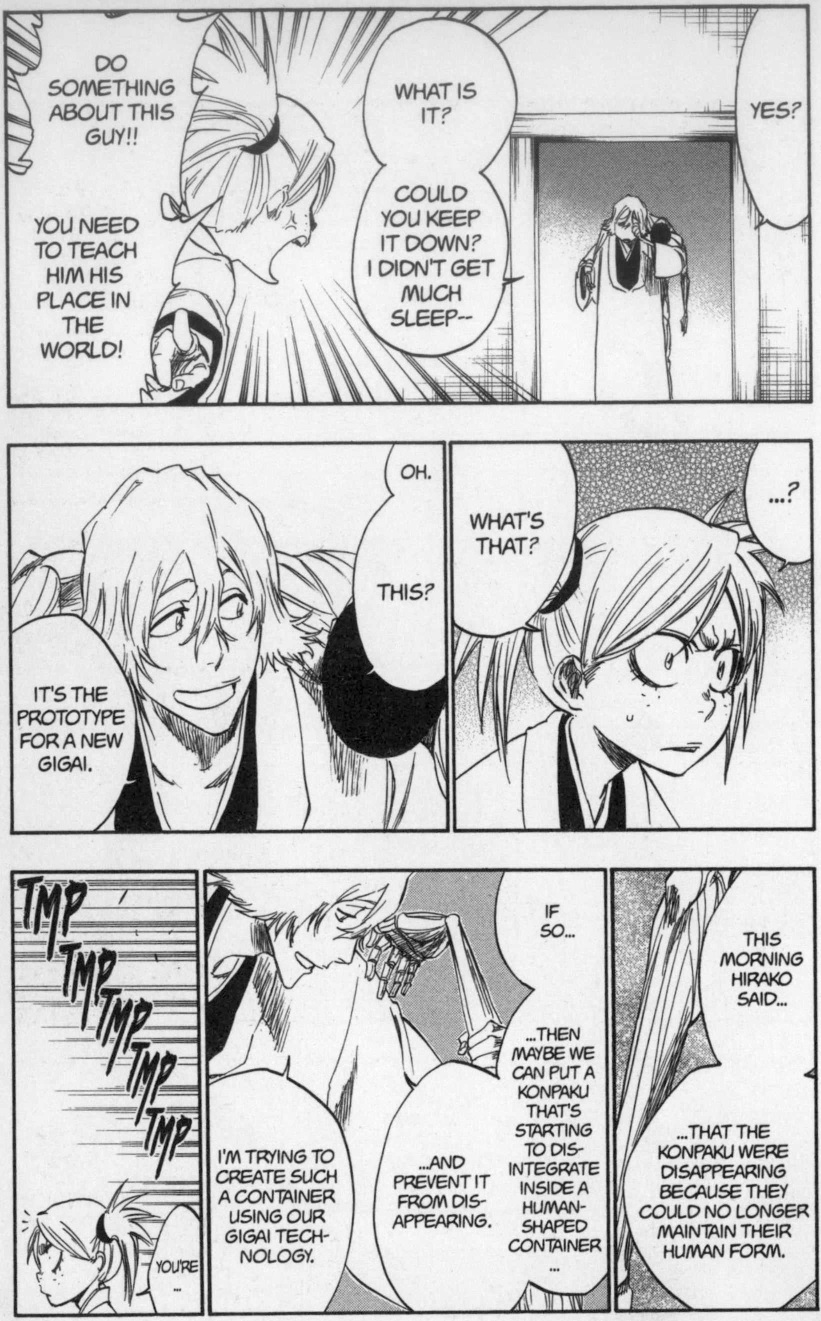
YES?
WHAT IS IT?
COULD YOU KEEP IT DOWN? I DIDN'T GET MUCH SLEEP--
DO SOMETHING ABOUT THIS GUY!!
YOU NEED TO TEACH HIM HIS PLACE IN THE WORLD!
...?
WHAT'S THAT?
OH.
THIS?
IT'S THE PROTOTYPE FOR A NEW GIGAI.
THIS MORNING HIRAKO SAID...
...THAT THE KONPAKU WERE DISAPPEARING BECAUSE THEY COULD NO LONGER MAINTAIN THEIR HUMAN FORM.
IF SO...
...THEN MAYBE WE CAN PUT A KONPAKU THAT'S STARTING TO DISINTEGRATE INSIDE A HUMAN-SHAPED CONTAINER...
...AND PREVENT IT FROM DISAPPEARING.
I'M TRYING TO CREATE SUCH A CONTAINER USING OUR GIGAI TECHNOLOGY.
TMP TMP TMP TMP TMP TMP
YOU'RE ...

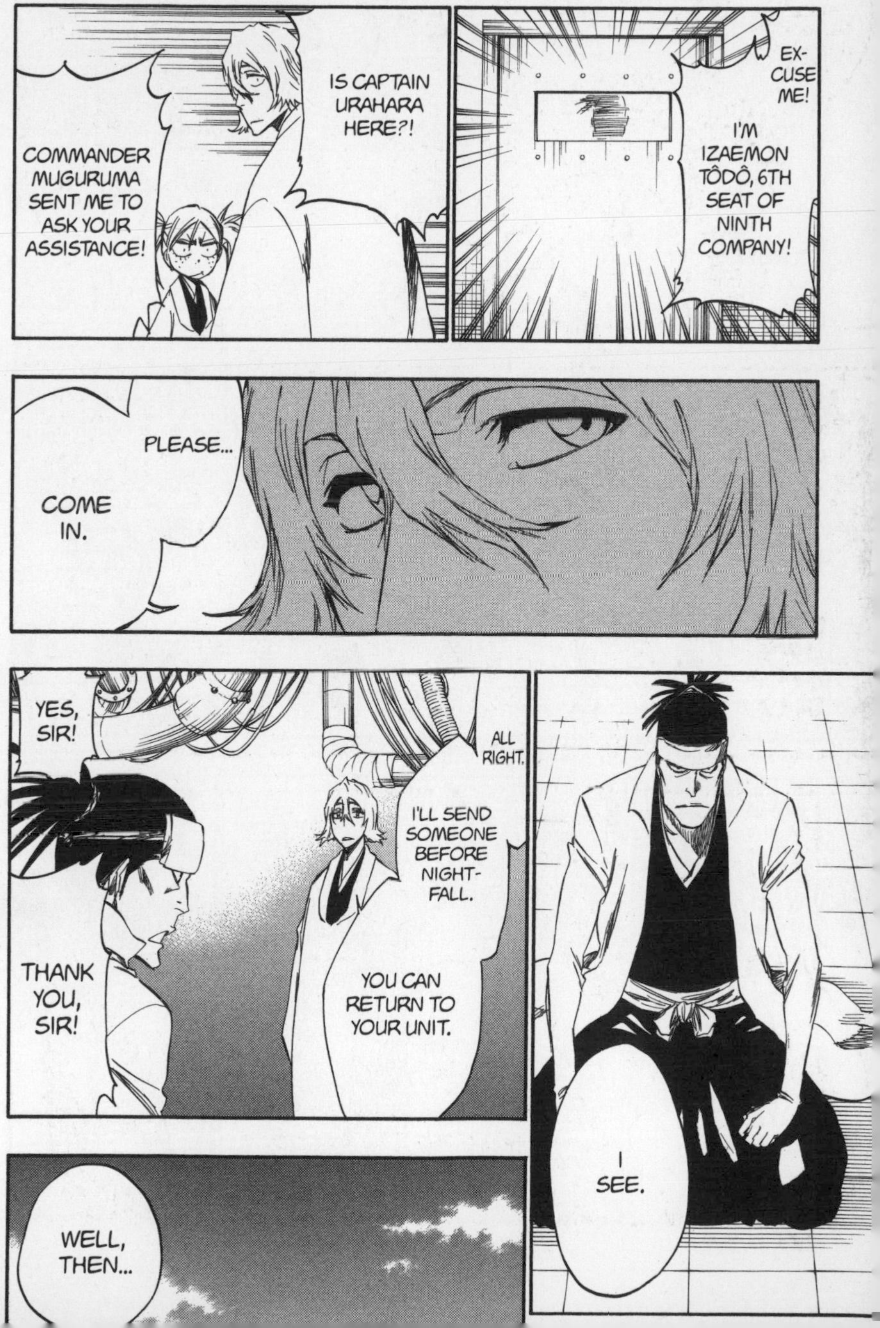
EX-CUSE ME!
I'M IZAEMON TÔDÔ, 6TH SEAT OF NINTH COMPANY!
IS CAPTAIN URAHARA HERE?!
COMMANDER MUGURUMA SENT ME TO ASK YOUR ASSISTANCE!
PLEASE...
COME IN.
I SEE.
ALL RIGHT.
I'LL SEND SOMEONE BEFORE NIGHT-FALL.
YOU CAN RETURN TO YOUR UNIT.
YES, SIR!
THANK YOU, SIR!
WELL, THEN...

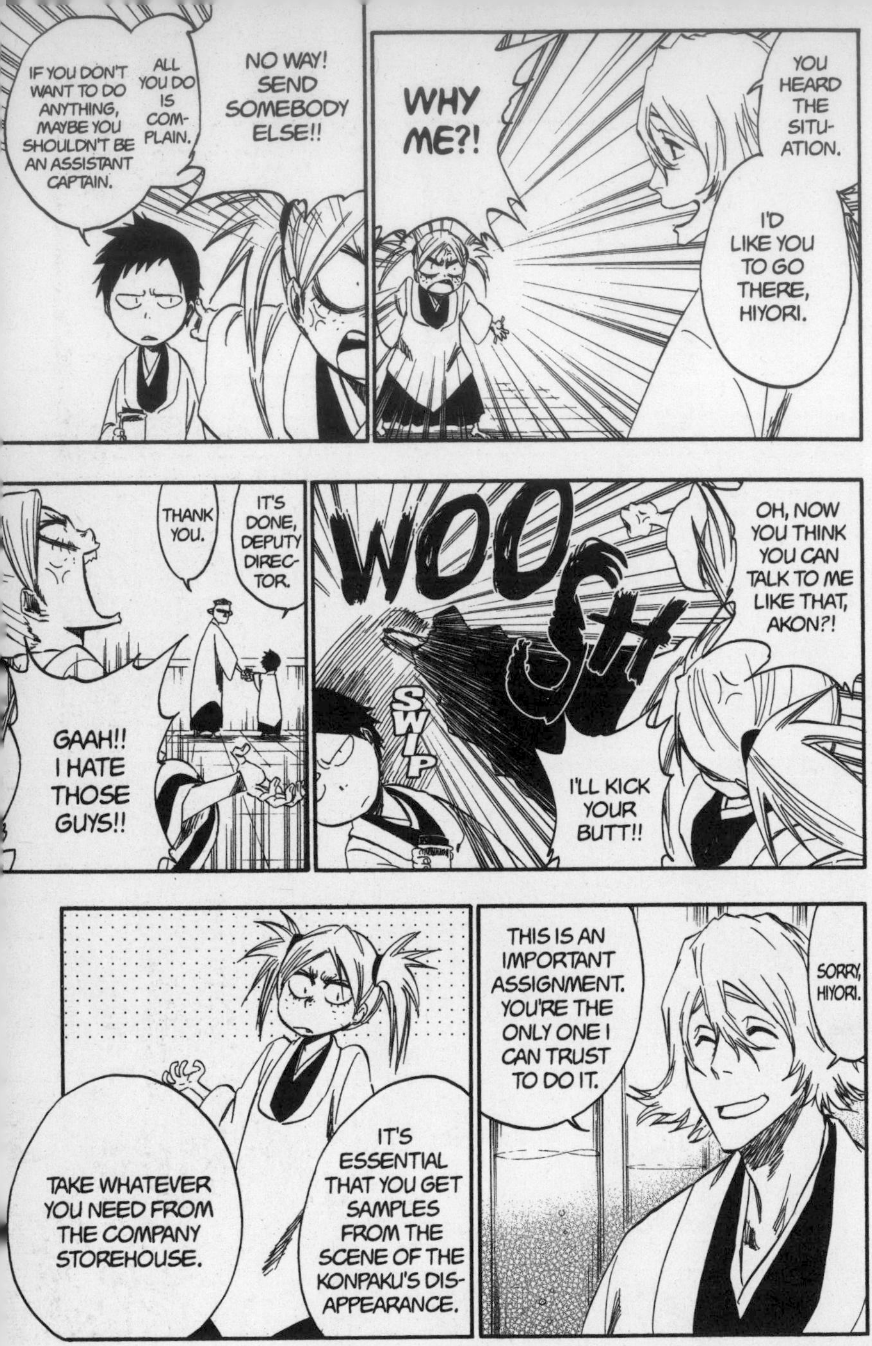
YOU HEARD THE SITU-ATION.
I'D LIKE YOU TO GO THERE, HIYORI.
WHY ME?!
NO WAY! SEND SOMEBODY ELSE!!
ALL YOU DO IS COM-PLAIN.
IF YOU DON'T WANT TO DO ANYTHING, MAYBE YOU SHOULDN'T BE AN ASSISTANT CAPTAIN.
OH, NOW YOU THINK YOU CAN TALK TO ME LIKE THAT, AKON?!
WOOSH
I'LL KICK YOUR BUTT!!
SWIP
IT'S DONE, DEPUTY DIREC-TOR.
THANK YOU.
GAAH!! I HATE THOSE GUYS!!
SORRY, HIYORI.
THIS IS AN IMPORTANT ASSIGNMENT. YOU'RE THE ONLY ONE I CAN TRUST TO DO IT.
IT'S ESSENTIAL THAT YOU GET SAMPLES FROM THE SCENE OF THE KONPAKU'S DIS-APPEARANCE.
TAKE WHATEVER YOU NEED FROM THE COMPANY STOREHOUSE.

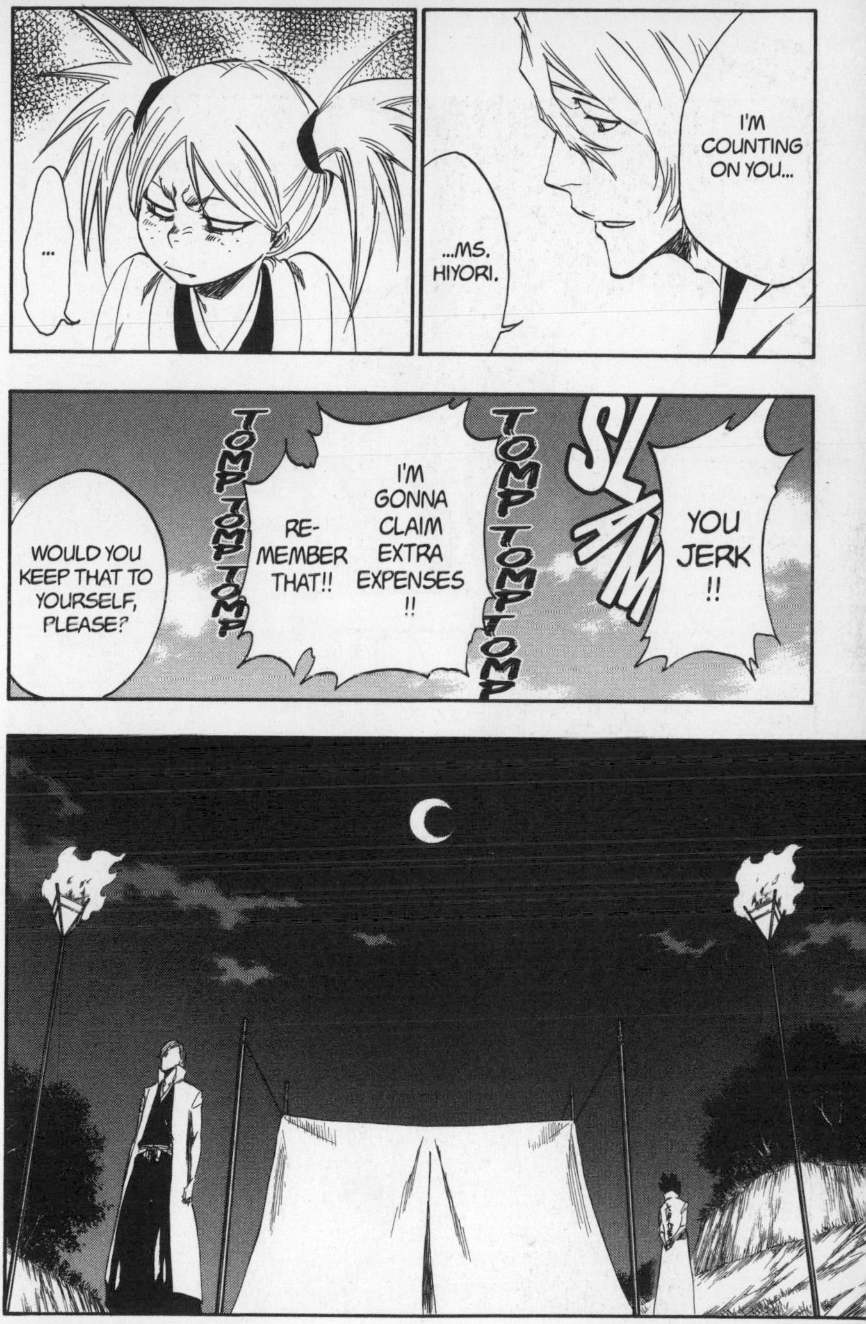
I'M COUNTING ON YOU...
...MS. HIYORI.
...
SLAM
YOU JERK!!
TOMP TOMP TOMP
I'M GONNA CLAIM EXTRA EXPENSES!!
RE-MEMBER THAT!!
TOMP TOMP TOMP
WOULD YOU KEEP THAT TO YOURSELF, PLEASE?

READ THIS WAY

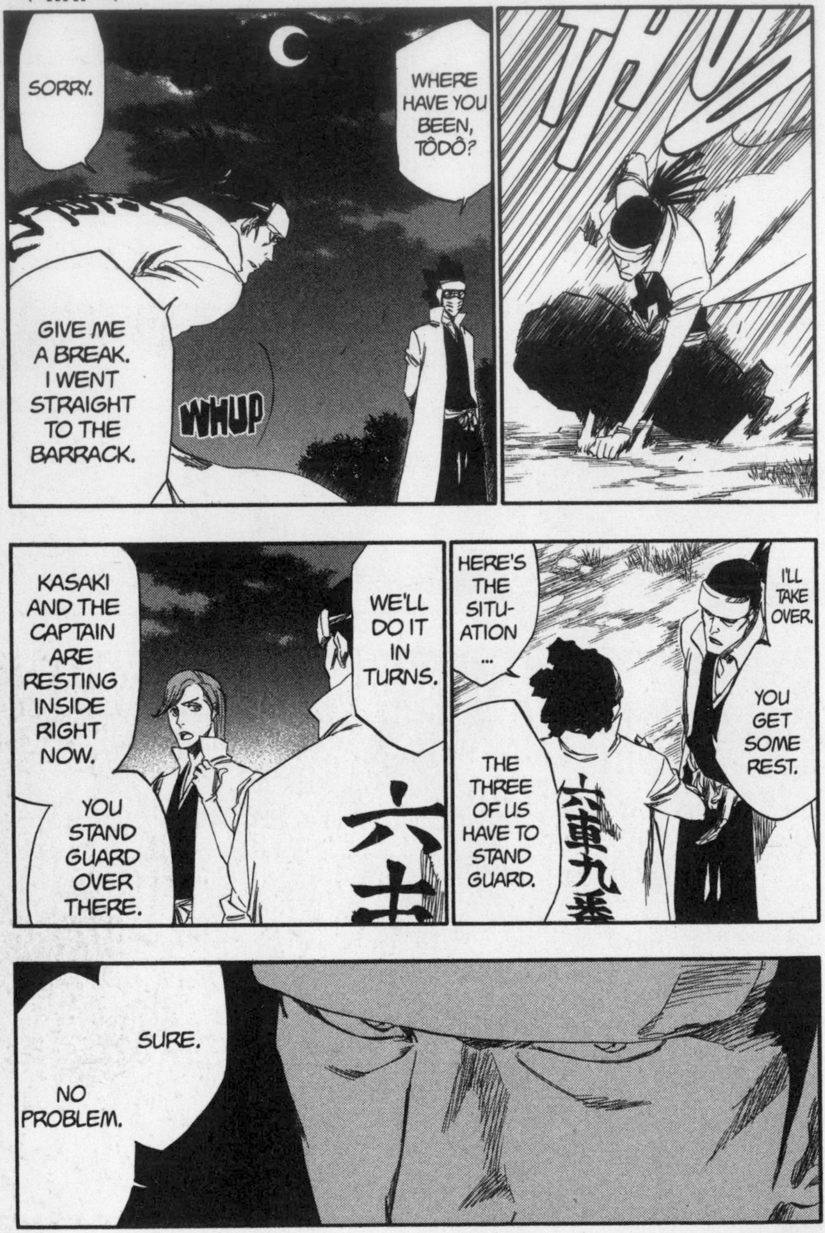
WHERE HAVE YOU BEEN, TÔDÔ?
SORRY.
GIVE ME A BREAK. I WENT STRAIGHT TO THE BARRACK.
WHUP
I'LL TAKE OVER.
YOU GET SOME REST.
HERE'S THE SITU-ATION ...
THE THREE OF US HAVE TO STAND GUARD.
六車九番
WE'LL DO IT IN TURNS.
KASAKI AND THE CAPTAIN ARE RESTING INSIDE RIGHT NOW.
YOU STAND GUARD OVER THERE.
SURE.
NO PROBLEM.

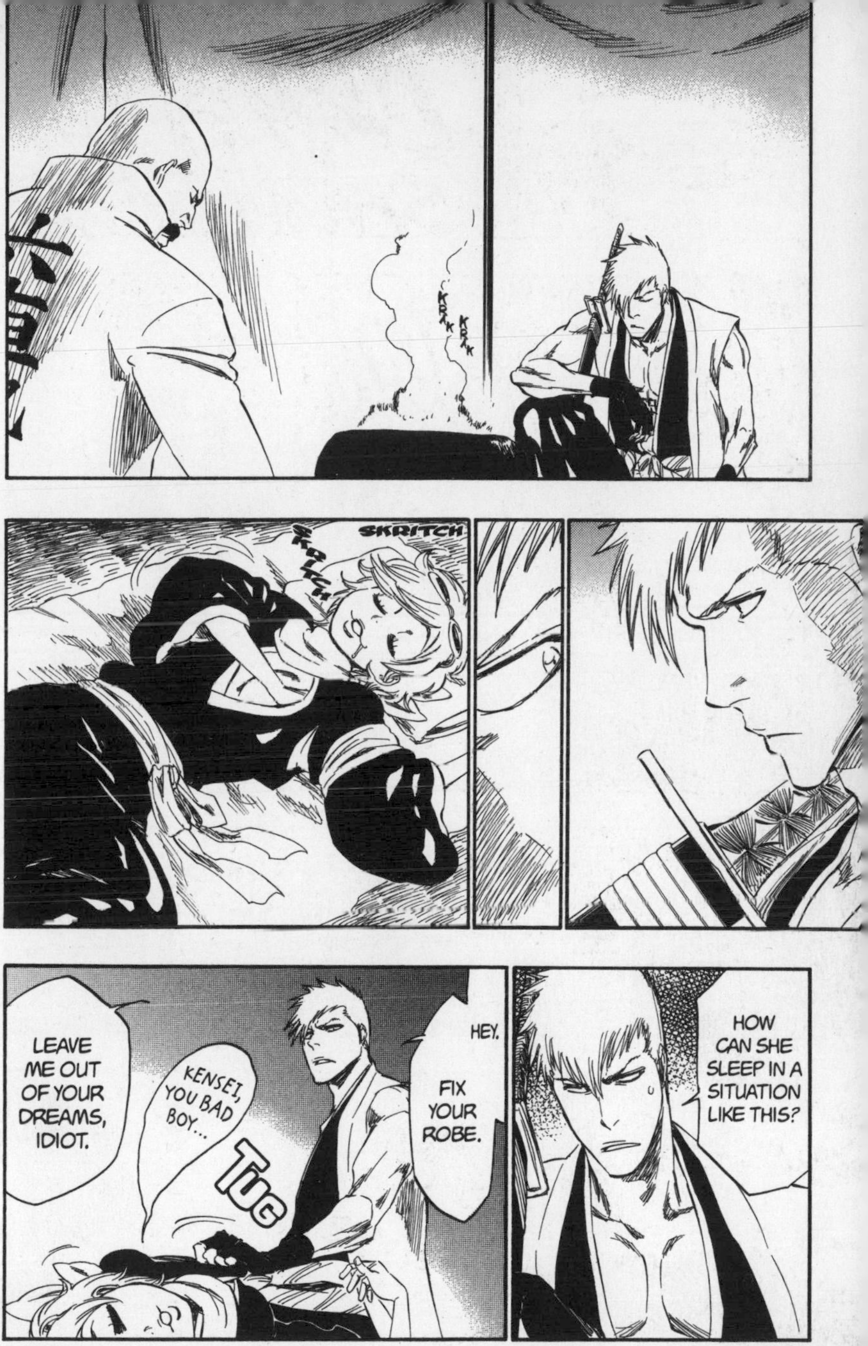
KRAK
KRAK
SKRITCH
SKRITCH
HOW CAN SHE SLEEP IN A SITUATION LIKE THIS?
HEY.
FIX YOUR ROBE.
KENSEI, YOU BAD BOY...
TUG
LEAVE ME OUT OF YOUR DREAMS, IDIOT.

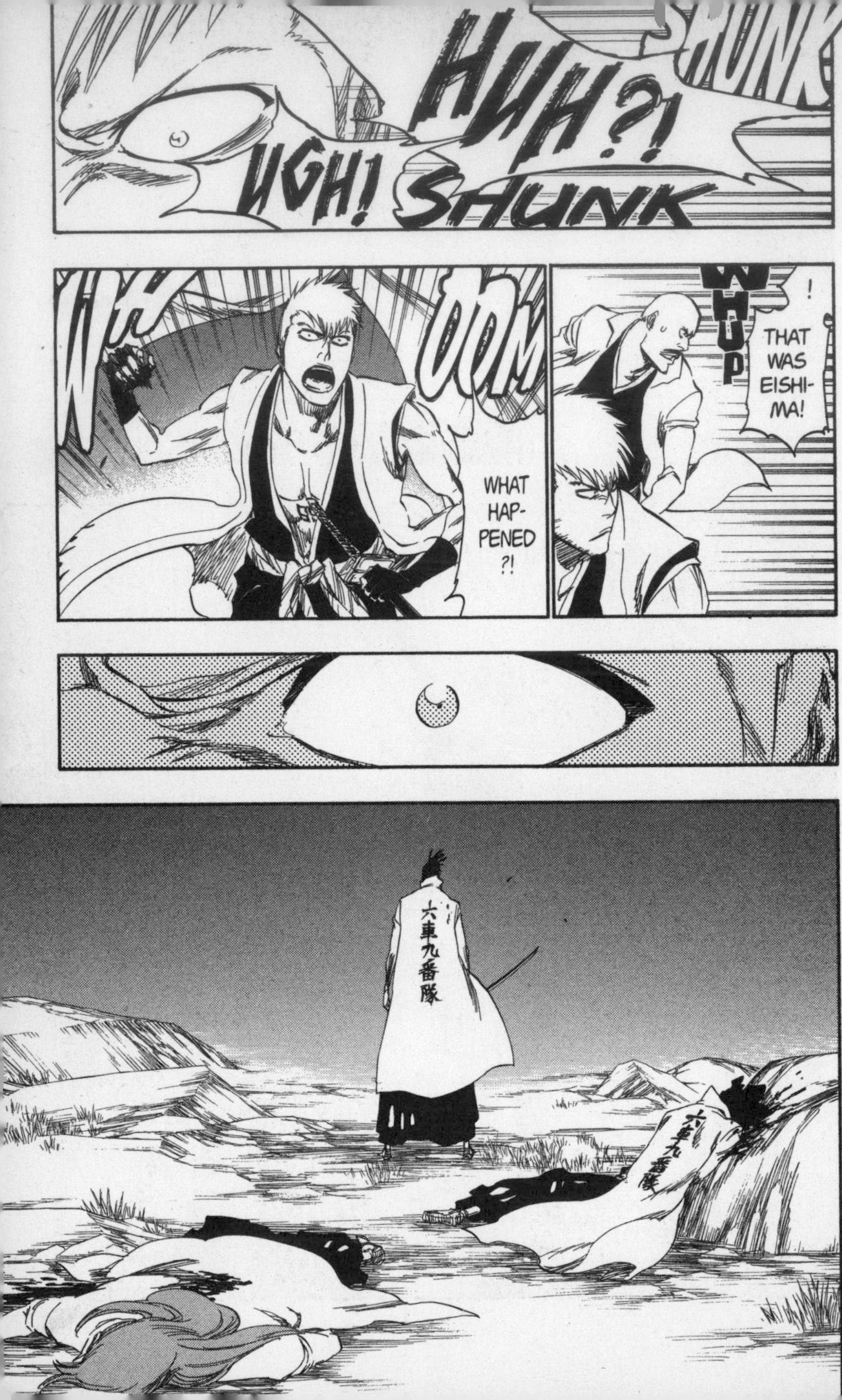
SHUNK
HUH?!
UGH!
SHUNK
WHUP
!
THAT WAS EISHI-MA!
WH
OOM
WHAT HAP-PENED ?!
六車九番隊
六車九番隊

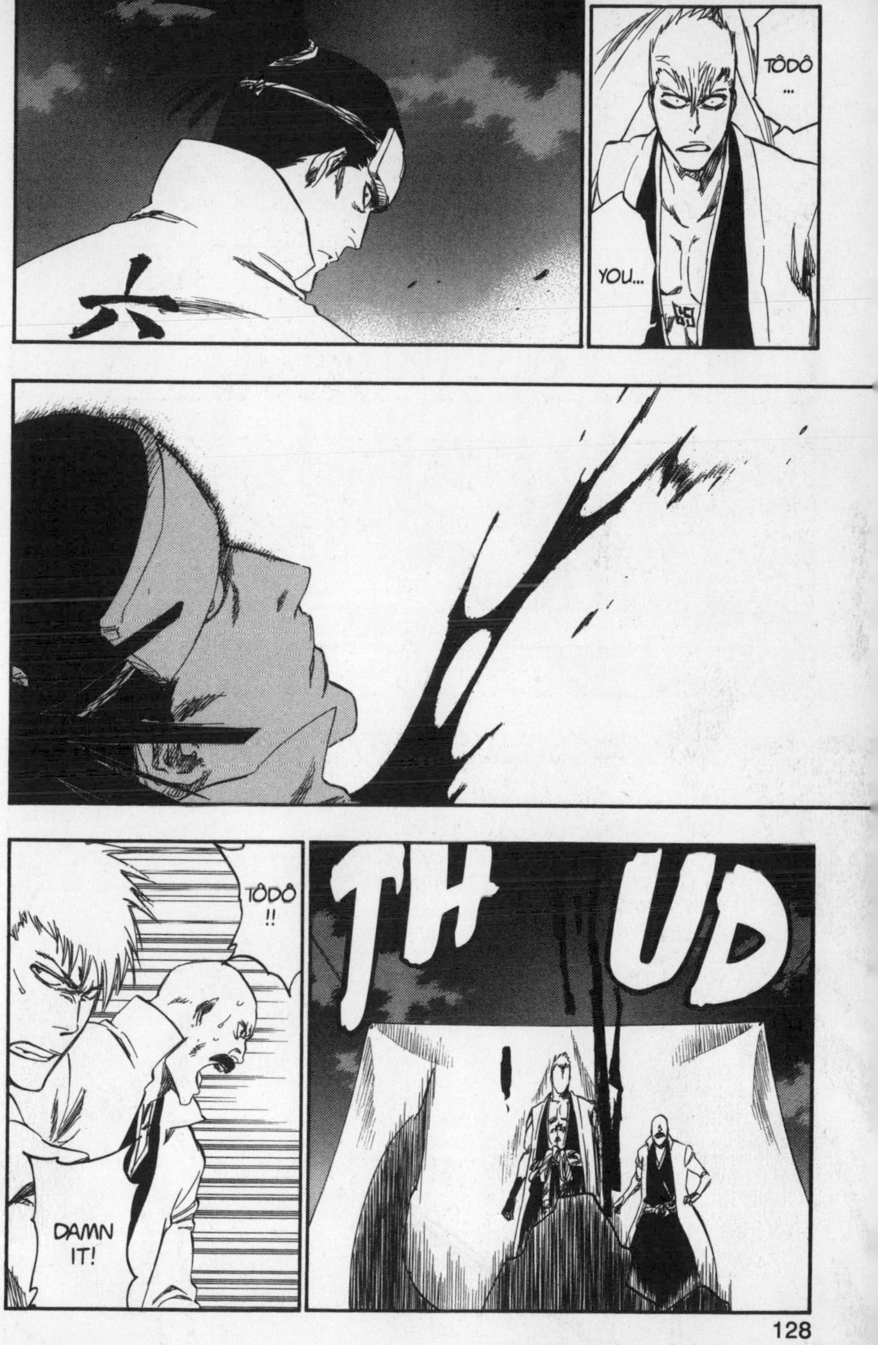
TÔDÔ ...
YOU...
THUD
TÔDÔ !!
DAMN IT!

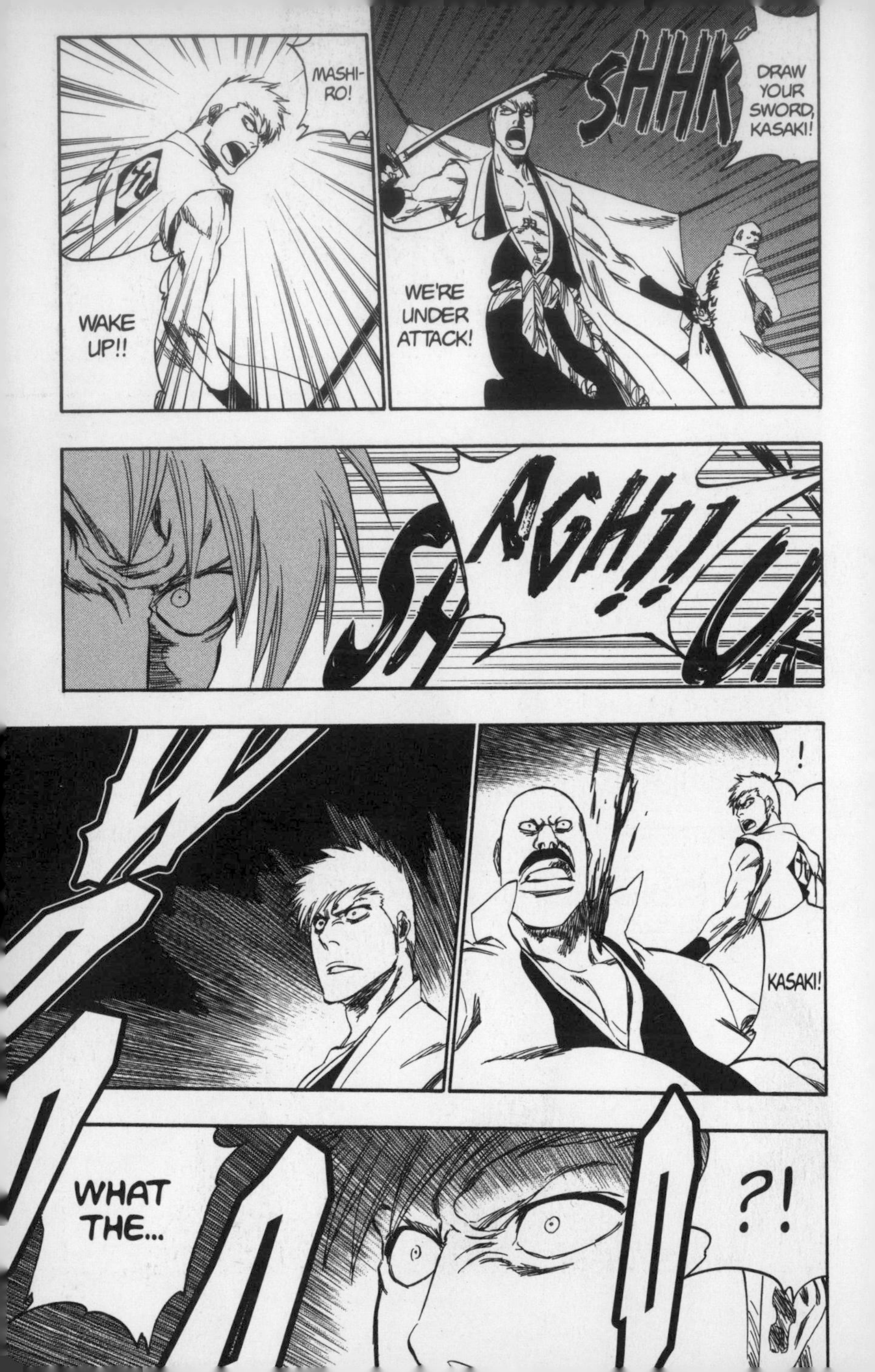
DRAW YOUR SWORD, KASAKI!
SHHK
WE'RE UNDER ATTACK!
MASHIRO!
WAKE UP!!
AGH!!
!
KASAKI!
?!
WHAT THE...

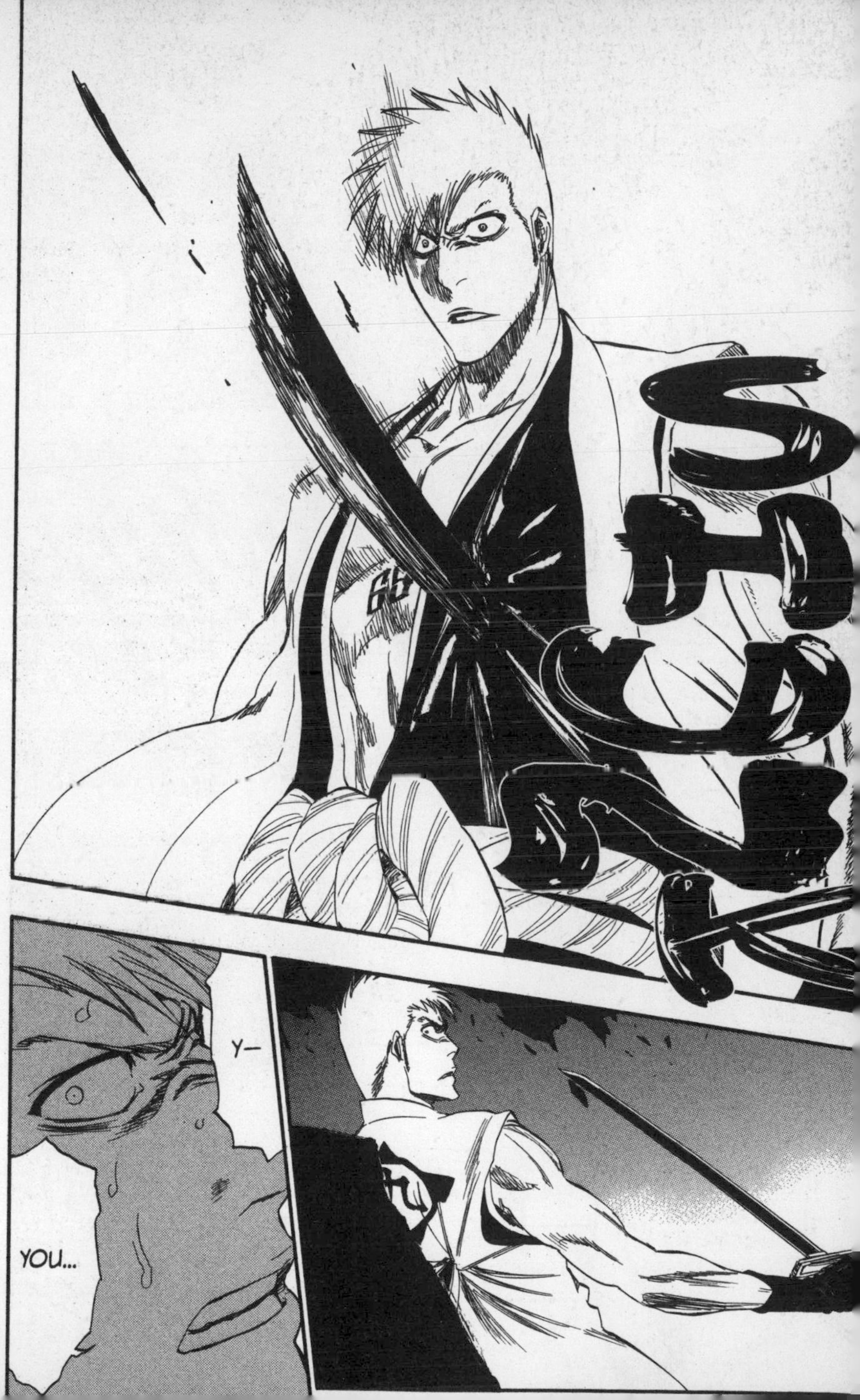
Y—
YOU...

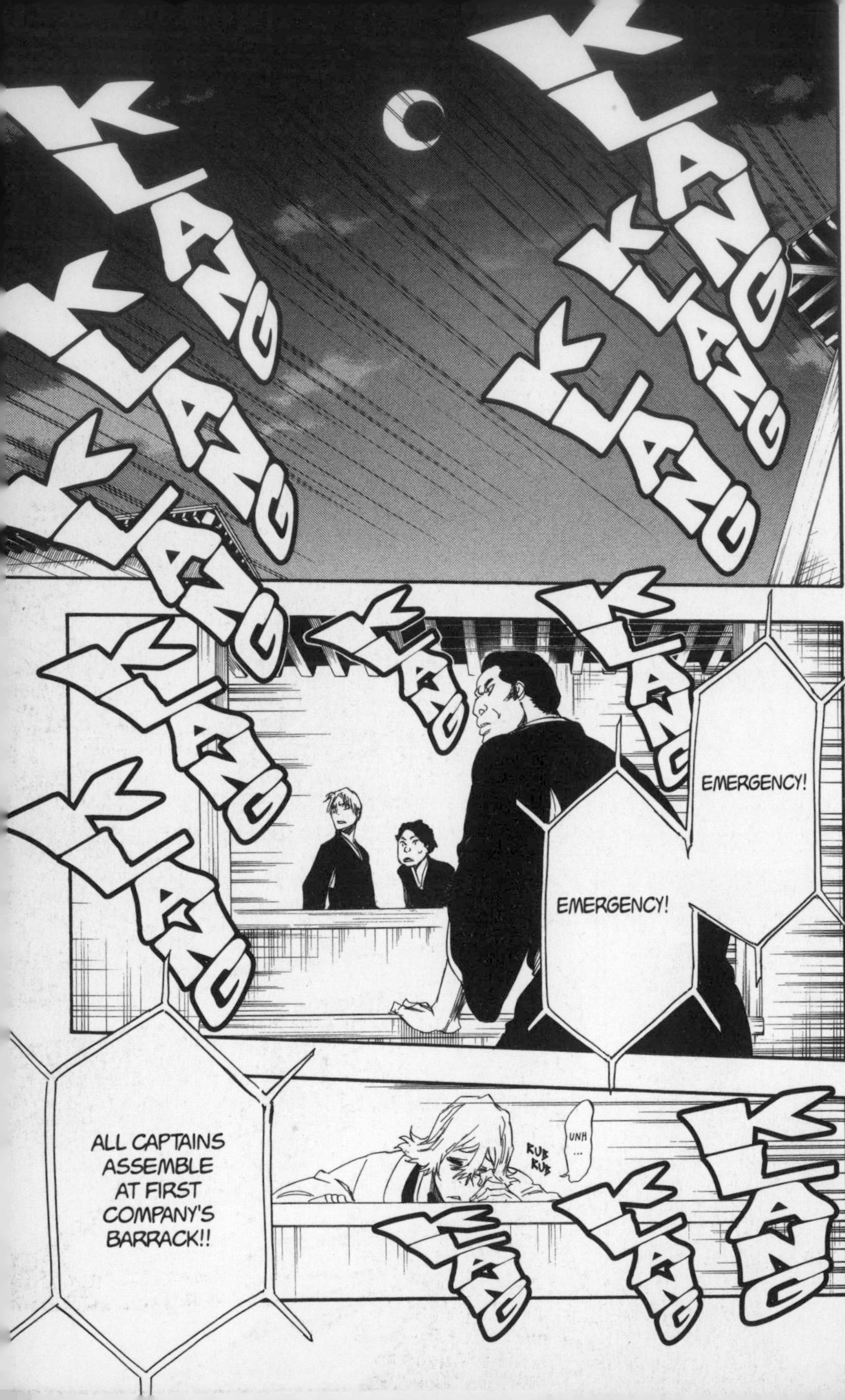
KLANG
KLANG
KLANG
KLANG
KLANG
KLANG
KLANG
KLANG
KLANG
KLANG
EMERGENCY!
EMERGENCY!
KLANG
KLANG
KLANG
UNH ...
RUB RUB
ALL CAPTAINS ASSEMBLE AT FIRST COMPANY'S BARRACK!!

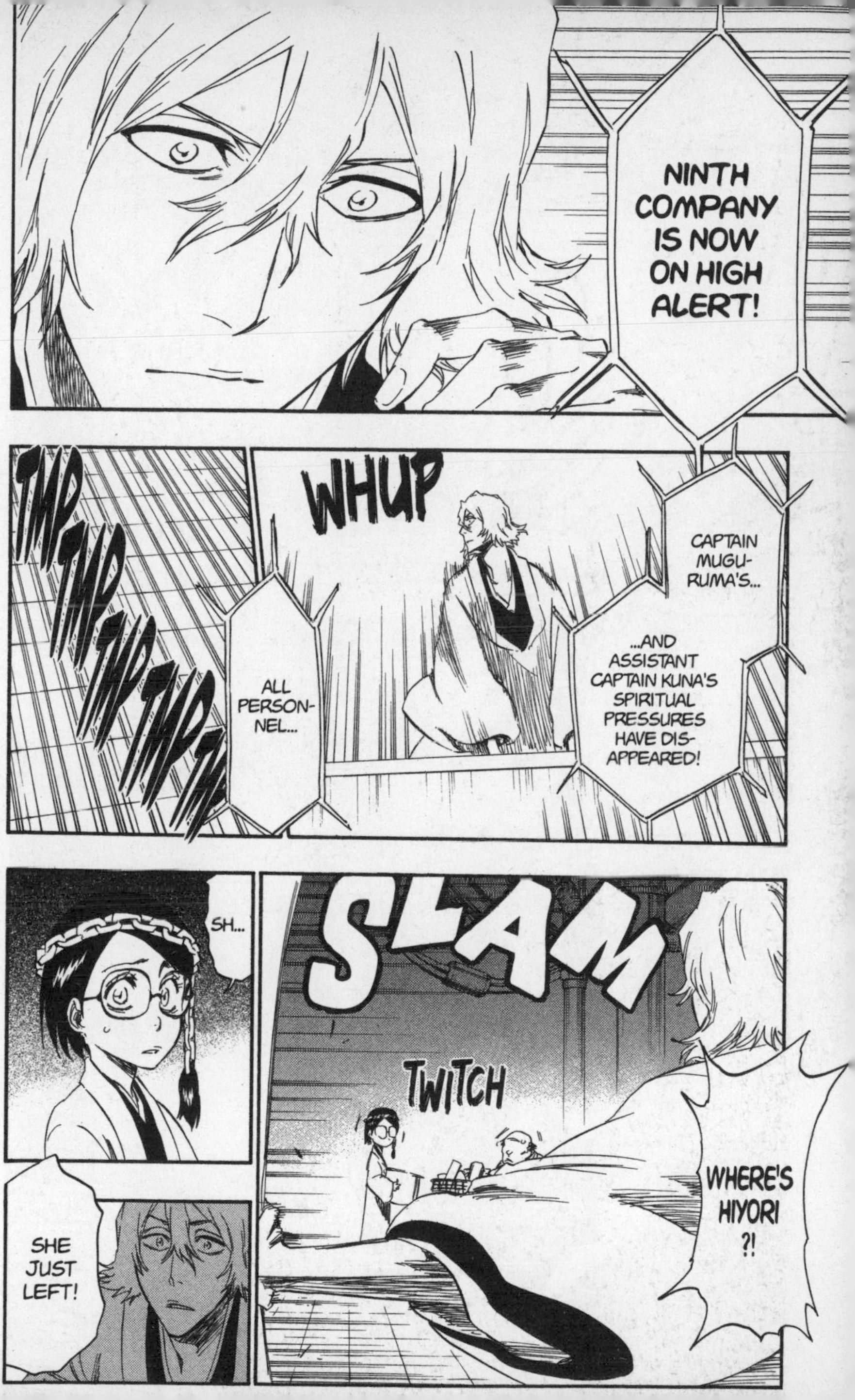
NINTH COMPANY IS NOW ON HIGH ALERT!
WHUP
CAPTAIN MUGU-RUMA'S...
...AND ASSISTANT CAPTAIN KUNA'S SPIRITUAL PRESSURES HAVE DIS-APPEARED!
ALL PERSON-NEL...
TMP TMP TMP TMP TMP
SLAM
WHERE'S HIYORI ?!
TWITCH
SH...
SHE JUST LEFT!

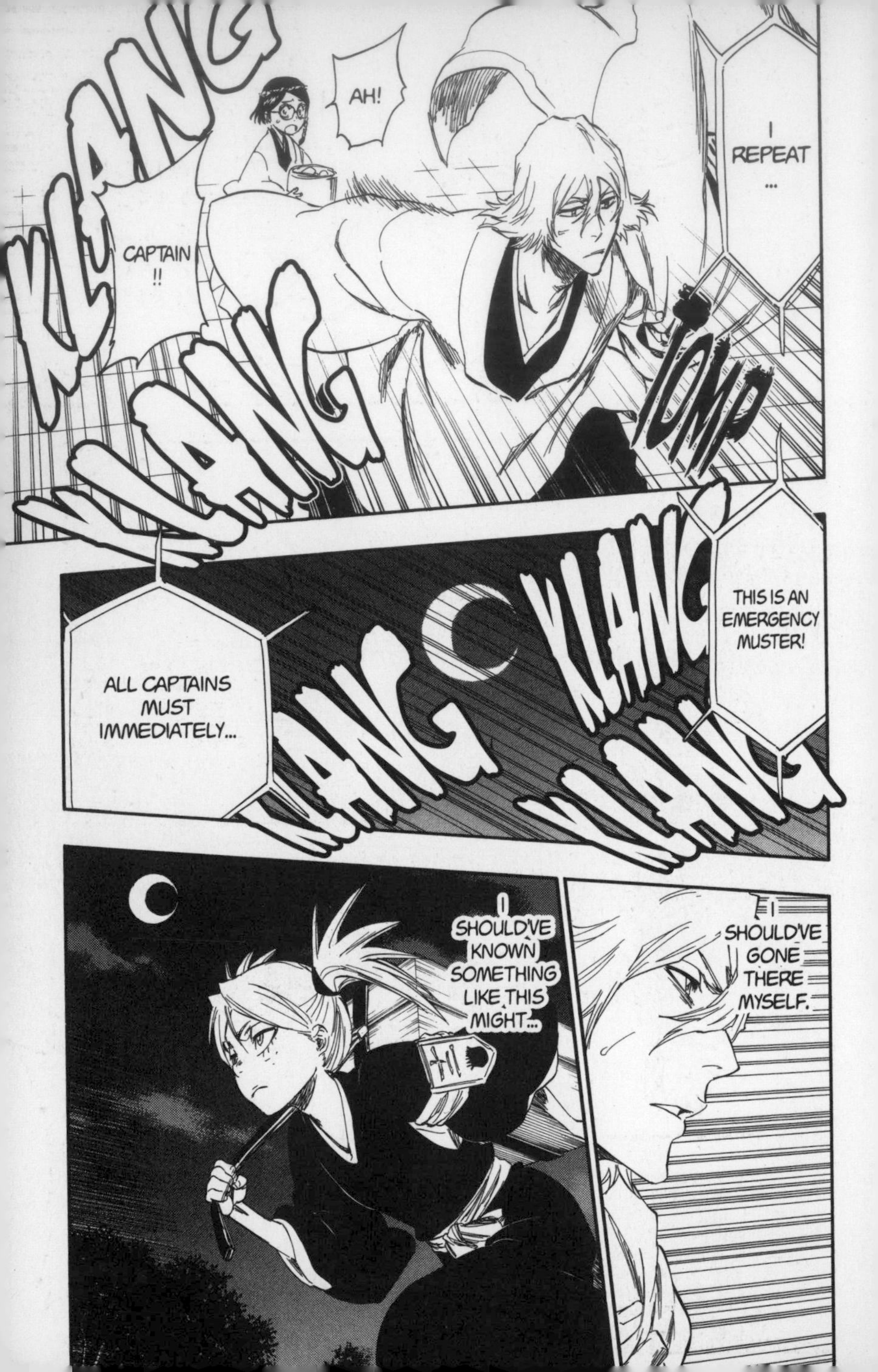
I REPEAT ...
AH!
TOMP
CAPTAIN !!
KLANG
KLANG
THIS IS AN EMERGENCY MUSTER!
KLANG
KLANG
KLANG
ALL CAPTAINS MUST IMMEDIATELY...
I SHOULD'VE GONE THERE MYSELF.
I SHOULD'VE KNOWN SOMETHING LIKE THIS MIGHT...

PRESENT
101 YEARS AGO
SAME PERSON

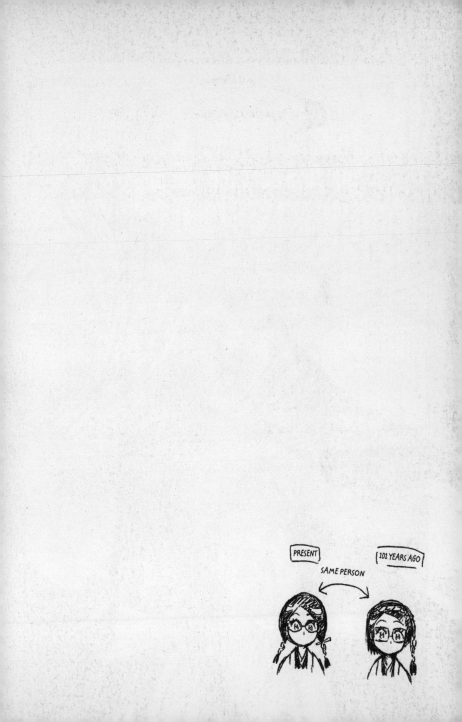

BLEACH

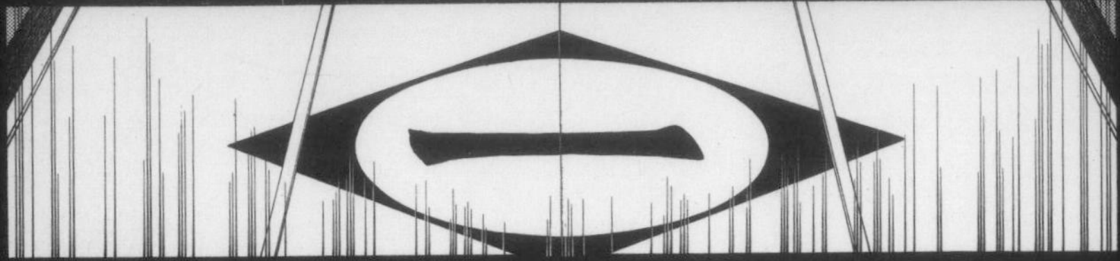

-102. Turn Back the Pendulum 7

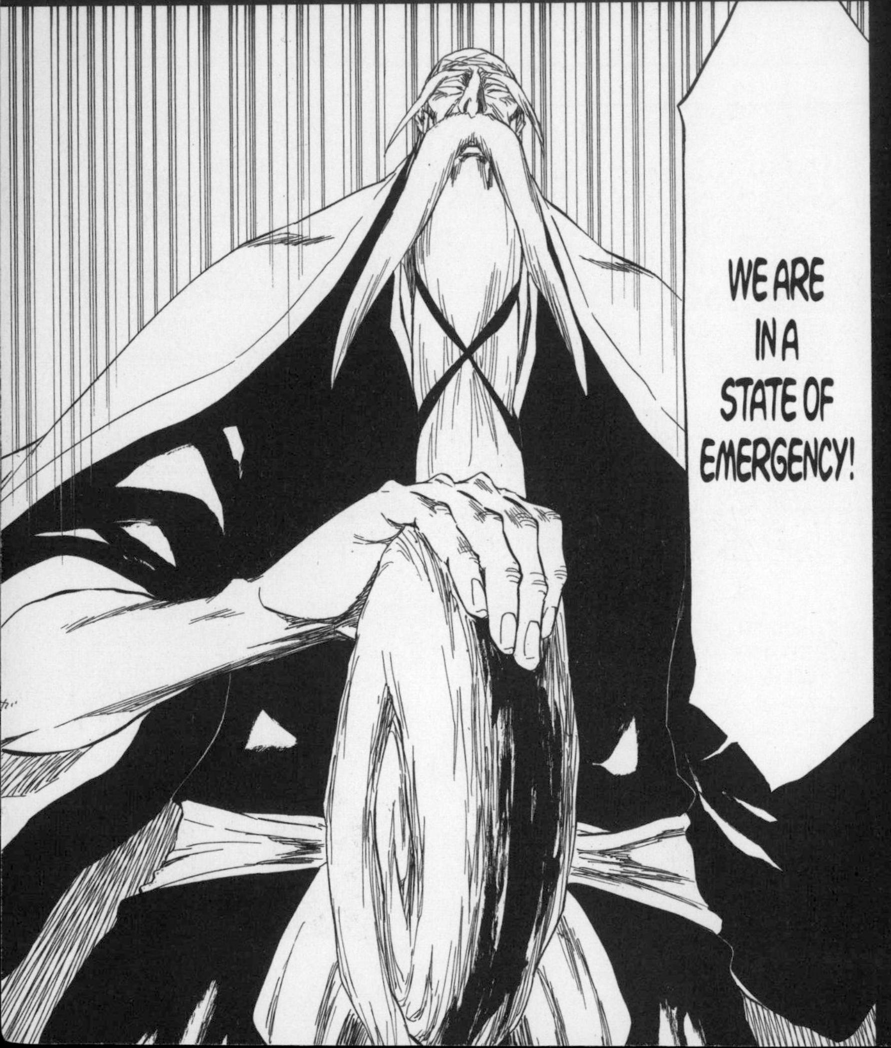
WE ARE IN A STATE OF EMERGENCY!

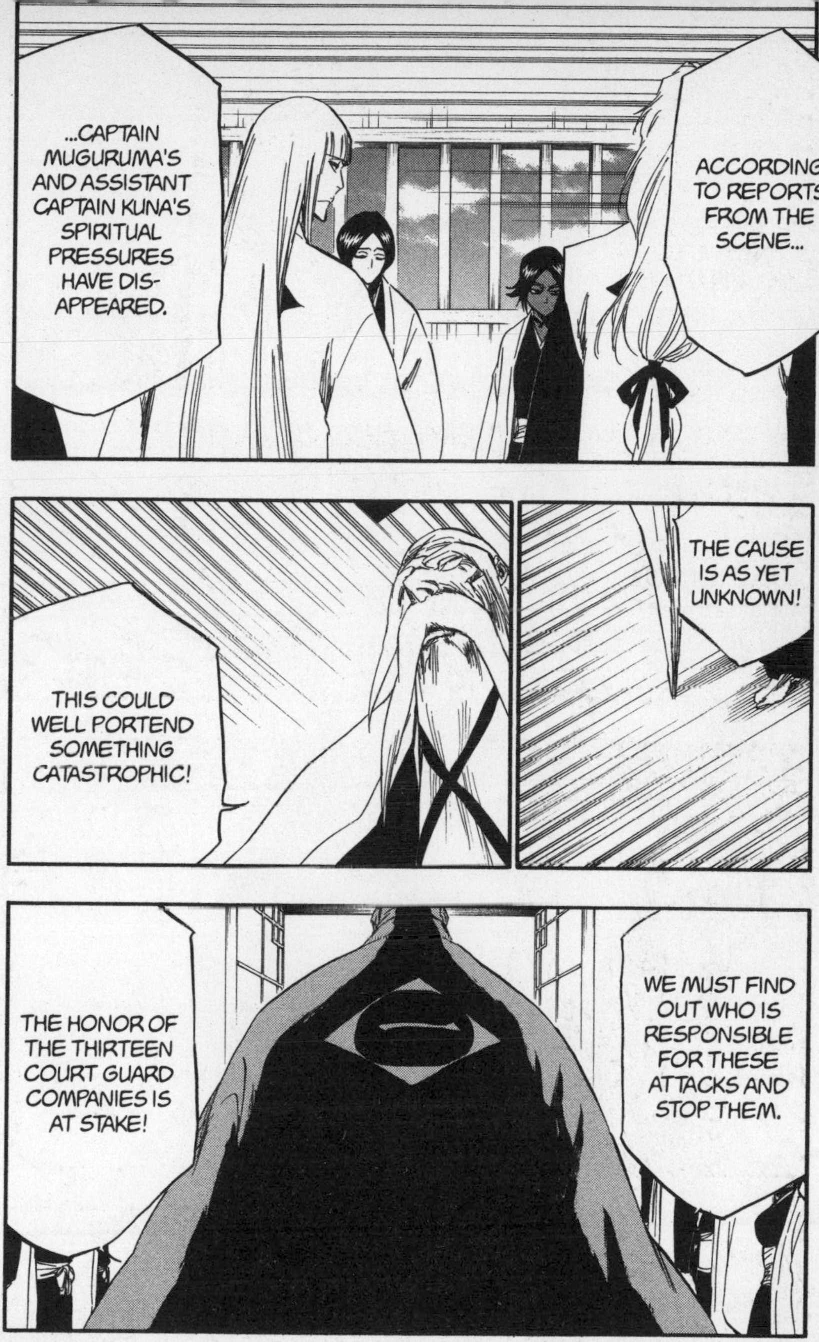
ACCORDING TO REPORTS FROM THE SCENE...
...CAPTAIN MUGURUMA'S AND ASSISTANT CAPTAIN KUNA'S SPIRITUAL PRESSURES HAVE DIS-APPEARED.
THE CAUSE IS AS YET UNKNOWN!
THIS COULD WELL PORTEND SOMETHING CATASTROPHIC!
WE MUST FIND OUT WHO IS RESPONSIBLE FOR THESE ATTACKS AND STOP THEM.
THE HONOR OF THE THIRTEEN COURT GUARD COMPANIES IS AT STAKE!

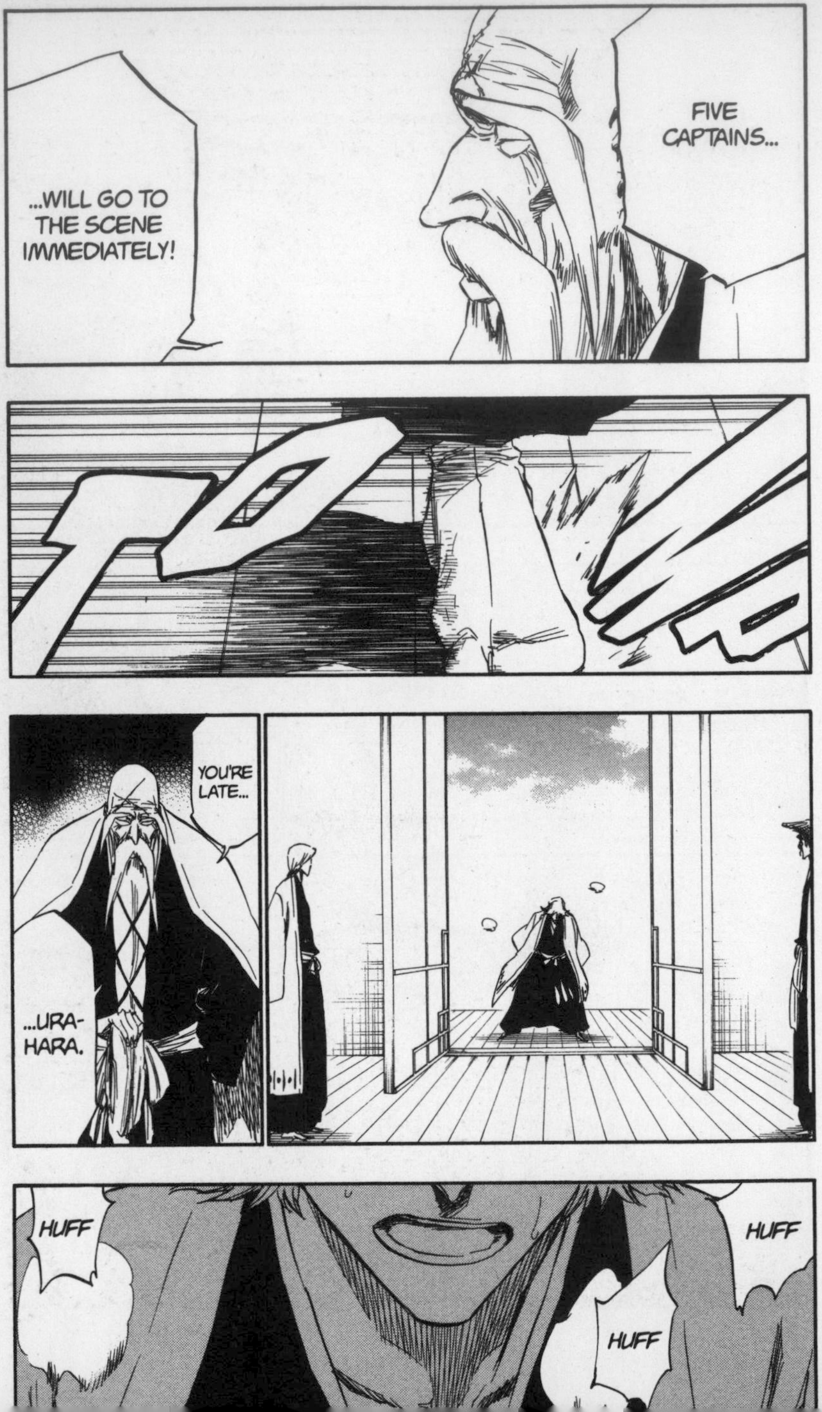
FIVE CAPTAINS...
...WILL GO TO THE SCENE IMMEDIATELY!
YOU'RE LATE...
...URA-HARA.
HUFF
HUFF
HUFF

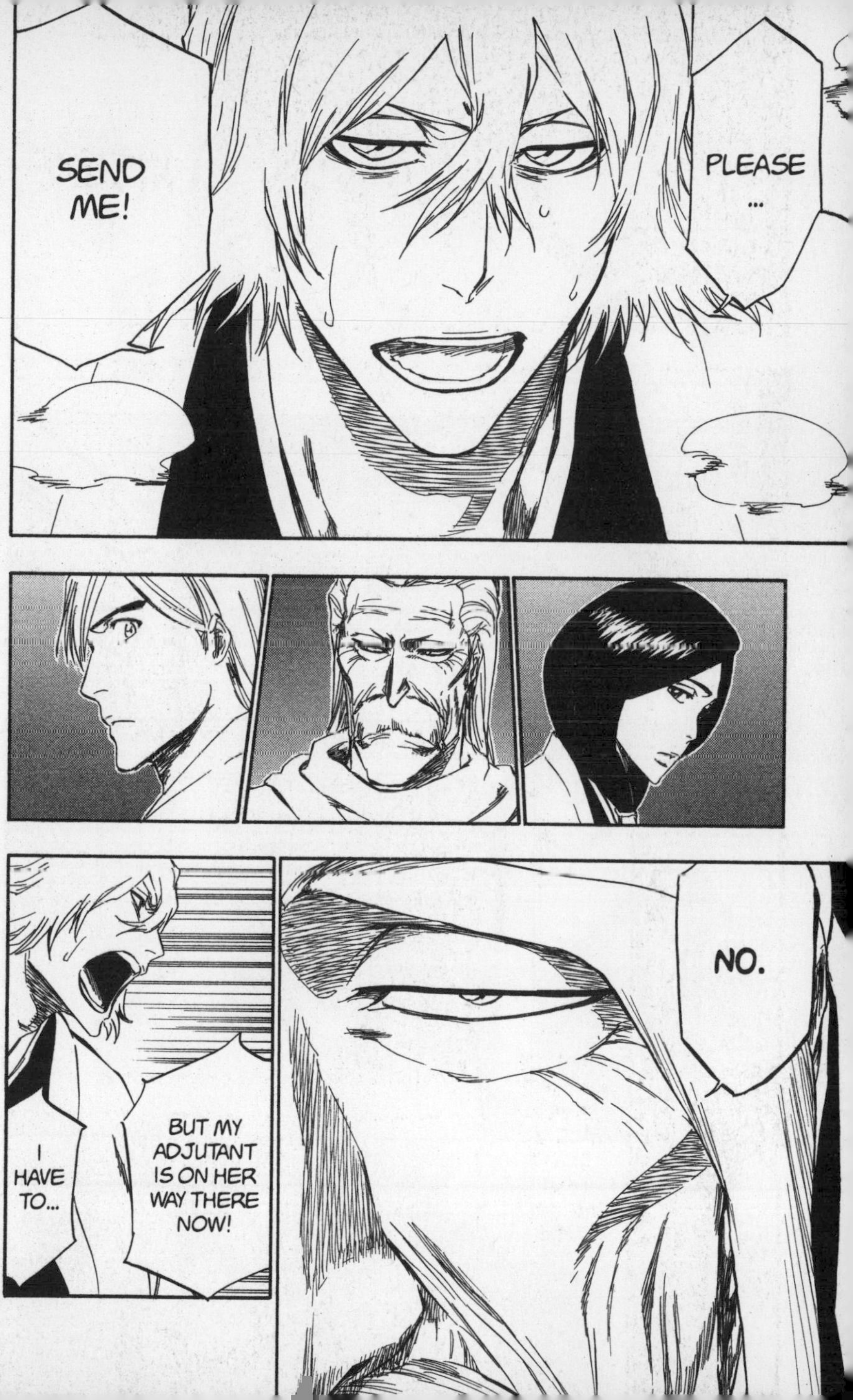
PLEASE ...
SEND ME!
NO.
BUT MY ADJUTANT IS ON HER WAY THERE NOW!
I HAVE TO...

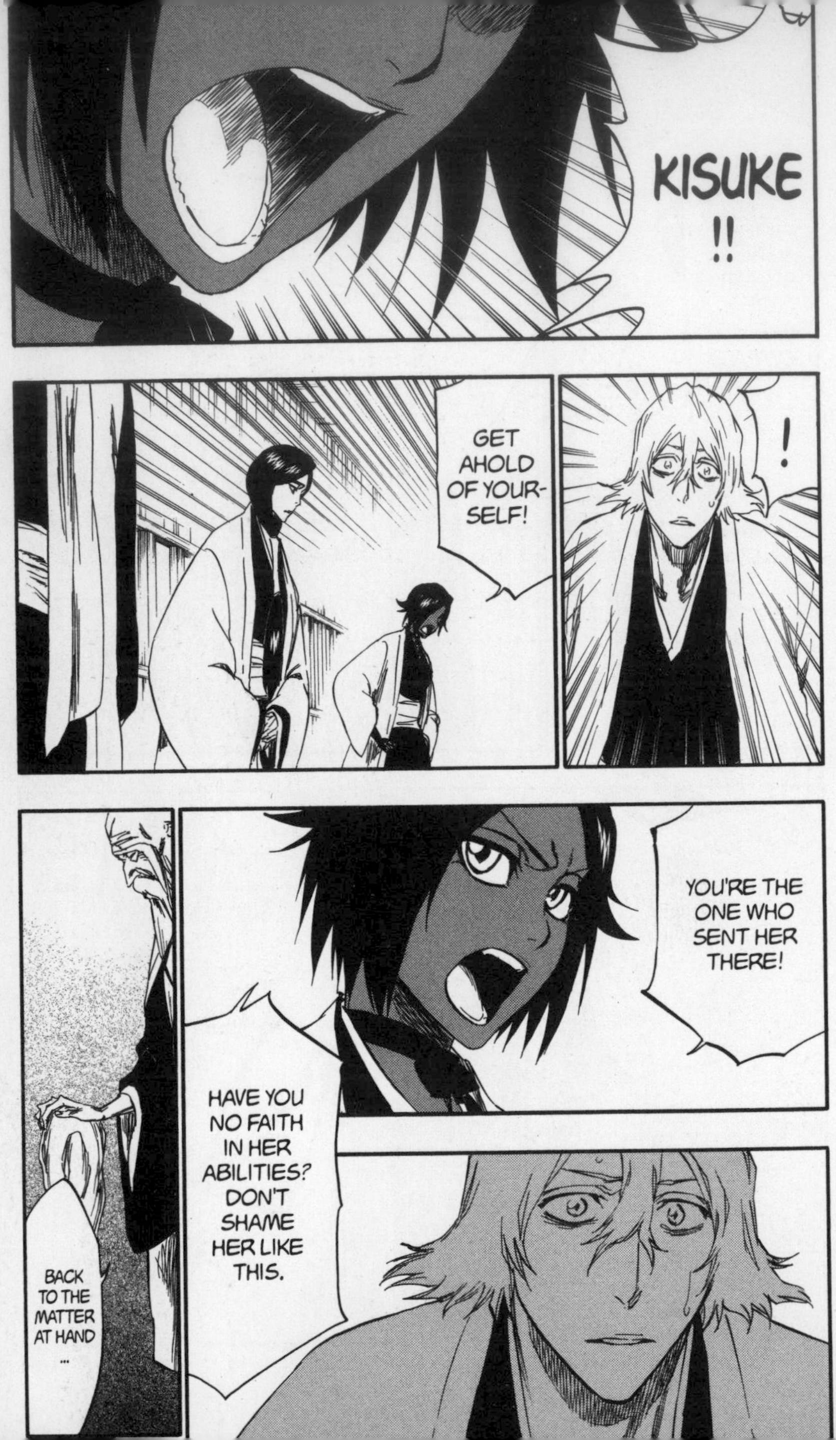
KISUKE !!
!
GET AHOLD OF YOURSELF!
YOU'RE THE ONE WHO SENT HER THERE!
HAVE YOU NO FAITH IN HER ABILITIES? DON'T SHAME HER LIKE THIS.
BACK TO THE MATTER AT HAND ...

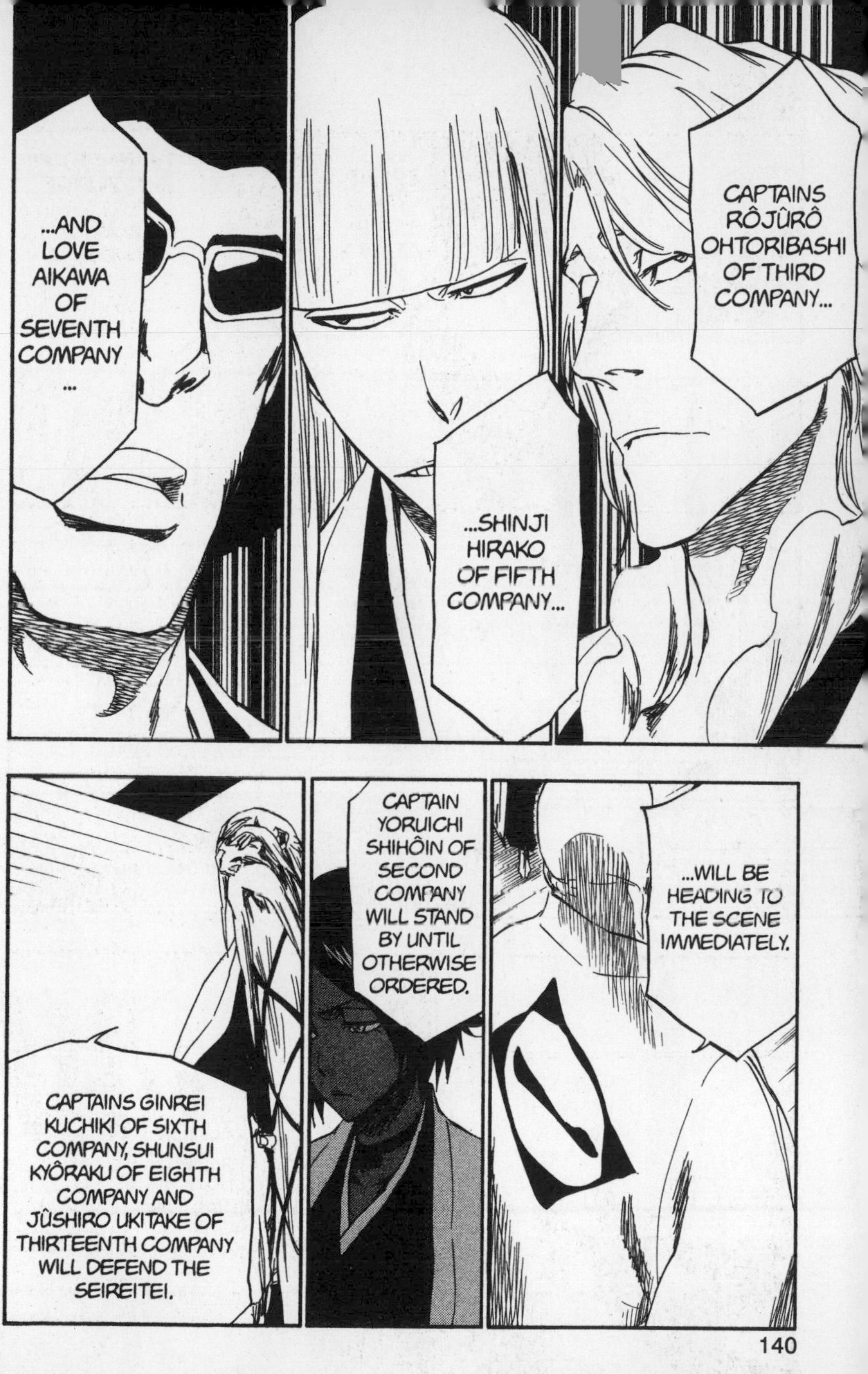
CAPTAINS RÔJÛRÔ OHTORIBASHI OF THIRD COMPANY...
...SHINJI HIRAKO OF FIFTH COMPANY...
...AND LOVE AIKAWA OF SEVENTH COMPANY ...
...WILL BE HEADING TO THE SCENE IMMEDIATELY.
CAPTAIN YORUICHI SHIHÔIN OF SECOND COMPANY WILL STAND BY UNTIL OTHERWISE ORDERED.
CAPTAINS GINREI KUCHIKI OF SIXTH COMPANY, SHUNSUI KYÔRAKU OF EIGHTH COMPANY AND JÛSHIRO UKITAKE OF THIRTEENTH COMPANY WILL DEFEND THE SEIREITEI.

READ THIS WAY

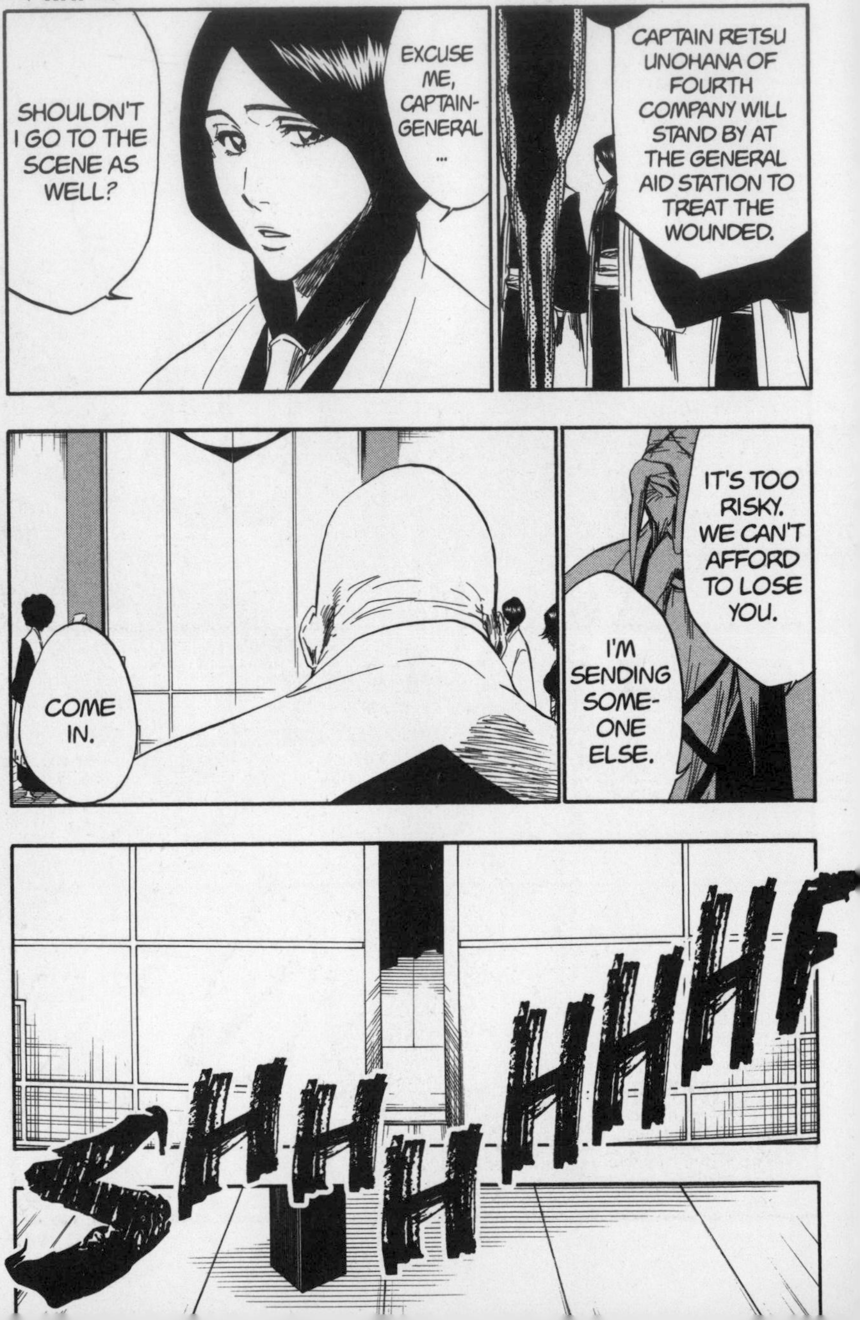
CAPTAIN RETSU UNOHANA OF FOURTH COMPANY WILL STAND BY AT THE GENERAL AID STATION TO TREAT THE WOUNDED.
EXCUSE ME, CAPTAIN-GENERAL ...
SHOULDN'T I GO TO THE SCENE AS WELL?
IT'S TOO RISKY. WE CAN'T AFFORD TO LOSE YOU.
I'M SENDING SOME-ONE ELSE.
COME IN.
SHHHHHHF

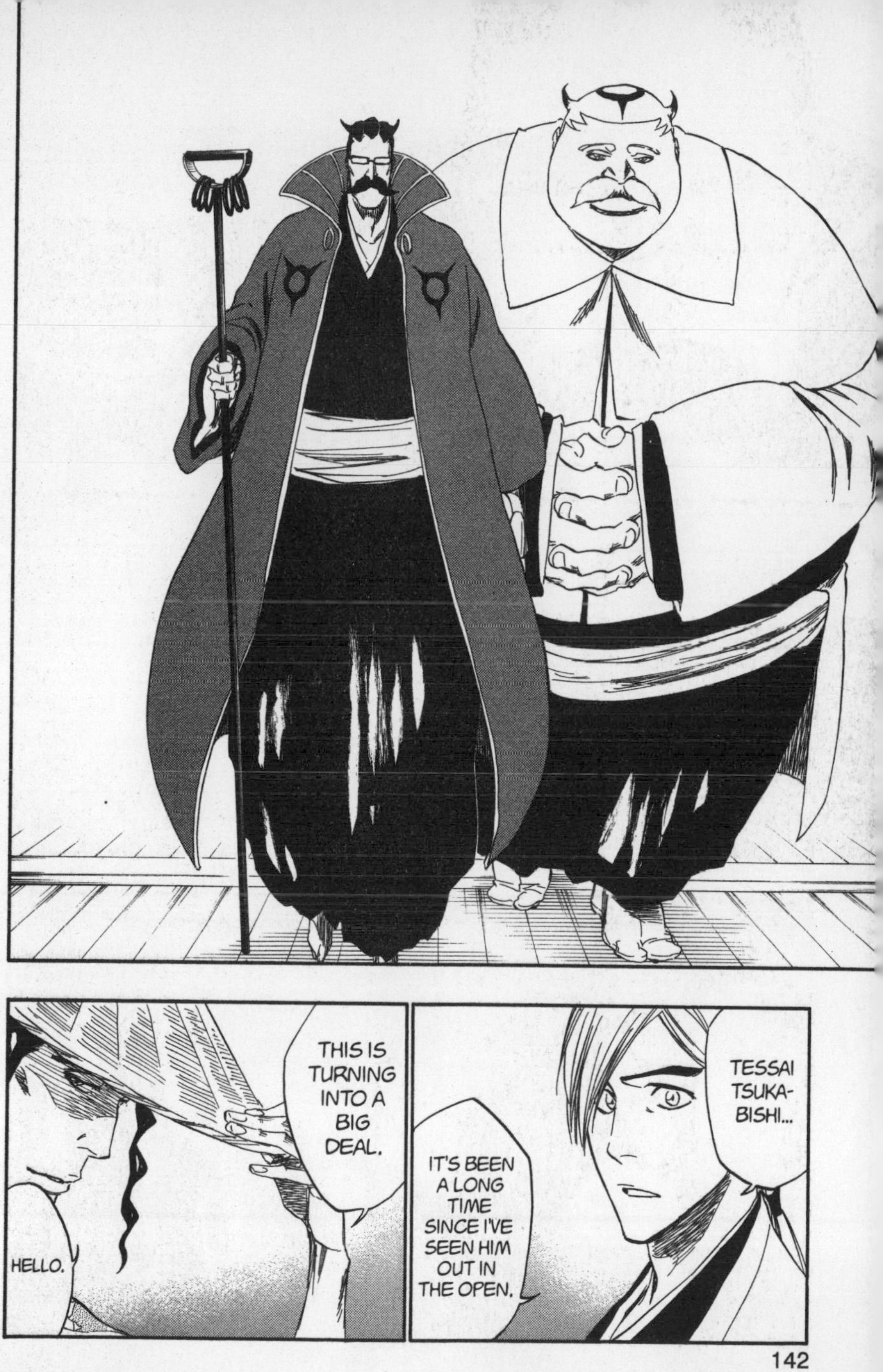
TESSAI TSUKA-BISHI...
IT'S BEEN A LONG TIME SINCE I'VE SEEN HIM OUT IN THE OPEN.
THIS IS TURNING INTO A BIG DEAL.
HELLO.

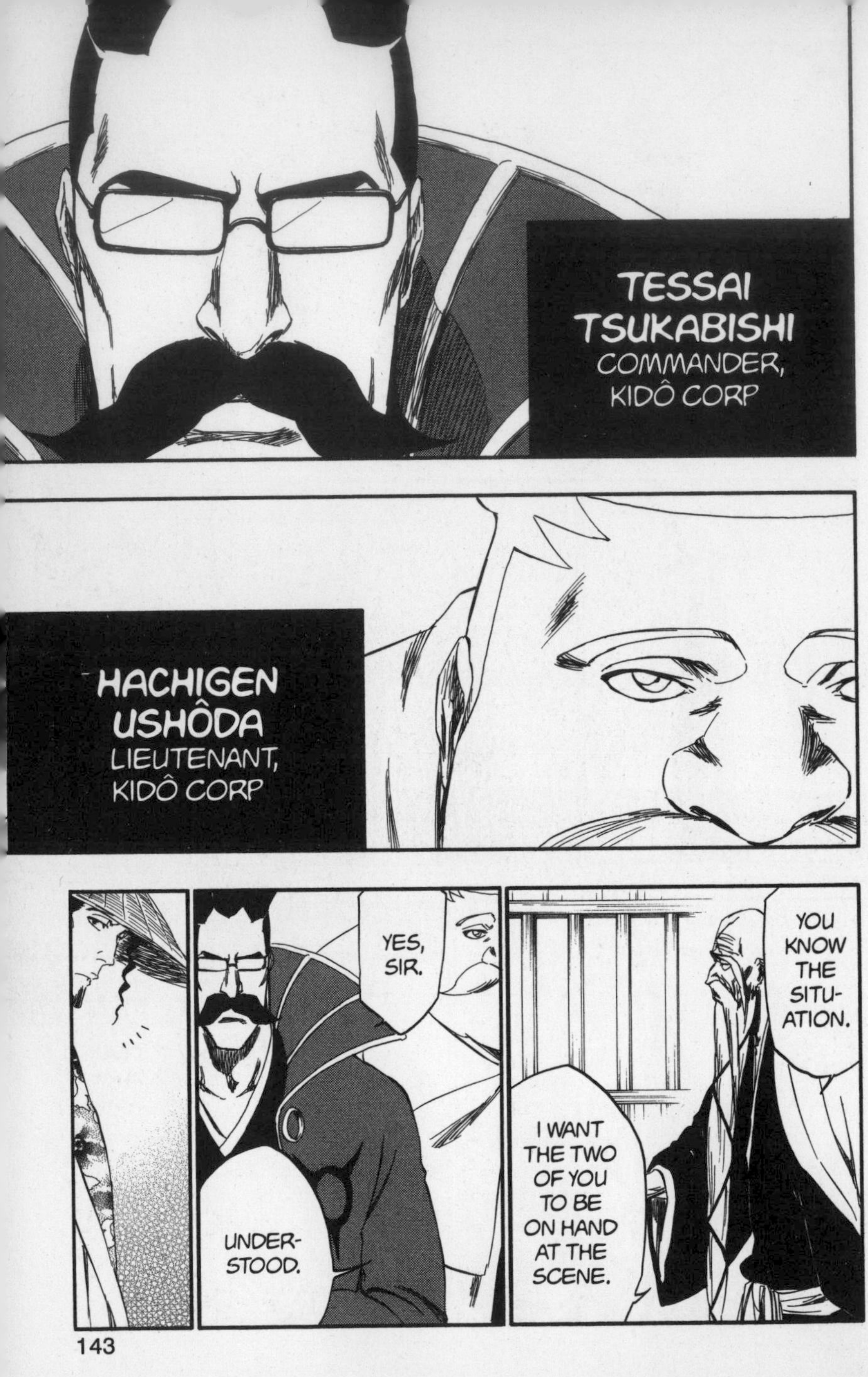
TESSAI TSUKABISHI
COMMANDER, KIDÔ CORP
HACHIGEN USHÔDA
LIEUTENANT, KIDÔ CORP
YOU KNOW THE SITU-ATION.
I WANT THE TWO OF YOU TO BE ON HAND AT THE SCENE.
YES, SIR.
UNDER-STOOD.

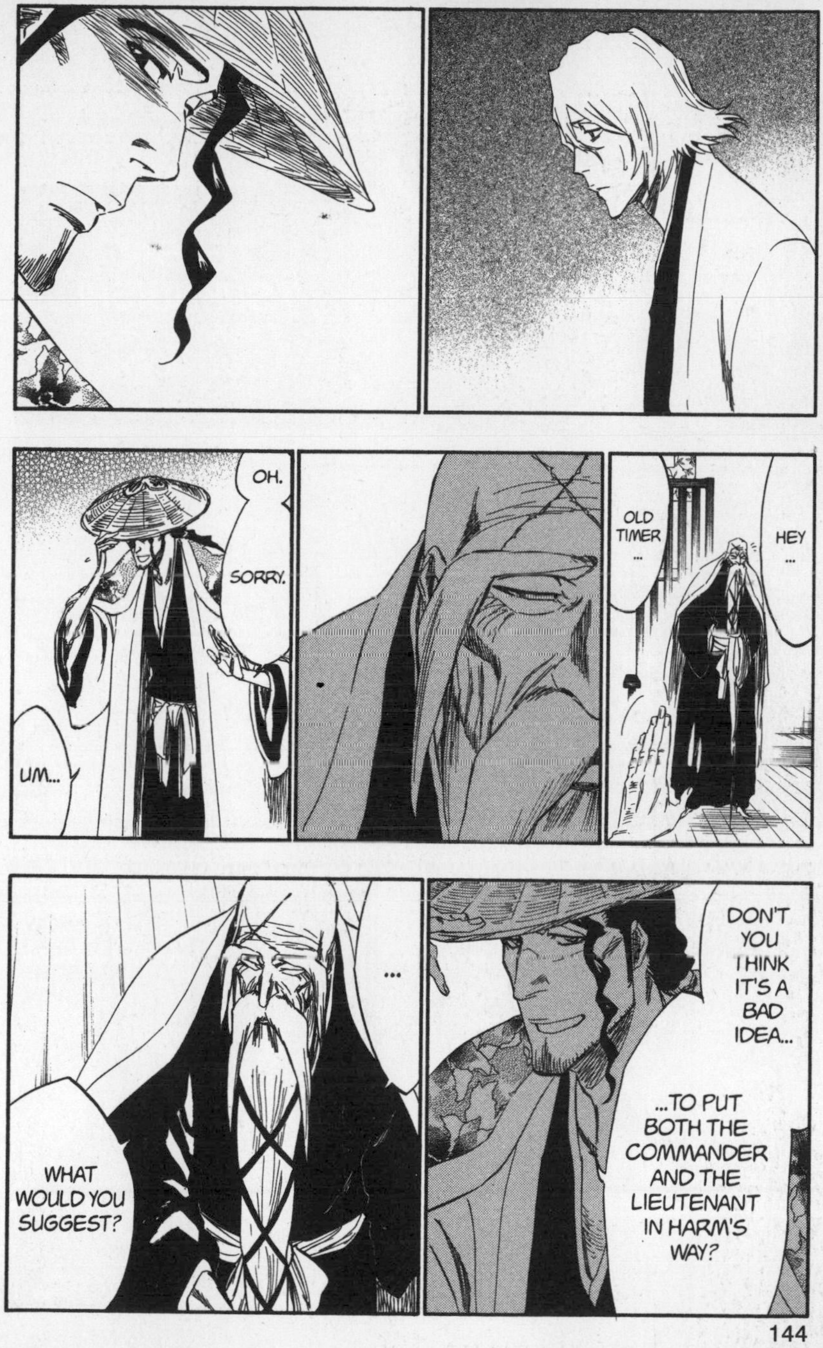
HEY ...
OLD TIMER ...
OH.
SORRY.
UM...
DON'T YOU THINK IT'S A BAD IDEA...
...TO PUT BOTH THE COMMANDER AND THE LIEUTENANT IN HARM'S WAY?
...
WHAT WOULD YOU SUGGEST?

READ THIS WAY

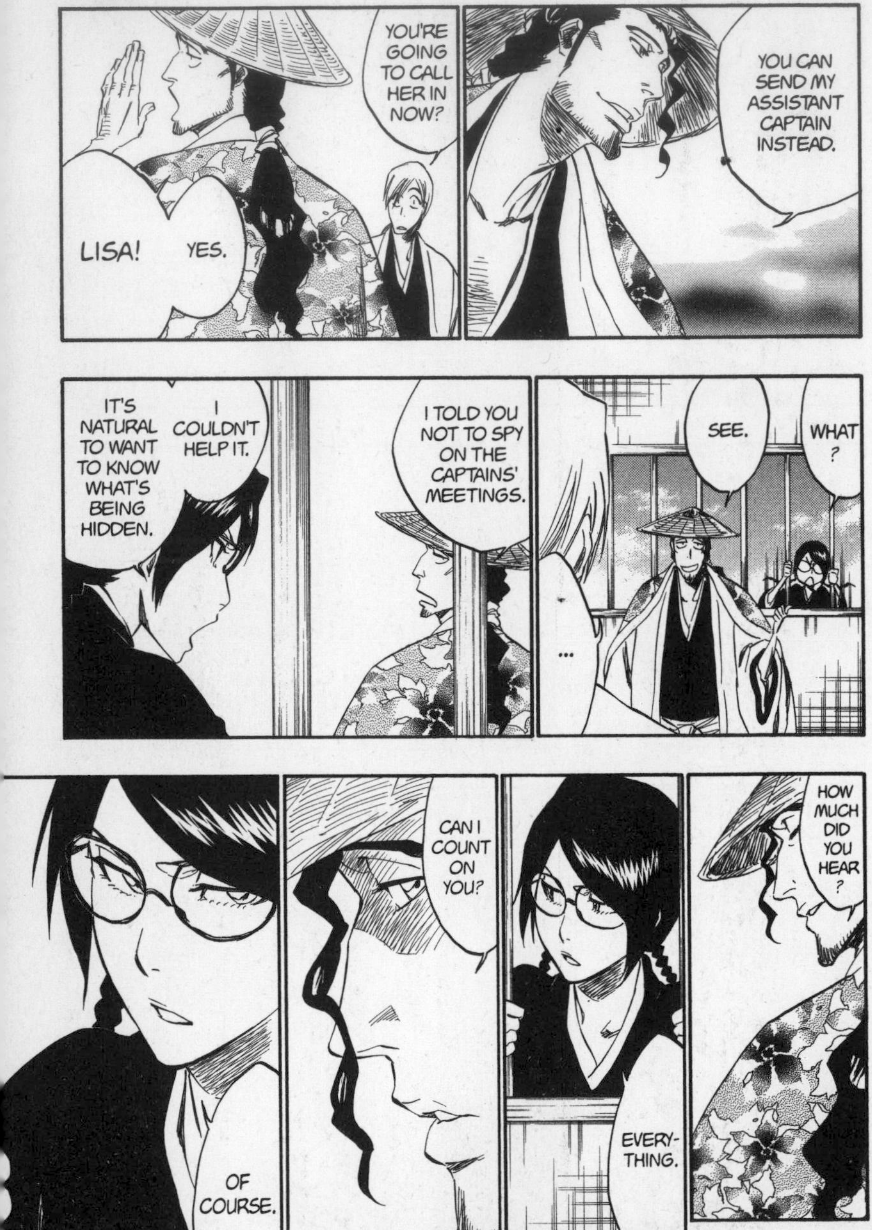

YOU CAN SEND MY ASSISTANT CAPTAIN INSTEAD.
YOU'RE GOING TO CALL HER IN NOW?
LISA!
YES.
WHAT?
SEE.
...
I TOLD YOU NOT TO SPY ON THE CAPTAINS' MEETINGS.
I COULDN'T HELP IT.
IT'S NATURAL TO WANT TO KNOW WHAT'S BEING HIDDEN.
HOW MUCH DID YOU HEAR?
EVERYTHING.
CAN I COUNT ON YOU?
OF COURSE.

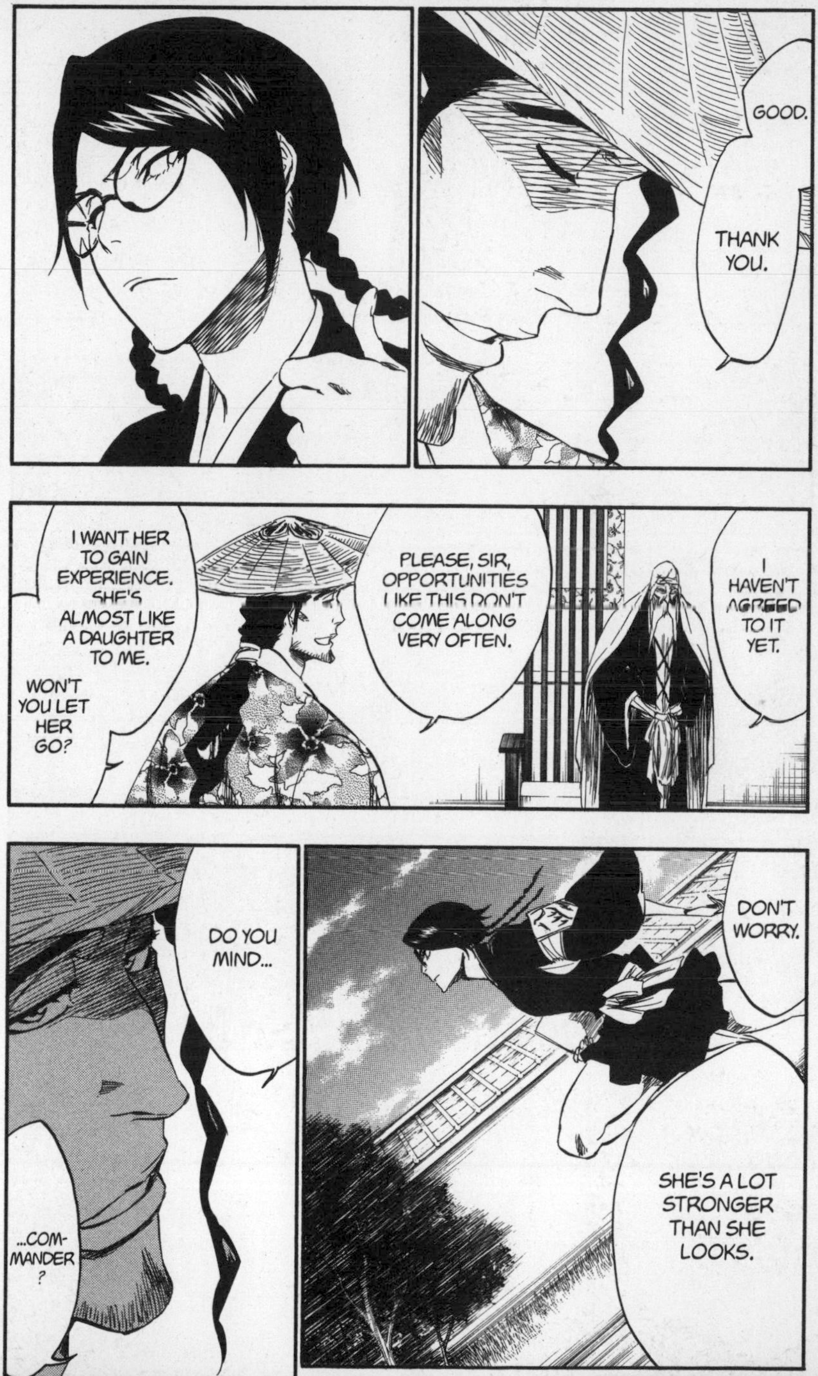
GOOD.
THANK YOU.
I HAVEN'T AGREED TO IT YET.
PLEASE, SIR, OPPORTUNITIES LIKE THIS DON'T COME ALONG VERY OFTEN.
I WANT HER TO GAIN EXPERIENCE. SHE'S ALMOST LIKE A DAUGHTER TO ME.
WON'T YOU LET HER GO?
DON'T WORRY.
SHE'S A LOT STRONGER THAN SHE LOOKS.
DO YOU MIND...
...COM-MANDER?

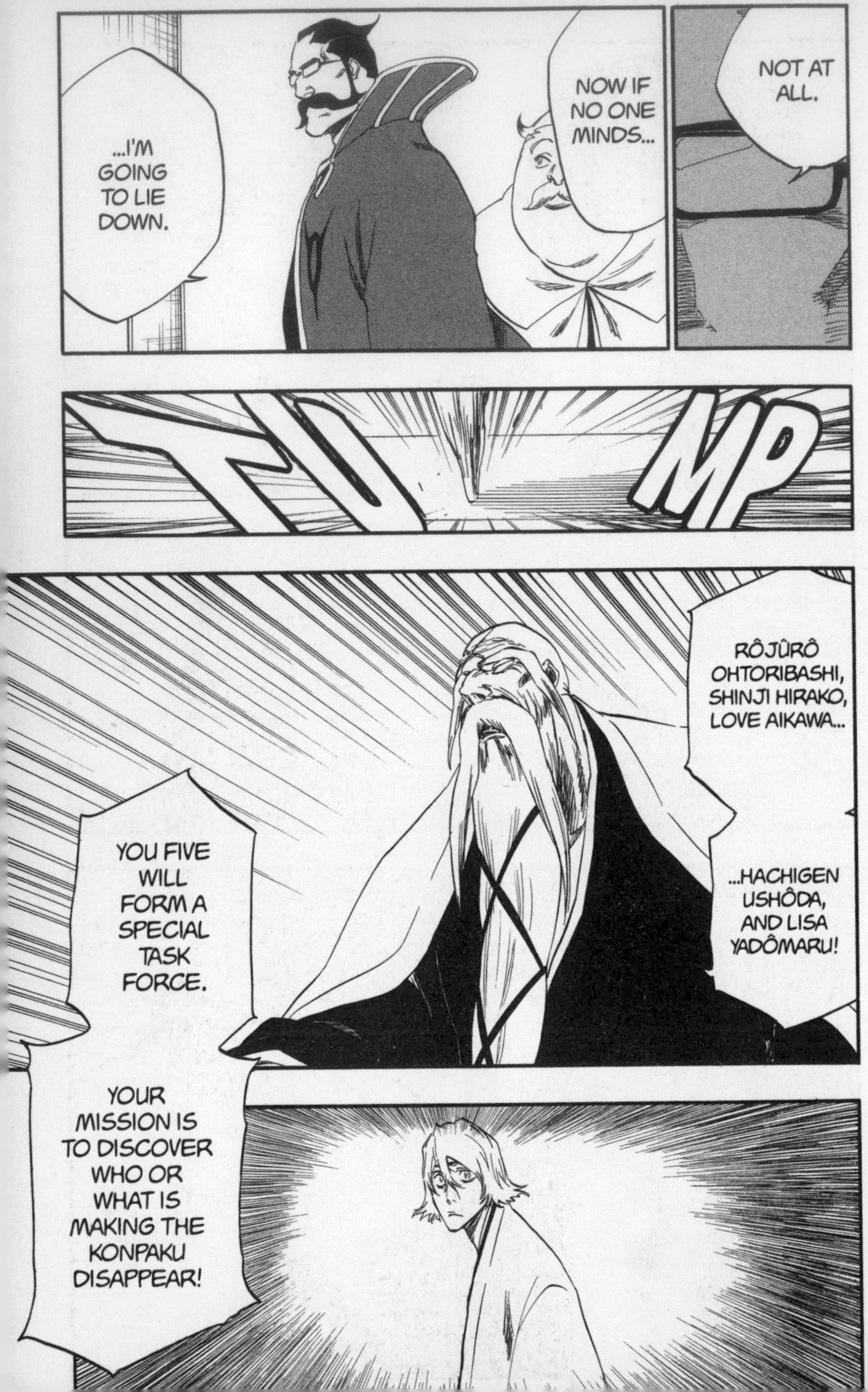
NOT AT ALL.
NOW IF NO ONE MINDS...
...I'M GOING TO LIE DOWN.
THUMP
RÔJÛRÔ OHTORIBASHI, SHINJI HIRAKO, LOVE AIKAWA...
...HACHIGEN USHÔDA, AND LISA YADÔMARU!
YOU FIVE WILL FORM A SPECIAL TASK FORCE.
YOUR MISSION IS TO DISCOVER WHO OR WHAT IS MAKING THE KONPAKU DISAPPEAR!

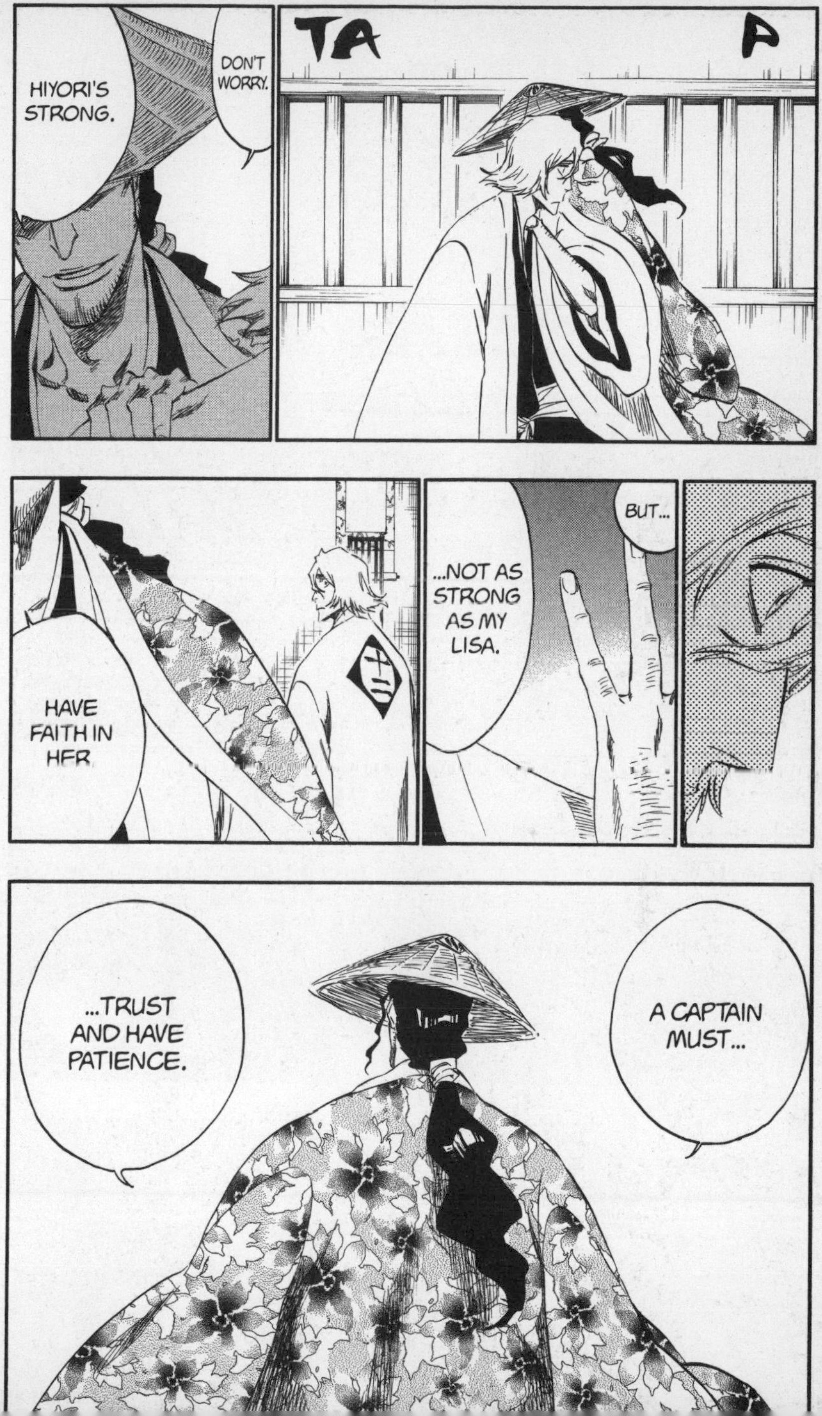
TA P
DON'T WORRY.
HIYORI'S STRONG.
BUT...
...NOT AS STRONG AS MY LISA.
HAVE FAITH IN HER.
A CAPTAIN MUST...
...TRUST AND HAVE PATIENCE.

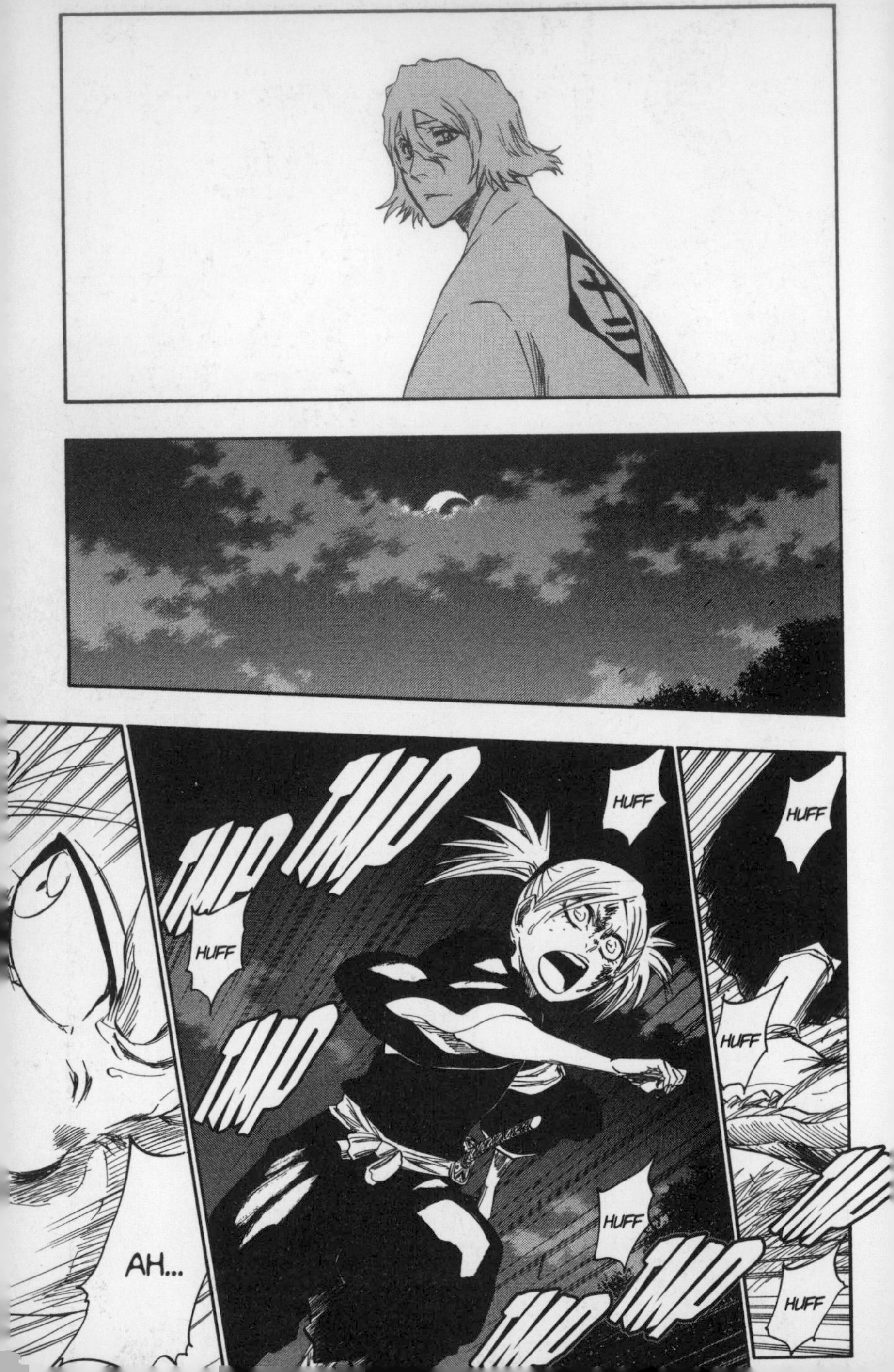
HUFF
HUFF
HUFF
HUFF
TMP TMP
HUFF
TMP
HUFF
TMP TMP
AH...

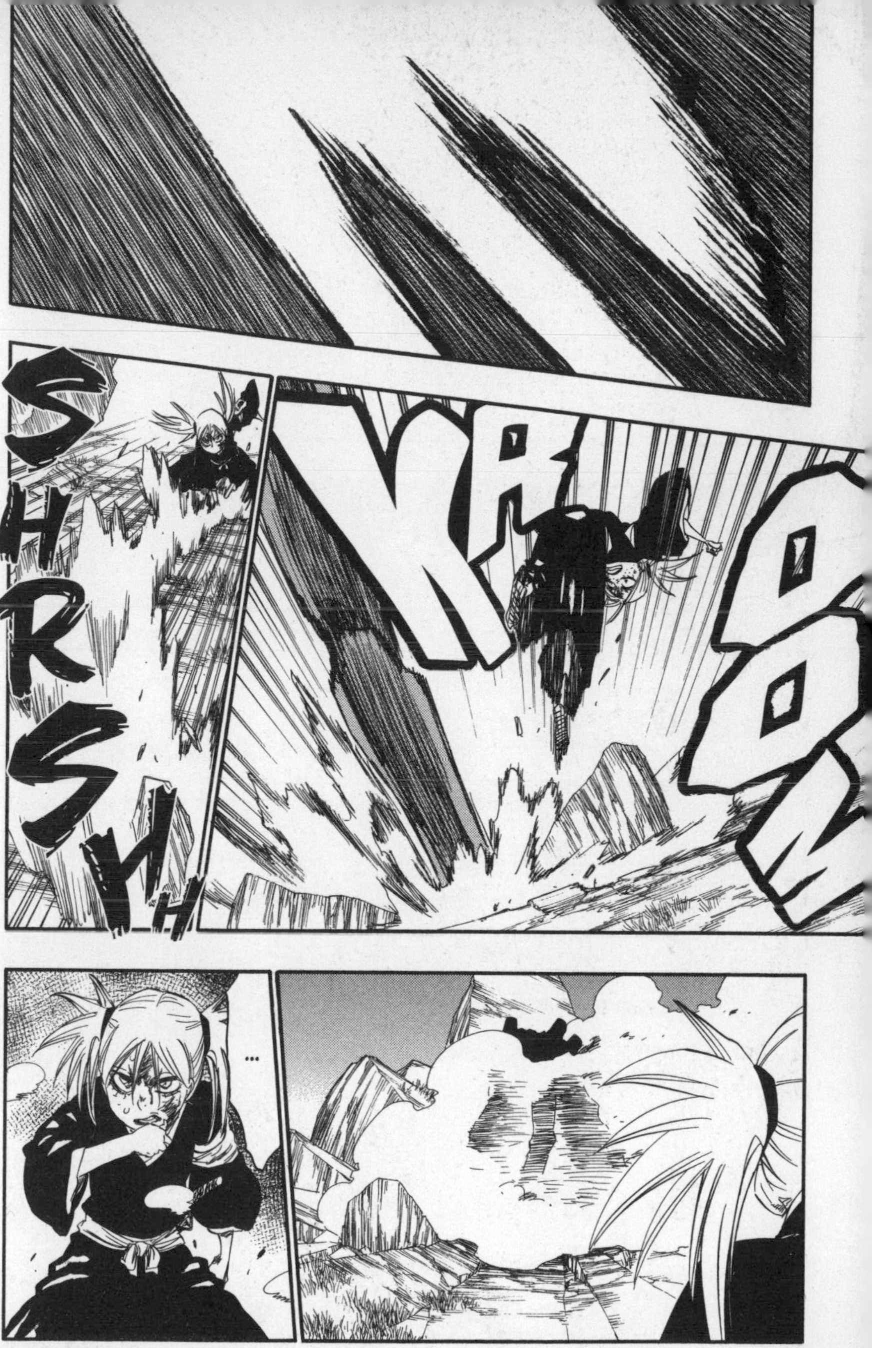
KRAOOM
SHRSHH
...

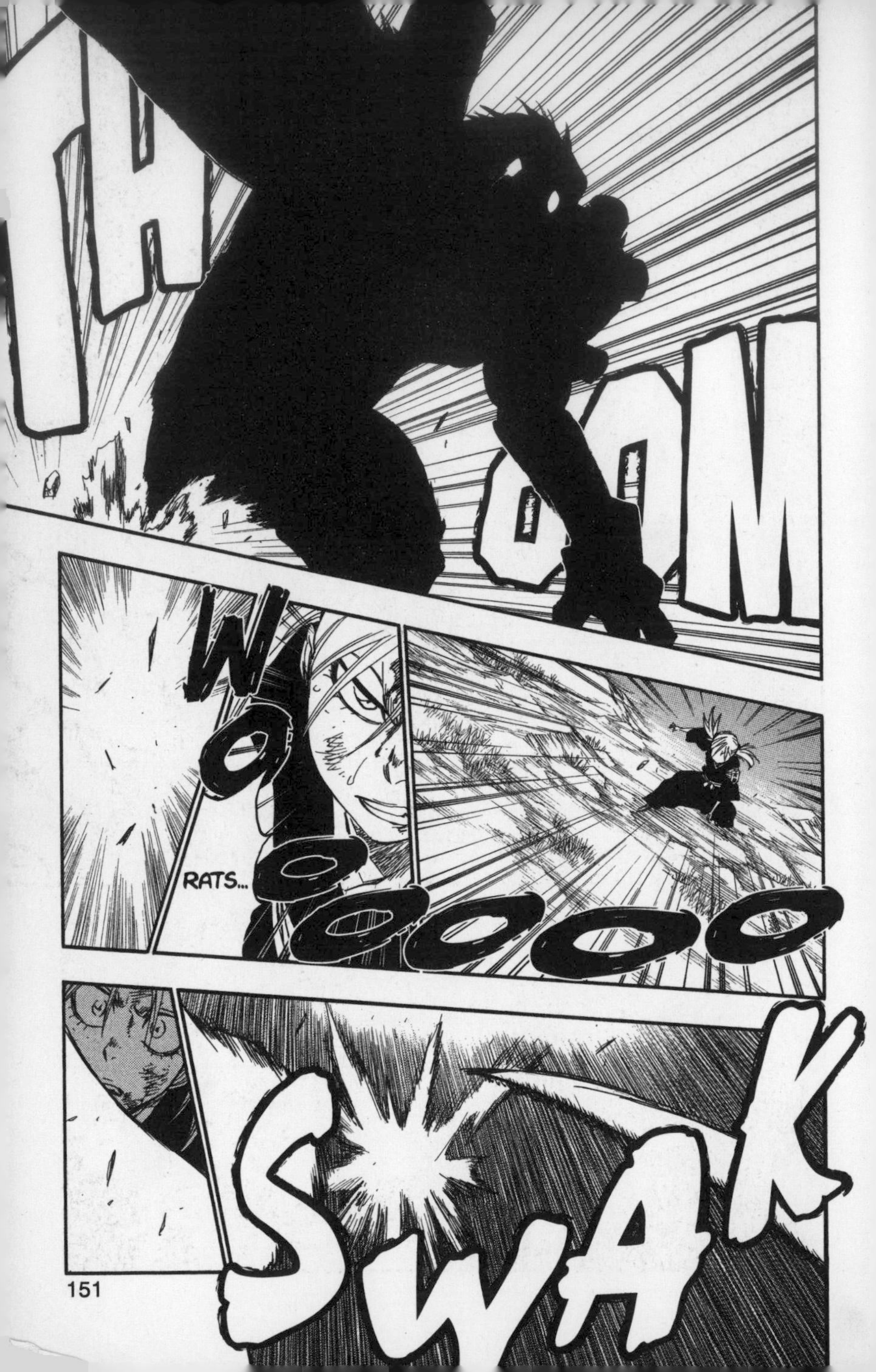
THOOM
WOOOOOOOO
RATS...
SWAK

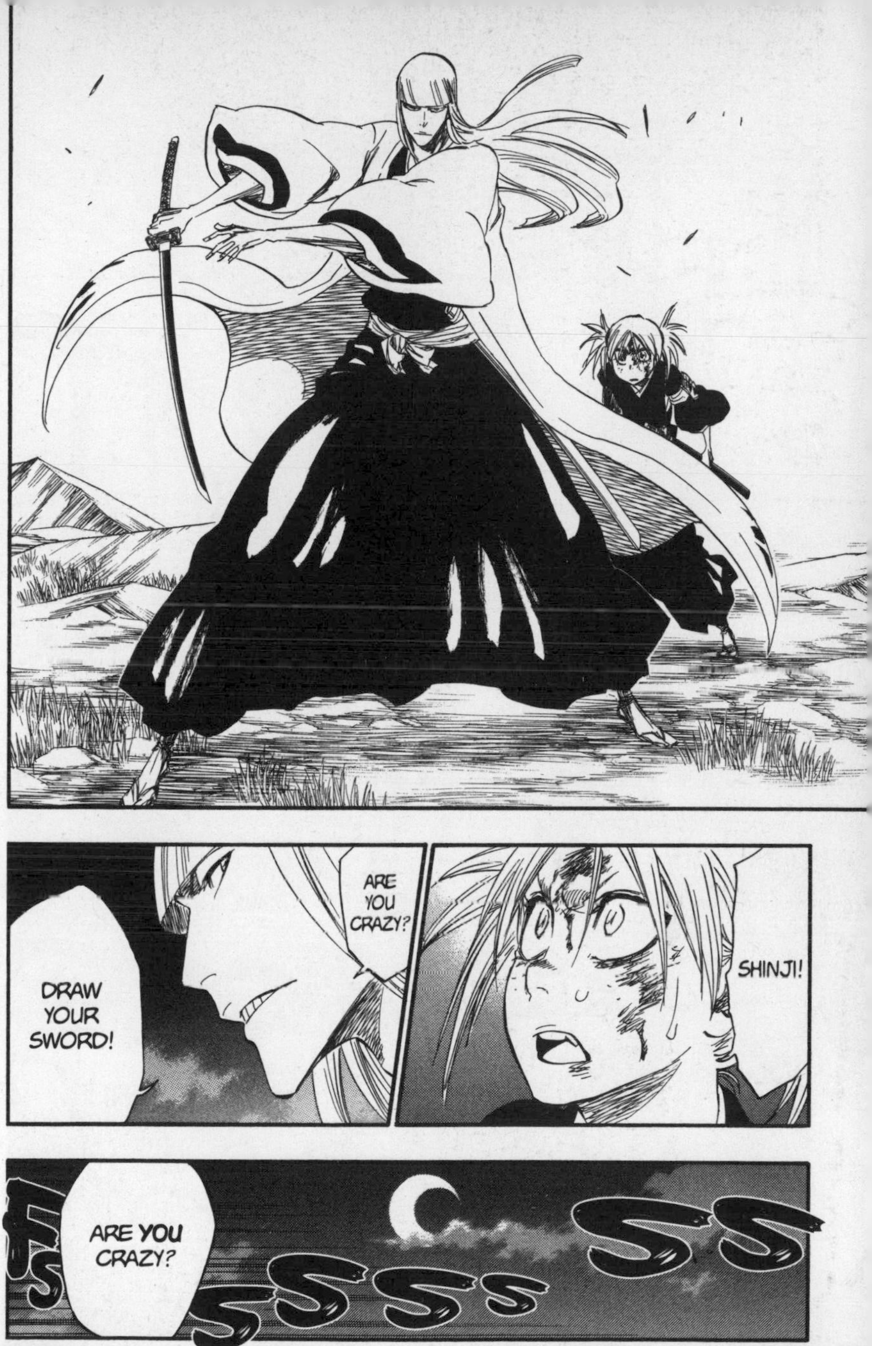
SHINJI!
ARE YOU CRAZY?
DRAW YOUR SWORD!
ARE YOU CRAZY?

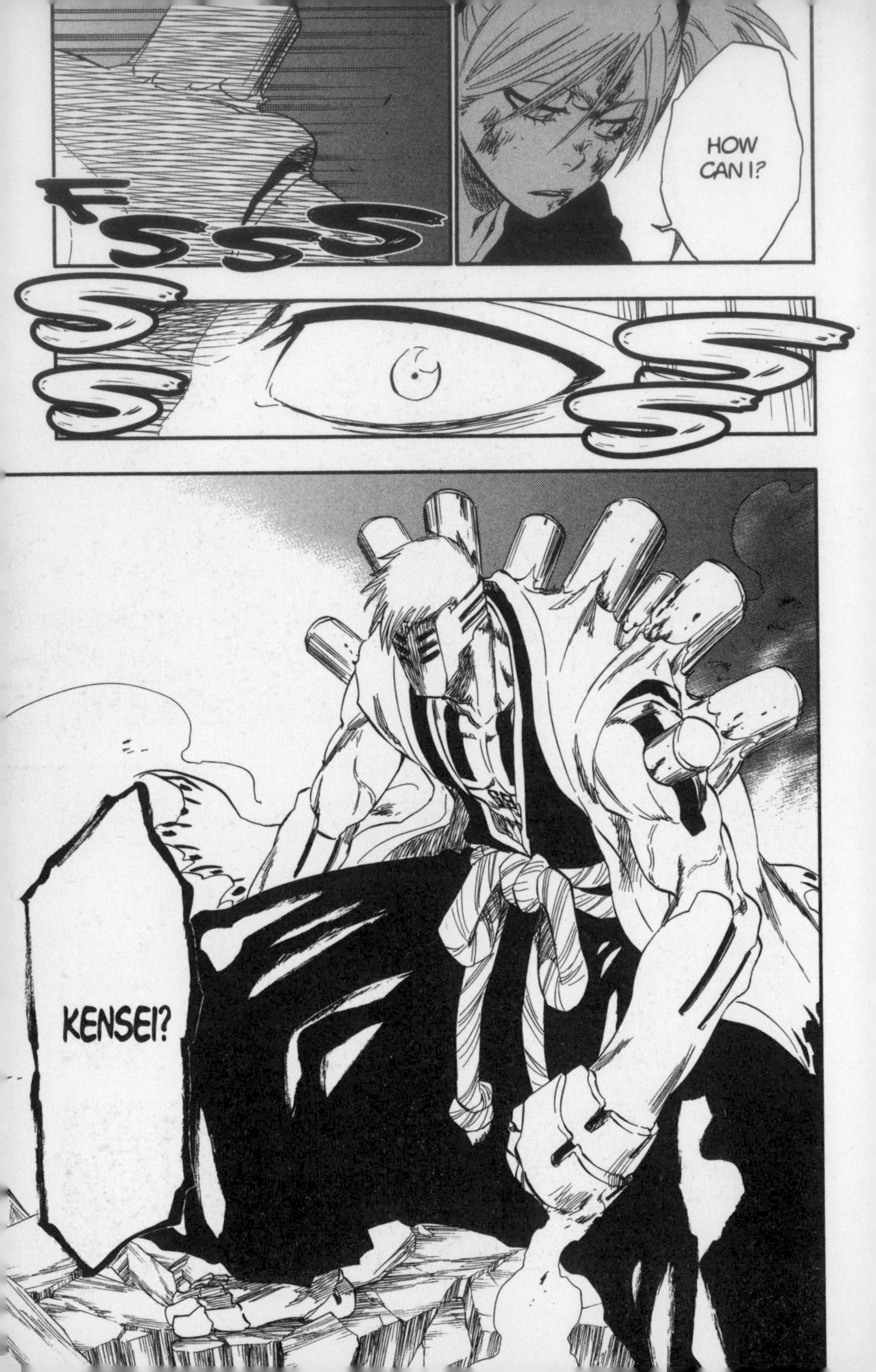
HOW CAN I?
FSSSS
SSSS
SSS
KENSEI?

HEIZÔ KASAKI
THIRD SEAT,
NINTH COMPANY LEADER,
MUGURUMA COMMANDO UNIT

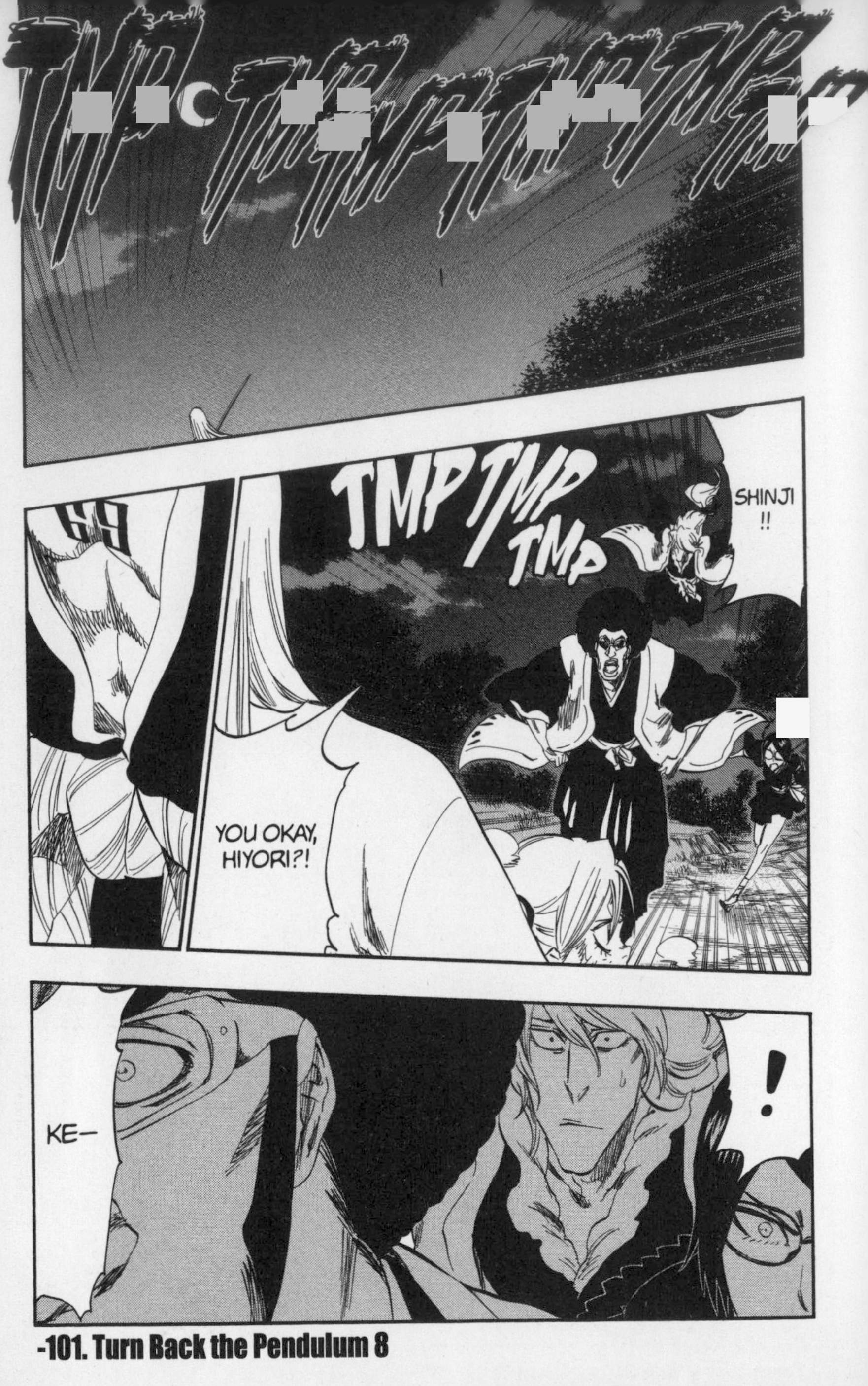
TMP TMP TMP TMP
SHINJI !!
YOU OKAY, HIYORI?!
!
KE—

-101. Turn Back the Pendulum 8

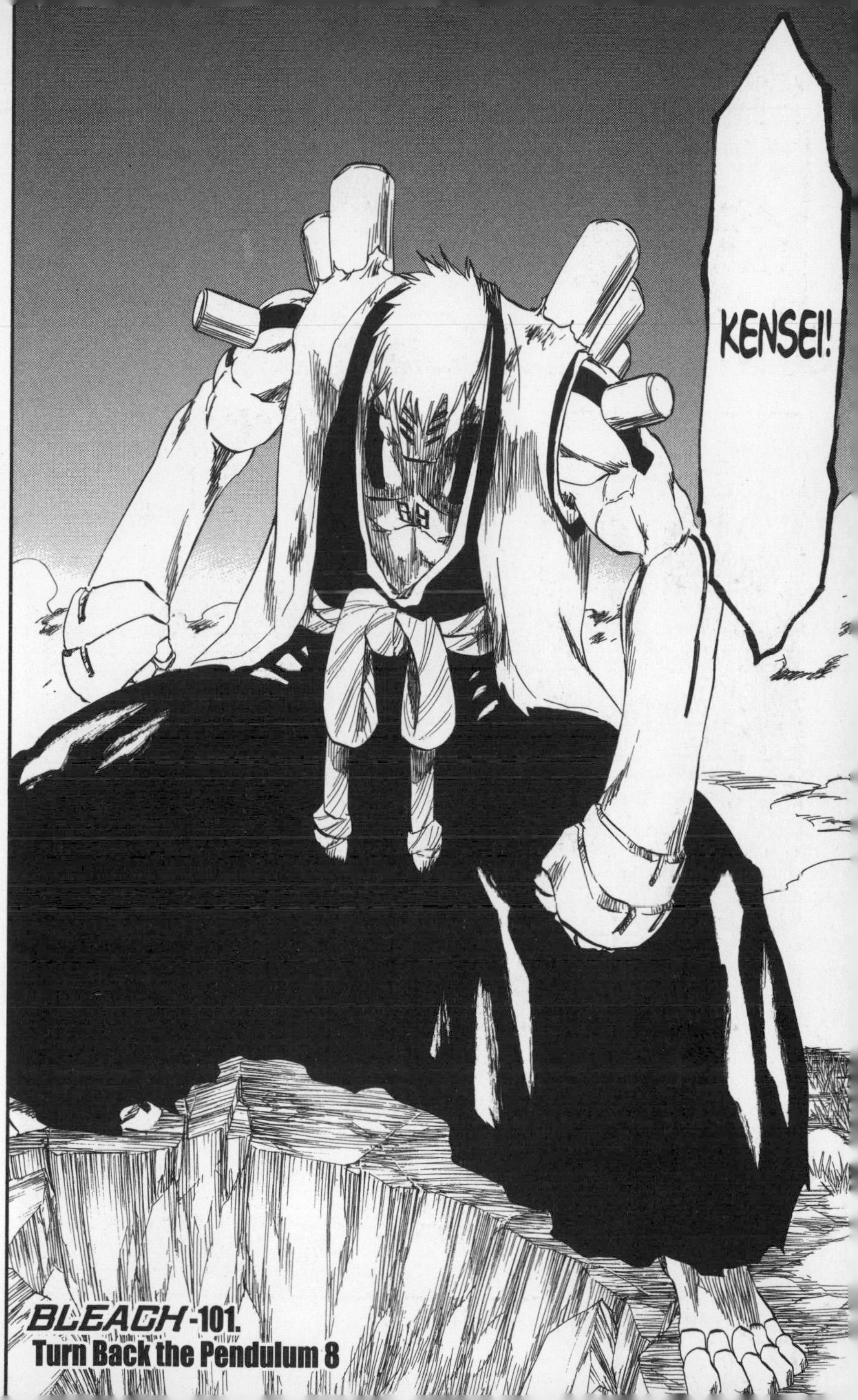
KENSEI!
BLEACH -101.
Turn Back the Pendulum 8

READ THIS WAY

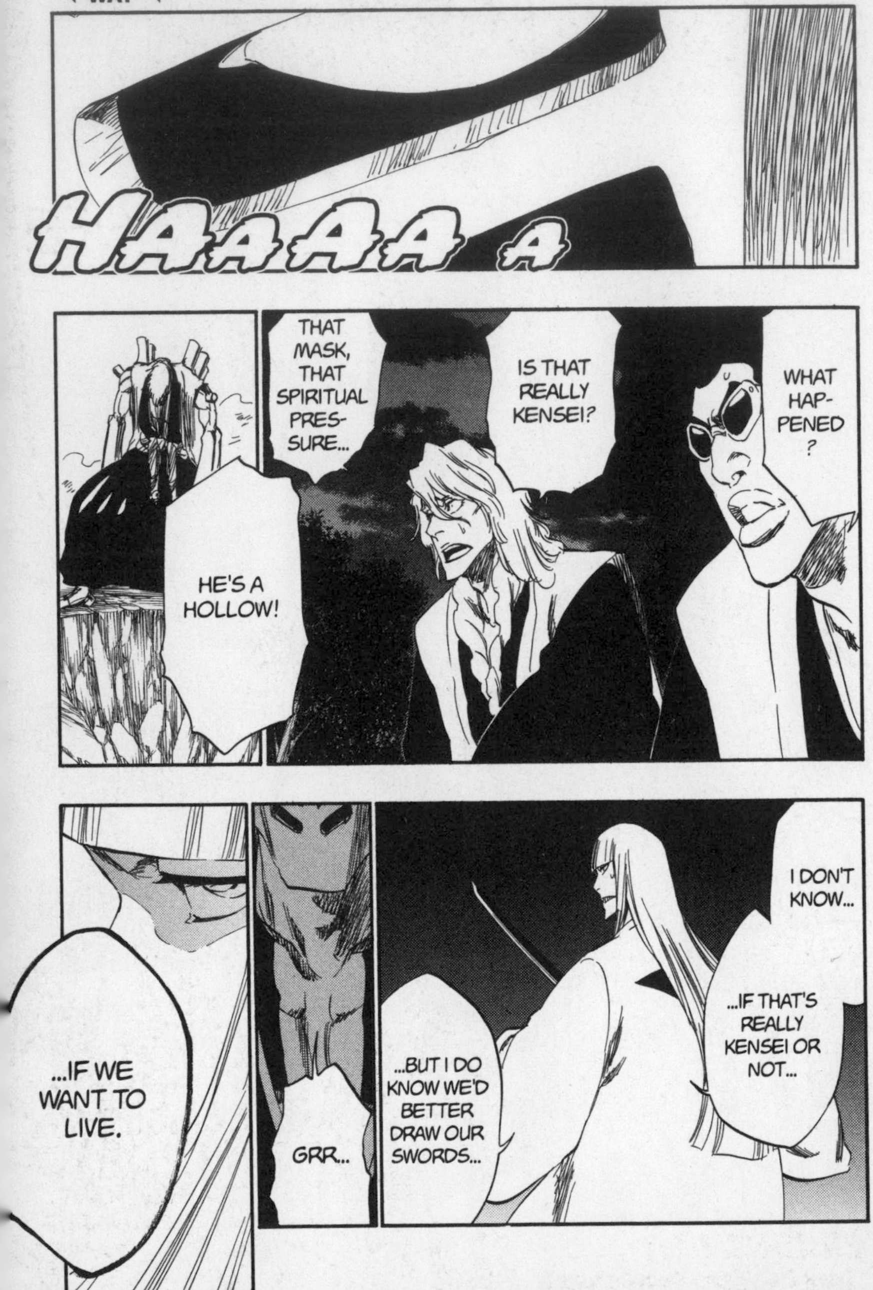
HAAAAA
WHAT HAPPENED?
IS THAT REALLY KENSEI?
THAT MASK, THAT SPIRITUAL PRESSURE...
HE'S A HOLLOW!
I DON'T KNOW...
...IF THAT'S REALLY KENSEI OR NOT...
...BUT I DO KNOW WE'D BETTER DRAW OUR SWORDS...
GRR...
...IF WE WANT TO LIVE.

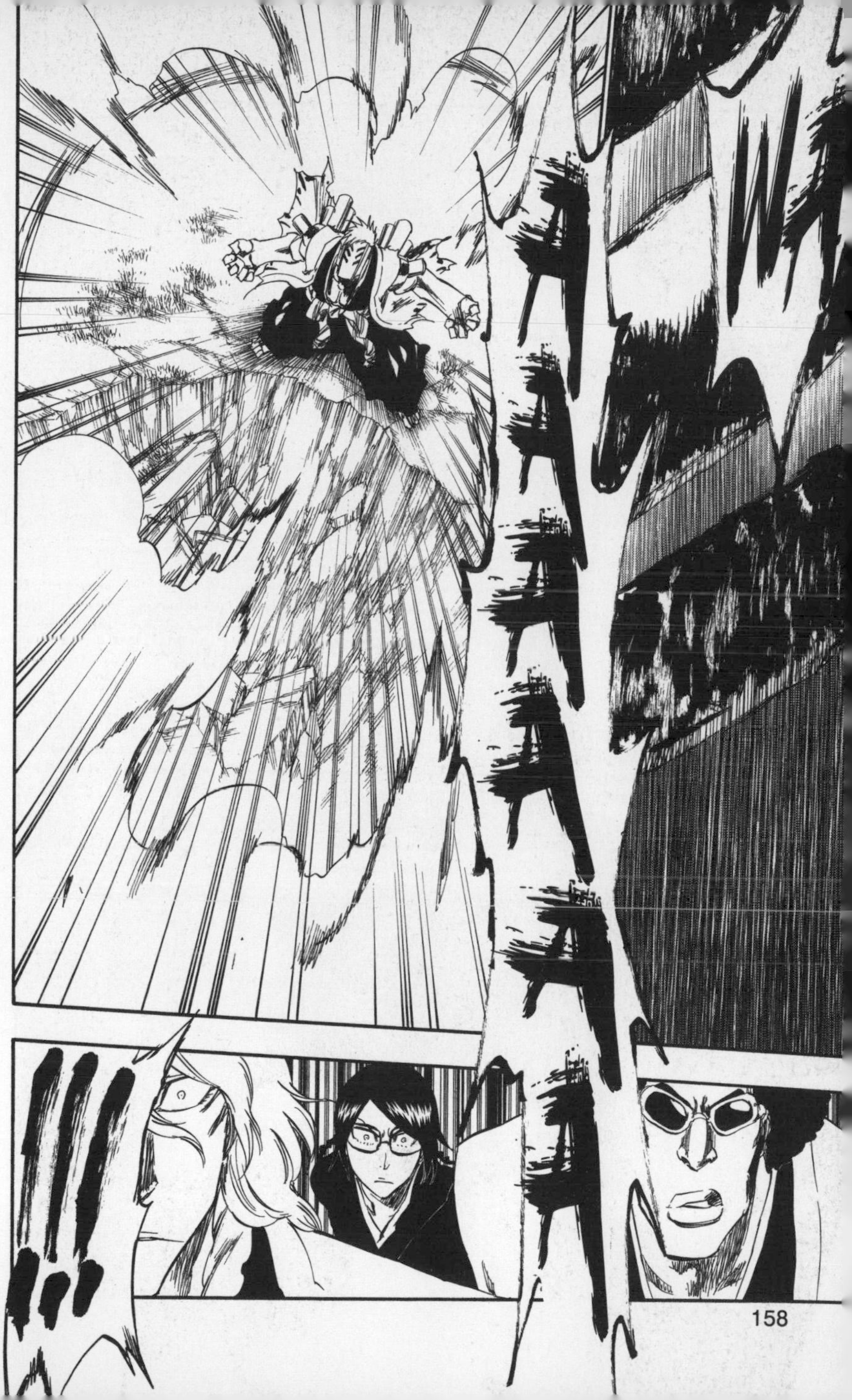
!!!

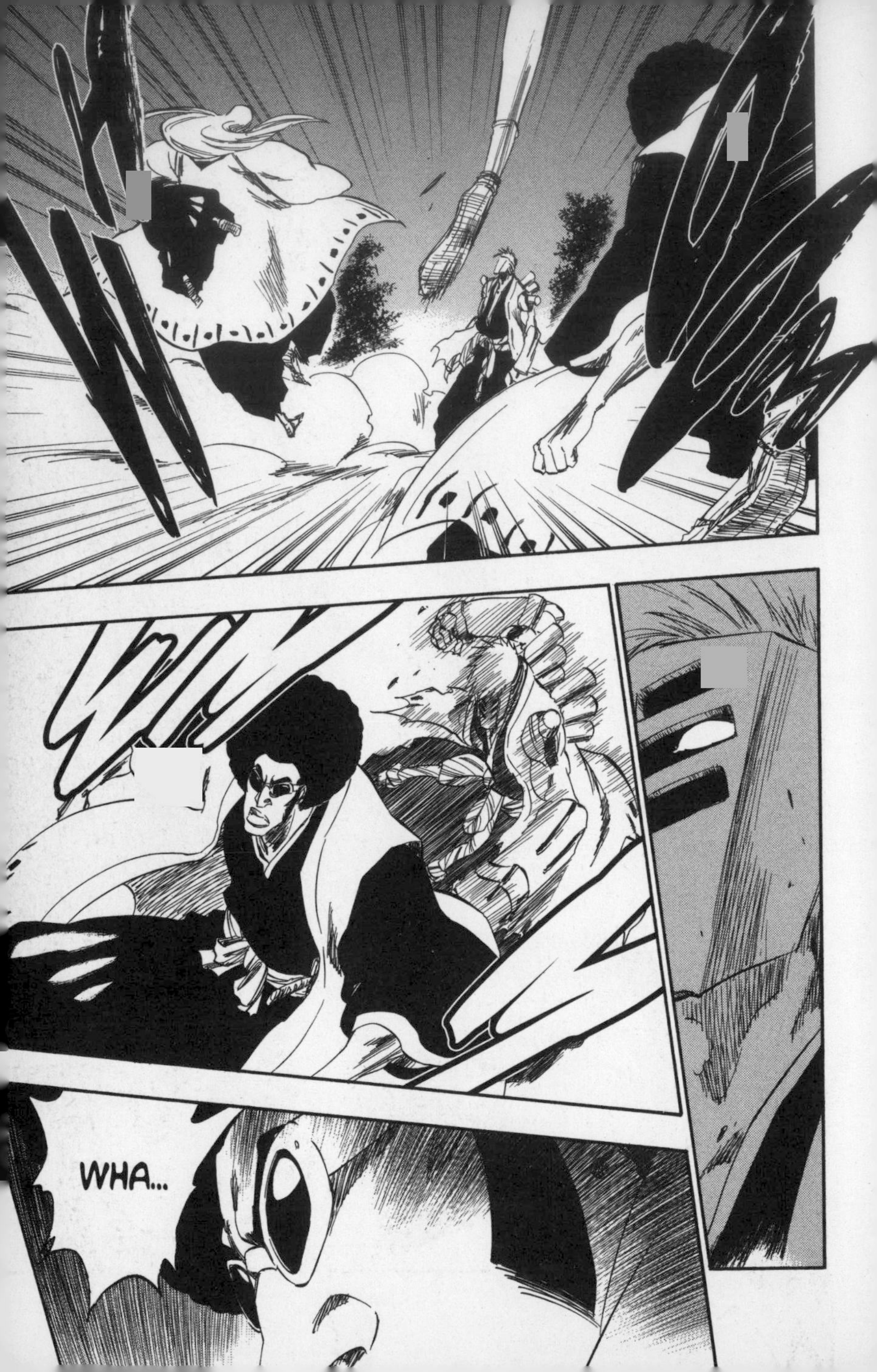
WHA...

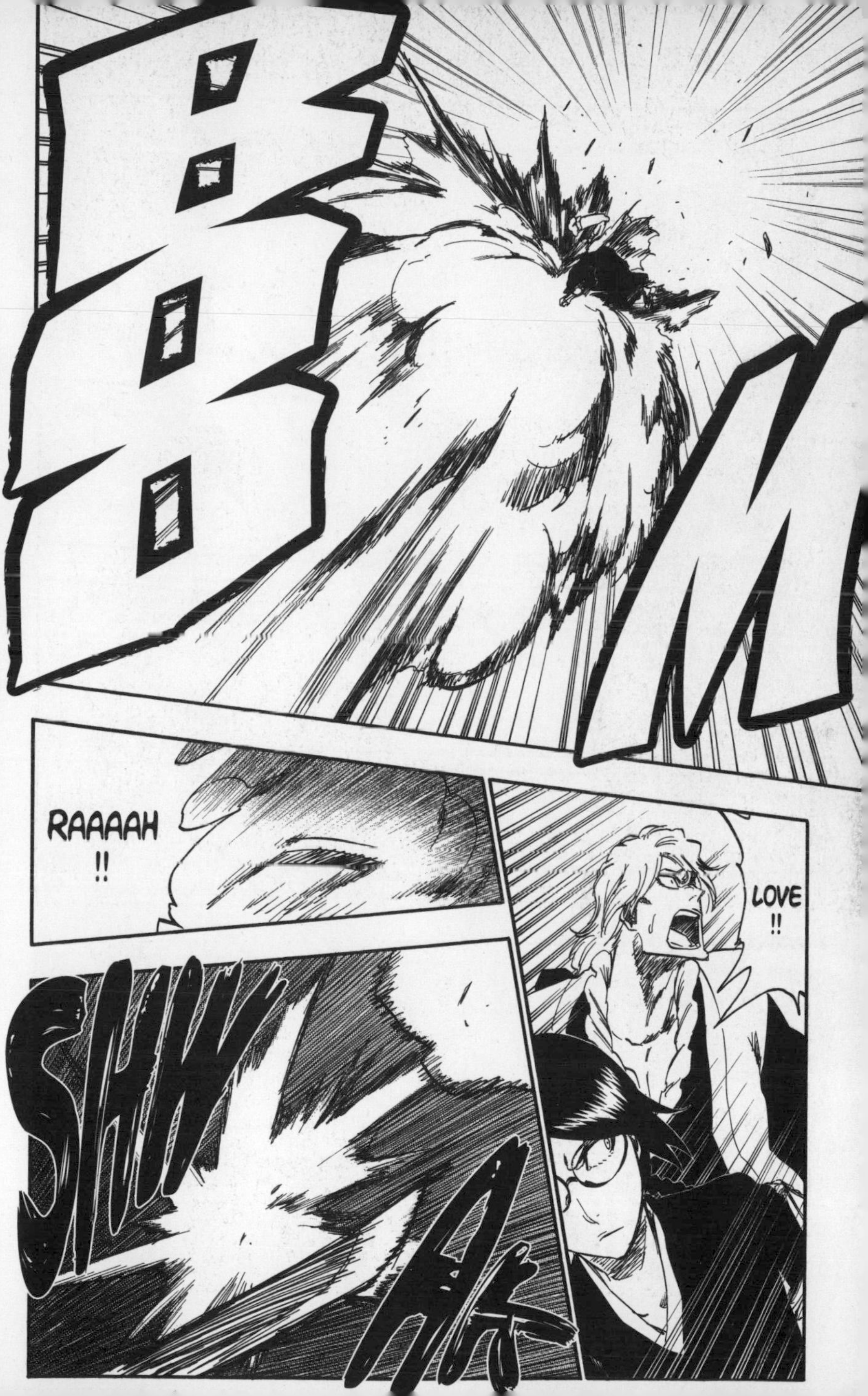
LOVE
!!
RAAAAH
!!

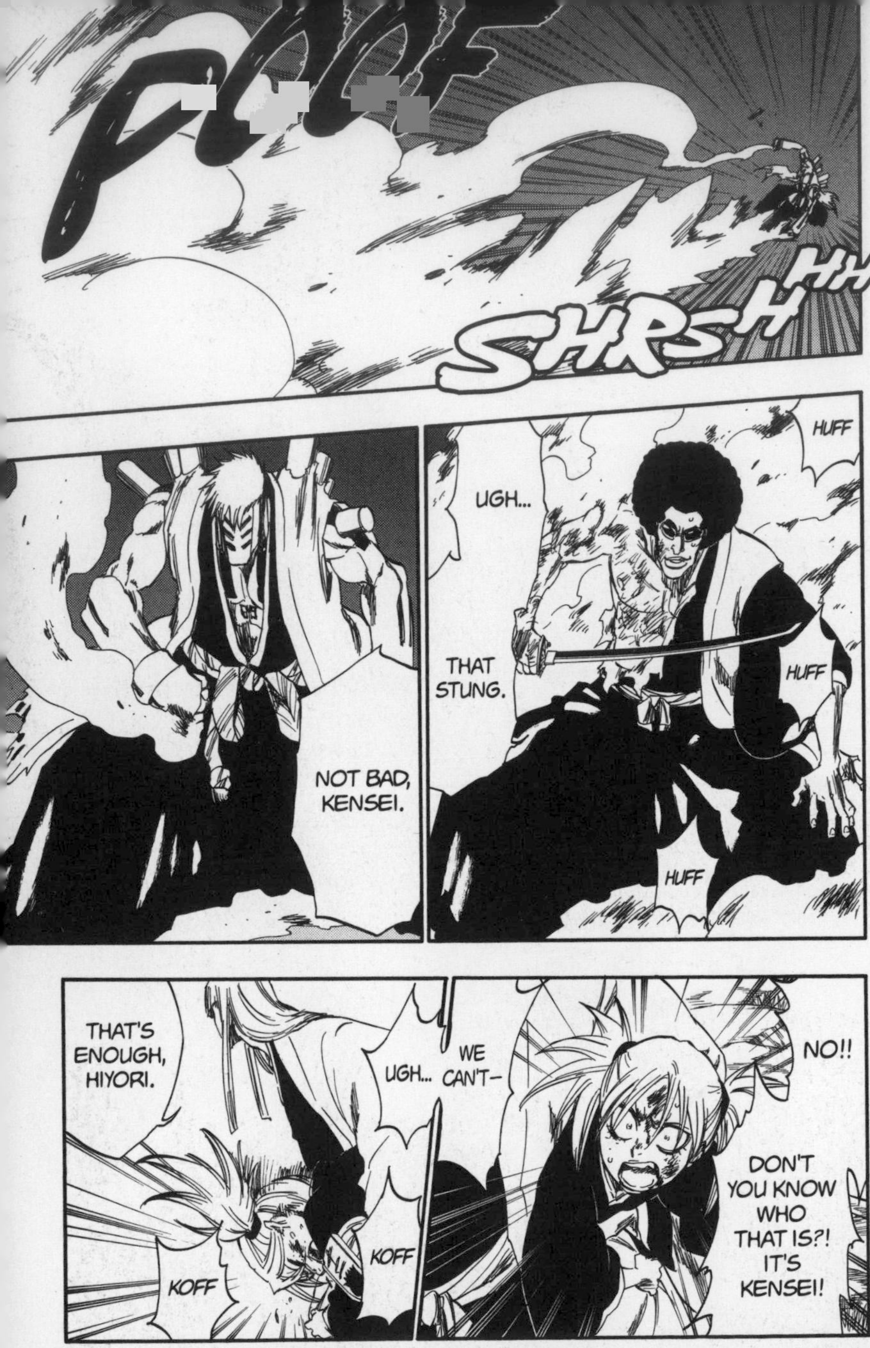
POOF
SHRSHHH
HUFF
UGH...
THAT STUNG.
HUFF
HUFF
NOT BAD, KENSEI.
NO!!
DON'T YOU KNOW WHO THAT IS?! IT'S KENSEI!
WE CAN'T-
UGH...
THAT'S ENOUGH, HIYORI.
KOFF
KOFF

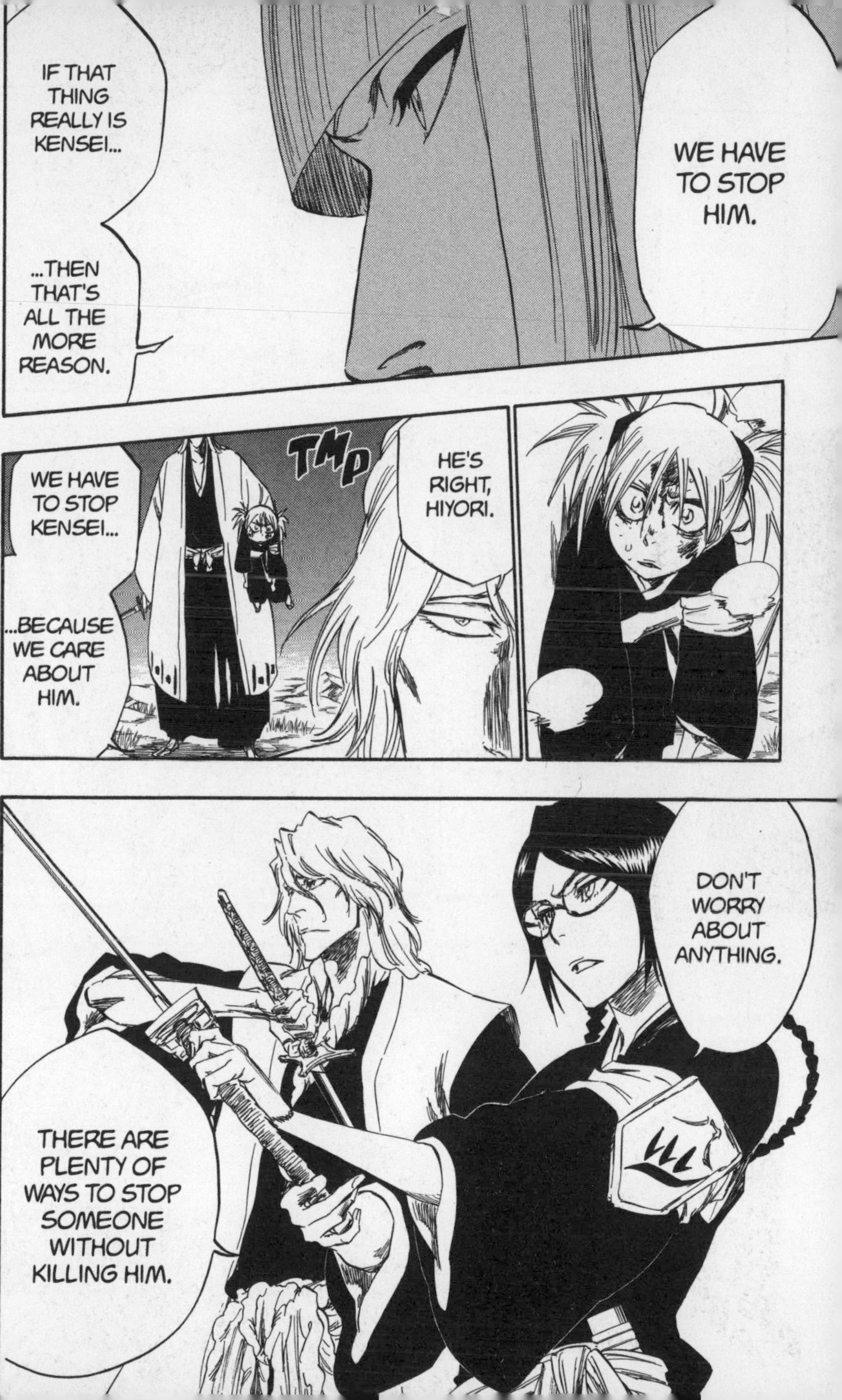
WE HAVE TO STOP HIM.
IF THAT THING REALLY IS KENSEI...
...THEN THAT'S ALL THE MORE REASON.
HE'S RIGHT, HIYORI.
TMP
WE HAVE TO STOP KENSEI...
...BECAUSE WE CARE ABOUT HIM.
DON'T WORRY ABOUT ANYTHING.
THERE ARE PLENTY OF WAYS TO STOP SOMEONE WITHOUT KILLING HIM.

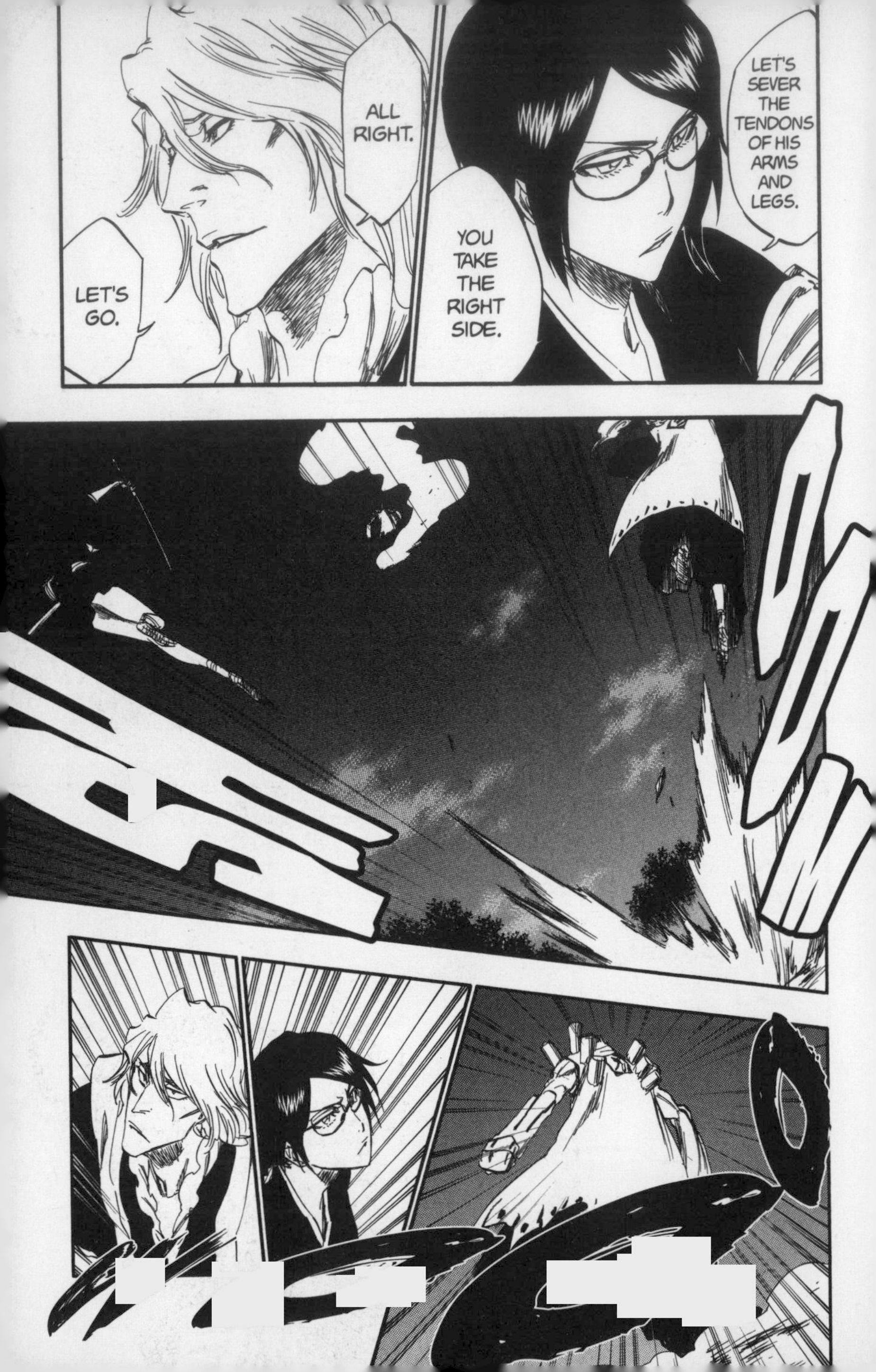
LET'S SEVER THE TENDONS OF HIS ARMS AND LEGS.
YOU TAKE THE RIGHT SIDE.
ALL RIGHT.
LET'S GO.

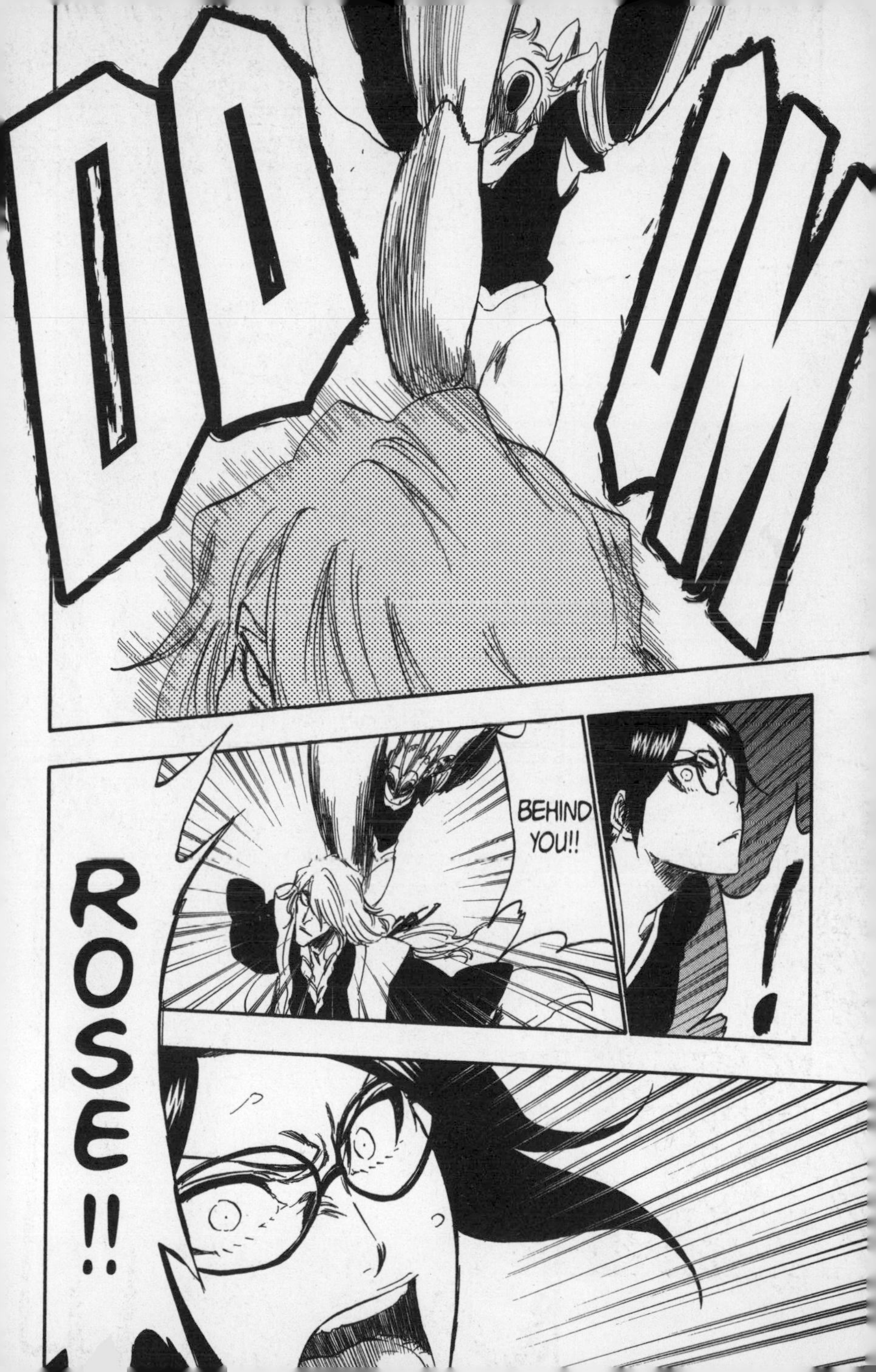
!
BEHIND YOU!!
ROSE!!

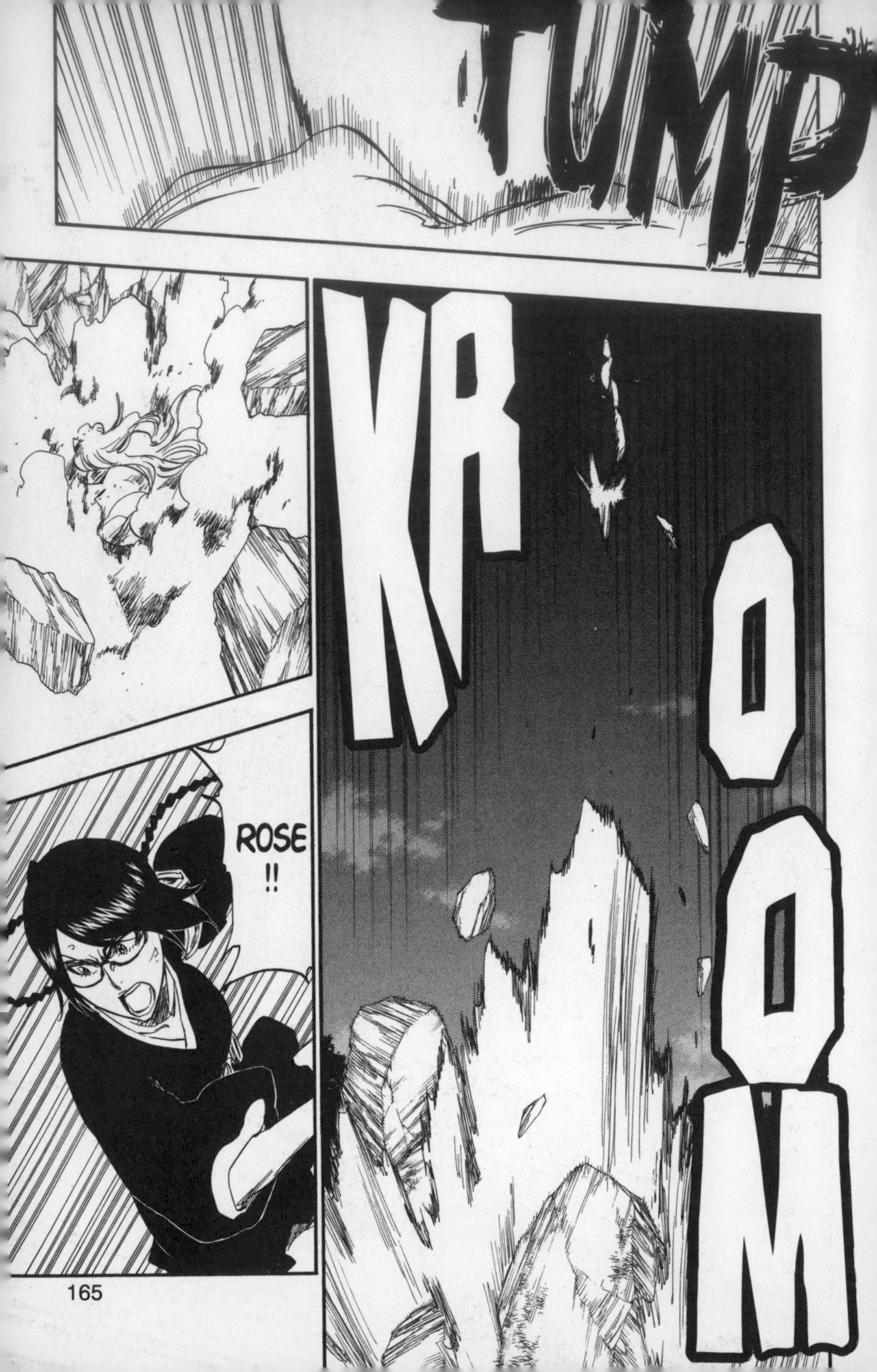
TUMP
KRAOOOM
ROSE !!

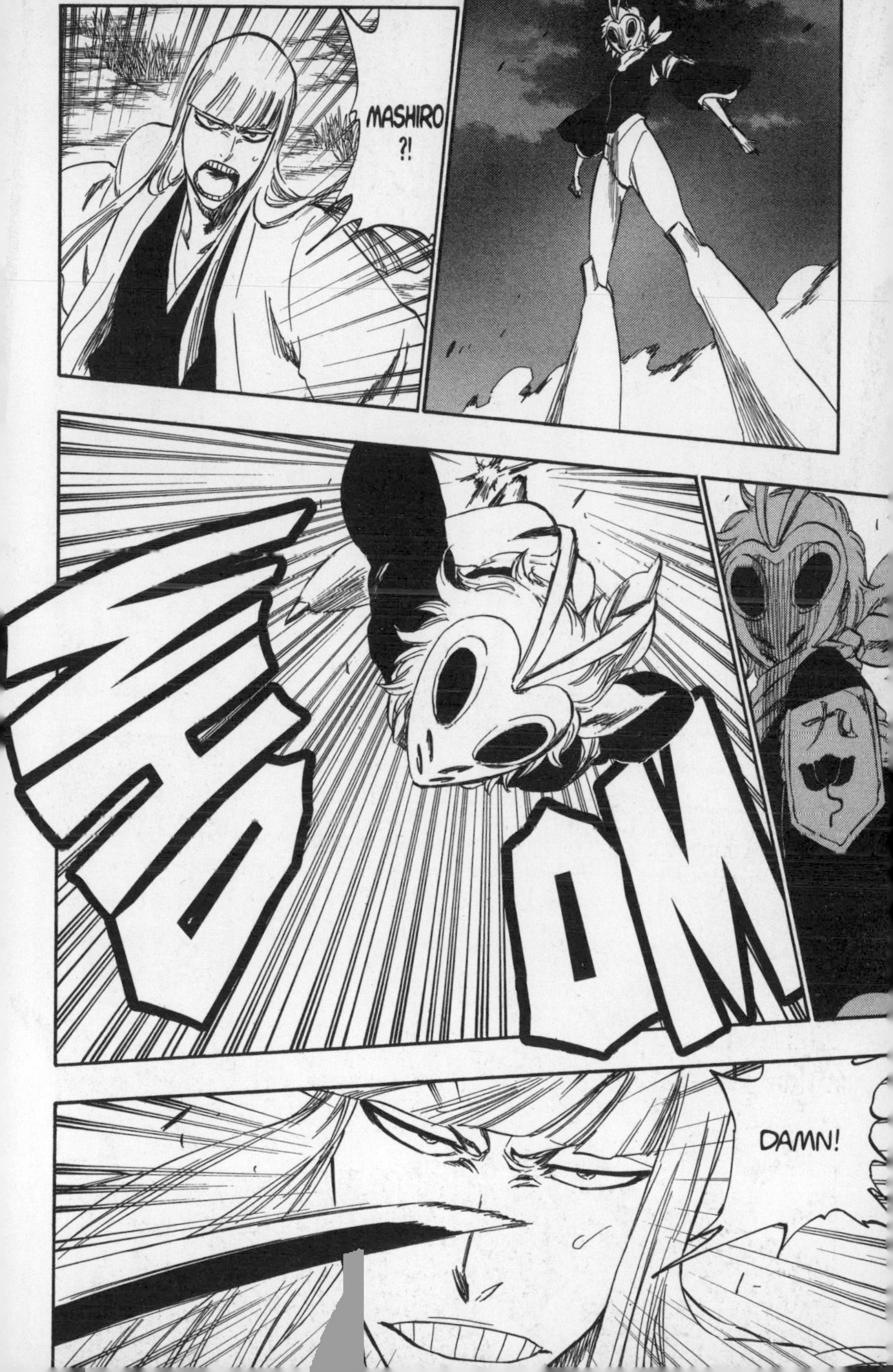
MASHIRO ?!
DAMN!

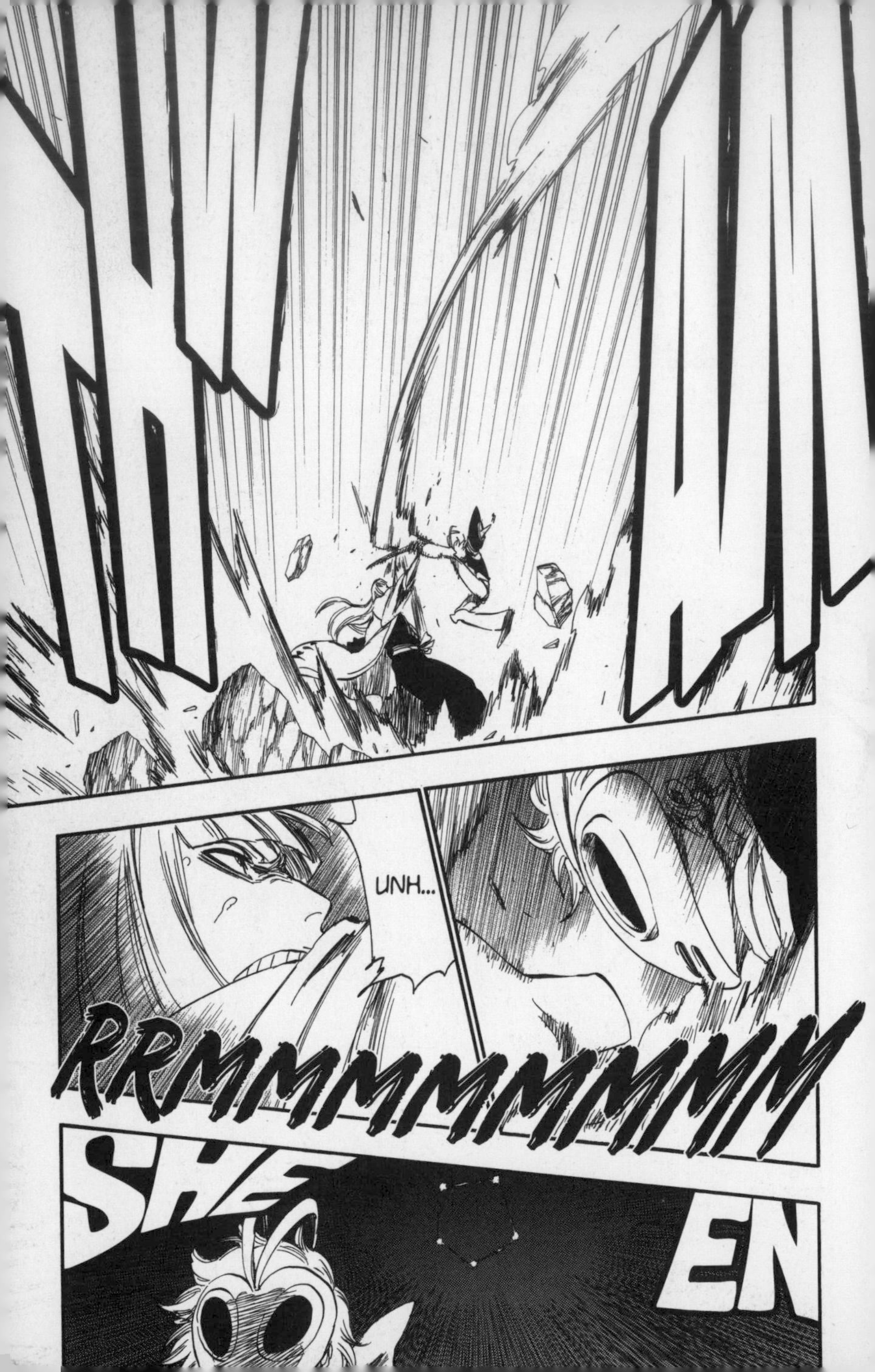
UNH...
RRMMMMMMMM
SHE
EN

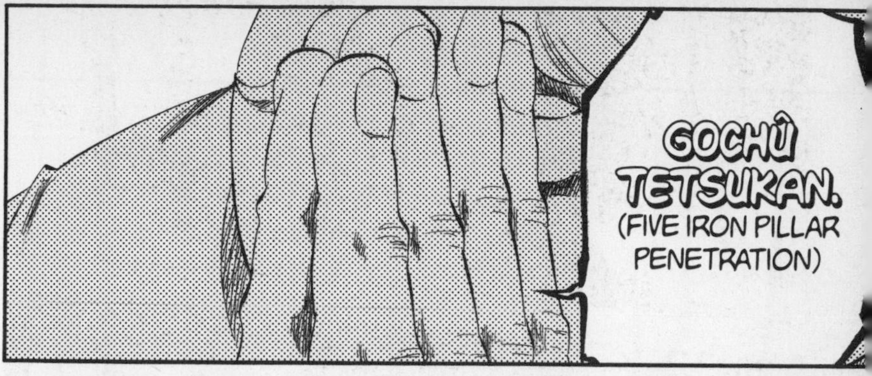
GOCHÛ TETSUKAN.
(FIVE IRON PILLAR PENETRATION)
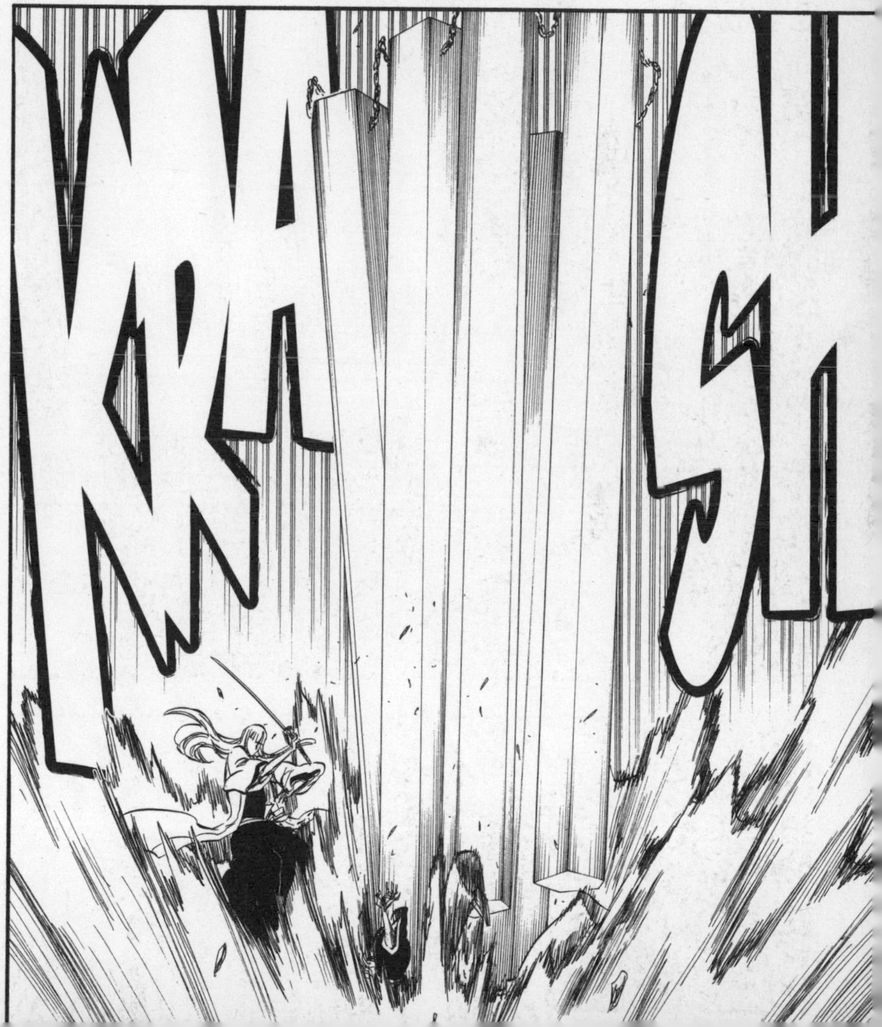

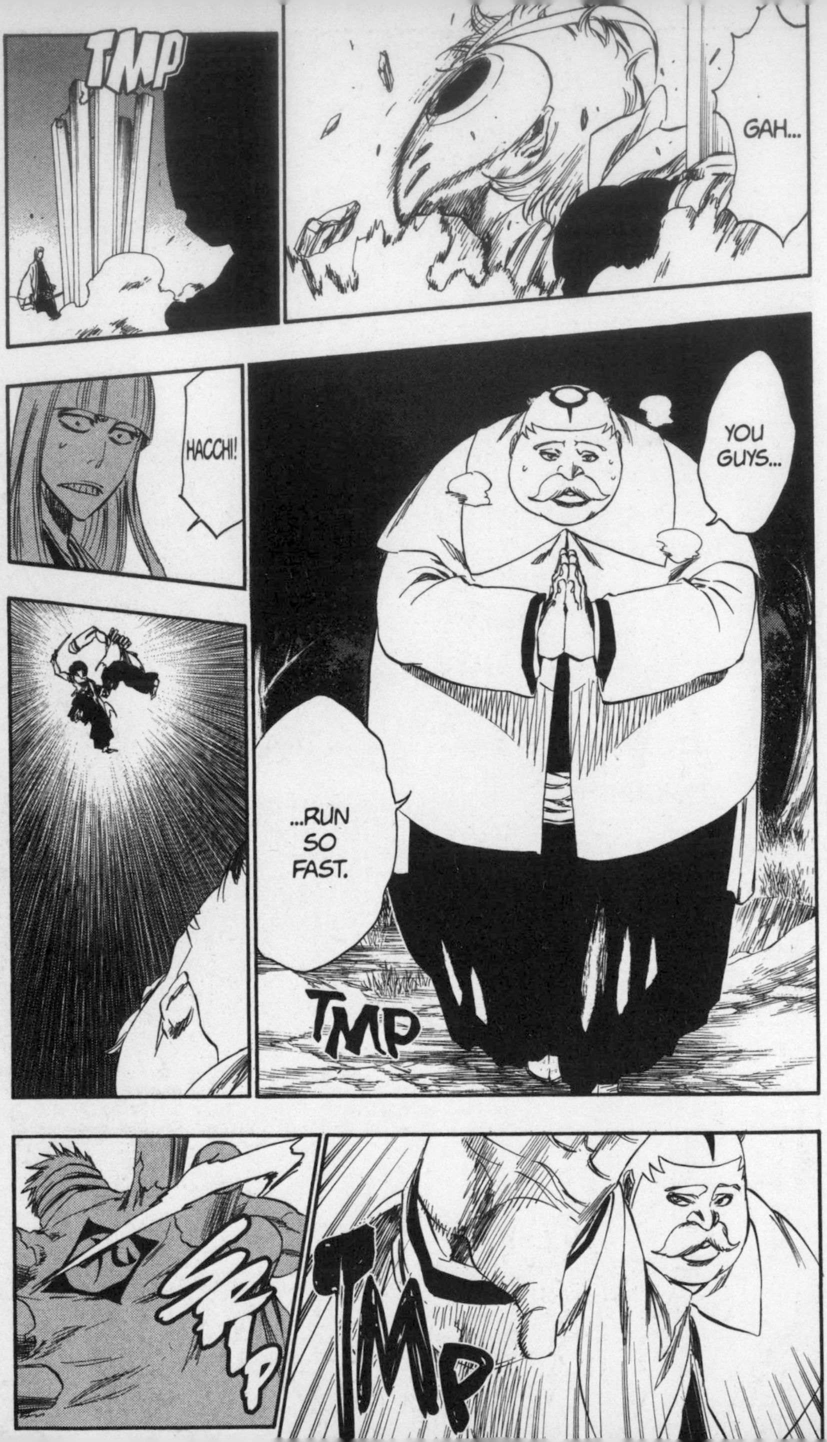
GAH...
TMP
YOU GUYS...
...RUN SO FAST.
TMP
HACCHI!
TMP

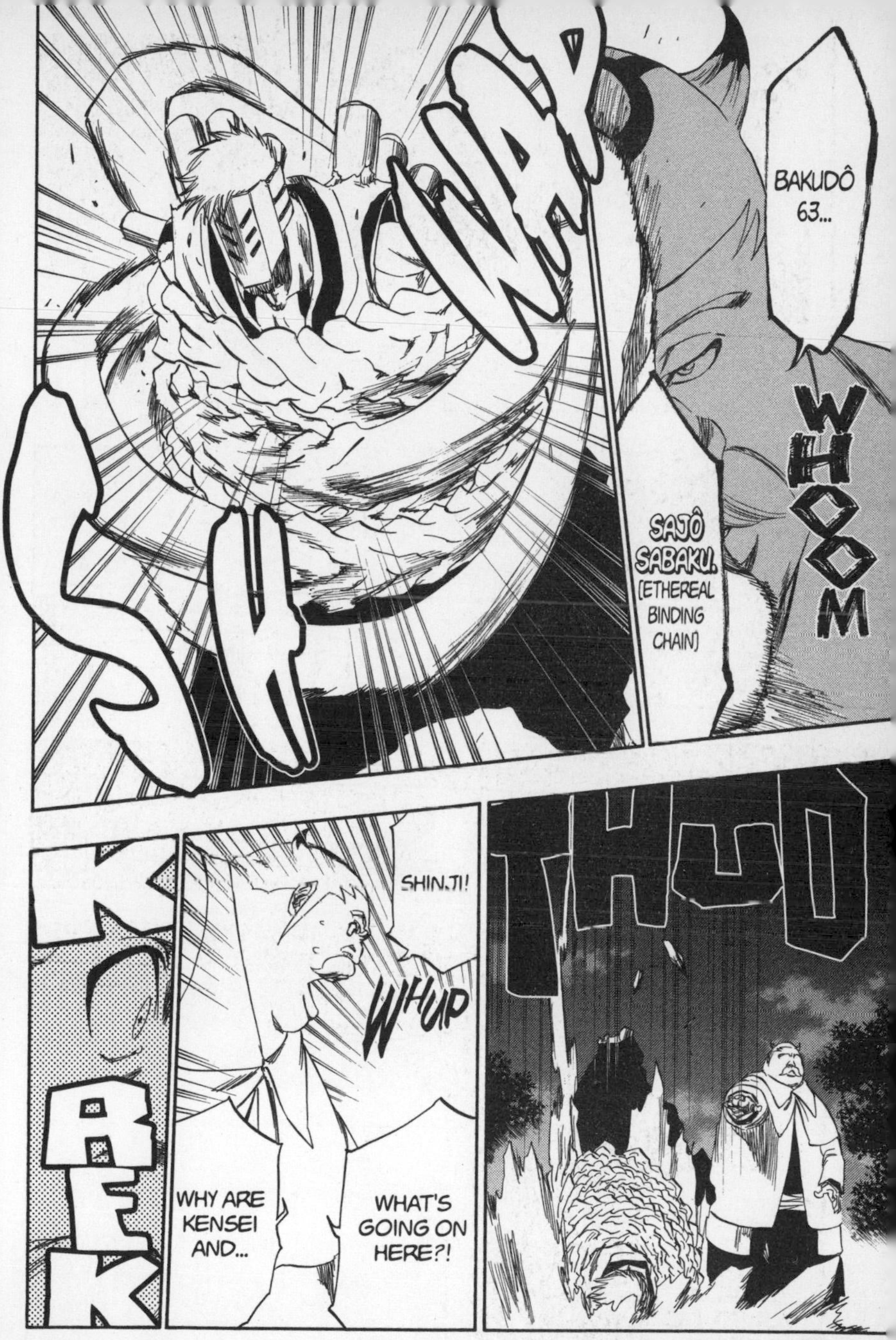
BAKUDÔ 63...
WHOOM
SAJÔ SABAKU.
[ETHEREAL BINDING CHAIN]
THUD
SHINJI!
WHUP
WHAT'S GOING ON HERE?!
WHY ARE KENSEI AND...

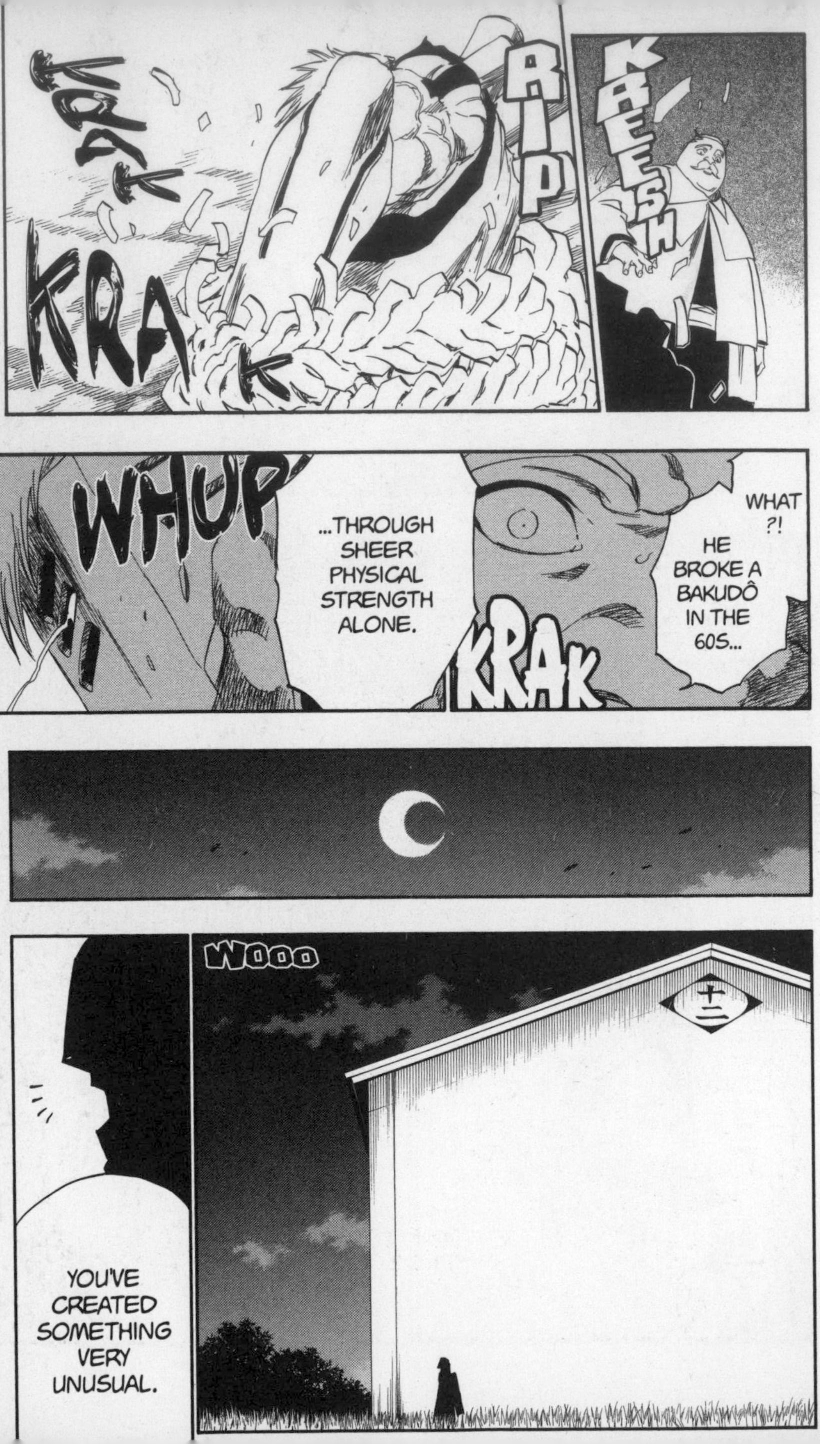
KREESH
RIP
KRA
WHAT?!
HE BROKE A BAKUDÔ IN THE 60S...
KRAK
...THROUGH SHEER PHYSICAL STRENGTH ALONE.
WHUP
WOOO
YOU'VE CREATED SOMETHING VERY UNUSUAL.

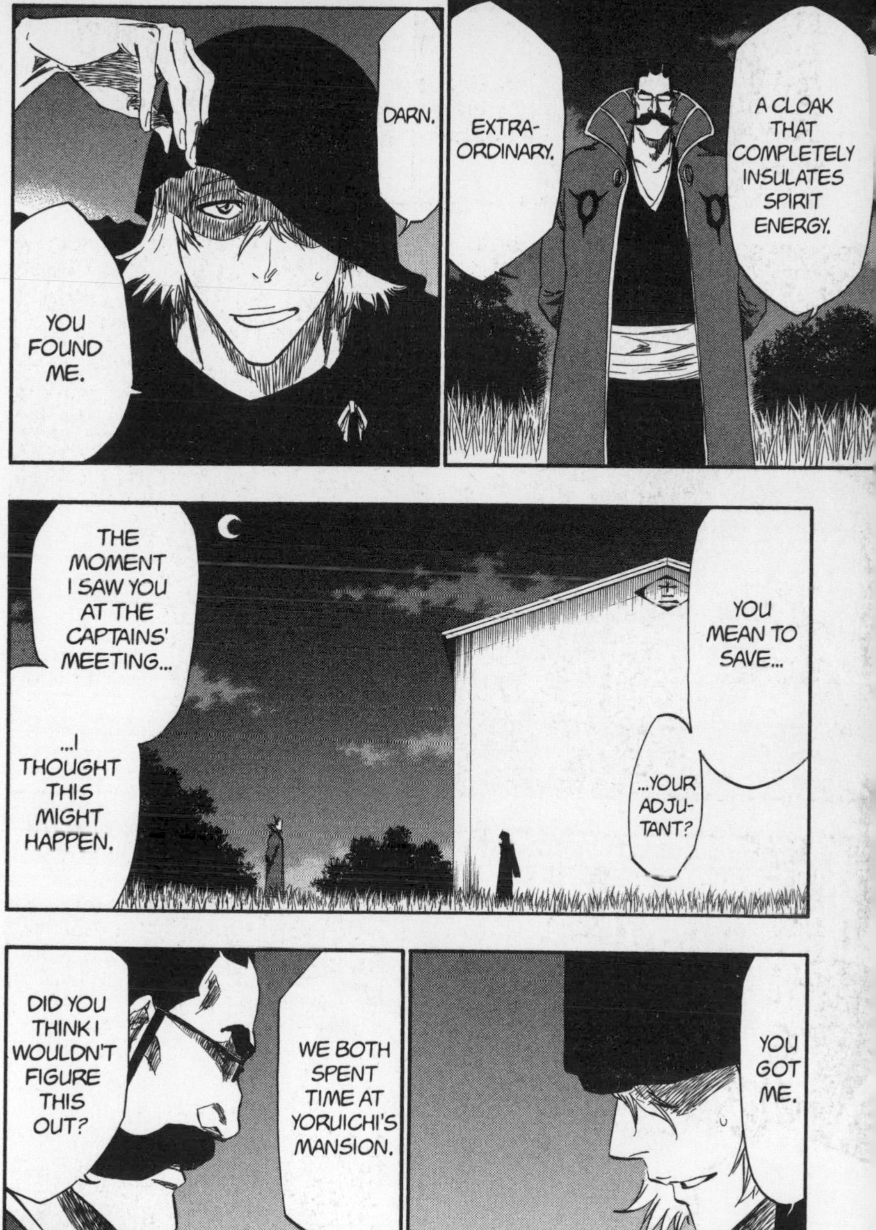
A CLOAK THAT COMPLETELY INSULATES SPIRIT ENERGY.
EXTRA-ORDINARY.
DARN.
YOU FOUND ME.
YOU MEAN TO SAVE...
...YOUR ADJUTANT?
THE MOMENT I SAW YOU AT THE CAPTAINS' MEETING...
...I THOUGHT THIS MIGHT HAPPEN.
YOU GOT ME.
DID YOU THINK I WOULDN'T FIGURE THIS OUT?
WE BOTH SPENT TIME AT YORUICHI'S MANSION.

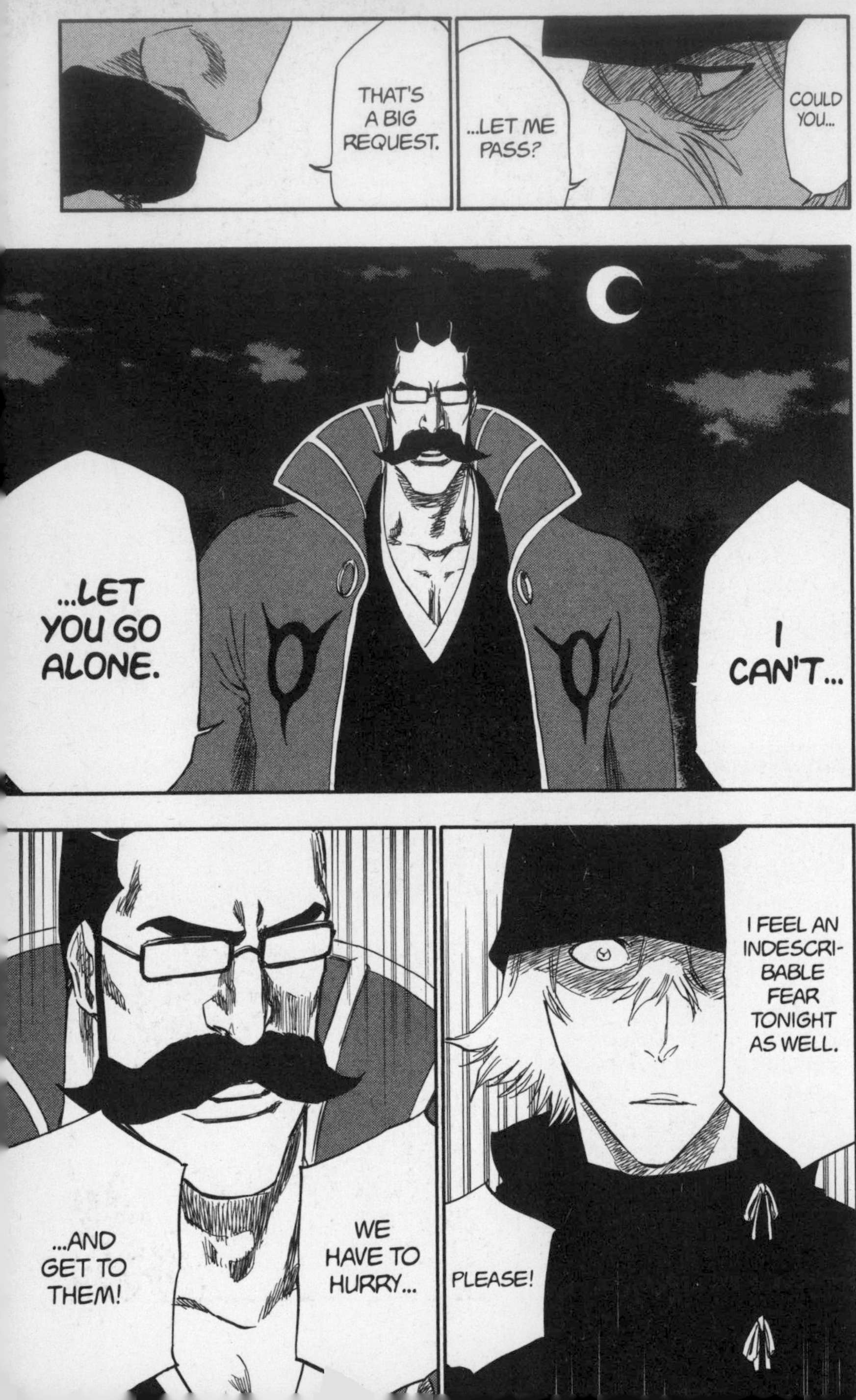
COULD YOU...
...LET ME PASS?
THAT'S A BIG REQUEST.
I CAN'T...
...LET YOU GO ALONE.
I FEEL AN INDESCRI-BABLE FEAR TONIGHT AS WELL.
PLEASE!
WE HAVE TO HURRY...
...AND GET TO THEM!

SHINOBU EISHIMA
FOURTH SEAT, NINTH COMPANY
MUGURUMA COMMANDO UNIT

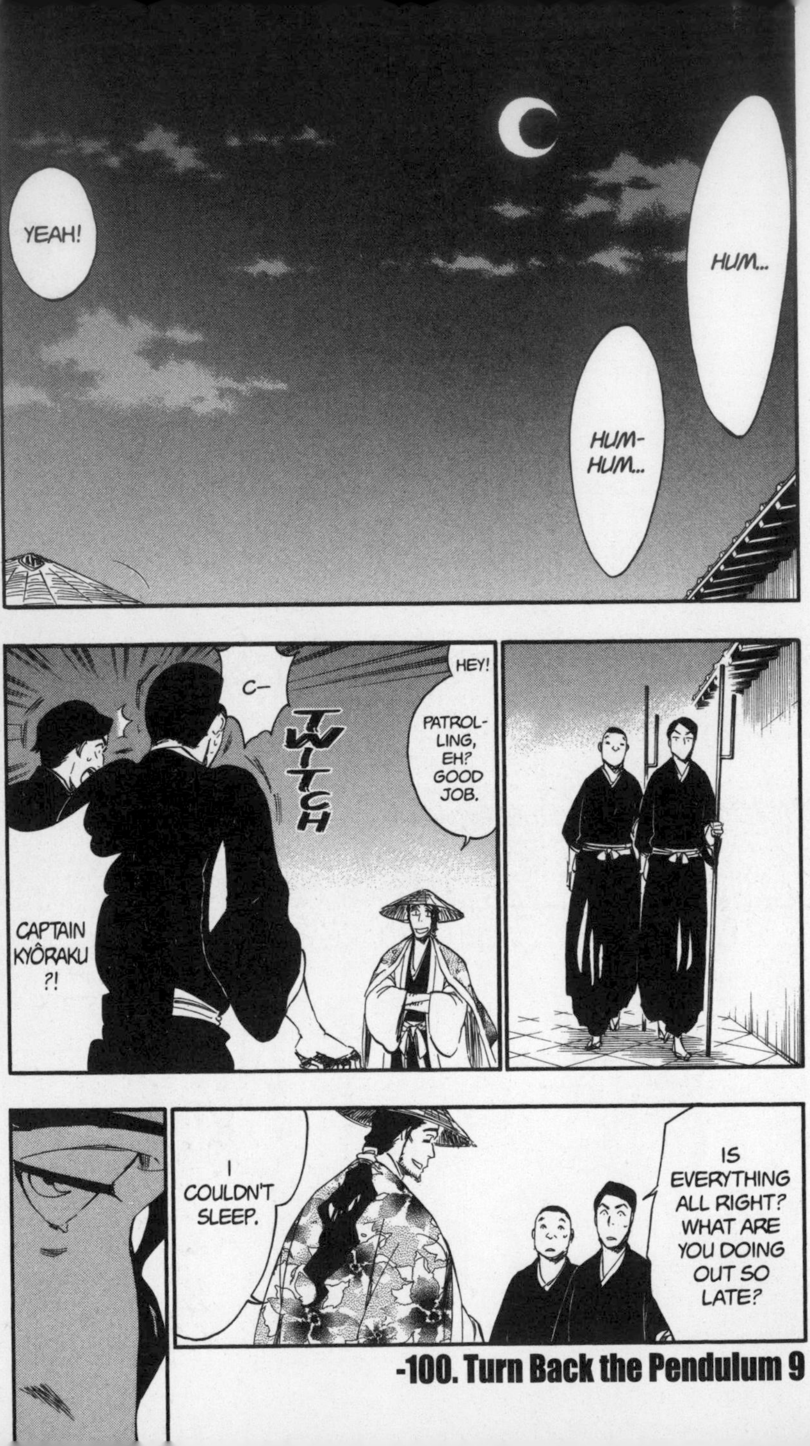
HUM...
HUM-HUM...
YEAH!
HEY!
PATROLLING, EH? GOOD JOB.
TWITCH
C—
CAPTAIN KYÔRAKU?!
IS EVERYTHING ALL RIGHT? WHAT ARE YOU DOING OUT SO LATE?
I COULDN'T SLEEP.

-100. Turn Back the Pendulum 9

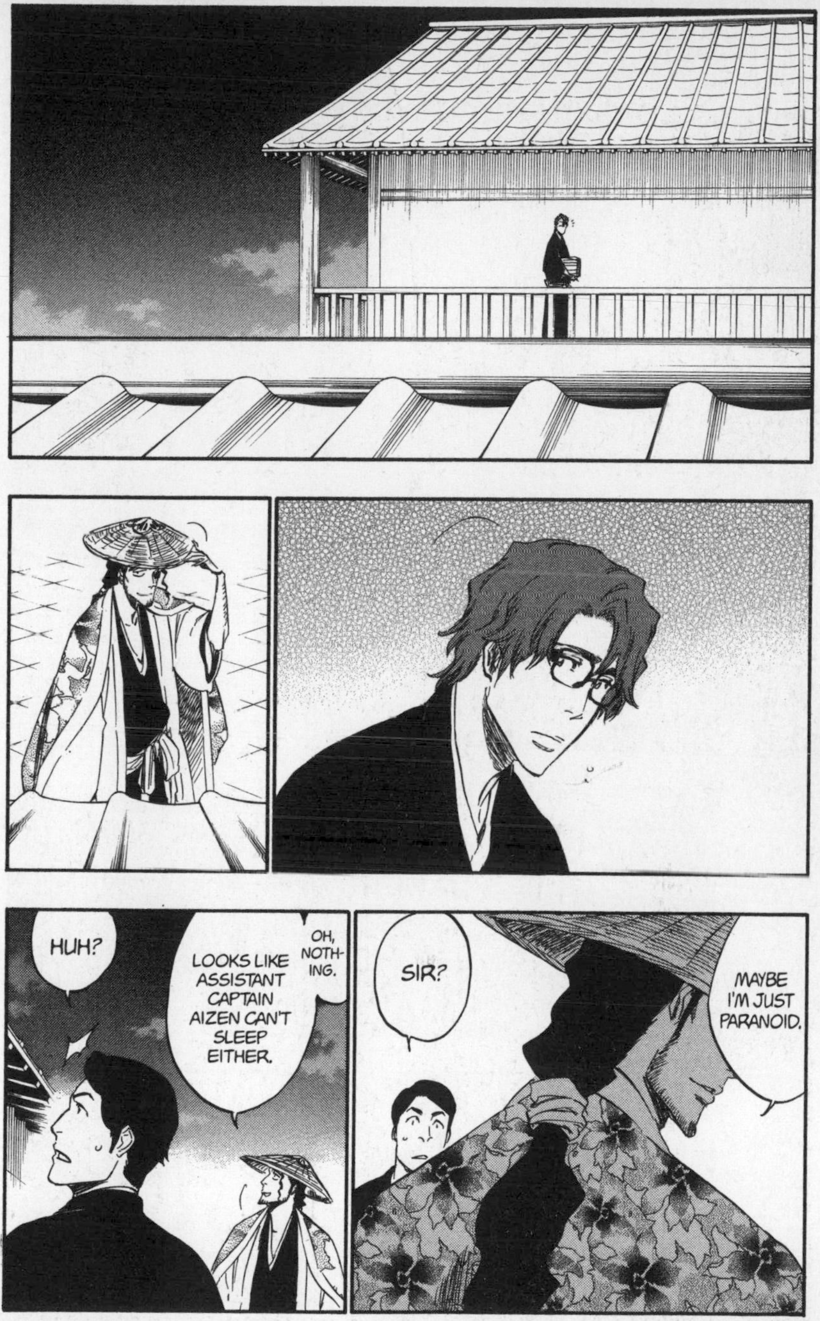
MAYBE I'M JUST PARANOID.
SIR?
OH, NOTHING.
LOOKS LIKE ASSISTANT CAPTAIN AIZEN CAN'T SLEEP EITHER.
HUH?

READ THIS WAY

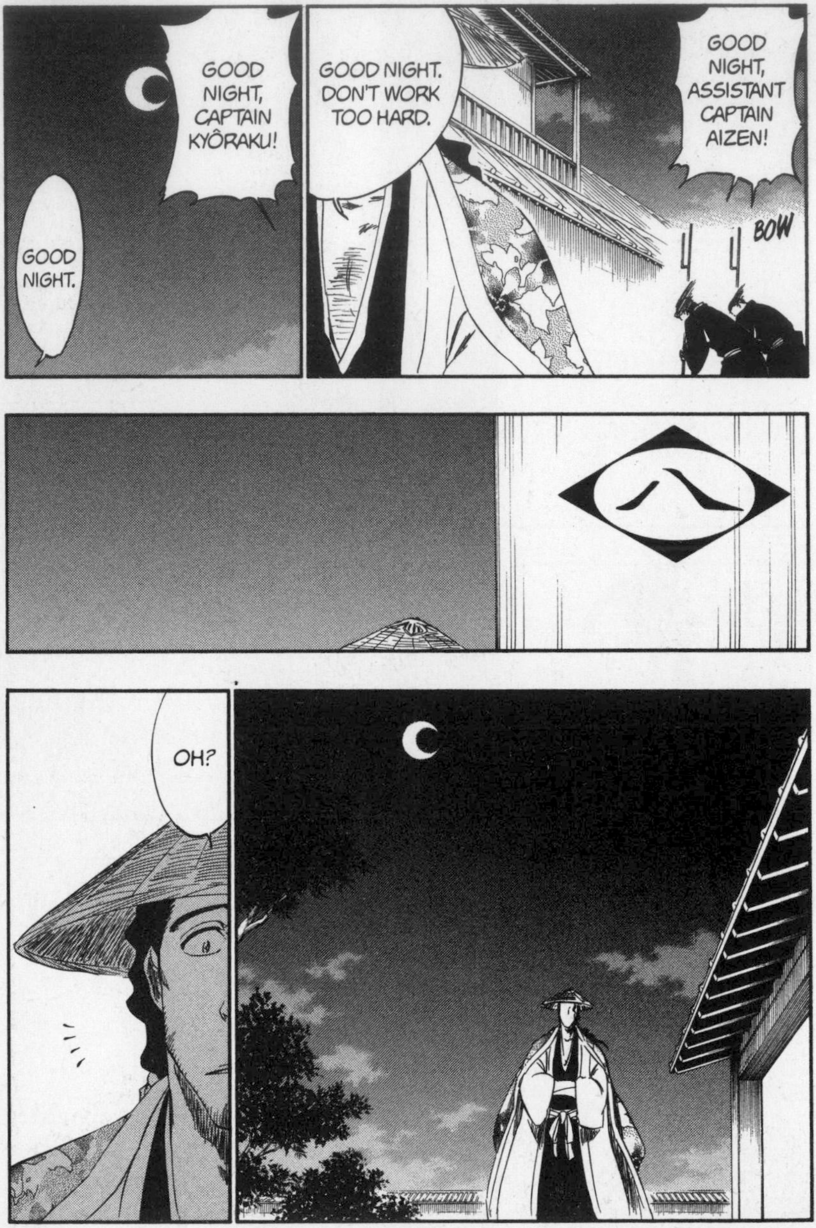
GOOD NIGHT, ASSISTANT CAPTAIN AIZEN!
BOW
GOOD NIGHT. DON'T WORK TOO HARD.
GOOD NIGHT, CAPTAIN KYÔRAKU!
GOOD NIGHT.
OH?

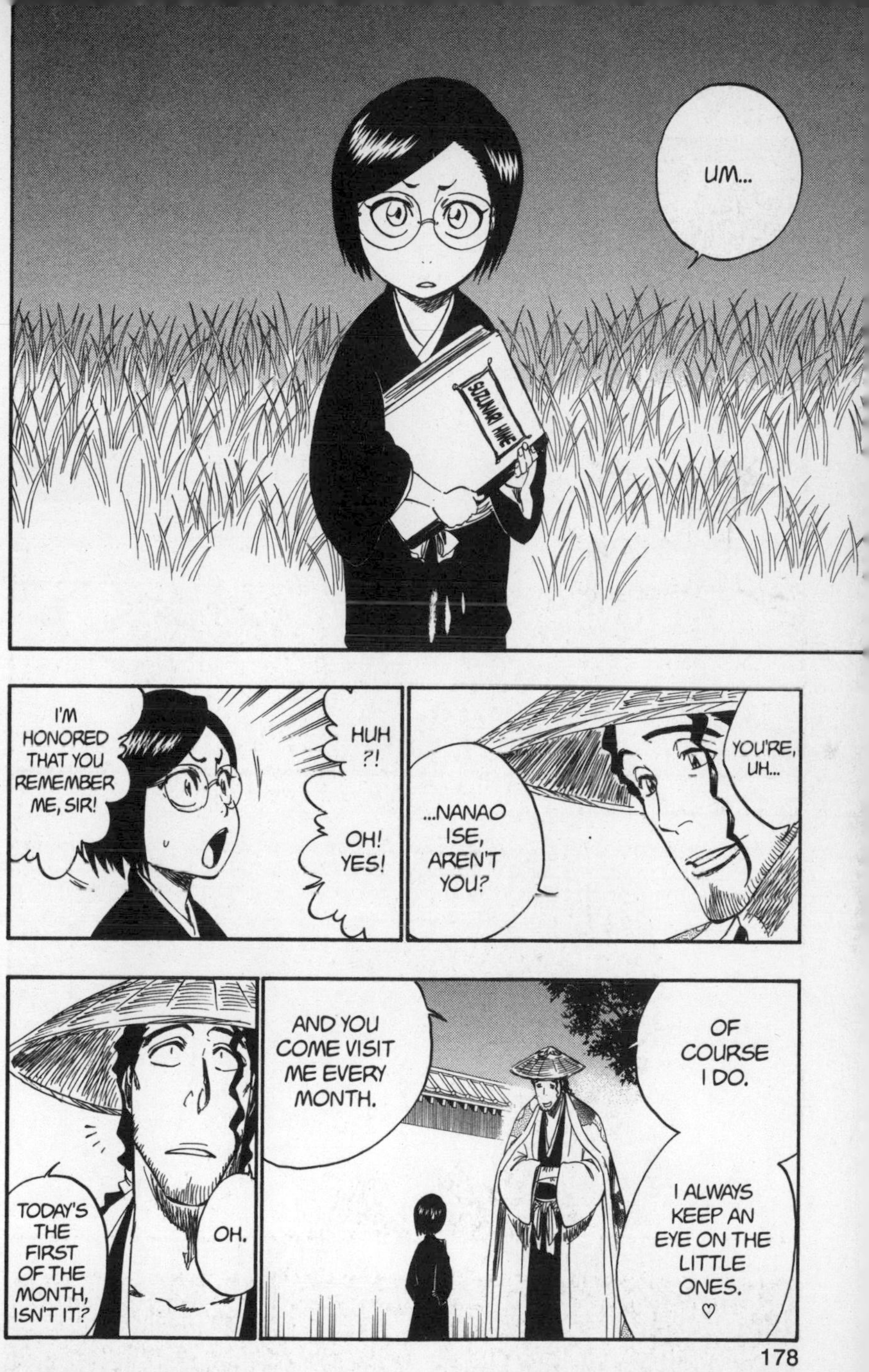
UM...
SUZUNARI HIME
YOU'RE, UH...
...NANAO ISE, AREN'T YOU?
HUH ?!
OH! YES!
I'M HONORED THAT YOU REMEMBER ME, SIR!
OF COURSE I DO.
AND YOU COME VISIT ME EVERY MONTH.
I ALWAYS KEEP AN EYE ON THE LITTLE ONES. ♡
OH.
TODAY'S THE FIRST OF THE MONTH, ISN'T IT?

READ THIS WAY

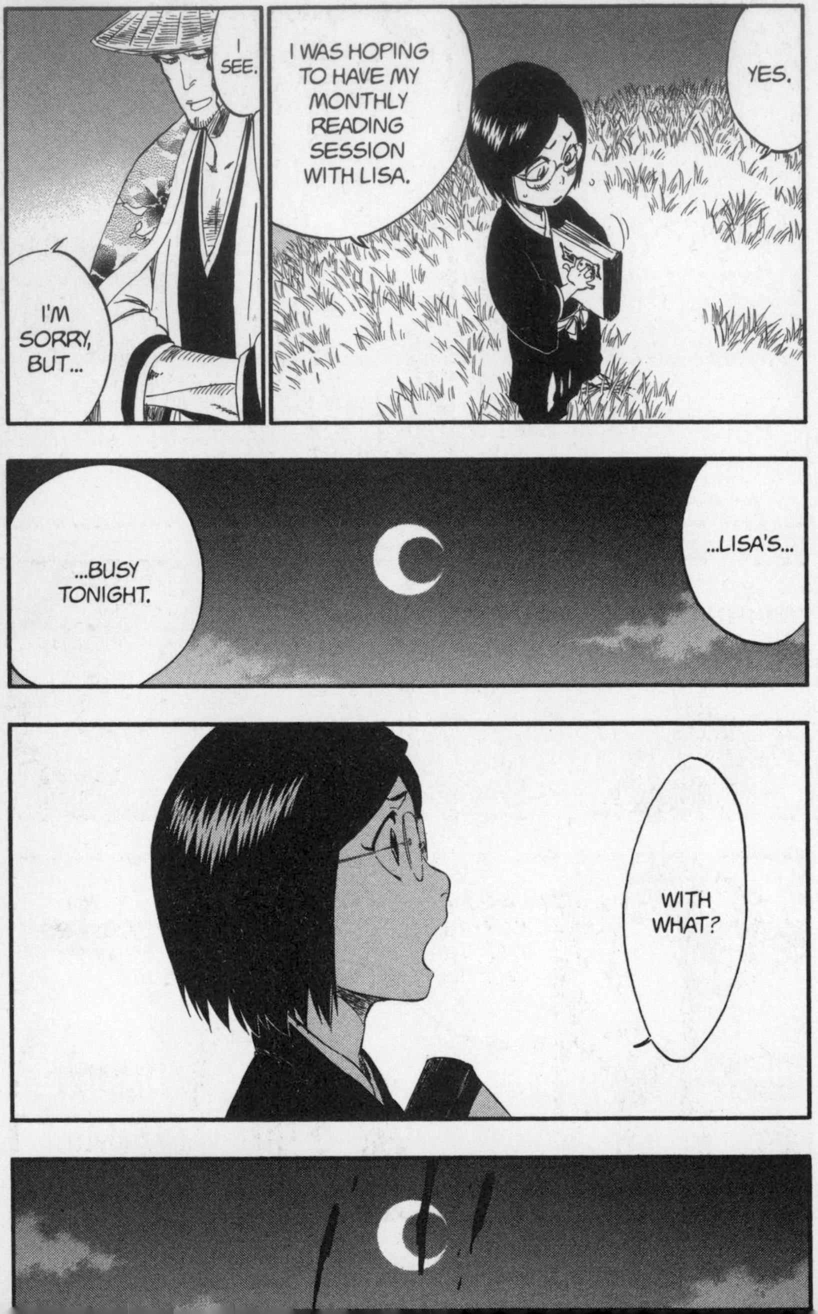
YES.
I WAS HOPING TO HAVE MY MONTHLY READING SESSION WITH LISA.
I SEE.
I'M SORRY, BUT...
...LISA'S...
...BUSY TONIGHT.
WITH WHAT?

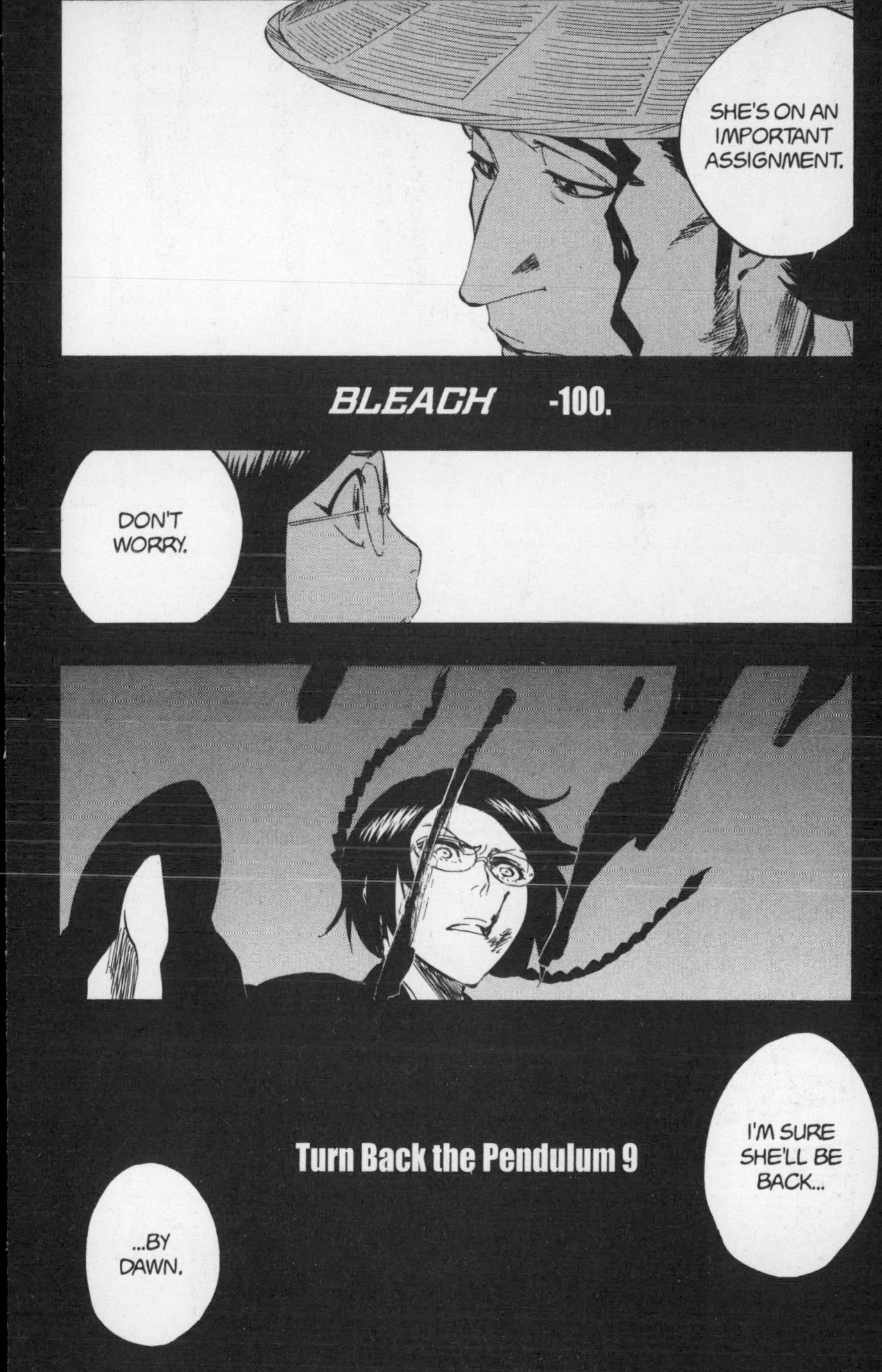
SHE'S ON AN IMPORTANT ASSIGNMENT.
BLEACH -100.
DON'T WORRY.
I'M SURE SHE'LL BE BACK...
Turn Back the Pendulum 9
...BY DAWN.

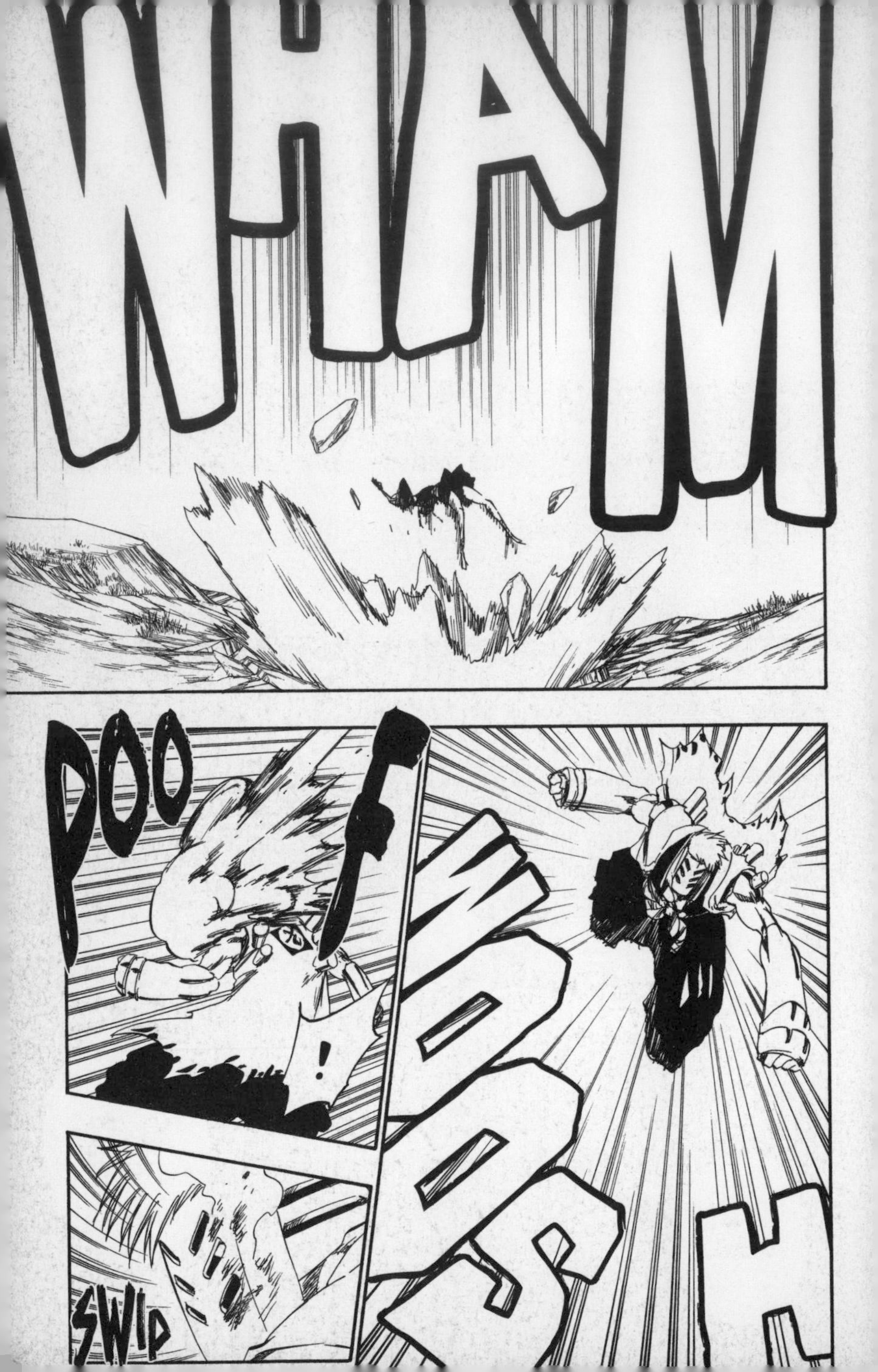
WHAM
WOOSH
POOF
!
SWIP

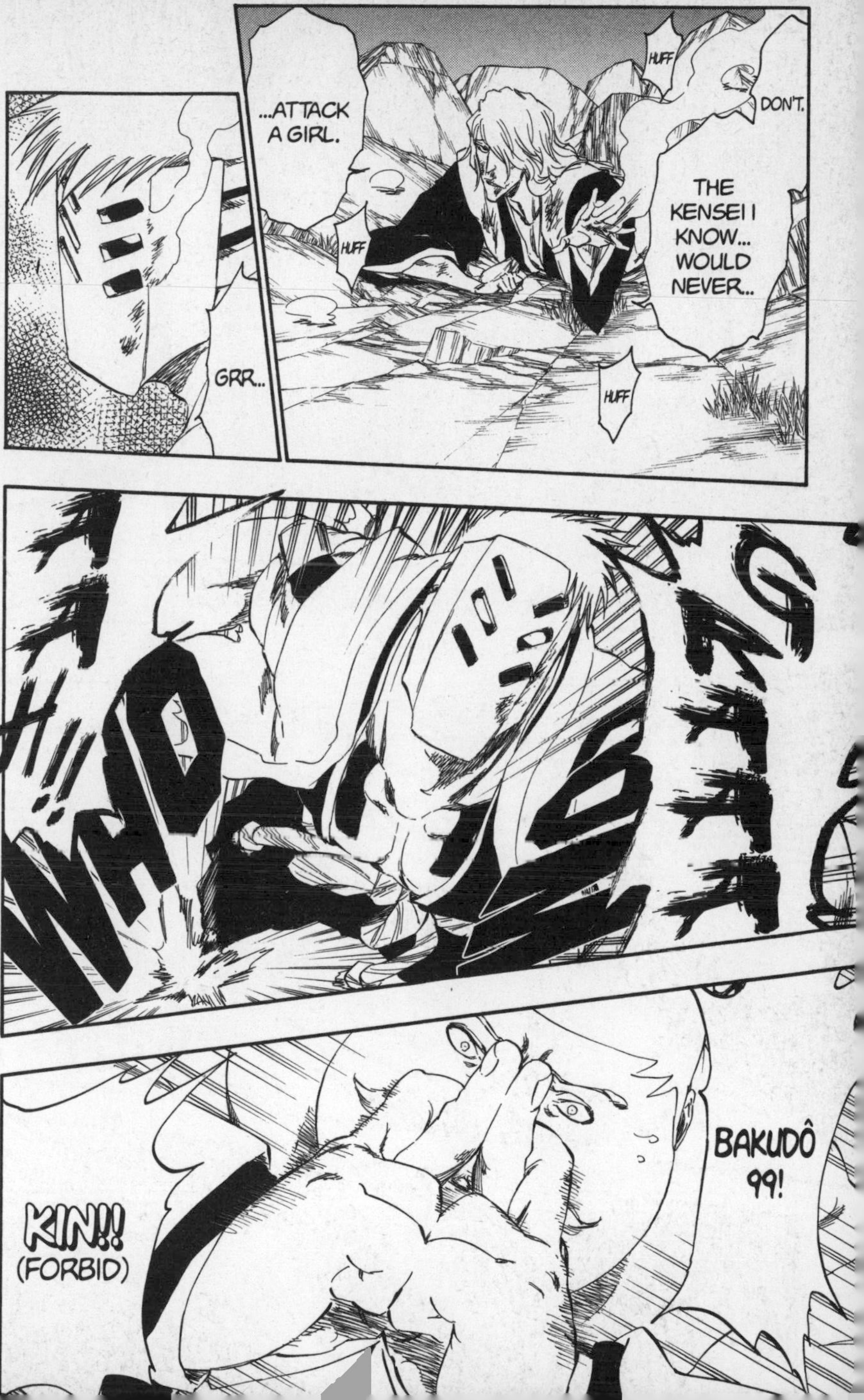
HUFF
DON'T.
THE KENSEI I KNOW... WOULD NEVER...
...ATTACK A GIRL.
HUFF
HUFF
GRR...
BAKUDÔ 99!
KIN!! (FORBID)

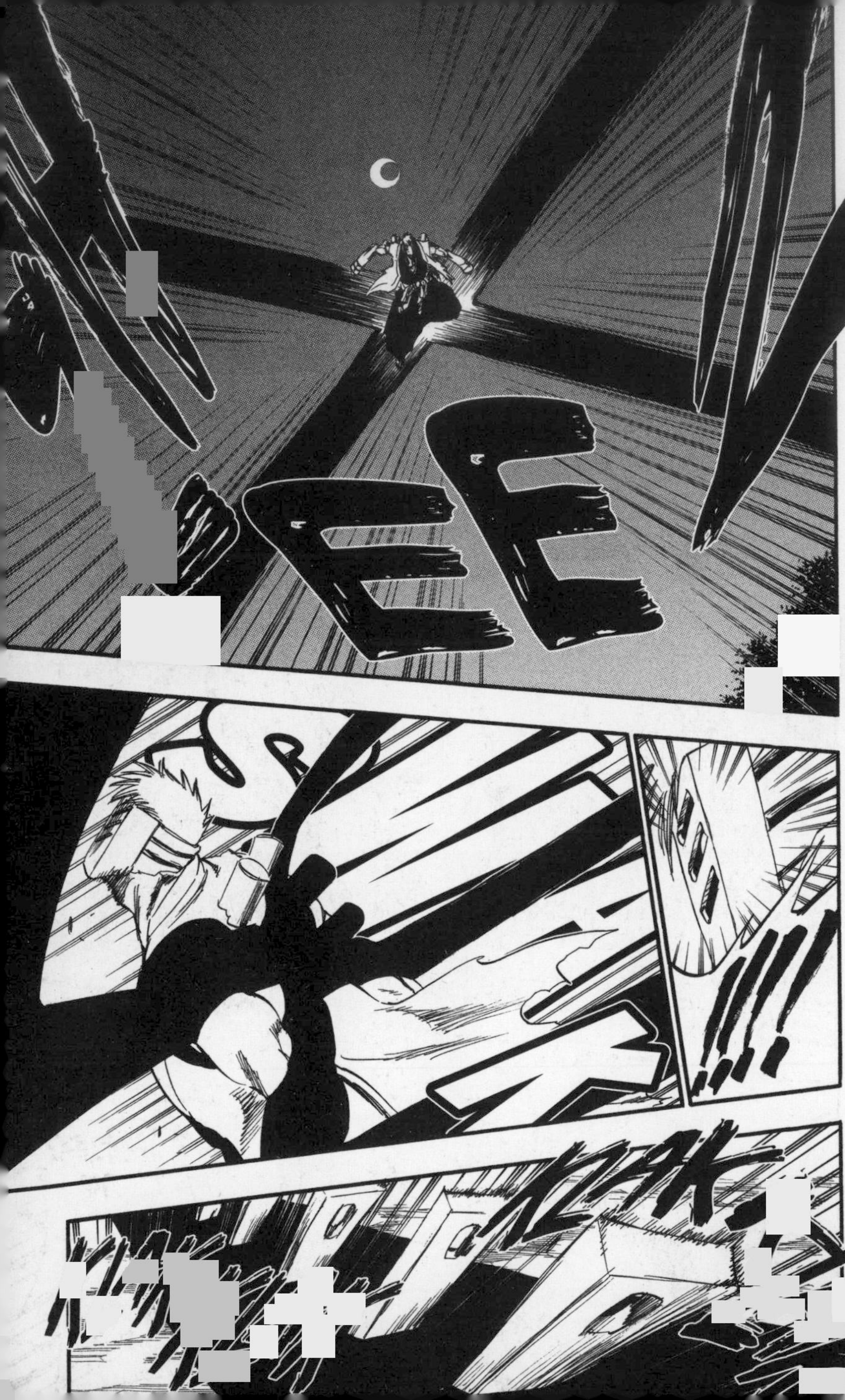

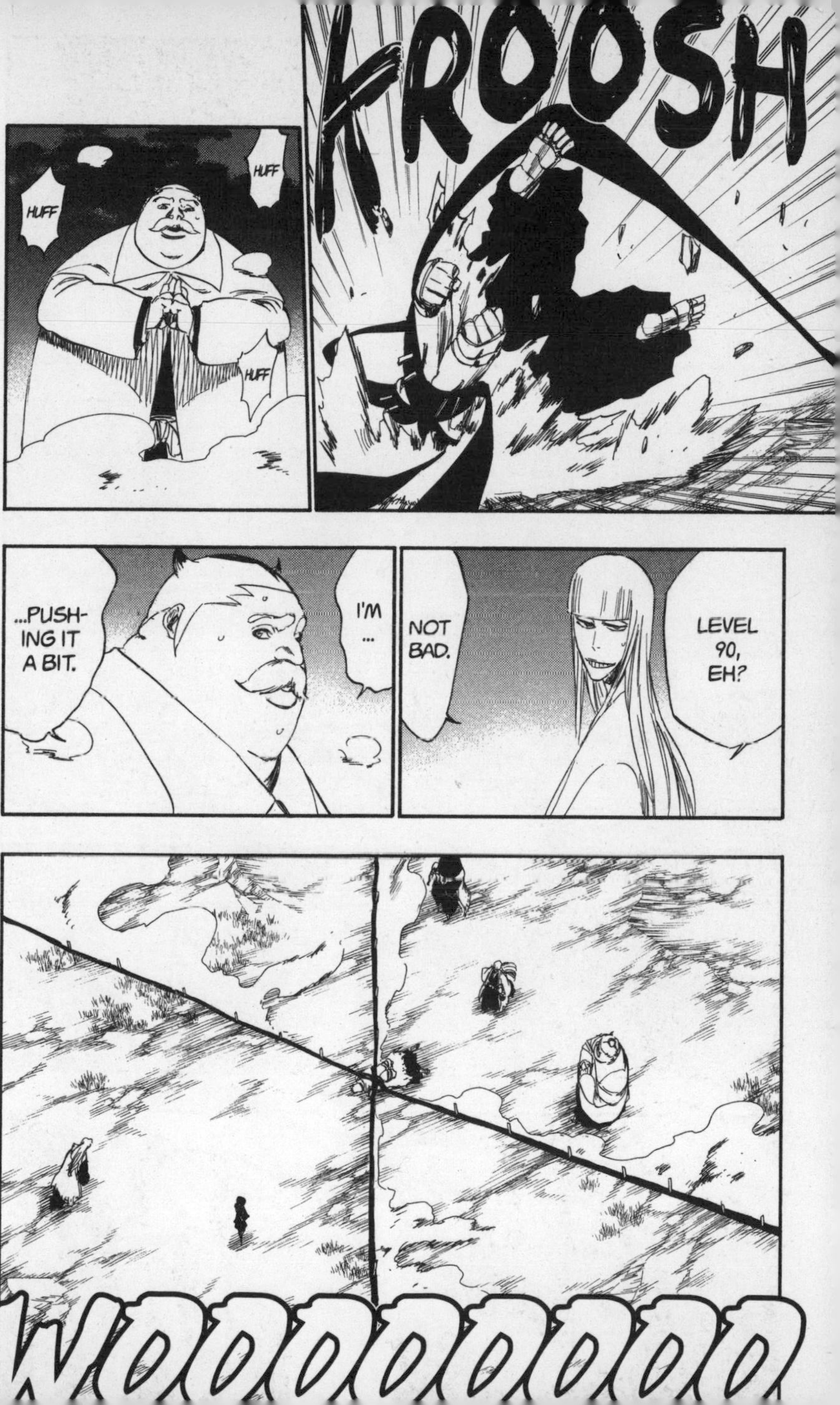
KROOSH
HUFF
HUFF
HUFF
LEVEL 90, EH?
NOT BAD.
I'M ...
...PUSHING IT A BIT.
WOOOOOOOO

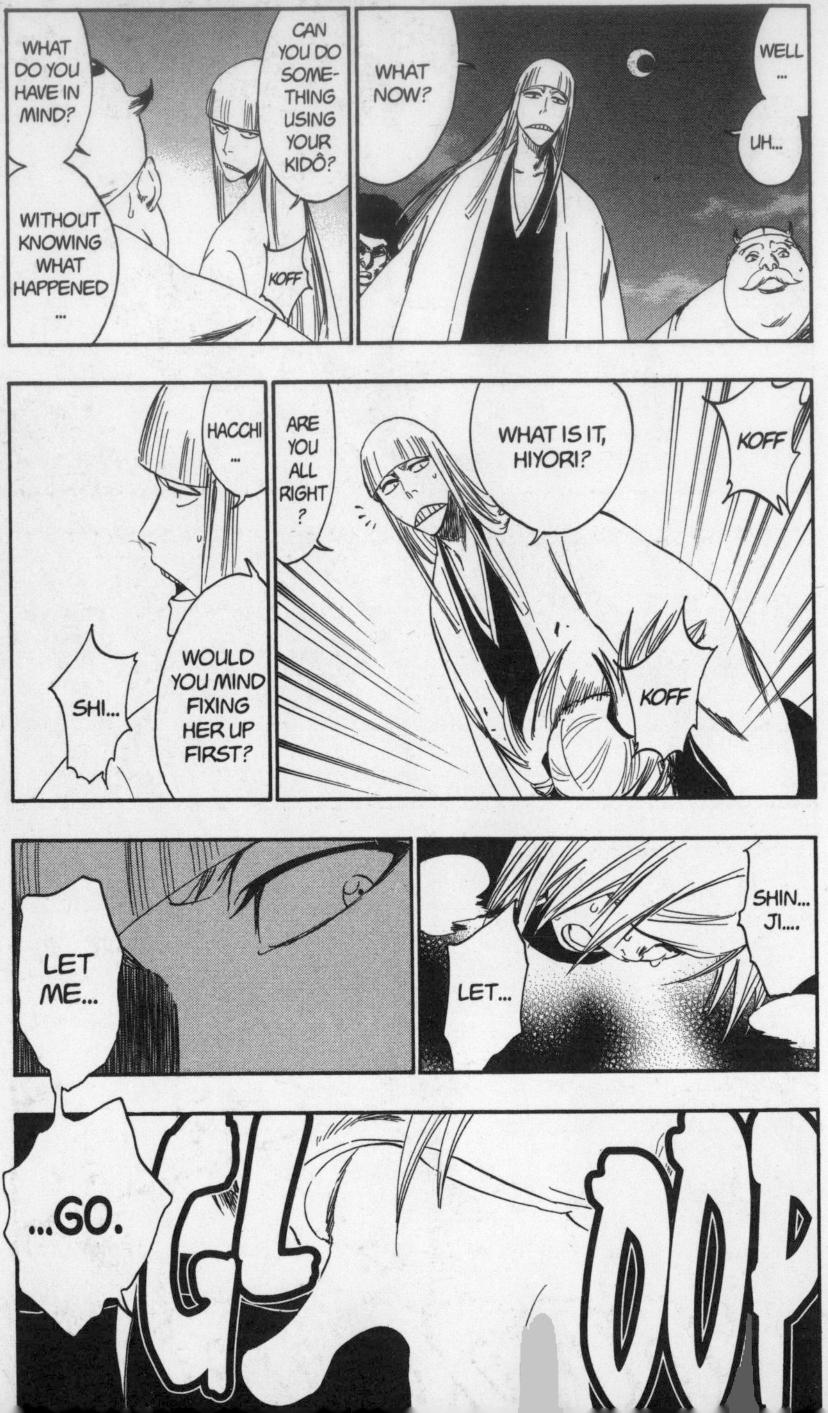
WELL ...
UH...
WHAT NOW?
CAN YOU DO SOME-THING USING YOUR KIDÔ?
WHAT DO YOU HAVE IN MIND?
KOFF
WITHOUT KNOWING WHAT HAPPENED ...
KOFF
WHAT IS IT, HIYORI?
ARE YOU ALL RIGHT ?
KOFF
HACCHI ...
WOULD YOU MIND FIXING HER UP FIRST?
SHI...
SHIN... JI....
LET...
LET ME...
...GO.
GL
OOP

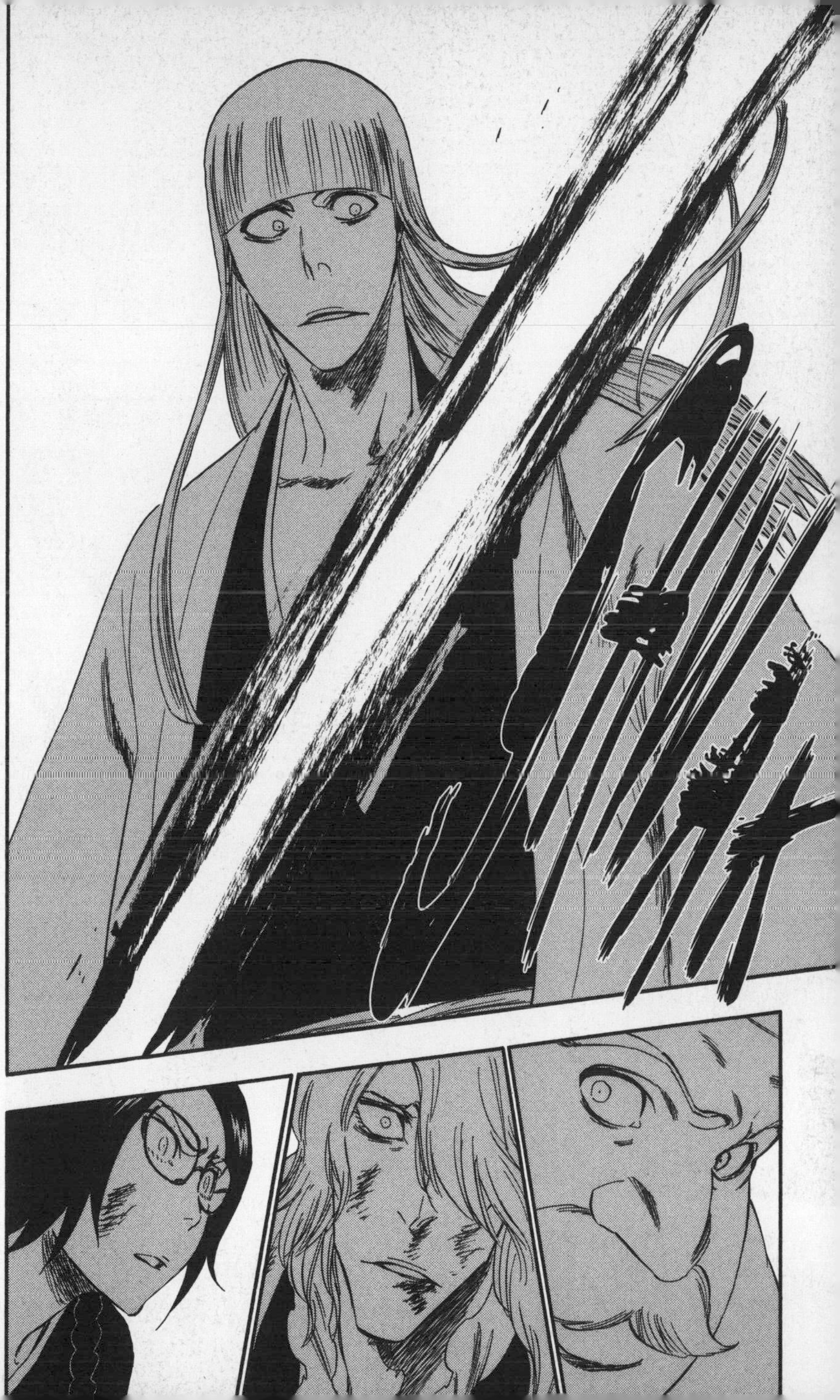

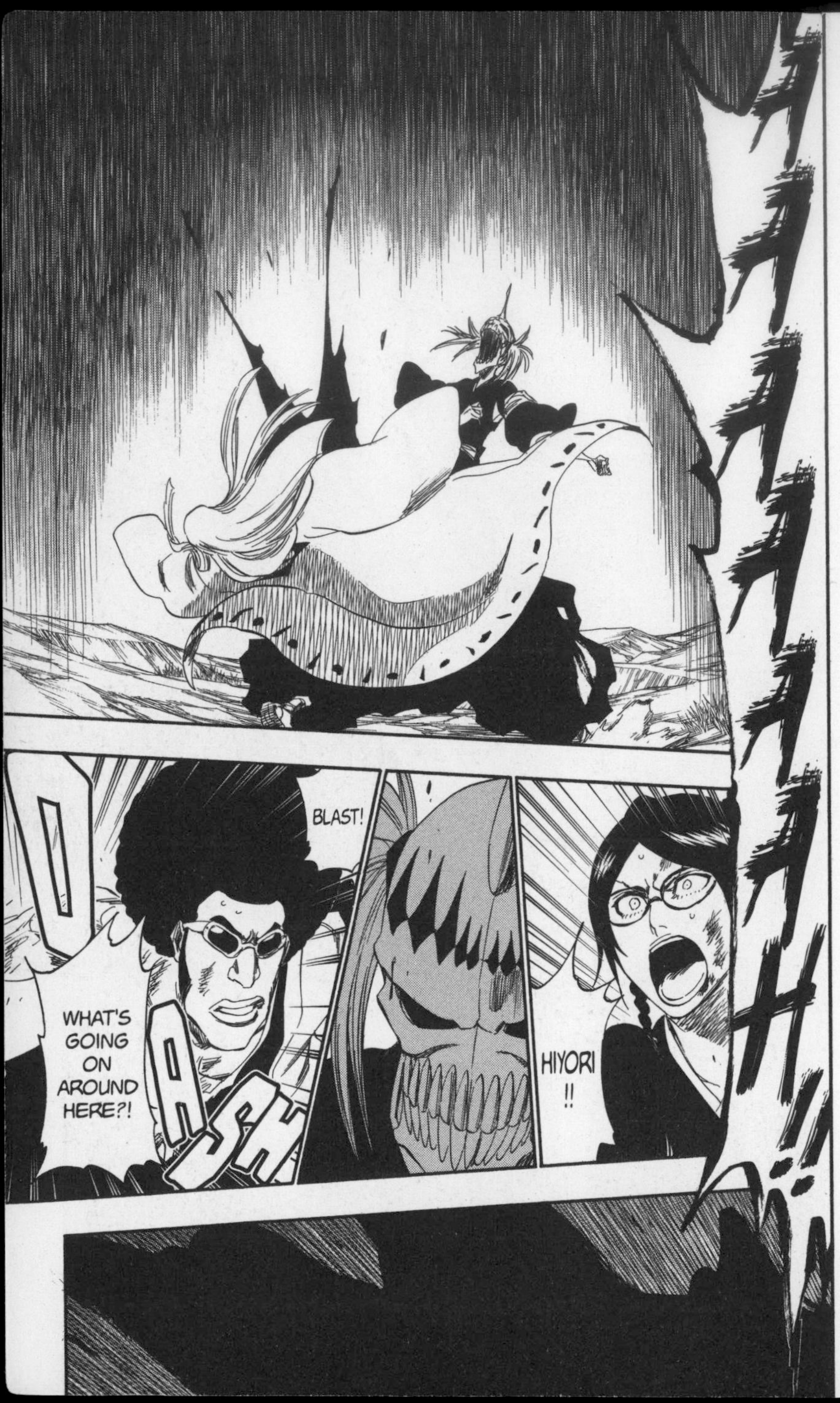
HIYORI !!
BLAST!
WHAT'S GOING ON AROUND HERE?!

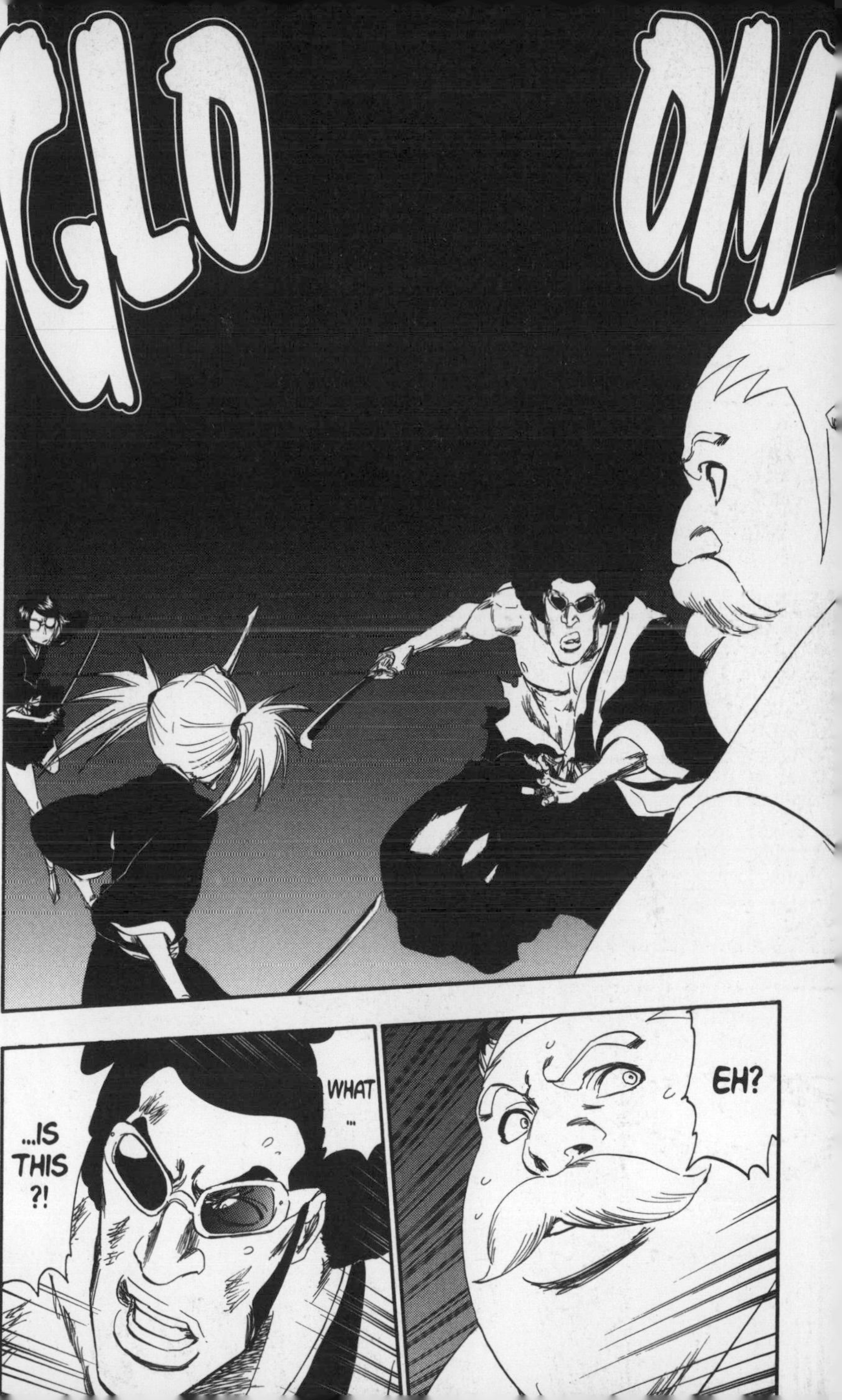
GLO
OM
EH?
WHAT ...
...IS THIS ?!

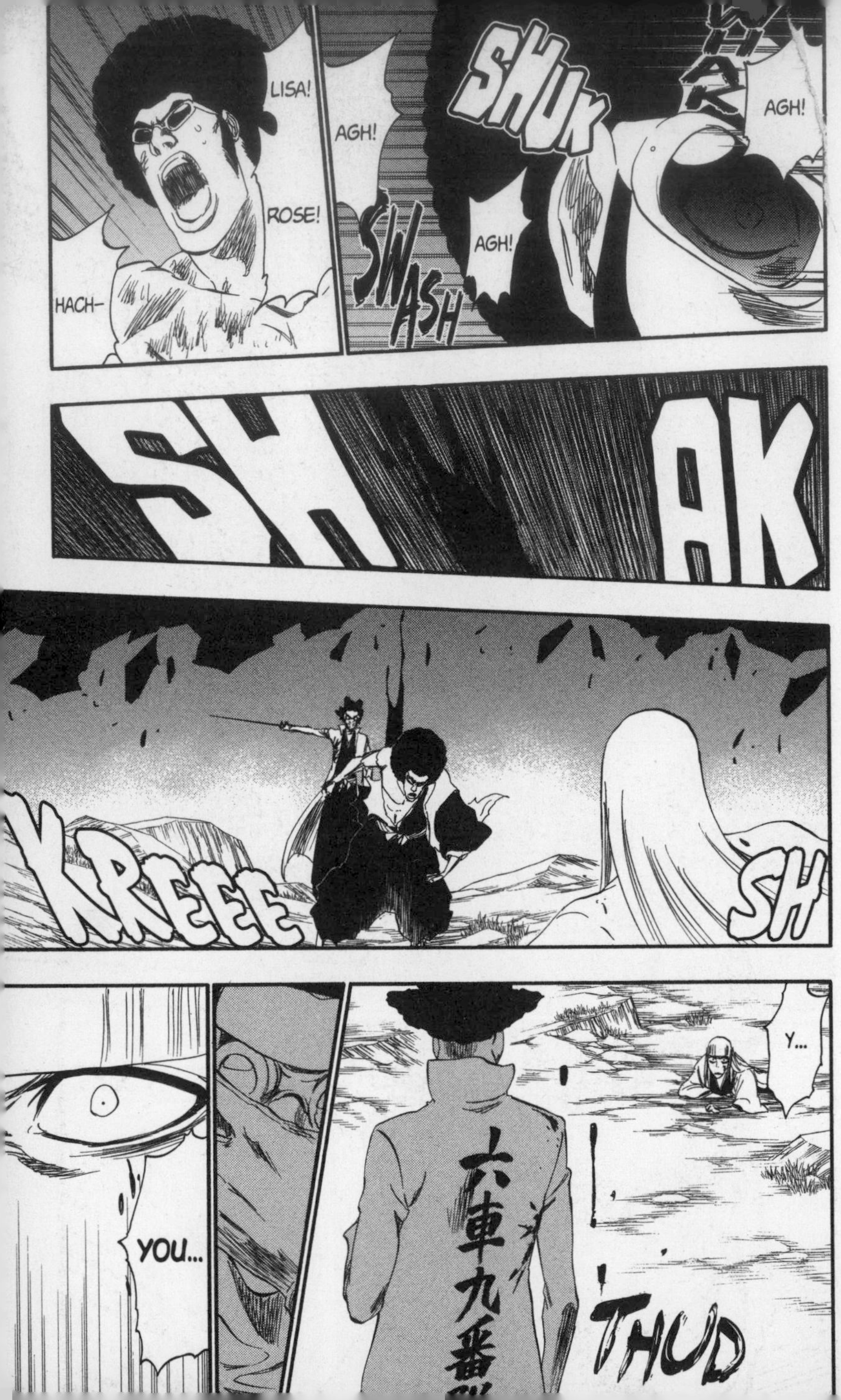
WHAK
AGH!
SHUK
AGH!
SWASH
AGH!
LISA!
ROSE!
HACH-
SH AK
SH
KREEE
Y...
THUD
YOU...

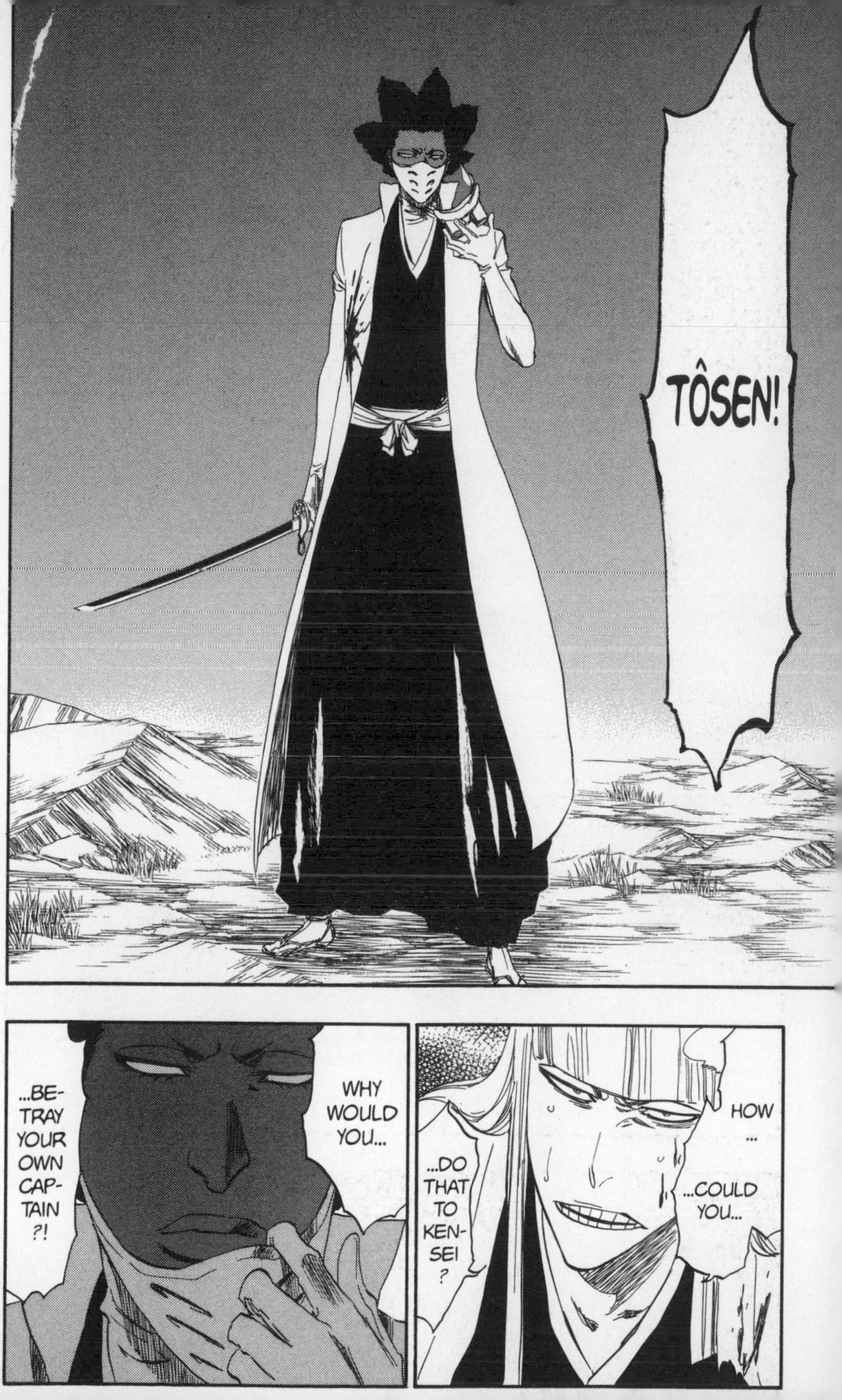
TÔSEN!
HOW ...
...COULD YOU...
...DO THAT TO KEN-SEI ?
WHY WOULD YOU...
...BE-TRAY YOUR OWN CAP-TAIN ?!

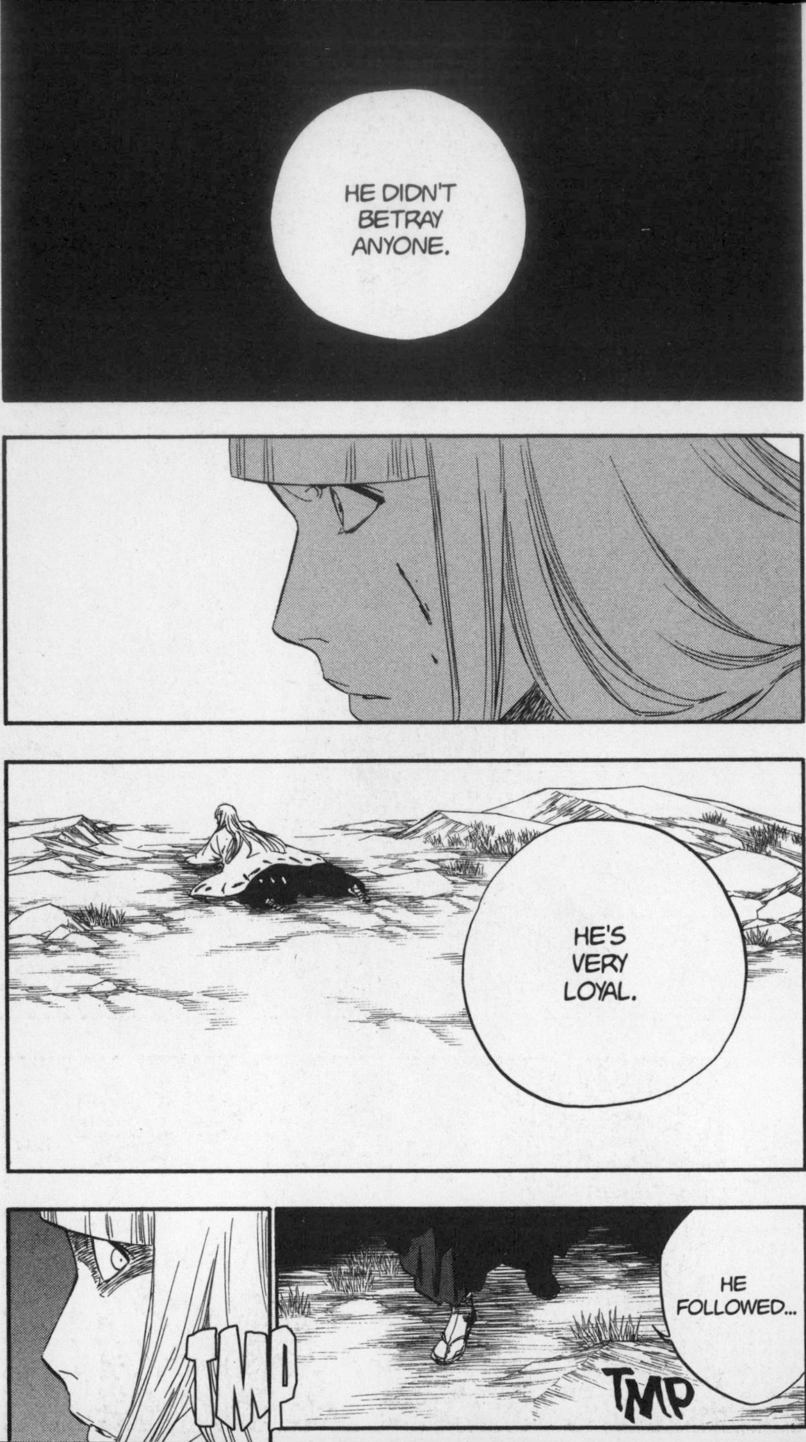
HE DIDN'T BETRAY ANYONE.
HE'S VERY LOYAL.
HE FOLLOWED...
TMP
TMP

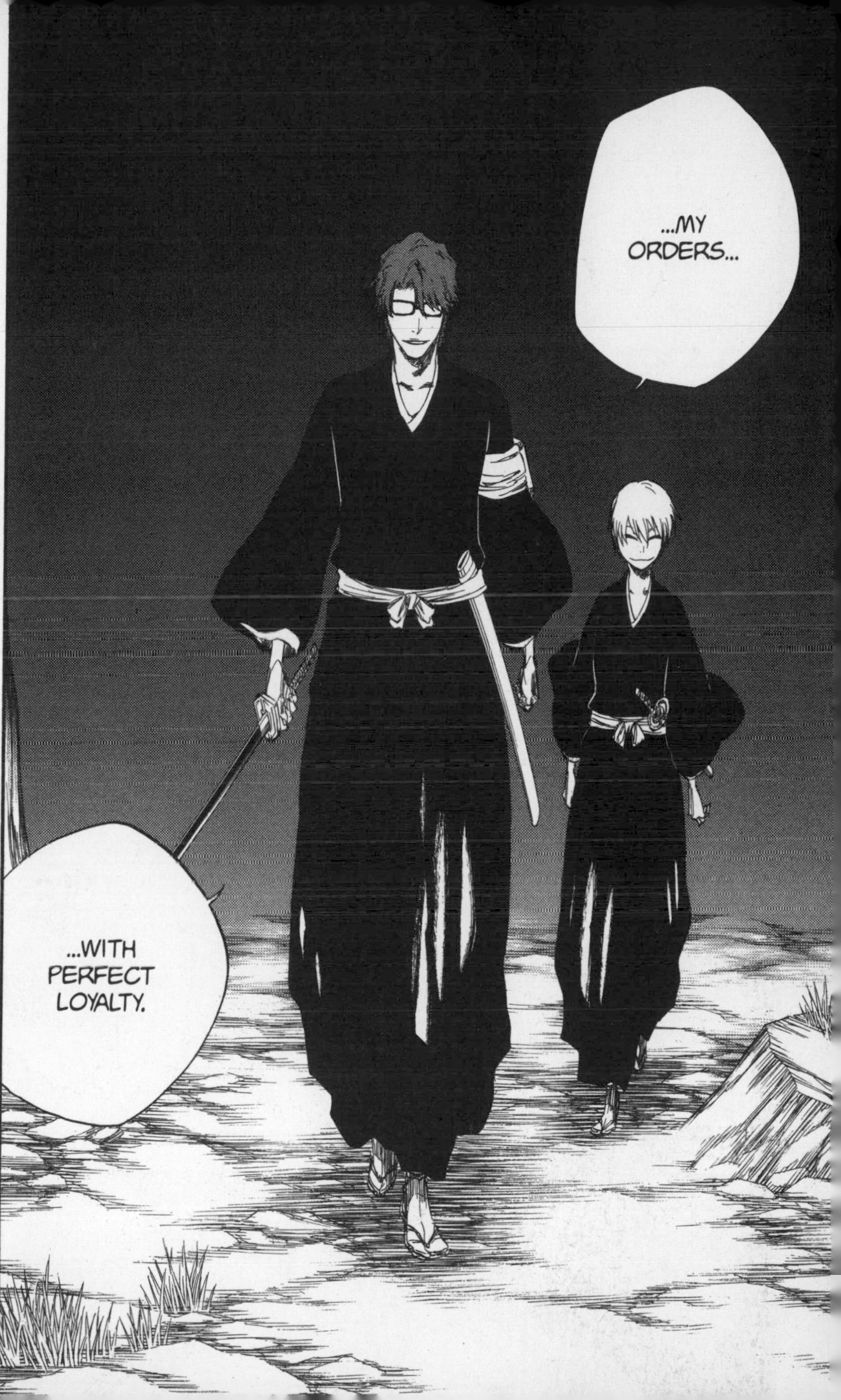
...MY ORDERS...
...WITH PERFECT LOYALTY.

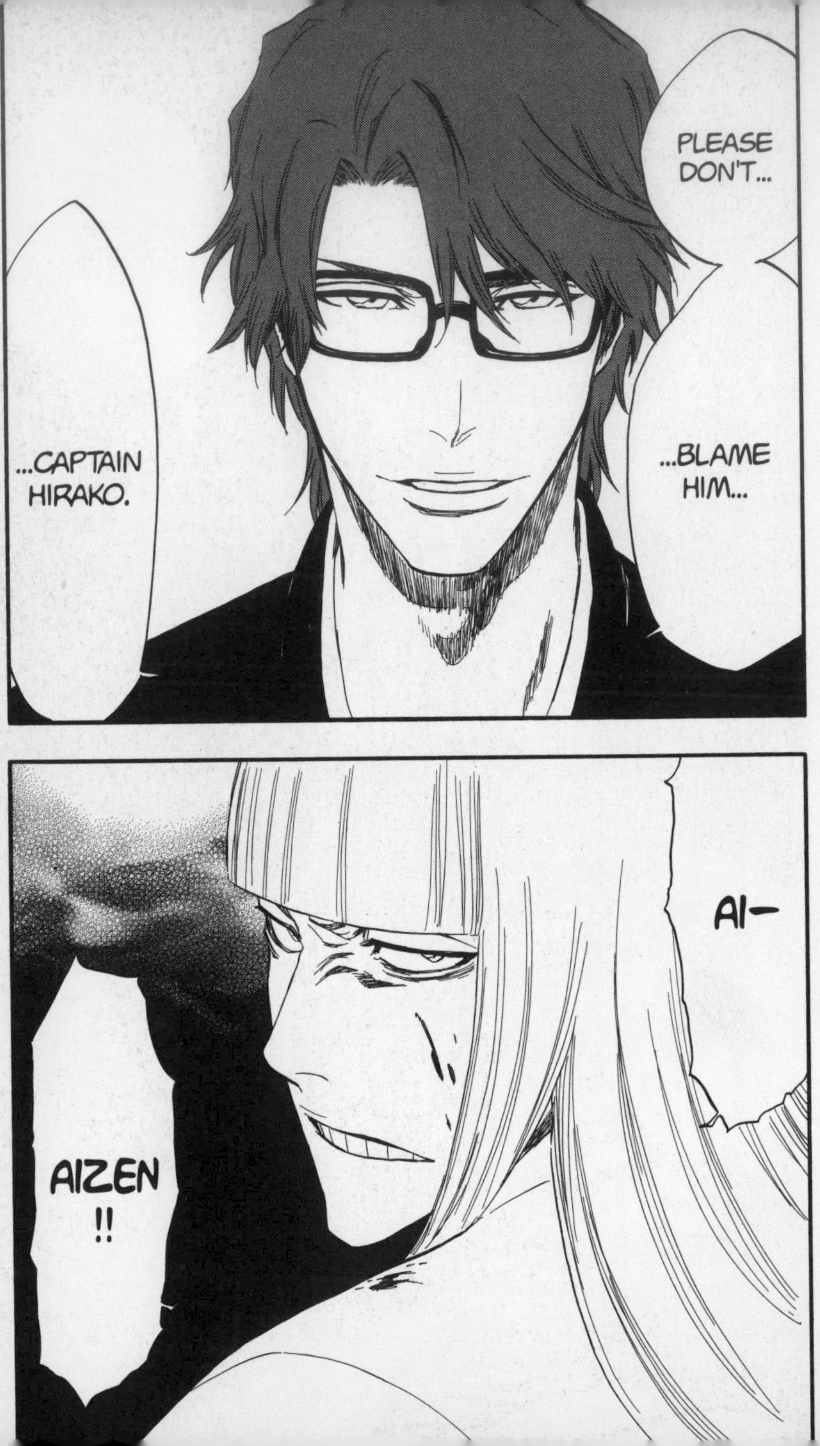
PLEASE DON'T...
...BLAME HIM...
...CAPTAIN HIRAKO.
AI-
AIZEN !!

THE PENDULUM KEEPS SWINGING

...IN BLËACH 37

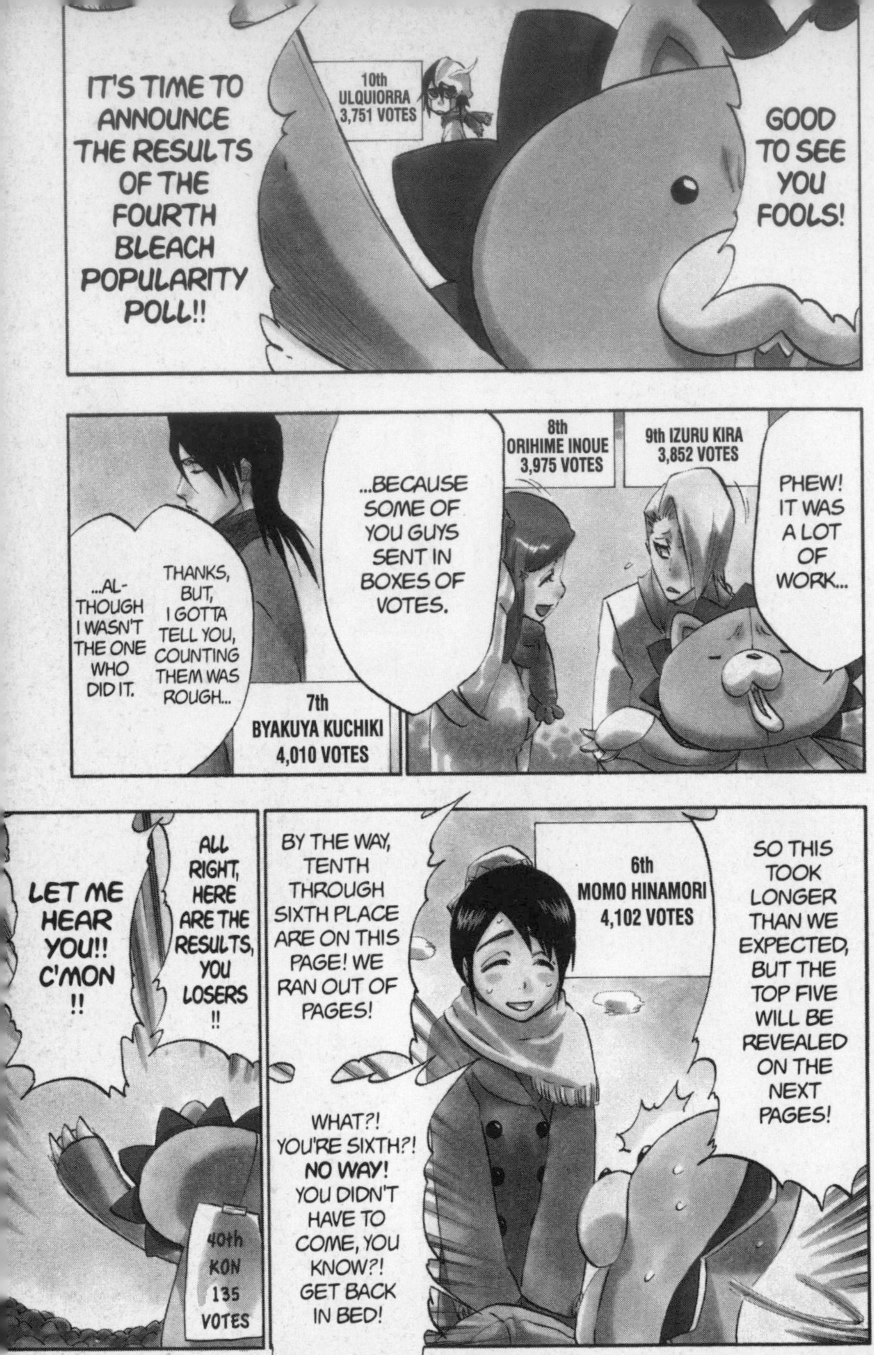
GOOD TO SEE YOU FOOLS!
10th ULQUIORRA 3,751 VOTES
IT'S TIME TO ANNOUNCE THE RESULTS OF THE FOURTH BLEACH POPULARITY POLL!!
PHEW! IT WAS A LOT OF WORK...
9th IZURU KIRA 3,852 VOTES
8th ORIHIME INOUE 3,975 VOTES
...BECAUSE SOME OF YOU GUYS SENT IN BOXES OF VOTES.
THANKS, BUT, I GOTTA TELL YOU, COUNTING THEM WAS ROUGH...
...AL-THOUGH I WASN'T THE ONE WHO DID IT.
7th BYAKUYA KUCHIKI 4,010 VOTES
SO THIS TOOK LONGER THAN WE EXPECTED, BUT THE TOP FIVE WILL BE REVEALED ON THE NEXT PAGES!
6th MOMO HINAMORI 4,102 VOTES
BY THE WAY, TENTH THROUGH SIXTH PLACE ARE ON THIS PAGE! WE RAN OUT OF PAGES!
WHAT?! YOU'RE SIXTH?! **NO WAY!** YOU DIDN'T HAVE TO COME, YOU KNOW?! GET BACK IN BED!
ALL RIGHT, HERE ARE THE RESULTS, YOU LOSERS!!
LET ME HEAR YOU!! C'MON!!
40th KON 135 VOTES

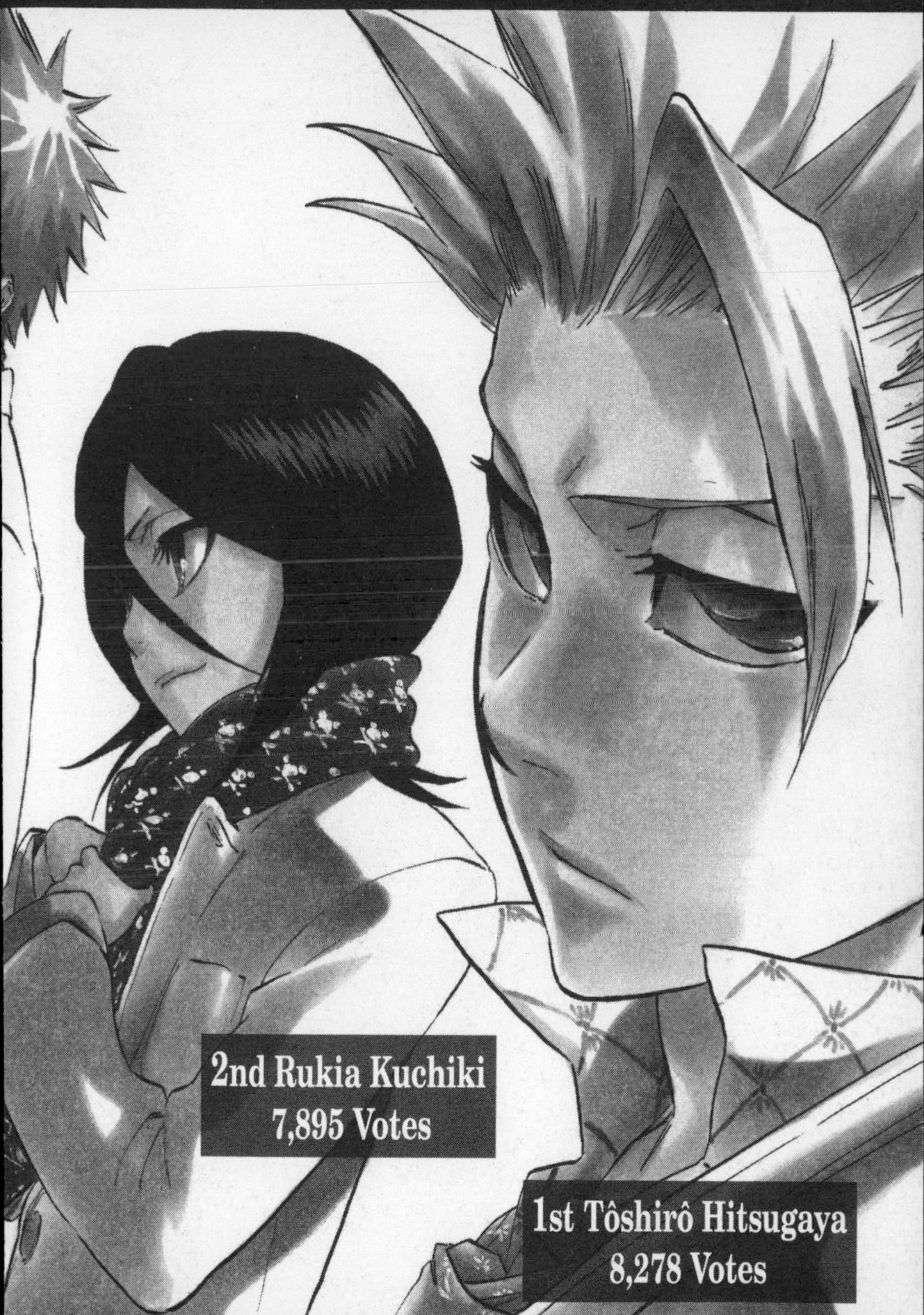
2nd Rukia Kuchiki
7,895 Votes
1st Tôshirô Hitsugaya
8,278 Votes

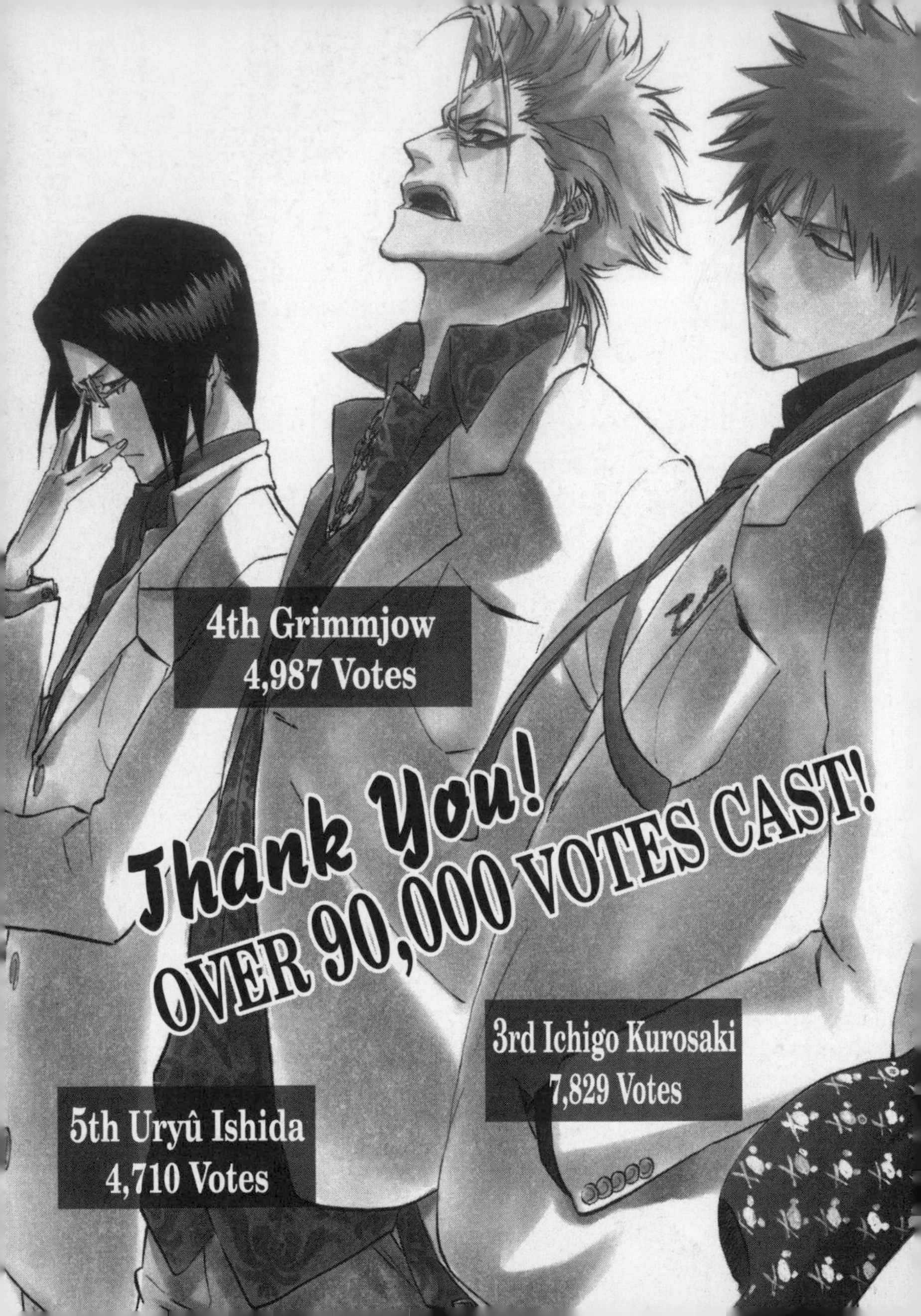
4th Grimmjow
4,987 Votes
Thank You!
OVER 90,000 VOTES CAST!
3rd Ichigo Kurosaki
7,829 Votes
5th Uryû Ishida
4,710 Votes

BLEACH POPULARITY POLL FOUR DETAILED RESULTS!

1	Tôshirô Hitsugaya	8,278 Votes
2	Rukia Kuchiki	7,895 Votes
3	Ichigo Kurosaki	7,829 Votes
4	Grimmjow	4,987 Votes
5	Uryû Ishida	4,710 Votes
6	Momo Hinamori	4,102 Votes
7	Byakuya Kuchiki	4,010 Votes
8	Orihime Inoue	3,975 Votes
9	Izuru Kira	3,852 Votes
10	Ulquiorra	3,751 Votes

11	Renji Abarai	3,746 Votes
12	Gin Ichimaru	3,699 Votes
13	Yumichika Ayasegawa	3,433 Votes
14	Shuhei Hisagi	3,400 Votes
15	Kenpachi Zaraki	3,385 Votes
16	Mizuiro Kojima	3,250 Votes
17	Shunsui Kyôraku	2,844 Votes
18	Yasutora Sado	2,477 Votes
19	Jûshiro Ukitake	2,003 Votes
20	Kisuke Urahara	1,752 Votes
21	Rangiku Matsumoto	1,666 Votes
22	Ikkaku Madarame	1,621 Votes
23	Sôsuke Aizen	1,423 Votes
24	Nnoitora	1,315 Votes
25	Soi Fon	1,228 Votes
26	Kaien Shiba	1,097 Votes
27	Yachiru Kusajishi	980 Votes
28	Yoruichi Shihôin	752 Votes
29	Szayelaporro	537 Votes
30	Nel	410 Votes
31	Soul Candy King	390 Votes
32	Akon	341 Votes
33	Kaname Tôsen	298 Votes
34	Nemu Kurotsuchi	246 Votes
35	Ashido	215 Votes
36	Sajin Komamura	190 Votes
37	White Ichigo	180 Votes
38	Hisana Kuchiki	162 Votes
39	Luppi	155 Votes
40	Kon	135 Votes
41	Shinji Hirako	118 Votes
42	Hanataro Yamada	107 Votes
43	Ryûgen Ishida	99 Votes
44	Kensei Muguruma	82 Votes
45	Cirucci	69 Votes
46	Ilfort	62 Votes
47	Ganju Shiba	58 Votes
48	Mayuri Kurotsuchi	53 Votes
49	Tesla	49 Votes
50	Isshin Kurosaki	45 Votes

BEST1 ▶160

51st(42 Votes) Tite Kubo/Stark 53rd(41 Votes) Senna 54th(39 Votes) Harunobu Ogidô/D Roy 56th(38 Votes) Tetsuzaemon Iba 57th(37 Votes) Ichigo Kurosaki(Hollowfied) 58 th(36 Votes) Uryû Ishida Exclusive Dressing Room 59th(35 Votes) Halibel/Seaweed Ambassador 61st(34 Votes) Keigo Asano 62nd(30 Votes) Hachigen Ushôda 63rd(26 Votes) Tatsuki Arisawa 64th(23 Votes) Retsu Unohana 65th(22 Votes) Kanisawa Senpai 66th(19 Votes) Fishbone D 67th(18 Votes) Aaroniero/Hiyori Sarugaki 69 th(17 Votes) Dordonii/Wonderweiss 71st(16 Votes) Yuzu Kurosaki 72nd(11 Votes) Nanao Ise/Chappy/Baishin 75th(9 Votes) Apache/Tatsuya Isaka/Karin Kurosaki/Zangetsu/Sode no Shirayuki/Rin Tsubokura/Ururu Tsumugiya/Noba/Chizuru Honshô/Lisa Yadômaru/Rikichi 86th(8 Votes)Eldorado/Mareyo Ohmaeda /Isane Kotetsu/Shawlong/Shuji Hayashi/Genryusai Shigekuni Yamamoto/Loli 93rd(7 Votes) Sun-Sun/Shrieker/Pesche 96th(6 Votes) Jinta Hanakari/Hiyosu/Ririn 99th(5 Votes)Iceringer/Kiyone Kotetsu/Shiba Home/Nakim/Hyôrinmaru (Tôshiro Hitsugaya)/Pesche's spit/Eye-glass cookies/Menos Grande/Yammy/Lilinette 109th(4 Votes) Arturo/Ulquiorra's eyeball/Ohshima Reiichi/Mihane Shirogane/Ichigo Kurosaki Bankai Version/Masaki Kurosaki/Kûkaku Shiba/Tsubaki/Lumina/Rock Musical Bleach 119th(3 Votes) Sosuke Aizen's glasses/Yasochika Iemura/Kisuke Urahara's hat/Marechiyo Ohmaeda/Misato Ochi/The cloth around Zangetsu's hilt/Don Kannonji/Dondochakka/Benihime (Kisuke Urahara)/Verona/Mashiro Kuna/Mila-Rose/Metazepi/Menoly 133rd(2 Votes) Mr. Af/The guy above Aaroniero/Aaroniero disguised as Kaien/The chair Sosuke Aizen sits on/Renji's eyebrow tattoo/Ichinose Maki/Tôshiro's bangs/Sora Inoue/Gantenbainne/Jin Kariya/Ginnosuke/Ginrei Kojaku/Rukia Kuchiki's drawings/Grantz Brothers/Grimmjow's left arm/Sentaro Kotsubaki/Yoruichi in Kiyone Kotetsu's imagination/Karakura Konsô Cop/Chôjirô Sasakibe/Demora/Midoriko Tôno/Poison Candy/Loincloth Denreishinki/Infinite Slick/The Arrancar that healed Yammy's arm/Roller Through Go-Go/Wabisuke/Yuichi Shibata161st(1 Vote) The Espada sitting next to Ulquiorra in Chapters 162 and 244/Sosuke Aizen(Black)/Aoga/Asano Touring/Renji Abarai's Tattoos/Renji Abarai's hair string/ Abarai dressed casually/Renji Abarai's goggles/Renji Abarai's washcloth/Renji Abarai's second pair of glasses/Renji Abarai's wristband/Abuelo/Yumichika Ayasegawa's Soul Candy/Ayame/Makizô Aramaki/Uryû's eyeglasses/Himawari Sewing Uryû was holding/Sôken Ishida/Uryû's cape (new version)/The chocolate Nanao tried to give Shunsui/The JUMP Nanao was holding/The dried persimmon that Gin gave Rangiku/Tôshiro Hitsugaya texting/The drawing of Komamura Iba drew/Visored/Ugendô/The blood Jûshiro Ukitake spits out/Ryo Udagawa/Enjôji's drawing of Soi Fon/Enraku/Oscar Joaquin De La Rosa/Onodera/Phantom Thief Neldonpe/Kamaitachi Uryû/The Hollow that appears in Karakura Cop/The sixth grader who beat up Karin/Ukitake in a coffin/The staff of the Research and Development Department in panda makeup/Dordonii drawn messily/The manju in shape of a fox/The Hollow that might be a cow or a pig/Kyôka Suigetsu/Shunsui's chest hair/Gillian/Ginjirô Shirogane/Training wheels on Yachiru Kusajishi's Zanpaku-tô/Tobiume embodied/Ryo Kunieda/Kurôdo/Grand Fischer/Grimmjow in Released state/Grimmjow in his Hollow days/Zennosuke Kurumadani/Hammer cut by Ichigo Kurosaki/Kon inside Ichigo Kurosaki/Ichigo Kurosaki's apron/The mask broken when Ichigo Kurosaki Hollowfies/Isshin Kurosaki (Soul Reaper)/Isshin Kurosaki's legendary chopsticks/Kurosaki Funeral Service/Mayuri Kurotsuchi's picture drawing song/Goro/Karakura Konsô Cop's transformation watch/The button on Kon's belly button/Kill-Phone/The little Hollow in the desert/Zabimaru/The right hand of the monkey grabs the star/Eleventh Company 4th Seat/Shuhei Hisagi's handmade riceball/Shuhei Hisagi's choker/Shunshun Rikka/Female Soul Reaper Society Ultra Rare Trading Card/Shinsô/The man who bought sushi/Justice Armor Justice Headband/General Captain's beard/Exequias/Yoshino Sôma/Hollow with sloppy face/Anti-Hollow Combat Simulation Training Machine/Kôichiro Takezoe/Keigo's desk tossed by Tatsuki/Small Ichigo (WJ 36/37 Cover)/Super Acceleration/Tessai Tsukabishi/Bowl with Tsubokura written on it/Ururu Tsumugiya's broom/Tensa Zangetsu/Denreishinki/ Tôsen Kaname's glove/Tôsen Kaname's goggles/Tôsen Kaname's female friend/Don Kannonji-like Hollow/Don Panini/Editor Mr. Nakano/Mahana Natsui Seven-colored shaved ice/Niimura/Rukongai's chief/Cat-shaped Bekkô candy(Honey flavor)/Twisted Headband Denreishinki/Nel's mask/Nnoitra's eyepatch/Haineko/Patros/Parfait bowl/Papyrus/Rose-colored Komichi/Halibel/Bawabawa/Tôshiro Hitsugaya's Haori/Hinagiku/The plastic bottle Shinji drank from/Shinji's Hollow mask/Shinji's bowl-cut/Raccoon hint/Felis Catus/Prince of Darkness/Bonny/Idiot/Madame Akiyama/Ikkaku Madarame's upper body muscles/Ikkaku Madarame's loincloth/Rangiku Matsumoto's necklace/Mabashi/Magic Girl Megalon/Marianne/Mihane Shirogane's eyeglasses/Mini-Gin Ichimaru/Infinite Chasing Game/Vegetable fanatic/Female Arrancar who gets her face crushed by Yammy/Yammy's back tooth/Yuki/Yoruichi (Soul Reaper)/Yoruichi (cat)/Yoshi/Las Noches/Love/The Erotic God that made Rangiku and Orihime's breasts bigger/Ran'Tao/Rukia Kuchiki's way of life/Rukia Kuchiki faking her identity/Rukia Kuchiki's area you can almost see but can't/Runuganga/

Next Volume Preview

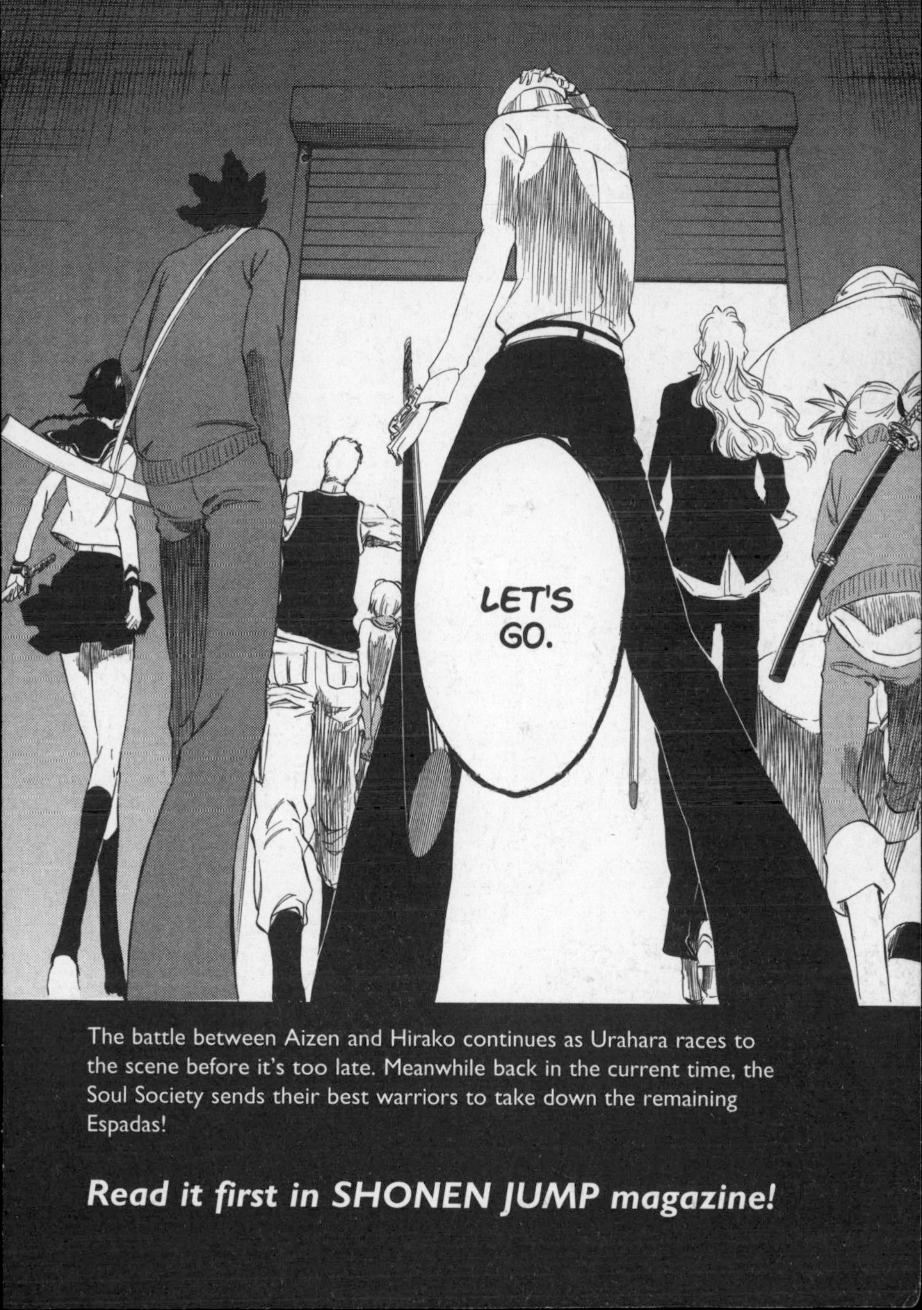
LET'S GO.

The battle between Aizen and Hirako continues as Urahara races to the scene before it's too late. Meanwhile back in the current time, the Soul Society sends their best warriors to take down the remaining Espadas!

Read it first in SHONEN JUMP magazine!

SEE INTO THE SOUL
OF *BLEACH*
WITH THE MANGA,
PROFILES AND ART BOOKS

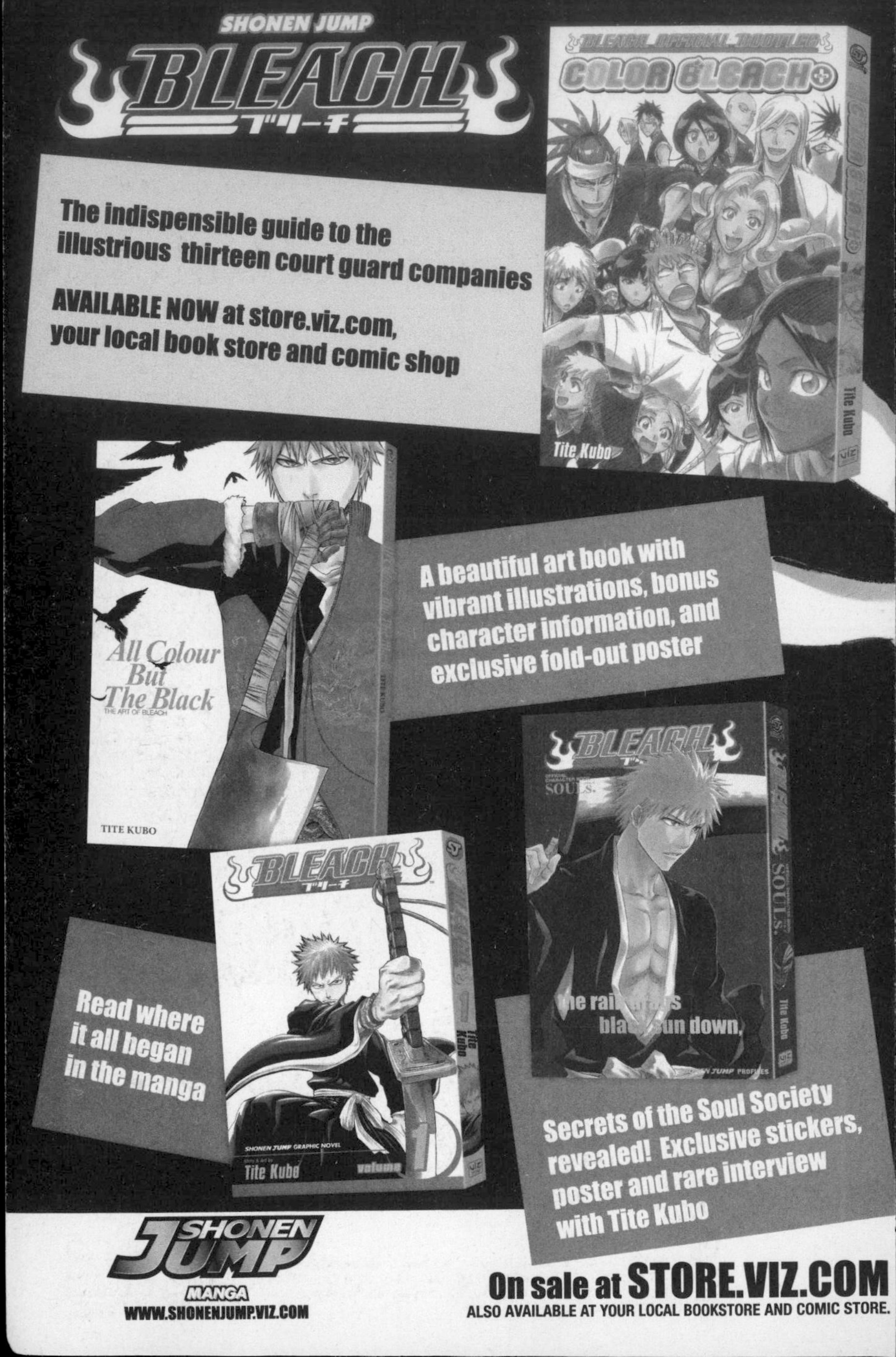
SHONEN JUMP
BLEACH
ブリーチ
COLOR BLEACH+
Tite Kubo
The indispensible guide to the illustrious thirteen court guard companies
AVAILABLE NOW at store.viz.com, your local book store and comic shop
All Colour But The Black
THE ART OF BLEACH
TITE KUBO
A beautiful art book with vibrant illustrations, bonus character information, and exclusive fold-out poster
BLEACH
SOULS.
Tite Kubo
BLEACH
ブリーチ
Tite Kubo
SHONEN JUMP GRAPHIC NOVEL
Read where it all began in the manga
Secrets of the Soul Society revealed! Exclusive stickers, poster and rare interview with Tite Kubo
SHONEN JUMP
MANGA
WWW.SHONENJUMP.VIZ.COM
On sale at STORE.VIZ.COM
ALSO AVAILABLE AT YOUR LOCAL BOOKSTORE AND COMIC STORE.

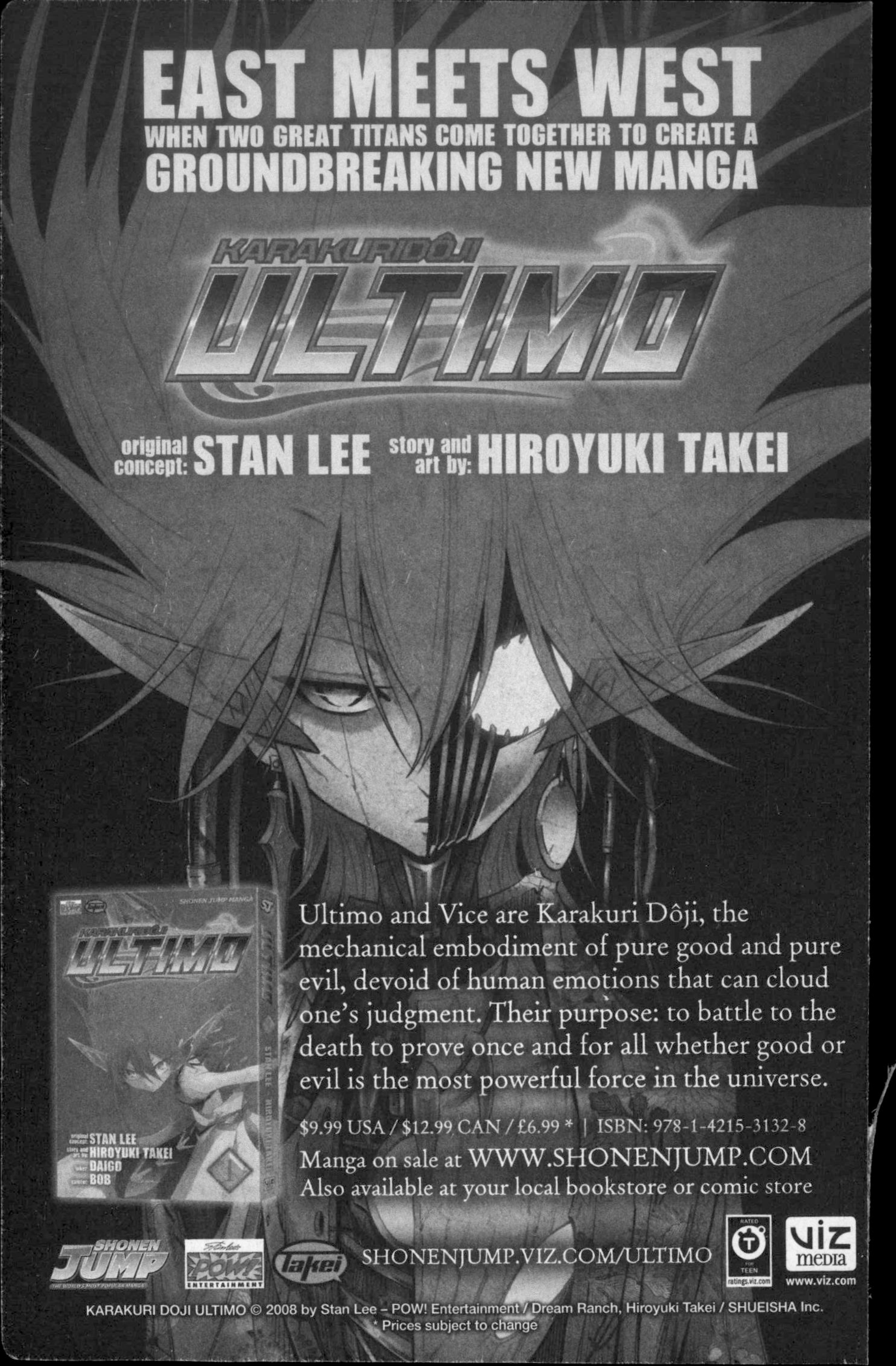
EAST MEETS WEST
WHEN TWO GREAT TITANS COME TOGETHER TO CREATE A
GROUNDBREAKING NEW MANGA
KARAKURIDÔJI
ULTIMO
original concept: STAN LEE
story and art by: HIROYUKI TAKEI
Ultimo and Vice are Karakuri Dôji, the mechanical embodiment of pure good and pure evil, devoid of human emotions that can cloud one's judgment. Their purpose: to battle to the death to prove once and for all whether good or evil is the most powerful force in the universe.
$9.99 USA / $12.99 CAN / £6.99 * | ISBN: 978-1-4215-3132-8
Manga on sale at WWW.SHONENJUMP.COM
Also available at your local bookstore or comic store
SHONENJUMP.VIZ.COM/ULTIMO
www.viz.com
KARAKURI DOJI ULTIMO © 2008 by Stan Lee – POW! Entertainment / Dream Ranch, Hiroyuki Takei / SHUEISHA Inc.
* Prices subject to change

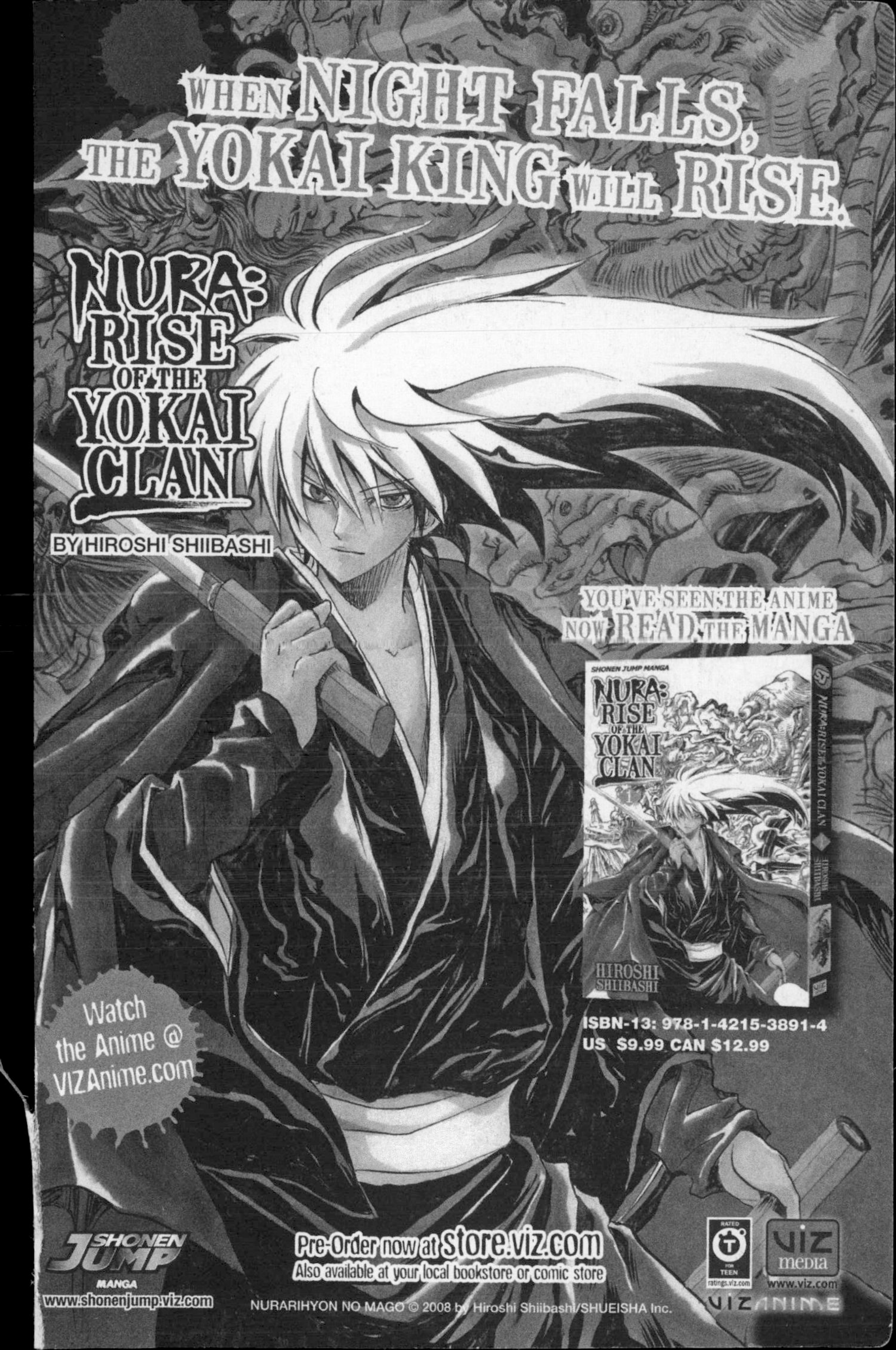

WHEN NIGHT FALLS, THE YOKAI KING WILL RISE.
NURA: RISE OF THE YOKAI CLAN
BY HIROSHI SHIIBASHI
YOU'VE SEEN THE ANIME NOW READ THE MANGA
SHONEN JUMP MANGA
NURA: RISE OF THE YOKAI CLAN
HIROSHI SHIIBASHI
ISBN-13: 978-1-4215-3891-4
US $9.99 CAN $12.99
Watch the Anime @ VIZAnime.com
SHONEN JUMP MANGA
www.shonenjump.viz.com
Pre-Order now at store.viz.com
Also available at your local bookstore or comic store
RATED T FOR TEEN
ratings.viz.com
VIZ media
www.viz.com
NURARIHYON NO MAGO © 2008 by Hiroshi Shiibashi/SHUEISHA Inc.
VIZANIME

SHONEN JUMP

The World's Most Popular Manga

OFF the cover price!

270+ pages of the **HOTTEST MANGA STORIES** every month combined with the latest in **GAMES, ANIME, TRADING CARDS**, and more!

PLUS Exclusive, **ULTRA-RARE PREMIUMS** in almost every issue—including **RED-HOT TRADING CARDS!**

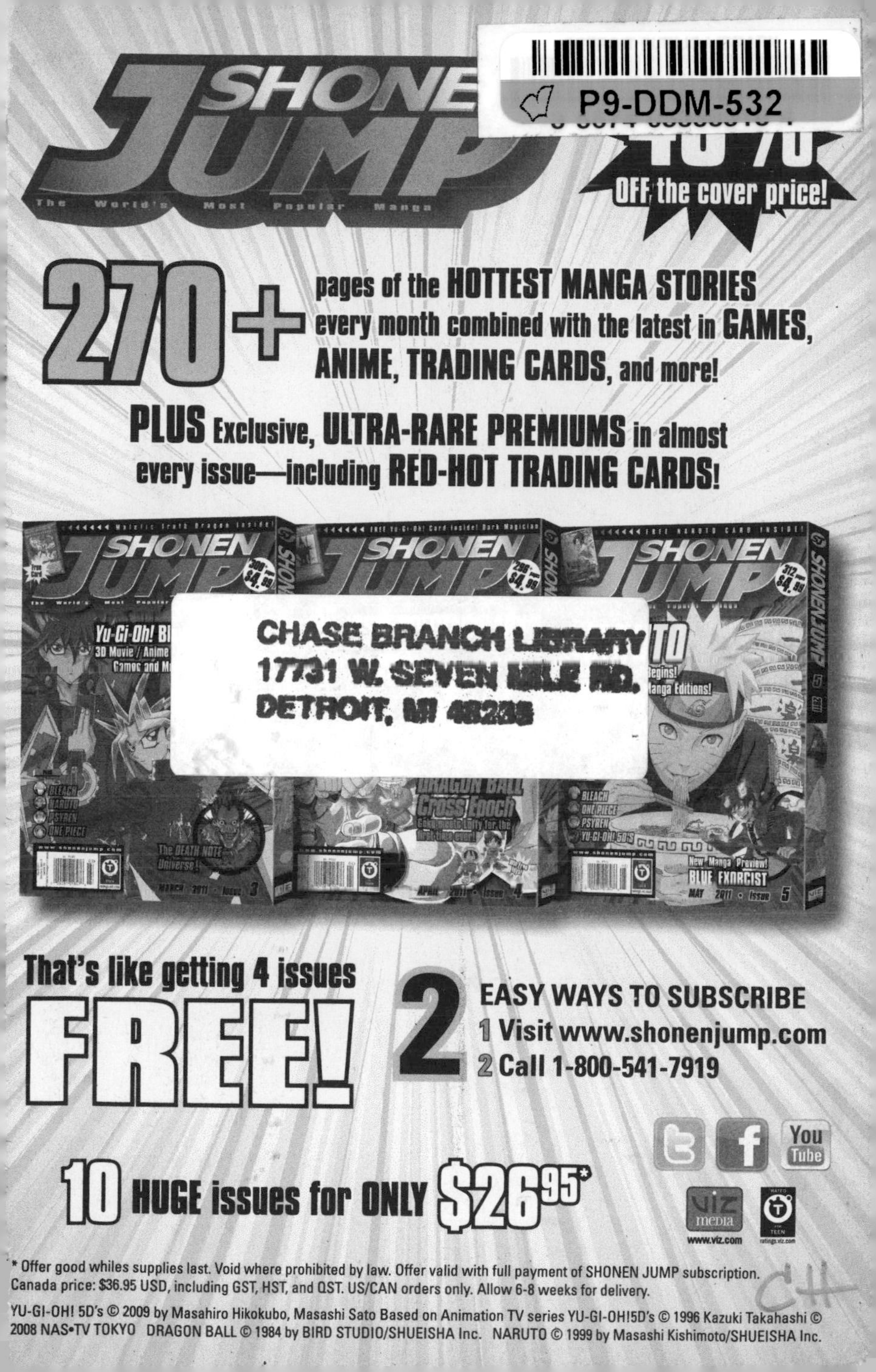
SHONEN JUMP
SHONEN JUMP
SHONEN JUMP
Yu-Gi-Oh!
BLEACH
NARUTO
PSYREN
ONE PIECE
The DEATH NOTE Universe!
MARCH 2011 · Issue 3
DRAGON BALL Cross Epoch
APRIL 2011 · Issue 4
BLEACH
ONE PIECE
PSYREN
YU-GI-OH! 5D'S
New Manga Preview!
BLUE EXORCIST
MAY 2011 · Issue 5

That's like getting 4 issues **FREE!**

2 EASY WAYS TO SUBSCRIBE

1 Visit www.shonenjump.com

2 Call 1-800-541-7919

10 HUGE issues for ONLY $26.95*

VIZ media www.viz.com

RATED T FOR TEEN ratings.viz.com

* Offer good whiles supplies last. Void where prohibited by law. Offer valid with full payment of SHONEN JUMP subscription. Canada price: $36.95 USD, including GST, HST, and QST. US/CAN orders only. Allow 6-8 weeks for delivery.